Hellenic Studies 56

IMPERIAL GEOGRAPHIES
IN BYZANTINE AND OTTOMAN SPACE

Recent Titles in the Hellenic Studies Series

Homer's Versicolored Fabric
The Evocative Power of Ancient Greek Epic Word-Making

Christianity and Hellenism in the Fifth-Century Greek East
Theodoret's Apologetics against the Greeks in Context

The Master of Signs
Signs and the Interpretation of Signs in Herodotus' Histories

The Epic Rhapsode and His Craft
Homeric Performance in a Diachronic Perspective

Eve of the Festival
Making Myth in Odyssey 19

Kleos in a Minor Key
The Homeric Education of a Little Prince

Plato's Counterfeit Sophists

Multitextuality in Homer's Iliad
The Witness of the Ptolemaic Papyri

Tragedy, Authority, and Trickery
The Poetics of Embedded Letters in Josephus

A Californian Hymn to Homer

Pindar's Verbal Art
An Ethnographic Study of Epinician Style

Iliad 10 and the Poetics of Ambush

The New Sappho on Old Age
Textual and Philosophical Issues

Hippota Nestor

Homer the Classic

Recapturing a Homeric Legacy
Images and Insights from the Venetus A Manuscript of the Iliad

http://chs.harvard.edu/chs/publications

IMPERIAL GEOGRAPHIES
IN BYZANTINE AND OTTOMAN SPACE

Edited by
Sahar Bazzaz, Yota Batsaki, and
Dimiter Angelov

CENTER FOR HELLENIC STUDIES
Trustees for Harvard University
Washington, D.C.
Distributed by Harvard University Press
Cambridge, Massachusetts, and London, England
2013

Imperial Geographies in Byzantine and Ottoman Space
 edited by Sahar Bazzaz, Yota Batsaki, and Dimiter Angelov
Copyright © 2013 Center for Hellenic Studies, Trustees for Harvard University
All Rights Reserved.
Published by Center for Hellenic Studies, Trustees for Harvard University,
 Washington, D.C.
Distributed by Harvard University Press, Cambridge, Massachusetts, and London, Eng-
 land
Production: Kristin Murphy Romano
Cover design and illustration: Joni Godlove
Printed by Edwards Brothers, Inc., Ann Arbor, MI

LIBRARY OF CONGRESS CATALOGING-IN-PUBLICATION DATA

Bazzaz, Sahar.
Imperial geographies in Byzantine and Ottoman space / by Sahar Bazzaz, Yota Batsaki,
 Dimiter Angelov.
 p. cm. -- (Hellenic studies ; 56)
Includes bibliographical references and index.
ISBN 978-0-674-06662-5 (alk. paper)
 1. Byzantine Empire--Historical geography. 2. Turkey--Historical geography. 3. Byz-
 antine Empire--History. 4. Turkey--History--Ottoman Empire, 1288-1918 I. Batsaki,
 Yota, 1974- II. Angelov, Dimiter, 1972- III. Title.
DF518.B39 2012
911'.4950902--dc23

                                                                          2012024437

Contents

Map 1: The Contraction of the Byzantine Empire
The Byzantine Empire in: 565, 1025, 1143, 1330. vii

Map 2: The Expansion of the Ottoman Empire
The Ottoman Empire in: 1300, 1481, 1512, 1683. viii

Introduction
Dimiter Angelov, Yota Batsaki, Sahar Bazzaz 1

1. Constantine VII and the Historical Geography of Empire
Paul Magdalino 23

2. "Asia and Europe Commonly Called East and West":
Constantinople and Geographical Imagination in Byzantium
Dimiter Angelov 43

3. Cartography and the Ottoman Imperial Project
in the Sixteenth Century
Pınar Emiralioğlu 69

4. Ferīdūn Beg's *Münşe'ātü 's-Selāṭīn* ('Correspondence of Sultans')
and Late Sixteenth-Century Ottoman Views of the Political World
Dimitris Kastritsis... 91

5. Imperial Geography and War: The Ottoman Case
Antonis Anastasopoulos 111

6. Ambiguities of Sovereignty: Property Rights and
Spectacles of Statehood in Tanzimat Izmir
Sibel Zandi-Sayek 133

Contents

7. Ottoman Arabs in Istanbul, 1860-1914:
   Perceptions of Empire, Experiences of the Metropole through
   the writings of Aḥmad Fāris al-Shidyāq, Muḥammad Rashīd Riḍā,
   and Jirjī Zaydān
      Ilham Khuri-Makdisi 159

8. Evading Athens:
   Versions of a Post-Imperial, National Greek Landscape
   around 1830
      Constanze Güthenke 183

9. Translation as Geographical Relocation:
   Nineteenth-Century Greek Adaptations of Molière in
   the Ottoman Empire
      Anna Stavrakopoulou... 207

10. In "Third Space": Between Crete and Egypt in
    Rhea Galanaki's *The Life of Ismail Ferik Pasha*
      Yota Batsaki 225

11. The Discursive Mapping of Sectarianism in Iraq:
    The Sunni Triangle in the Pages of *The New York Times*
      Sahar Bazzaz 245

Contributors...263

Index..265

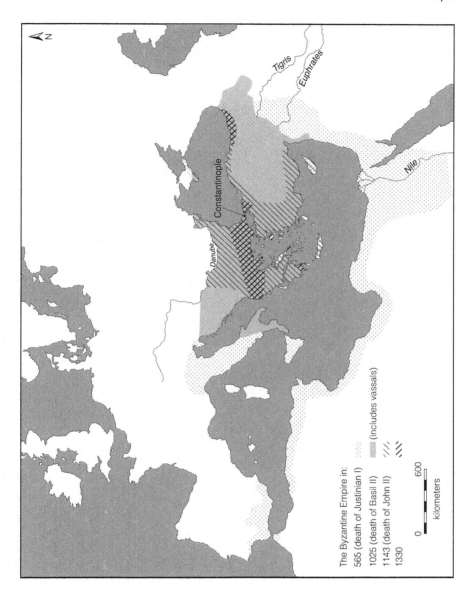

Map 1: The Contraction of the Byzantine Empire in: 565, 1025, 1143, 1330.

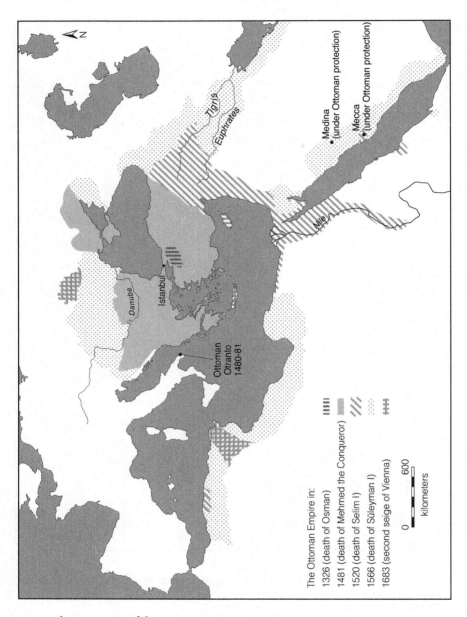

Map 2: The Expansion of the Ottoman Empire in: 1300, 1481, 1512, 1683.

Introduction

Imperial Geographies
in Byzantine and Ottoman Space

Dimiter Angelov, Yota Batsaki, Sahar Bazzaz

THE DIALECTICAL RELATIONSHIP between empire and geography has long been recognized. Empires are beneficiaries or prisoners of their geography, while specific imperial projects have shaped the content and effects of geographical knowledge across different periods. The essays in this volume represent a collaboration between historians and literary critics with intersecting interests in the imperial geographies of the medieval and modern eastern Mediterranean. These geographies are set within the extensive imperial and post-imperial space of the Byzantine and Ottoman Empires, two political and cultural formations which themselves contributed to perceptions of local and world geography. Although the comparative study of empire has received much impetus in recent years, it remains to a large extent focused on examples from the classical world or the modern European era.[1] This volume's attention to the space of the eastern Mediterranean centers instead on two empires that do not fit this chronological scheme, and whose contribution to the construction of imperial space has been relatively neglected, even though in terms of duration and territorial extension they are both remarkable.

The volume approaches geography, or rather the multiple geographies of the area (the plural is necessitated by the divergent geographical notions and experiences), as a socially constructed body of knowledge. This means that the volume will largely leave aside problems of Mediterranean environmental history and historical ecology that have recently attracted considerable attention.[2] Nor is cartography of central concern to this volume, even though some of the papers engage with questions of maps and mapping. The focus lies instead on the strategies, ideological contexts, and effects of the production of

---

[1] Two recent exceptions are: Bang and Bayly 2011; Bang and Kolodziejczyk 2012.
[2] McNeill 1992; Horden and Purcell 2000:45–49.

geographical knowledge, both material and imaginary. Through texts as diverse as Ottoman *kadı* court records and chancery manuals, imperial treatises on administration and works of fiction, travel literature, and dramatic adaptations, the essays explore ways in which the production of geographical knowledge supported imperial authority or revealed its precarious mastery of geography. Our interest lies mainly in the discursive construction of imperial space, and we bring to it a variety of methodologies: historical and literary, textual and theoretical, but in all cases explicitly "spatial."

The Byzantine and Ottoman Empires succeeded each other and came to view themselves, and to be viewed, as oppositional, yet they share a number of distinctive characteristics. They both exercised their rule on what came to be near-identical geographical space, namely Asia Minor and the Balkans, and from the vantage point of the same city: Constantinople/Istanbul. As several of the essays discuss, they both saw themselves poised between East and West, while their notions of imperial geography to a certain extent shaped those very categories. They both created narratives of imperial legitimacy in which they presented themselves as the heirs of the region's classical empires, especially Rome. And they both had to negotiate the significant challenges of Mediterranean geography. Because these distinctive and shared characteristics have been relatively neglected in the comparative study of imperial geographies, the following section provides a brief historical and geographical overview of the region from the medieval to the modern period.

Historical and Geographical Specificity: The Byzantine and Ottoman Empires

The Byzantine and Ottoman Empires dominated the politics of the eastern Mediterranean throughout its late antique, medieval, and modern history until 1922. The two empires shared profound similarities and common traditions. Both were highly centralized multiethnic polities. Both were governed from Constantinople/Istanbul and maintained imperial ambitions for most of their histories. Some essential differences must also be noted at the outset. Byzantium after the seventh century was a medieval state, whose history was closely entwined with the politics and culture of the Middle Ages: for example, the crusades and the transmission of ancient Greek philosophy to the Muslims and the West. By contrast, the history of the Ottoman Empire spans the early modern and modern periods after a brief late medieval phase, a circumstance that makes issues of modernity directly relevant to the Ottomans in ways that do not apply to Byzantium. The Byzantine Empire was, and certainly saw itself as, a thoroughly Christian polity. While being the direct continuator of the Roman

Empire in the East, Byzantium underwent a period of transformation between the fourth and the seventh centuries that turned it into a thoroughly Christian and medieval society. One of the principal turning points was the foundation of Constantinople in 330, accompanied by the introduction of Christianity as the official religion. Byzantium was to foster continually the spread of the Christian religion beyond its borders through state-sponsored missionary activities, notably in central and eastern Europe. By contrast, the Ottoman Empire—which was formed in the aftermath of the collapse of the Seljukid sultanate of Rum in Asia Minor in the second half of the thirteenth century under the twin pressure of Mongol invasions and Turcoman migration—was a state with an ethnically mixed but primarily Muslim elite. While both empires were ethnically and culturally diverse, their diversity manifested itself in different ways. The Byzantine Empire wove together in a unique way the Judeo-Christian religious tradition with elements of classical culture, such as: the ancient Greek literature and philosophy; Roman law and institutions; and the revived ideological tradition of Hellenistic kingship. The Ottoman Empire was constructed mostly by adapting preexistent cultural and political practices in Islamic states in the Near East and Asia Minor, notably those of the Seljuks of Rum. A larger proportion of the population of the Ottoman Empire were religious minorities, towards whom the Ottomans followed a general policy of tolerance in accordance with the Islamic tradition. The incorporation of massive religious minorities and the permission granted to these minorities to practice their own laws distinguishes the cultural hybridity of the Ottoman Empire from the Byzantine case.

The Byzantine and the Ottoman Empires, like most imperial formations in history, adopted and adapted political and cultural traditions of preceding civilizations. By virtue of chronology and conquest, Ottoman state-builders had Byzantine, Seljuk, and Near Eastern models of administration and imperialism from which to pick and choose, while the subject Christian population inherited directly its church institutions and elements of its literary culture from Byzantium. Continuity in imperial administration has been identified in the fiscal institutions of *pronoia* and *timar*, while Byzantine borrowing from the Ottoman taxation practices during the early fifteenth century has also been observed.[3] Studying the continuities between the two empires is neither easy nor unproblematic. Christians and Muslims had a long history of contacts in the eastern Mediterranean before the rise of the Ottoman Empire, which raises numerous possibilities for intermediate stages of influence.[4] The concept of influence itself is a loaded one, and is sometimes seen to carry connotations

---

[3]   Vryonis 1969/70:273–275; Oikonomides 1985.
[4]   Vryonis 1969/70:254–255.

of cultural superiority and agency.[5] At the level of ideological claims of universality constructed through spatial language, the similarities between the two empires were mostly a function of their common geographical location and the role of Constantinople/Istanbul, rather than of direct influence from one empire on the other, as shown by several essays in this volume (Angelov, Magdalino, Kastritsis, Khuri-Makdisi).

The geography of the eastern Mediterranean has traditionally been seen both as conducive to the formation of imperial networks and as a limit to further imperial expansion. In the case of Byzantium, parallels have been drawn with its immediate ancestor, imperial Rome. The expansion of the Roman Empire is thought to have reached its natural geographical boundaries with the Sahara desert to the south or the Rhine-Danube frontier to the north. Seen from the viewpoint of Rome, the Mediterranean served as a highway of communication and trade ("the Roman Lake") rather than a barrier. Similar kinds of geographical boundaries, this time of contraction and defense rather than of expansion, have also been noted for Byzantium. Thus, after the collapse of the Rhine frontier in the fourth century, the Danube formed the boundary between the eastern Roman Empire and its tribal neighbors in the north. Medieval historians have studied the Mediterranean both for the opportunities for travel, commerce, and communications it continually presented, as well as for the challenges posed by sea currents, wind patterns, and a winter season hostile to navigation.[6] Increasingly after the seventh century, Byzantium was confined to the Balkans in the west and Asia Minor in the east, whose mountainous landscapes posed natural barriers. It has been estimated that around two-thirds of the Balkans are mountains. When, in the seventh century, the Bulgars settled south of the Danube, the Haimos, or Balkan, Mountains became a natural frontier. The estimate for Asia Minor is that nine-tenths consist of a large elevated plateau and mountains lying mostly to the east and the south. Coastal plains, of which the largest ones are in the west, and punctuating river valleys, amount to about one-tenth of the territory of Asia Minor.[7] The geographical relief of Asia Minor influenced patterns of invasion and settlement. The Taurus and the Anti-Taurus Mountains were natural barriers to the expansion of the Arabs from the south and the southeast during the seventh and eighth centuries—the same period when Byzantium lost forever its territories in the Levant, Egypt, and North Africa.[8] The one major exception is the strategic city of Antioch, the seat of one of the five patriarchs, which the Byzantines recaptured in 969 and held

[5]   Kafadar 1995:24–25.
[6]   Pryor 1988; McCormick 2001.
[7]   Hendy 1985:26; Geyer 2002:32–33.
[8]   Whittow 2008:223.

until 1084 when it fell to the Seljuks. Once the Seljuk Turks migrated into Asia Minor during the eleventh century, the large mountainous plateau provided the nomadic Turkmen with the necessary environment for raising livestock.[9] Notably, this is an area that the Byzantines, with a traditionally sedentary lifestyle, did not succeed in recovering in the twelfth century. Their reconquest was confined mostly to the plains in western Asia Minor and some of the river valleys extending inland.

The territories of the Byzantine and Ottoman Empires fluctuated throughout the centuries (see Figure 1 and Figure 2). The Byzantine Empire generally tended to defend and gradually lose the lands it inherited from imperial Rome except for limited periods of reconquest. The loss of massive territories to the Arabs, Slavs, and Bulgars in the seventh century was followed by imperial expansion between the ninth and the early eleventh centuries, culminating in the annexation of Bulgaria during the reign of Basil II (976–1025) and the restoration of the Danube as the Balkan frontier. The settlement of the Seljuk Turks in Asia Minor deprived the empire of much of its remaining eastern territory. In the year 1071, Byzantium suffered a heavy double-blow: a spectacular defeat by the Seljuks at Manzikert and the loss of its last territorial possession in southern Italy. The reassertion of Byzantine authority in western Asia Minor during the twelfth century was mostly successful, but nothing more could be achieved. The empire disintegrated under internal pressures in the late twelfth century and collapsed with the crusader conquest of Constantinople in 1204. The restored Byzantine Empire, after the recapture of Constantinople in 1261, was a fragmented, smaller, and less resourceful state. By contrast, the Ottoman Empire rose from a frontier principality, first attested in about 1300, to an empire encompassing by the late sixteenth century the entire eastern Mediterranean, parts of central Europe, Arabia, Iraq, and North Africa. The core land of the two empires, territorial changes notwithstanding, remained generally the same and was centered on the Balkans and Asia Minor. It has been pointed out that the territorial extent of the Byzantine Empire at the time of the death of Basil II roughly coincided with the empire of Mehmed the Conqueror and included most of the Balkans and Anatolia.[10] Constantinople was always the capital city of both the Byzantine and the Ottoman Empires, with the notable exceptions of the period 1204–1261, when a Latin power held the city, and the early period of Ottoman history until 1453, when Constantinople was still Byzantine.

The importance of Constantinople, the city of "New Rome," can hardly be overestimated. The ruler of Constantinople, whether Byzantine or Ottoman,

9   Vryonis 1976.
10   Kafadar, 2007:8.

was set in a continuum leading back to imperial Rome. The city played a crucial administrative role as the seat of the civil and military bureaucracies, and as the permanent residence of the Byzantine emperors and the Ottoman sultans. The geographical location of Constantinople itself was capable of influencing the military history of the two empires. The patterns of involvement of Ottoman armies in Europe and Asia, for instance, have been seen as depending to a large extent on distances from Constantinople.[11] The Byzantine road networks leading from Constantinople to the frontier and the logistics of army movement have also drawn heightened attention.[12] The Byzantine emperors and the Ottoman sultans coopted outlying areas, which were far from Constantinople and therefore difficult to administer directly, as client states and tributary vassals. Such was the case in the Ottoman period with the Crimean Khanate; the territories north of the Danube including Moldavia, Transylvania, and Wallachia; Georgia; and the Sharifate of Mecca. The role of the metropolis in setting the parameters of imperial geography is a reason why several papers in the volume deal with the imperial center and discuss its spatial and geographical perspectives. The thematic focus on the center rather than the periphery is naturally not intended to challenge the recent and profitable upsurge of interest among Byzantinists in provincial areas and perspectives. For instance, historians of the twenty-first century have examined Byzantium's Balkan frontier during the middle Byzantine period and the reception of the Christian Parthenon in medieval Athens until 1204.[13] The archaeology of Byzantine urban centers, such as Ephesos and Pergamon, to mention only two, has produced, and doubtless will continue to produce, fruitful and illuminating results.[14] Much scope remains for the study of material culture and the mental outlooks, spatial attitudes in particular, of people living in the provinces and along the frontiers of the Byzantine Empire.

By contrast to the shrinking trajectory of the Byzantine Empire, from their emergence at the turn of the fourteenth century the Ottomans succeeded almost continually in bringing new territories under their domain. Despite intermittent (and during the Ottoman Civil War in the early fifteenth century near-catastrophic) setbacks, the Ottoman state evolved from a small principality (*beylik*) in northwestern Asia Minor (Bithynia) to a state straddling large parts of the Balkans and western Asia Minor, with Constantinople as its capital. In its written form, the Ottomans knew the city as "Istanbul" and in its spoken form as "Stambol," both of which are derived from the Greek εἰς τὴν πόλιν. Sultan

[11]   Murphey 1999:xiv, 20–25.
[12]   Haldon 1999:51–60; Belke 2002; Haldon 2006.
[13]   Stephenson 2000; Kaldellis 2009.
[14]   Foss 1979; Rheidt 1991, 2002.

Mehmed II, who captured Constantinople for the Ottomans in 1453, is known to have called the city "Islam-bol," that is, "where Islam abounds." In later centuries, Ottoman literate society viewed "Islam-bol" as the proper Ottoman name for the city. Despite these various usages, the Ottomans continued to refer to Constantinople as "Ḳonṣṭantiniyya"—an Arabized/Persianized version of the Greek original—in chancery and other official documents, in deeds for pious endowments issued by the *kadı* courts, and on coins.[15]

Following the conquest of Constantinople, Mehmed II took the titles "sultan of the two lands" (Anatolia and the Balkans) and "emperor of the two seas" (Black and Aegean Seas), thereby indicating his desire to revive the legacy of Byzantium.[16] These geographical titles (i.e. "sultan of the two lands and emperor of the two seas") were inscribed on the Imperial Gate of Mehmed's newly commissioned Topkapı palace, which was built on a hill chosen for its "omnivoyant, spectacular site as a metaphor for world dominion."[17] By the mid-sixteenth century, the Ottomans had become a world power, dominating the Mediterranean and Black Seas and demonstrating their capacity to wage war on numerous fronts simultaneously. They challenged the Portuguese in the Indian Ocean, Red Sea, and the Straits of Hormuz; battled Safavid Shi'ite co-religionists and their Turkmen supporters in eastern Anatolia and Iran; faced the Habsburgs over the imperial domination of central Europe and the Balkans on the western frontier; and, finally, defeated Spain, whose incursions in North Africa since the early fifteenth century had stood in the way of Ottoman naval hegemony in the Mediterranean.[18]

Until the early sixteenth century, Ottoman political military ambitions were directed both eastward into what is today western Iran and westward into the lands of the former Roman Empire. Evidence suggests that Mehmed II intended to launch a campaign against Rome following the landing of Ottoman troops in Otranto on the southeastern shore of the Italian Peninsula in AD 1480. From 1516 until the mid-sixteenth century, conquests in the "Arab Lands" introduced into the Ottoman dominions a massive region roughly half the size of the continental United States.[19] The Ottomans now controlled the Muslim holy cities of Mecca (Mekka) and Medina in the western Arabian Peninsula, the pilgrimage city of Jerusalem sacred to Muslims, Christians, and Jews and, intermittently, the two most important Shi'ite pilgrimage sites, Najaf and Karbala in modern day Iraq. These conquests "thrust [the Ottomans] into an entirely different

---

15 Inalcik 2010.
16 Inalcik 1994:274–275; Karateke 2005:24.
17 Necipoğlu 1991:13.
18 Hess 1978; Casale 2010.
19 Hathaway 2008:23.

symbolic universe." They were now overlords of large populations of Muslims and, moreover, they could legitimately claim the title *Khādim al-Ḥaramayn* or protector of the two holiest sites of Islam, Mecca, and Medina.[20] As the major Muslim power in the region, the Ottomans were poised to assume the role of defenders of Sunni Orthodoxy against enemy Christian powers and the Safavid Shi'ites, whom the Ottomans viewed as heterodox Muslims and therefore as enemies.

The Ottomans provide a rare example of an imperial formation that evolved from a premodern and preindustrial to a modern state. In order to remain viable in the context of an emerging international state system in the early to mid-nineteenth century, on the one hand, and an increasingly globalized, capitalist economy, on the other, Ottoman society experienced important socioeconomic, political, military, and cultural transformations.[21] Responding to internal and external political and intellectual challenges, the Ottomans embarked on modernization and reform (Tanzimat). This set in motion a drive toward state centralization, implementation of a new secular law code, reform of the tax system to eliminate rapacious tax-farming practices, creation of an Ottoman citizenship that removed legal distinctions separating Muslims from non-Muslims, and urban renewal and provincial administrative reform, to name only a few. These reforms, in turn, shaped the experience of modernity in the Ottoman Empire and, later, in the nation-states that emerged out of its disintegration and dismemberment in the nineteenth and twentieth centuries, including Turkey, the Arab states (Egypt, Syria, Lebanon, Jordan, and Iraq), Greece, the other Balkan states, and the Palestine mandate/Israel.[22]

Broadly speaking, these transformations occurred against the backdrop of, and in conversation with, the shifting balance of power between the Ottomans and European states such as Russia and Austria (and later, Great Britain and France) during the eighteenth and nineteenth centuries, which challenged the Ottoman "Great Power" status. Territorial losses to Russia in the eighteenth century set in motion the first decisive effort on the part of the Ottoman officialdom to examine and reconsider foundational Ottoman institutions of governance, administration, and warfare which had endured even as they evolved and changed over time since the early Ottoman period (known in Ottoman historiography as the "Classical Age").[23] Meanwhile, Napoleon's invasion and occupation of the Ottoman province of Egypt in 1798 brought France, and soon

---

[20] Karateke 2005:25.
[21] Aydin 2006; Inalcik 1994:777; Owen 1993.
[22] Hanioğlu 2008.
[23] For an overview of the historiography of the "decline paradigm" in Ottoman Studies, see Sajdi 2007.

after Great Britain, into the Ottoman lands of the eastern Mediterranean—a new arena for their competing national and imperial ambitions to conquer territory and expand their spheres of influence on the European continent and in Asia and Africa in the nineteenth century.[24] In 1830, Ottoman Algeria fell to the French followed by the fall of Tunis in 1881. Great Britain occupied Egypt in 1882, effectively ending its already greatly diminished allegiance to the imperial center, Istanbul. By the end of the nineteenth century, the European powers referred to the Ottoman state as the "Sick Man of Europe." European commitments to preservation of the territorial integrity of the empire had given way to a virtual land-grab, with individual powers vying for control of the already greatly reduced Ottoman territory.

Threats to Ottoman authority also came from within the realm. In 1803, supporters of the religiopolitical movement led by the Saud family and their Wahhabi allies occupied the holy sites of Mecca and Medina after launching attacks several years earlier against Ottoman towns in Iraq and the Hijaz (the region along the western coast of the Arabian Peninsula where Medina and Mecca are located). In so doing, the Wahhabis challenged Ottoman claims of authority and legitimacy that, since the early sixteenth century, had been linked to the dynasty's commitment to protect the pilgrimage routes and ensure the smooth running of the annual pilgrimage to the holy cities.[25]

Finally, increased trade and circulation of people and ideas associated with the French Revolution provided new opportunities for *dhimmis* (protected non-Muslim subjects of the empire) to renegotiate their status within and commitments to the Ottoman imperial order, where they had traditionally occupied a second-class legal status vis-à-vis their Muslim counterparts.[26] For some, like the Phanariots—Greeks who occupied positions in Ottoman government whether in the capital, Istanbul, or in provinces such as Wallachia—these changes did not necessarily weaken their commitment to the empire, while for others, such as leaders of the Greek *Philikē Hetaireia*, revolutionary ideas emanating from France and other centers of Enlightenment led to a complete rejection of Ottoman suzerainty over Greek lands and helped fuel calls for Greek independence.[27] The nineteenth century brought heightened mobility due to steamship transportation and broader circulation of information through printing and the telegraph. Reformist ideas found expression throughout the Ottoman realms in the form of news journals and, in the Levant and Egypt, in the rise of an Arabic-language

---

[24] Jasanoff 2005.
[25] Hanioğlu 2008:12.
[26] Göçek 1996; on the *millet* system and its transformation, see Karpat 1982.
[27] On the Greek Enlightenment, see Kitromilides 1992; Philliou 2010; on Ottoman Jews, see Mazower 2005.

literary movement known as the *Nahḍa*, or "Arab Awakening."[28] Meanwhile, western-oriented intellectuals, reform-minded administrators and bureaucrats, and Islamic legal scholars (*ulama*), military men, and laborers debated the pressing issues of the day: What was the secret of European economic and political power? How should Ottoman society evolve while staying true to its essence? What was the role of religion in the reformed Ottoman state and society? Did language and ethnicity form the basis for a new kind of polity—a national one? How could the poor of society be raised out of their misery? What role should women play in a reformed society?[29]

One outcome of these multiple social and political developments was the creation of an Ottoman nationality based on the modern principle of equality before the law. Hoping to reduce the threat of nationalist break-away movements within the empire and demonstrate to increasingly meddlesome European powers their commitment to reform, the Ottomans issued the 1839 Imperial Edict of the Rose Garden (and renewed the principles embodied therein in another decree issued in 1856), which expressed the state's commitment to level the playing field among its "citizens." This was a seemingly paradoxical notion for a society historically structured in part by legal distinctions between the Ottoman non-taxpaying military-bureaucratic elite (*askeri*) and the largely tax-paying peasantry (*reaya*); between Muslims and non-Muslims; between slaves and slave-owners; and between men and women.[30] Although ultimately unsuccessful at preventing the loss of most Ottoman territory in the Balkans to nationalist movements and their Great Power backers, short-lived experiments with parliamentary governance between 1876 and 1878 and briefly again in 1908 (after the Young Turk Revolution) fueled enthusiasm for the Ottoman polity among its remaining minority citizenry, including Ottoman Greeks, Armenians, and Arabs.[31] Meanwhile, Sultan Abdülhamid's (r. 1876–1909) calls for unity under an Ottoman Caliphate among Muslims worldwide highlighted the numerous and sometimes competing and contradictory strands of prevailing thought about the future of the Ottoman Empire, the form it would take, and who would be included in it.

The Ottoman Empire sided with Germany in World War I, and as a consequence, was made to pay the price of defeat. This meant the loss of its remaining territories in the Middle East to France and Britain, who then proceeded to create the boundaries that formed the basis for the modern nation-states of the region.

---

[28] Ayalon 1995; Khuri-Makdisi 2010.
[29] Hourani 1983.
[30] Philliou 2010
[31] Hanioğlu 2008; Kayali 1997.

Academic and Imaginary Geographies

Ottoman modernization and European imperial expansion in the nineteenth century coincided with the rise of academic geography. The progress and content of this new discipline reflects some of the historiographical assumptions about modernity and empire that have drawn attention away from developments in the eastern Mediterranean. Often viewed as a predominantly European or even Eurocentric enterprise, the rise of academic geography in the nineteenth century is also regarded as largely complicit with European colonial expansion, to which it contributed through the production of cartographic knowledge, but also by generating "imagined geographies" that mediated the spatial appropriation and colonial subjection of other cultures. An example of the first form are the often state-sponsored nineteenth-century projects of exploration and mapping of Africa, Asia, and Latin America; an example of the second are the geographical theories about the impact of environment and climate on racial difference that provided an ideological underpinning for colonialism as a "civilizing mission." This instrumental and situated character of the discipline has been widely explored in recent scholarship,[32] which in turn has been influenced by developments in postcolonial theory.

The work of Edward Said marked a turning point in the understanding of how "imagined geographies" served to essentialize difference by establishing binary oppositions (self/other, rational/irrational, progressive/backward, normative/perverse, etc.) at the service of colonial domination.[33] Said also emphasized the extent to which imperialism is defined by a "struggle over geography" and probed the ideological representations of this struggle in the sphere of culture, opening up the geographical imagination to the fields of cultural studies and literary criticism.[34] Geographers have responded by exploring the multiple ways in which their discipline can engage with postcolonial questions of identity, legitimation, and resistance.[35] However, despite its seminal impact, the contribution of Said (and of historians such as Eric Hobsbawm)[36] has had the effect of pinning the "age of empire" to the nineteenth century, as well as conceiving the European imperial project as a relatively monolithic enterprise. In order to provide a corrective to this narrow conceptualization of geography as a discourse and discipline of modern empire, scholars have been concentrating on a wider chronological range as well as differentiating between

---

[32] Gregory 1994; Bell, Butlin and Heffernan 1995; Godlewska and Smith, 1994; Driver 1992; Harley 2001; Edney 1997; Lewis and Wigen 1997.

[33] Said 1978.

[34] Said 1993.

[35] Blunt and McEwan 2000.

[36] Hobsbawm 1989.

colonial enterprises in terms of their attitudes to space, culture, race, etc.[37] This shift can nuance the idea of empire as "the creation of sharp alterity"[38] by showing that imperial space is a varied and fluid site of contestation and by incorporating alternative models of—and resistances to—imperial sovereignty.

This collection takes up these questions of longue durée and difference in order to contribute to the novel interrogation of empire, which has traditionally been seen as a western project associated with modernity. This does not mean forgetting about European imperialism and its aftermath; rather, it entails freeing the discussion of empire and geography from its Eurocentric focus in order to consider other spaces and practices. Several of the contributions to this volume engage with the ways in which both Orientalist and counter-Orientalist discourses have failed to provide a nuanced account of imperial formations and experiences in the eastern Mediterranean. One side effect of Said's powerful binaries in *Orientalism* has been to downplay the ways in which the Orient was also a vocal and internally differentiated participant in empire. Paying attention to Ottoman representations of the West, for instance, untethers the "Muslim discovery of Europe" from narratives of belatedness and decline, while showing that relationships to the other can be marked by ambivalence but also partial or shifting identification, and that they have to be understood across a spectrum that changes with political and historical circumstances.

Our focus on geography as a vehicle for understanding empire is partly informed by the "spatial turn" in the humanities and the social sciences. Here, too, the discipline of geography has become an arena of heated debate about the methods of inquiry into political and social experience. Drawing on Michel Foucault and Henri Lefebvre, Edward Soja has provocatively argued that spatiality since the nineteenth century has been repressed in favor of the historicist narratives favored by modernity.[39] Spatiality, according to Soja and other theorists, needs to be recovered as an important third term that mediates the dialectic between historicity and sociality. From this perspective, "Reflecting the uneven development of historical versus spatial discourse, the Spatial Turn is fundamentally an attempt to develop a more creative and critically effective balancing of the spatial/geographical and the temporal/historical imaginations."[40]

A helpful distinction emerging from these theoretical debates is one between material geographies (amenable to quantitative and mathematical methodologies), imagined or mental geographies (that invite discursive and

---

[37] Pagden 1995; McKee 2000; Kamen 2002; Lieven 2002.
[38] Cooper 2004:269n33.
[39] Soja 1996.
[40] Soja 2009:12.

ideological analysis), and the harder to define category of "lived space" that is the hybrid product of social, intellectual, and bodily experiences. Although the boundaries among these spatial categories and definitions are permeable, they provide a helpful way of organizing and balancing alternative approaches to space. Nevertheless, and by contrast to the trend towards socioeconomic methodologies in the comparative study of empires, this volume is predominantly interested in the narrative and representational aspects of imperial geographies. Their implications for this volume are thought-provoking, given that the contributors are predominantly historians and literary critics whose disciplinary parameters sometimes tolerate a relative neglect of the spatial dimension. At the same time, our focus on the eastern Mediterranean immediately entails a different chronological and cultural perspective, which is particularly important given that the application of spatial thinking to questions of colonialism has largely focused on the modern European powers. The nineteenth-century triumph of historicism has often been considered as instrumental to imperialism by generating teleological narratives of Western progress, supported by advances in transportation and communication, that "robbed the understanding of social change of any sense of contingency."[41] This volume's attention to the often recalcitrant, contested, or indeterminate nature of geographical space can enhance our understanding of how historical narratives of empire are themselves dynamic, overlapping, and sometimes conflicting.

Description of Contents

The critical focus on space as a key analytical category has promoted interdisciplinary inquiry across the fields of cultural studies, geography, political science, history, and art history, to name but a few.[42] Still, the collaboration between historians and literary critics is an unusual feature of this collection. Methodologically, it has generated substantial debate among the contributors about what the two approaches can say to one another, and how they can jointly contribute to an understanding of imperial geographies. Given the focus on narrative and representation as legitimizing or subversive practices of empire, contributors have had to think hard about what narrative means across their different disciplines. While for the historians, for example, narrative needs to be set as concretely as possible in the contemporary historical context, for the literary critics narrative entails metaphor—literally a process of semantic transfer—that encourages substitution, displacement, and a degree of

---

[41] Warf 2008:129.
[42] Warf and Arias 2008:2.

indeterminacy. Translated into a reading of geographical space, this combination of approaches has encouraged both a grounding of representations in their institutional and political matrices (Magdalino, Angelov, Kastritsis, Bazzaz), and an awareness that spatial practices and experiences are often provisional, precarious, or subject to conflicting jurisdictions (Zandi-Sayek, Güthenke, Batsaki). The metaphor of translation as cultural transfer of meaning across space is driven home in the essay by Stavrakopoulou, which analyzes theatrical translations/adaptations of Molière across the Greek diasporic communities of Izmir and Istanbul.

The essays examine specific phenomena associated with empire (such as travel; social, commercial, and cultural exchange and conflict; and processes of identity formation) through an interdisciplinary approach that is both synchronic and diachronic. One important aim of the volume is to elucidate the ways in which different groups or individuals (for example, sovereigns, intellectuals, political and financial élites, or travelers from the imperial "periphery") imagined and articulated their relationship to empire through spatial and geographical language and metaphors. One of the organizing polarities of any understanding of empire is the center-periphery relation. Several essays in this volume are in dialogue with one another to show that this model varies according to the specific historical, political, and geographical contexts. Dimiter Angelov and Paul Magdalino discuss the Byzantine Empire as predominantly centered in Constantinople, the imperial metropolis. Angelov shows that Constantinople served as a Greenwich zone and determined the spatiality of the East and West, which were identified with the continents of Asia and Europe. The imagined geography, according to which the imperial metropolis dominated over Europe and Asia, prevented the continents from becoming oppositional cultural categories as occurred in Renaissance Italy. Magdalino's detective-like reading of Constantine VII's *On the Themes* and *On the Administration of the Empire* reveals an "optic of power" through which Constantine conceived the geographical dimension of his empire and sought to share his vision with his successor. This power perspective on geography accounts, Magdalino suggests, for the highly selective and strategic nature of Constantine's narrative, focusing, for example, on naptha-producing regions important to military strategy, or on areas with significant potential for dynastic intervention.

But this centripetal model of empire is also modified and challenged by perspectives on the metropolis from other regions, as demonstrated by recent scholarship on the relationship between the Ottoman imperial center and its provinces.[43] In her account of writings about Istanbul by journalists (both

---

[43] Mikhail 2011:24–25.

travelers and residents) hailing from Egypt and the Levant (modern day Syria and Lebanon), Ilham Khuri-Makdisi complicates the notion of the "periphery" within the Ottoman Empire. She shows that encounters with the metropolis were often informed assessments of modernization and urban reform, enriched by comparative perspectives from European centers such as London and Paris. Devoid of provincialism, such accounts suggest instead a critique and even a "banalization of Istanbul." In conjunction with the essays by Sibel Zandi-Sayek and Anna Stavrakopoulou, Khuri-Makdisi's contribution paints a picture of a multi-centered empire where processes of modernization occurred at different paces and across crisscrossing trade, diplomatic, and travel networks.

The collective preoccupation with strategies of representation is fuelled by a common interest in questions of imperial self-legitimation. How are imperial ambitions inscribed in the texts and practices treated in this volume? A recurrent strategy is based on the universalist claims of empire. Usual examples of such claims include the "White Man's Burden" and the *mission civilisatrice*—concepts grounded in the Enlightenment ideal of the "triumph and development of reason" in all realms of public and private life—and are most often associated with late eighteenth- and nineteenth-century British and French imperialism in Asia and Africa.[44] However, the Byzantines and Ottomans also developed and then sought to project their own notions of imperial universalist claims. The Byzantines enriched the tradition of imperial self-presentation inherited from Rome and were receptive to Hellenistic and ancient Near Eastern ideas and historical memories of rulership. Old ideas of empire were adapted to a new context and enhanced by Christian interpretations.[45] For example, the early Byzantine emperors followed their Roman predecessors in placing an orb on their coins symbolizing their global dominion, though with a Christian cross added on top of the orb (*globus cruciger*).[46] Byzantium was imagined to be the last in a series of four world empires referred to in the Book of Daniel.[47] The actual capacity of Byzantium to carry out imperial policies on a large scale, in the sense of ambitious military campaigns and massive public works, varied through the centuries and diminished dramatically in 1204. Yet the fantasy of imperialism and world rule persisted in oratorical performances at the court well into the late Byzantine period, largely in contradiction to the political realities.[48]

For the Ottomans, imperialist universalist claims were based on the appropriation and synthesis of three traditions of universal sovereignty: the Islamic,

---

[44] Conklin 1997:2.
[45] Dvornik 1966.
[46] Papamastorakis 2005.
[47] Podskalsky 1972.
[48] Angelov 2007.

the Turko-Mongol (Central Asian), and that of Byzantium.[49] These claims could take nonviolent forms, such as the "soft empire" strategies of trade and diplomacy.[50] Dimitris Kastritsis's essay in this volume examines Ottoman imperial ideology as expressed in a late-sixteenth-century chancery manual designed to represent the history of Ottoman diplomacy at the highest level. His analysis reveals that "soft power" strategies were articulated in the hierarchy of titulature and honorific titles meant for use in epistolary exchange between the Ottomans and the wider world. Universalist claims could also be expressed through expansionism and, therefore, war. Indeed, in the early Ottoman period, the Ottomans advanced the boundaries of their territory along the western coast of Asia Minor and in the Balkans by drawing on the *gazi "ethos"* as warriors for the faith (Islam). By the sixteenth century, Ottoman universalist claims had evolved to reflect territorial expansion. Focusing on a rich body of sixteenth-century *portolan* charts, atlases, and *isolaria* in Ottoman-Turkish, Pinar Emiralioğlu demonstrates how the development of a heightened Ottoman sensitivity to geographical knowledge about the Mediterranean (following the conquest of lands in the eastern Mediterranean, the North African littoral, and the territories bordering the Red Sea) reflected the importance of the Roman *Mare Nostrum* as a model to be emulated by the Ottomans in the quest for imperial domination. Despite strategies of "soft power," war remained the preeminent resource for imperial expansion. Antonis Anastasopoulos shows how geographical constraints become particularly prominent, and affect imperial authority and policy, when considering the movement of troops or the difficulties of imperial tax collecting.

Several essays address the issue of the transition from empire to nation-state in terms of a model of space as contested or subject to overlapping jurisdictions (Sayek, Güthenke, Batsaki). Subjects within that space are shown to have similarly malleable identities. Focusing on two spatial practices where imperial and foreign sovereignties conflicted and overlapped in the urban environment of Izmir/Smyrna, (foreign) property ownership and diplomatic protocol, Zandi-Sayek shows that during the Tanzimat, the Ottoman state was working to strengthen its control of property and diplomatic transactions that had traditionally enabled foreign states to exercise privileges and secure exemptions in Ottoman territory. Changing the scene to a former Ottoman dominion negotiating its new identity as nascent nation-state in the 1830s, Constanze Güthenke notes how the choice of Athens over Nafplio for the capital of the Greek state stumbled against the vague legal status of public land. Examining space through

---

[49]   Göçek 1993.
[50]   Casale 2010.

the peregrinations of two literary characters, Güthenke stresses "the indeterminacy and the volatile locations of identity that attach to a Greek territory that
is to a large extent first realized in writing." Focusing on a literary depiction
of Egypt and Crete as "third spaces" between the nascent Greek state and the
Ottoman Empire, Yota Batsaki shows how strategies of triangulation in a late-
twentieth-century Modern Greek novel revisit the question of national identity
against the background of the region's colonial legacies.

The current vogue of empire in cultural studies is related to the contemporary world of transnational economic networks, political alliances, and military
interventions. A substantial literature addresses the lingering sense that global
relations are still structured by imperial dynamics, for better or worse.[51] The
concluding essay, by Sahar Bazzaz, on the "Sunni Triangle" and the surprising
persistence of Orientalist rhetoric in the coverage of the Iraq War in, *The New
York Times*, moves us forward to the present, to ponder the continuing hold of
imagined geographies and their real-life political implications.

A Note on Transliterations

*The transcription of Greek words adheres to the style guide of the Harvard Center for
Hellenic Studies, Washington, DC. The transcription of Arabic, Persian, Ottoman and
Turkish words follows the normal practices.*

---

[51] Ferguson 2004; Harvey 2005; Hardt and Negri 2000.

Works Cited

Angelov, D. 2007. *Imperial Ideology and Political Thought in Byzantium, 1204-1330.* Cambridge.

Ayalon, A. 1995. *The Press in the Arab Middle East: A History.* New York.

Aydin, C. 2007. *The Politics of Anti-Westernism in Asia: Visions of World Order in Pan-Islamic and Pan-Asian Thought.* New York.

Bang, P. and Bayly, C., eds. 2011. *Tributary Empires in Global History.* Houndmills and New York.

Bang, P. and Kolodziejczyk, D., eds. 2012. *Universal Empire: A Comparative Approach to Imperial Culture and Representation in Eurasian History.* Cambridge.

Belke, K. 2002. "Roads and Travel in Macedonia and Thrace in the Middle and Late Byzantine Periods." In Macrides 2002:73-90.

Bell, M., Butlin R. and Heffernan M., eds. 1995. *Geography and Imperialism 1820-1940.* Manchester.

Blunt, A. and McEwan C., eds. 2002. *Postcolonial Geographies.* London.

Braude B. and Lewis, B., eds. 1982. *Christians and Jews in the Ottoman Empire: The Functioning of a Plural Society.* New York.

Casale, G. 2010. *The Ottoman Age of Exploration.* Oxford.

Chrysos, E., ed. 2005. *Byzantium as Oecumene.* Athens.

Conklin, A. 1997. *A Mission to Civilize: The Republican Idea of Empire in France and West Africa, 1895-1930.* Stanford.

Cooper, F. 2004. "Empire Multiplied: A Review Essay." *Comparative Studies in Society and History* 46:247-272.

Driver, F. 1992. "Geography's Empire: Histories of Geographical Knowledge." *Environment and Planning D: Society and Space* 10:23-40.

Dvornik, F. 1966. *Early Christian and Byzantine Political Philosophy: Origins and Background.* 2 vols. Washington, DC.

Ferguson, N. 2004. *Colossus: the Rise and Fall of the American Empire.* London.

Foss, C. 1979. *Ephesus after Antiquity: A Late Antique, Byzantine and Turkish City.* Cambridge.

Edney, M. 1997. *Mapping an Empire: The Geographical Construction of British India, 1765-1843.* Chicago.

Geyer, B. 2002. "Physical Factors in the Evolution of the Landscape and Land Use." In Laiou 2002: 31-45.

Göçek, F. Müge. 1993. "The Social Construction of an Empire: Ottoman State under Sülaymân the Magnificent." In Inalcik and Kafadar 2010:93-108.

———. 1996. *Rise of the Bourgeoisie, Demise of Empire: Ottoman Westernization and Social Change.* New York.

Godlewska, A. and Smith N., eds. 1994. *Geography and Empire.* Oxford.

Gregory, D. 1994. *Geographical Imaginations*. Oxford.

Haldon, J. 1999. *Warfare, State and Society in the Byzantine World*. London.

——, ed. 2006. *General Issues in the Study of Medieval Logistics: Sources, Problems and Methodologies*. Leiden.

Hanioğlu, Ş. 2008. *A Brief History of the Late Ottoman Empire*. Princeton.

Hardt, M. and Negri, A. 2000. *Empire*. Cambridge, MA.

Harley, J.B. 2001. *The New Nature of Maps: Essays in the History of Cartography*. Baltimore.

Harvey, D. 2005. *The New Imperialism*. Oxford and New York.

Hathaway, J. 2008. *The Arab Lands under Ottoman Rule, 1516-1800*. Harlow.

Hess, A. 1978. *The Forgotten Frontier: A History of the Sixteenth-Century Ibero-African Frontier*. Chicago.

Hendy, M. 1985. *Studies in the Byzantine Monetary Economy, c. 300-1450*. Cambridge.

Hobsbawm, E. 1989. *The Age of Empire, 1875-1914*. New York.

Holden, S. 2009. *The Politics of Food in Modern Morocco*. Gainsville, Florida.

Horden, P. and Purcell, N. 2000. *The Corrupting Sea: A Study of Mediterranean History*. Oxford.

Hourani, A. 1983. *Arabic Thought in the Liberal Age, 1798-1939*. New York and Cambridge.

Inalcik, H. 2010. "Istanbul." *Encyclopaedia of Islam,* Second edition eds. P. Bearman, Th. Banquis, C.E. Bosworth, E. van Donzel, W.P. Heinrichs. Brill Online. Harvard University. December 21, 2010. <http://www.brillonline.nl/subscriber/entry?entry=islam_COM-0393>

Inalcik, H. et al., eds. 1994. *Social and Economic History of the Ottoman Empire, 1300-1600*, 2 vols. Cambridge.

Inalcik, H. and Kafadar C., eds. 1993. *Sülaymân the Second and His Time*. Istanbul.

Jasanoff, M. 2005. *Edge of Empire: Lives, Culture, and Conquest in the East, 1750-1850*. New York.

Jeffreys, E., Haldon, J. and Cormack, R., eds. 2008. *Oxford Handbook of Byzantine Studies*. Oxford.

Kafadar, C. 1995. *Between Two Worlds: The Construction of the Ottoman State*. Berkeley.

——. 2007. "A Rome of One's Own: Reflections on Cultural Geography and Identity in the Lands of Rum." *Muqarnas* 24:7-26.

Kaldellis, A. 2009. *The Christian Parthenon: Classicism and Pilgrimage in Byzantine Athens*. Cambridge.

Kamen, H. 2003. *Empire: How Spain Became a World Power, 1492-1763*. New York.

Karateke H. T. and Reinkowski M., eds. 2005. *Legitimizing the Order: the Ottoman Rhetoric of State Power*. Leiden.

Karateke, H. 2005. "Legitimizing the Ottoman Sultanate: A Framework for Historical Analysis." In Karateke and Reinkowski 2005:13-52.

Karpat, K. 1982. "Millets and Nationality: the Roots of the Incongruity of Nation and State in the Post-Ottoman Era." In Braude and Lewis 1982:141–170.

Kayali, H. 1997. *Arabs and Young Turks: Ottomanism, Arabism and Islamism in the Ottoman Empire, 1908–1918.* Berkeley.

Kitromilides, P. 1992. *The Enlightenment as Social Criticism: Iosipos Moisiodax and Greek Culture in the Eighteenth Century.* Princeton.

Khuri-Makdisi, I. 2010. *The Eastern Mediterranean and the Making of Global Radicalism, 1860–1914.* Berkeley.

Laiou, A., ed. 2002. *Economic History of Byzantium*, 3 vols. Washington, DC.

Lewis, M. W. and Wigen, K. 1997. *The Myth of Continents: A Critique of Metageography.* Berkeley.

Lieven, D. 2002. *Empire: The Russian Empire and its Rivals.* New Haven.

Macrides, R., ed. 2002. *Travel in the Byzantine World.* Aldershot.

Mazower, M. 2005. *Salonika, City of Ghosts: Christians, Muslims and Jews, 1430–1950.* New York.

McCormick, M. 2001. *Origins of the European Economy: Communications and Commerce, AD 300–900.* Cambridge.

McKee, S. 2002. *Uncommon Dominion: Venitian Crete and the Myth of Ethnic Purity.* Philadelphia.

McNeill, J. R. 1992. *Mountains of the Mediterranean: An Environmental History.* Cambridge.

Mikhail, A. 2011. *Nature and Empire in Ottoman Egypt: An Environmental History.* Cambridge.

Murphey, R. 1999. *Ottoman Warfare, 1500–1700.* London.

Necipoğlu, G. 1991. *Architecture, Ceremonial and Power: The Topkapi Palace in the Fifteenth and Sixteenth Centuries.* Cambridge, MA.

Oikonomides, N. 1985. "Ottoman Influence on Late Byzantine Fiscal Practices." *Südost-Forschungen* 45:1–24.

Owen, E.R. 1993. *The Middle East in the World Economy, 1800–1914.* London.

Papamastorakis, T. 2005. "Orb of the Earth: Images of Imperial Universality." In Chrysos:79–105.

Pagden, A. 1995. *Lords of All the World: Ideologies of Empire in Spain, Britain and France c.1500–c.1800.* New Haven.

Philliou, C. 2010. *Biography of an Empire: Governing Ottomans in the Age of Revolution.* Berkeley.

Podskalsky, G. 1972. *Byzantinische Reichseschatologie: Die Periodisierung der Weltgeschichte in den vier Grossreichen (Daniel 2 und 7) und dem tausendjährigen Friedensreiche (Apok. 20).* Munich.

Pryor, J. 1988. *Geography, Technology, and War: Studies in the Maritime History of the Mediterranean, 649-1571.* Cambridge.

Rheidt, K. 1991. *Die Stadtgrabung,* II. *Die byzantinische Wohnstadt.* Altertümer von Pergamon, 15. Berlin.

Rheidt, K. 2002. "The Urban Economy of Pergamon." In Laiou 2002:623–629.

Said, E. 1993. *Culture and Imperialism.* New York.

———. 1978. *Orientalism.* New York.

Sajdi, D., ed. 2007. *Ottoman Tulips, Ottoman Coffee: Leisure and Lifestyle in the Eighteenth-Century.* London and New York.

———. 2007. "Decline, its Discontents, and Ottoman Cultural History: By Way of Introduction." In Sajdi:1-40.

Soja, E. 2009. "Taking Space Personally." In Warf and Arias 2009:11–35.

———. 1996. *Thirdspace. Journeys to Los Angeles and Other Real-and-Imagined Places.* Oxford.

Stephenson, P. 2000. *Byzantium's Balkan Frontier: A Political Study of the Northern Balkans, 900-1204.* Cambridge.

Vryonis, S. 1969/70. "The Byzantine Legacy and Ottoman Forms." *Dumbarton Oaks Papers* 23/24:51–308.

———. 1976. "Nomadization and Islamization in Asia Minor." *Dumbarton Oaks Papers* 29:41–71.

Warf, B. 2008. *Time-Space Compression: Historical Geographies.* New York.

Warf, B. and Arias, S., eds. 2009. *The Spatial Turn: Interdisciplinary Perspectives.* New York.

Whittow, M. 2008. "Geographical Survey." In Jeffreys, Haldon and Cormack 2008:219–231.

1

Constantine VII and the Historical Geography of Empire

Paul Magdalino

HISTORY AND GEOGRAPHY were fundamental to the identity of Byzantium as an ecumenical empire with a long existence in time and an outreach that extended to three continents. Yet while the Byzantine elite maintained a long and distinguished tradition of history writing, it produced no geographers and travel writers to compare with those of antecedent and neighboring or comparable cultures. There was no Byzantine equivalent of Strabo, Ptolemy, Pausanias, Ibn Hawqal, al-Idrisi, Gerald of Wales, William of Rubruck, Marco Polo, or Evliya Çelebi. Byzantine geographical theory did not rise above the level of commentary on Strabo and Ptolemy, and geographical treatises were almost nonexistent.[1] The three main works date from the sixth century, a period that was as much Late Roman as it was Byzantine, and none of them contains much discussion of real geography. The *Ethnika* of the Constantinopolitan teacher (grammarian) Stephanos of Byzantium (ca. 528–535), which apart from a few fragments survives mainly in a later epitome, is essentially a list of ethnic names related, where appropriate, to the places from which they derive; the geographical information it contains is largely incidental, uneven, and derived from ancient literature.[2] The *Synekdēmos* of another grammarian, Hierokles, is a list of imperial provinces with the cities belonging to each.[3] The *Christian Topography* (Χριστιανικὴ Κοσμογραφία), written slightly later, does not live up to the geographical promise of its title, or of the name attributed to its author, the so-called "Cosmas Indicopleustes" or "Cosmas the Indian sailor."[4] The author's firsthand experience of tropical travel contributes very little to the work, which consists mainly

[1] Hunger 1978: I, 507–542.
[2] Meineke 1849; entries A–Γ in Billerbeck 2006.
[3] Honigmann 1939.
[4] Wolska-Conus 1968–1973.

23

of a lengthy demonstration from Scripture that the earth is a box-like structure with a semi-cylindrical upper story corresponding to the heavens.[5] Yet, in the poverty of their geographical research, these non-geographies are not atypical of Byzantine attitudes to the geography of the world beyond Constantinople, as reflected in Byzantine literature. Byzantine literature as a whole not only reveals a deafening lack of curiosity about the empire's provincial territories, let alone the lands beyond its borders; several authors notoriously express a positive distaste for life and travel anywhere outside the capital.[6]

In spite of this, Byzantines had to think geographically, and many of them had to travel, whether they liked it or not.[7] There were two central facts of their culture that held them to a geographical outlook, beyond the basic functions of agriculture and trade. The first was the topography of holiness: the network of *loca sancta*, emanating from Jerusalem, through which the Gospel of Christ's Resurrection had been preached throughout the world by the apostles, and the power of faith in the Christian God had been made manifest, first by martyrs in the towns, and then by holy monks in the desert fringes of agricultural society.[8] The diffusion of apostles, martyrs, and ascetics created a *hagio-geography* of sacred sites where their bodily presence was venerated, in death as in life, and their miraculous intervention was sought. This hagio-geography partly replaced, and partly redrew, the map of the pagan cult centers of the ancient Roman world. Like its ancient predecessor, it did not correspond exactly to the map of imperial power and administration, and it generated much movement in search of holiness. Pilgrimage never stopped, and the ultimate pilgrimage destination remained Jerusalem and the Holy Land. Monasteries drew visitors seeking spiritual benefits and physical therapy. Monks themselves were often on the move in search of spiritual opportunities. Byzantine hagiography indeed constitutes a not inconsiderable body of travel literature,[9] whose perception of travel is not negative even though its information on places is minimal and marginal—just as the splendid locations of most Byzantine monasteries barely rate a mention in the accounts of their foundation. The most positive and geographically informative piece of travel literature surviving from Byzantium is a late twelfth-century *Description of the Holy Places*.[10]

---

[5] Wolska-Conus 1962.
[6] Galatariotou 1993; Magdalino 2000 [2007].
[7] Macrides 2002.
[8] Kazakou and Skoulas 2008.
[9] Malamut 1993.
[10] PG, vol. 133:923–962; Wilkinson 1988:315–336. Messis 2011 has shown that this text has been wrongly attributed to the priest John Phokas, and that the real author was a high-ranking imperial official under Manuel I, the *sebastos* John Doukas.

However, the second and primary impulse to geographical thinking in Byzantium came from the mechanisms and logistics of empire. The measurement and evaluation of landed resources,[11] the planning and execution of defensive and offensive warfare, the management of communications and supplies, the dispatch and reception of embassies, the gathering of foreign intelligence, the deployment of administrative personnel in the provinces and the frontier areas, and the referral of decisions from the periphery to the center: all of these activities required a conception of differences and distances between spaces and places. The geography of empire lay behind most of the perceptions of peoples and places expressed in Byzantine non-religious sources. This is obviously true of the Byzantine historians, whose geographical information is linked to their narratives of war, civil war, and diplomacy. But even the "geographical denial" which, as we have seen, typifies Byzantine literary attitudes to life and travel outside Constantinople, reflects the geographical dimension of the imperial experience. It reflects, first of all, the enormous attraction of Constantinople as a magnet of ambition, a cultural metropolis, and a center of consumption on a global scale. It also reflects the extent to which displacement from Constantinople was a function of imperial power, for the intellectuals who complained about the wretchedness of foreign travel or provincial residence were all officially assigned to their locations—whether as members of diplomatic missions, as civil administrators, as bishops of remote episcopal sees, or simply as political exiles.[12]

Was geography, then, like trade, something that the Byzantine elite accepted as a practical necessity, but deemed unworthy of theoretical formulation, and preferred not to get involved in directly? Did they lack a systematic, coherent conception of imperial geography in the way that they arguably lacked a view of the monetary economy as a coherent system?[13] For the late antique/early Byzantine period, there are several pieces of evidence that the imperial response to geographical logistics was not merely piecemeal and *ad hoc*. There are the rare surviving maps, such as the *Tabula Peutingeriana* and the Madaba mosaic, that reflect a cartographic habit.[14] There is the early fifth-century *Notitia* of Constantinople, a detailed description of the city, quarter by quarter, which could serve as the specification for a map.[15] There are the massive imperial building projects of the Later Roman Empire, from the foundation of new

---

[11] Lefort et al. 1991.
[12] Mullett 1996:22–23.
[13] Laiou and Morrisson 2007:1–7.
[14] Talbert 2010, Bowersock 2006.
[15] Seeck 1876:229–243.

imperial capitals in the early fourth century to the comprehensive fortification program of Anastasios and Justinian two hundred years later. All these projects required a sophisticated knowledge of local geography, as well as expertise in civil engineering. In particular, we may mention the long-distance aqueduct system of Constantinople, which has recently been investigated in detail; it extended over 200 kilometers, and involved careful mapping of the geology, hydrology, and elevation of the entire region.[16] Finally, it should be noted that Procopius' book on the *Buildings* of Justinian, though a shameless panegyric with a heavy emphasis on church building, also contains much information on harbors, bridges, and baths, and provides a comprehensive overview of the empire's defense infrastructure that must have been based on government records.[17] It shows that Justinian himself not only had a global vision of imperial geography but liked to have it put in writing. In the light of this observation, the two geographical treatises of the grammarians Stephanos and Hierokles, disappointing though they are in terms of information, take on significance from the fact that both were composed in the early years of Justinian's reign.

To what extent did this geographical vision of empire, and the desire to articulate it, survive the collapse of the ancient world and the transition to the smaller, poorer, and culturally deprived Byzantine Empire of the Middle Ages? The answer is to be sought in the official literature of the tenth century that may be loosely characterized as treatises on government. By far the largest group in this category is the series of military treatises, starting with the *Taktika* of the emperor Leo VI from 905–906 and ending with the *Taktika* of Nikephoros Ouranos from 1010–1011.[18] These texts, which include manuals on naval and siege warfare, necessarily pay close and detailed attention to the geography of military operations and cover a full range of possibilities. Some of them are explicitly concerned with particular regions. However, on the whole they deal in general, transferable geographical features, and rarely refer to the unique geography of a specific area. For a specific focus on imperial geography as the principal object of attention (and not as a transferable model), we have to turn to the two treatises in which the emperor Constantine VII Porphyrogenitus (913–959) discussed the empire's provinces and the foreign peoples with whom the empire had to deal. These works are, respectively, the *De thematibus* (DT)[19] and the so-called *De administrando imperio* (DAI).[20] It should be noted that the latter

[16] Crow, Bardill and Bayliss 2008.
[17] Dewing 1914–1940, vol. 7.
[18] See e.g. PG, vol. 107: 671–1120, Dennis 1985; Dennis 2010, McGeer 1995, Sullivan 2000.
[19] Pertusi, A., ed. 1952. *Costantino Porfirogenito, De thematibus.* Rome, Città del Vaticano.
[20] Ed. Moravcsik, trans. Jenkins 1967, commentary in Jenkins 1962.

work has no Greek title apart from the address to the emperor's son Romanos.[21] Between them, these works offer a rich, comprehensive, and quintessentially Byzantine historical geography of empire.

The *DT* is a survey of the administrative divisions ("themes" or *themata*) that had replaced the provinces of the Later Roman Empire.[22] Book 1, devoted to the eastern themes (i.e. the Aegean islands and Cyprus) is dateable to ca. 934; Book 2, on the European provinces, shows signs of having been added in a revision of the original version some 80–90 years later. In his Preface (DT:59–60), Constantine emphasizes that the themes were an innovation, which he rightly connects with the great territorial losses that the empire suffered from the reign of Heraclius, but wrongly explains as a result of the emperors no longer leading their troops in battle. His 17 chapters on the Anatolian and Aegean themes vary greatly in length, from more than two pages in Pertusi's edition on the great central Anatolian provinces of Anatolikon and Armeniakon to only a few lines on some of the newly formed units on the eastern frontier. The type of coverage can also be inconsistent and random. Over half of the entry on Paphlagonia in Pertusi's Chapter 7 is devoted to a rant, based on Homer, against the despicable Paphlagonians.[23] The six lines on the theme of Mesopotamia in Pertusi's Chapter 9 merely record its recent upgrading from the status of a frontier outpost (*kleisoura*) after the local Armenian lords had surrendered their castles to Constantine's father, the emperor Leo VI (DT:73). The eleven-line entry on the theme of Sebasteia, by contrast, consists entirely of an explanation of the etymology of the name Caesar, the derivation of Sebasteia from Sebastos-Augustus having apparently triggered an association with the parallel derivation of the name Caesarea.[24] To some extent, this uneven treatment reflects the uneven nature of Constantine's sources. While he clearly relied regularly on the *Synekdēmos* of Hierokles for the provincial divisions and distribution of towns before the institution of the themes, he otherwise gives the impression of using whatever materials happened to come to hand or to mind—whether it was Homer, the Bible, Strabo, Stephanos, the *De magistratibus* of John the Lydian, or epigrams from the poetic anthology of Kephalas (DT:66, 70), soon to be re-edited under Constantine's patronage as the Palatine Anthology.

---

[21] I find the most convincing explanation to be that of Signes Codoñer 2004, who postulates that the section headings and the individual entries in the form of source excerpts (usually introduced by ἐκ) or specially composed notices (introduced by ὅτι or ἰστέον ὅτι) are as Constantine left them, but that the chapter headings (introduced by περί) were originally marginal comments of a later reader that were subsequently copied into the main text.

[22] Haldon 1999:71–85.

[23] DT:72; Magdalino 1998.

[24] See Chapter 11, DT:74; also see Chapter 2, DT:65.

Occasionally, Constantine quotes a totally random source. Thus in his attempt to relate the theme of Anatolikon with the former Roman province of Asia, he cites two inscriptions commemorating provincial governors: one from the tombstone/sarcophagus in Smyrna of a certain proconsul Publius, and the other from a set of repoussé silver plates in the imperial treasury that had belonged to, or been donated by, one Jordanes "commander of the East and of the other nations in Asia Minor" (DT:61–62). Later, in Chapter 12, on the newly created theme of Lykandos, Constantine quotes a rather more dubious inscription that Justinian had supposedly set up on the city walls to honor the local mayor, Thomas.[25] Justinian, not yet emperor, had been passing through as commander in chief of the imperial forces, and Thomas had made him a little gift of 10,000 sheep in ten different colors.

Nevertheless, the *DT* is not without method. Constantine is consistently concerned to relate the present theme system to the ancient administrative and human map that it overlays. In a number of entries, he goes through a checklist of points: he explains the name of the theme where this is not self-evident, he outlines the boundaries of the province, and he lists its towns. He also, intriguingly, describes the inhabitants of Asia Minor in terms of their ancient ethnic names. One might be tempted to dismiss this as an affected or unthinking anachronism but for the insistence with which he uses the present tense and repeats the words ἔθνη and γένη; as we shall see, the units of "nation" and "people" are basic to Constantine's geographical thinking in the *DAI*. In other ways, too, the *DT* anticipates the presentation of geographical information in the later treatise. While it frequently defines territories in terms of coasts and rivers, it almost never mentions mountains and plains. It notes the presence of architectural wonders: Justinian's great bridge over the Sangarios river,[26] the Mausoleum at Halikarnassos, and the temple of Aphrodite at Knidos (DT:78). It registers places associated with famous ancient people and events: the river Granikos as the site of Alexander's famous victory (DT:69), Amaseia as the birthplace of Strabo (DT:63), and Kotyaeion as the birthplace of Aesop (DT:69). Repeated attention is given to hagiography. Under the theme of Armeniakon, Cappadocia is highlighted as the homeland of numerous saints, including St. Gregory of Nazianzos whose relic, as Constantine observes, he had brought to Constantinople for reburial in the church of the Holy Apostles (DT:66). In the theme of Thrakesioi, Constantine mentions the famous sanctuary of the Archangel Michael at Chonai (DT:68). Under Seleukeia, Constantine records that the shield of St. Theodore the Great Martyr hangs under the dome of the church at Dalisandos (DT:77),

---

[25] See Chapter 12, DT:76.
[26] DT:70; Whitby 1985.

while the mention of Myra, in the theme of Kibyrraiotai, occasions the remark that this is where the great St. Nicholas, the servant of God, exudes an unguent (*myron*) according to the name of the city (DT:78).

The mention of the translation of St. Gregory of Nazianzos points to another, unmistakably imperial, aspect of Constantine VII's geographical outlook. It is centered on Constantinople, and Constantinople is the constant point of reference. Characteristic is Constantine's explanation for the name of the Anatolikon *thema*. "This theme is called Anatolikon not because it properly belongs to the eastern parts, where the sun rises, but because it is east for us the inhabitants of Byzantium and the land of Europe" (DT:60). In fact, the *thema* derived its name from the field army of Oriens who had been stationed there after their withdrawal from the eastern frontier in the face of the Arab onslaught.[27]

The Constantinopolitan perspective is maintained in Constantine's main geographical work, the *DAI*, which can be dated on internal evidence to the years 949–952. This text remains one of the most enigmatic compositions in the whole of Byzantine literature, and there is still no consensus as to the reason for its infuriating inconsistencies. Were these due to imperfect editing, incomplete filing, or careless copying, as most scholars believe (although there is no consensus as to exactly how or when the dossier was constituted)?[28] Or do they mask a highly sophisticated and devious agenda, as one scholar has maintained in an elaborate argument that has been consistently ignored but never effectively refuted?[29] In this view, Constantine did not feel able to express himself directly even in a private memorandum to his son and heir, and was deliberately oblique in advocating policies that he knew to be controversial and contested, notably his policy of "limited ecumenicity" in regard to Byzantine imperial claims—the effective renunciation of Roman sovereignty and even suzerainty over most of western Europe and Italy.

The problems of decoding the *DAI* begin with the earliest and only seriously important manuscript, Parisinus Graecus 2009. This was copied in the late eleventh century for a very important political figure, the Caesar John Doukas, and Brigitte Mondrain has thrown out the intriguing hypothesis that Doukas and his scribe, Michael Rozaites, were responsible for the arrangement of the material in its present form.[30] This form can only be described as opaque. The treatise combines prescriptive advice with ethnographical descriptions, which, it has been suggested, derive from a separate work, a Περὶ ἐθνῶν. Up-to-the

---

[27] Haldon 1999:73.
[28] For a sample of divergent recent interpretations, see Sode 1994, Howard-Johnston 2000, Signes Codoñer 2004.
[29] Lounges 1990.
[30] Mondrain 2002.

minute information is juxtaposed with antiquated and often fanciful historical material, raw documentary data with worked-up narratives, original reports with passages lifted from the ninth-century chronicles of Theophanes and George the Monk. There are enormous distortions in the historical perspective, with Diocletian mentioned more frequently than Constantine, who appears in a mainly legendary role, and Justinian I glaringly absent. Yet, as in the *DT*, there is method amid the apparent chaos, and the *DAI* in fact has a clearly defined structure, which it declares up front. In the Preface that Constantine addresses to his son and co-emperor, he outlines a clear five-point agenda. His work, it is stated, will set out information and advice under the following headings:

> Nations that are useful and dangerous to the empire, and how to use them against each other (Chapters 1-13).

> Their insatiable demands (Chapter 13).

> Differences between other nations: "their origins and customs and manner of life, and the position and climate of the land they dwell in, its geographical description and measurement" (Chapters 14–46).

> "Events which have occurred at various times between the Romans and various nations" (Chapters 47–48).

> Changes that have been introduced at various times in "our state/city" and throughout the whole Roman Empire (Chapters 49–53).

Throughout the work, this structure is formally adhered to. The headings are reiterated in almost identical terms, and on the whole they recognizably correspond to the material that follows them. Although it is not always clear why some chapters fall under one rubric rather than another, the classification scheme generally makes more than less sense of apparent inconsistencies, and notably the fact that the geographical information on the Black Sea region is divided among three different sections. Indeed, if the work has a concealed agenda, the key to unlocking this may lie in matching the section headings exactly to the section contents. More prosaically, and perhaps more plausibly, the occasional mismatch between contents and headings, and the generally disjointed character of the work as a whole, may be explained by reading the headings as the titles of files into which Constantine sorted his materials with the intention—which he never realized—of connecting them into a continuous narrative.

The multiplicity of files and the unprocessed heterogeneity of their contents create not only a moving lens but also an abruptly shifting depth of focus and angle of vision, which together present a highly fragmented tableau of imperial geography: a series of animated vignettes with a bewildering variety of scales and legends, rather than a uniform panorama. The camera dwells first on the area north of the Black Sea (Chapters 1–13, DAI:44–65), then switches to record some scenes of policy-making at imperial headquarters (Chapter 13, DAI:66–77), before taking a rapid tour of the Islamic Mediterranean (Chapters 14–25, DAI:77–109). Coming around to Italy, it lingers there a little (Chapters 26–28, DAI:109–121), as a preliminary to shooting detailed footage on Dalmatia and the Balkan Slavs (Chapters 29–36, DAI:122–165), and revisiting the Black Sea area (Chapters 36–42, DAI:166–189). Then there are some equally close-up shots of the Armenian, Arab, and Georgian principalities on the eastern frontier (Chapters 43–46, DAI:189–223). This is followed by brief shots of Cyprus and Cyzicus (Chapters 47–48, DAI:224–227), after which the focus shifts inside the empire to register administrative changes in the Peloponnese (DAI:228–237, 256–257), Asia Minor (DAI:237–243), and the imperial entourage (DAI:244–257). The final scene is a long piece of action set in Cherson, in the Crimea, so that the coverage ends where it began, north of the Black Sea (Chapter 53, DAI:258–287).

The difference in coverage lies not just in the degree of zooming and lingering, but also in the depth of the historical dimension and the relative density of topographical and genealogical information. The first 12 chapters, which concern the importance of maintaining good relations with the Pechenegs, contain no history but report current steppe politics and diplomacy, and Chapter 9 consists of a long, detailed topographical description of the river and sea route taken by the Rus from the Baltic area to the Black Sea. The greater part of Chapter 13, which forms the second section of the work, contains absolutely no geography but fabricates much bogus history, invoking mythical curses of Constantine the Great to fob off the importunate northern barbarians who come asking for precious state assets like crowns, Greek fire, and imperial daughters.

The long, central, ethnographic section 3 (Chapters 14–46), which sweeps clockwise around the Mediterranean and Black Sea from Syria to Armenia, is full of the history of the peoples who occupy these former imperial territories and the genealogies of their rulers. But the history varies considerably in timespan, emphasis, originality, and accuracy. Chapters 14–25, covering the Islamic world, are primarily the history of the Arabs, except for Chapters 23–25, where the focus is more on the territory of Spain and on all the peoples who have occupied it since its loss to the empire. All these chapters, however, are lifted mainly from chronicles and, in the case of Spain, from Stephanos of Byzantium.

Chapters 26–28 contain three original narratives on the history of Italy from the time of the Lombard invasions, all probably deriving from oral accounts of Italian visitors to Constantinople. Constructed to make sense of the present territorial status quo, they are reasonably accurate on the history of the recent past, but degenerate into pure fantasy when they try to explain the more remote origins of the political divisions of the Italian peninsula between the imperial provinces and dependencies, notably Venice, on the one hand, and the Lombard and Frankish controlled areas on the other.[31] The sixth-century Lombard occupation is effectively transposed to the eighth century. This is one of several instances where Constantine should have known better, and perhaps did, but chose to propagate, or to go along with, a version of history that suited his diplomatic agenda—in this case a division of Italy into Frankish and Byzantine spheres of domination.

Chapters 29–36, on Dalmatia and the western Balkans, are similarly constructed to rationalize the presence of the Croats and Serbs on former imperial territory. However, here the story begins much earlier and is told in much greater detail. It has four main phases:

1. The settlement of Romans in Dalmatia by Diocletian because he greatly loved the country.

2. The expansion of these *Rhōmanoi* as far as the Danube and their wars with the Avars, equated with the Slavs, who eventually broke through the frontier, overran the land, and drove the *Rhōmanoi* back on the coastal cities and islands.

3. The arrival of the Croats and Serbs and their settlement authorized by the emperor Heraclius, who had some groups baptized.

4. The genealogy of the Croat and Serb rulers in the past century. Constantine must have obtained the elements of this narrative from both Dalmatian and Serbo-Croatian informants. The earlier parts of it are fanciful, but there is little reason to doubt the basic authenticity of the agreements between Heraclius and the Serbs and Croats, and none at all to question the facts, if not the chronology, of more recent events.

The ultimate purpose of the historical narrative is hinted at in those passages where Constantine records the achievement of his own ancestor, Basil I, in regaining imperial control of Dalmatia, and where he asserts, in identical wording, both for the prince of Croatia and the prince of Serbia, that each "has from the beginning, that is, ever since the reign of Heraclius the emperor, been in servitude and submission to the emperor of the Romans, and was never made subject to the prince of Bulgaria" (DAI:150–151, 160–161). This reminds us that the Christian kingdom of Bulgaria, the empire's closest political neighbor, firmly

---

[31] See von Falkenhausen 1989.

established on former imperial territory, was as conspicuous for its powerful presence in the Balkans and Black Sea region as it is for the massive absence of a chapter devoted to it in the *DAI*.

The looming absence of Bulgaria at the center of Constantine VII's imperial geography is palpable in the next few chapters of the ethnographic section (Chapters 36–42), which provide the historical background to the steppe nomad peoples whose strategic value to the empire was discussed in section 1. These are essentially the all-important Pechenegs and the Magyars, whom Constantine calls Turks. The emergence of both these groups from the area of the former Chazar empire north of the Black Sea occasions several references to the Chazars and the Uz, and the final settlement of the Magyars on the territory of Greater Moravia prompts a short chapter on the demise of that principality (Chapter 41). The history of these peoples, derived presumably from their own oral memories, begins relatively recently and concerns their clans and their migrations. The only exception is an account (in Chapter 42), reproduced from the contemporary history of *Theophanes Continuatus*, of the mission of a certain imperial official, Petronas Kamateros, sent by Theophilos to help the Chazars build the city of Sarkel.

The last chapters in the ethnographic section (Chapters 43–46) concern the recent history of the minor Caucasian principalities—Armenian, Arab, and Georgian—in the northern sector of the empire's eastern frontier. They are certainly not in any sense ethnographies of the nations in question, since the Arab caliphates have been dealt with at the start of the section, and the main kingdoms of Georgia and Armenia are barely mentioned at all. The principalities in question are clearly included because of their strategic importance to the empire, whether for blocking the advance of invading armies or for capturing the important Arab-held city of Erzerum (Theodosiopolis), and the desirability of keeping their princely dynasties, and indeed their towns and castles, under close imperial control. In these chapters, Constantine thus anticipates the future imperial policy of annexing Armenian and Georgian principalities as a result of more or less voluntary bequests by their rulers. In terms of his own filing system, he also anticipates the next section that is labeled "relations between the empire and foreign powers," so one might ask whether these Caucasian chapters have not been wrongly filed. As for the historical dimension, although the Georgian chapters are introduced with the myth of the nation's descent from King David, the real dynastic history in each case effectively covers no more than the last three generations: in other words, the period of oral memory. Constantine could have had his information from more than one source: from the imperial agents, like Constantine Lips, who were dispatched to deal with the princes, as well as from the various members of the princely families themselves who spent time in Constantinople.

Like the historical coverage of the ethnographic section, the topographical and geographical focus is uneven. Most of the chapters on Italy and eastern Europe end with lists of the main cities, but otherwise the section as a whole provides no consistent geographical information, and very few parts of it supply all the data promised in the section heading: "knowledge of the difference between other nations, their origins and customs and manner of life, and the position and climate of the land they dwell in, and its geographical description and measurement." While the origins of nations are regularly covered, and most chapters end with a list of the main towns in the area, the other aspects really only feature in the chapters on Dalmatia and the region north of the Danube and Black Sea.

The last two sections of the *DAI* can be dealt with more rapidly. Section 4, on "events which have taken place at various times between the Romans and different nations," consists of two chapters dealing with Justinian II's policy with regard to Cyprus. Section 5, on "internal reforms," is concerned mainly with administrative changes in the Peloponnese, Asia Minor, and the staff of the imperial palace. With one exception, it contains little geographical description, and refers to no events earlier than the ninth century, with its main focus being on the reigns of Constantine's immediate predecessors, Leo VI, Alexander, and Romanos I. The exception is the long, last Chapter 53, on the ancient history of the city of Cherson. Although the greater part of this seems highly inappropriate to the section where it has been filed, the notices appended at the end (DAI:284–287) point to a basic relevance. The first five of these notices indicate the locations east of the Crimea of various sources of naphtha, the inflammable petroleum that was vital for the manufacture of ὑγρὸν πῦρ (Greek fire), Byzantium's secret weapon.[32] The remaining three notices detail the reprisals that are to be taken if the Chersonitai revolt against the emperor. So the whole chapter is really about the need to keep a tight control over the city of Cherson, and it is in the file on internal reforms because, as we have been told in an earlier section (§3, Chapter 42), since the reign of Theophilos "it has been the rule for military governors in Cherson to be appointed from here [i.e. Constantinople]."

So what is the vision of imperial geography that the *DAI* presents us with? The text is plainly not a flat, diaphanous window, or even a single distorting lens, through which to view the geographical vista of the tenth-century Byzantine Empire; and it is certainly not the legend for a coherent, homogenous map, such as we do get in the sixth-century geographical list of Hierokles.

---

[32] Haldon 2006.

Rather it is a densely packed, intricate mosaic of unequal and highly refractory gemstones, offering a multiple split focus on a spatial image that is as much a reflection of the viewing subject as it is an objective vision of the landscape beyond. But in this aspect, it is not unlike the representation of spatial reality in Byzantine paintings of landscapes, or indeed in all medieval maps. And in its very patchwork of distortions, the *DAI* may accurately represent the optics of power by which Constantine VII viewed his empire in its geographical dimension and sought to share his vision with his son. It is analogous to his other main political compilation, the *Book of Ceremonies*, in the way that it states a comprehensive, general idea through the accumulation of highly specific prescriptions and descriptions. Both works are statements of power: this is what unites them, together with the *DT*, and this is what gives sense and coherence to their internal inconsistencies. Both are studies in the topography of power. The *De cerimoniis* builds up a picture of the demonstration of power in the ritual spaces of Constantinople; the *DAI* evokes the exercise of power in the geographical space of the *oikoumenē*. However, being a more personal and confidential document, apparently destined for the emperor's son and successor, it is also more partial, in every sense, although it hides its partiality under a discourse of objective, comprehensive reporting. It does not say everything, and it does not state the obvious, leaving its reader to infer the importance of what is being said.

That its selectivity is coded and deliberate, and not just the result of incomplete or unprocessed filing, must surely be concluded from the way the treatise downplays or totally ignores the empire's current relations with what we regard as the most important foreign powers on the mid tenth-century horizon—the Arab caliphates and emirates (including Crete), the German empire, and Bulgaria—while paying what seems like inordinate attention to the western Balkans, the peoples to the north of the Danube and Black Sea, and petty Caucasian princes. That Constantine's discourse is deliberately opaque can be inferred from the way that he keeps coming, in different contexts and from different angles, at the strategic importance of Greek fire and the security of the region that produces its main ingredient, naphtha. Section 1 prescribes the diplomacy among the northern peoples needed to keep the region secure. Section 2 provides the argument needed to prevent these northern peoples from gaining the secret of Greek fire. In Section 3, Constantine includes the invention of Greek fire in his account of Arab history taken from Theophanes, and later in that section (Chapter 42) he describes in detail the route, circumventing Bulgaria, from Thessalonike via the Danube to Cherson and the regions to the east of it. This is the only part of Section 3 that fulfills the heading's promise to provide distances. Then we learn, at the very end of Section 5, that the areas at the end of that route are none other than those where the naphta-yielding wells are located.

The power perspective of the *DAI*, which is surely the key to understanding the work, needs further investigation in terms of the power politics at the court of Constantine VII. In particular, Section 4, with its details of court appointments and administrative changes under Leo VI and Romanos I, needs to be examined in the light of Constantine's intention, which he expressed but never realized, of writing a sequel to his *Life of Basil* that would deal with the reigns of Basil's successors.[33] But we can safely conclude, for present purposes, that his geographical perspective in the *DAI* is a function of the power perspective. Constantine applies to each geographical area on the imperial horizon the degree of historical narrative and topographical description that is appropriate to his imperial and, we should add, dynastic interests. The depth and angle of coverage varies not only according to the quantity and quality of his sources and the degree of processing, but also, and I would argue primarily, according to the potential for imperial intervention and domination, both inside and outside the empire.

Thus the *DAI* may be seen to represent Constantine VII's considered and coherent view of the historical geography of empire, despite its inaccuracies, inconsistencies, and omissions, which are indeed an important part of the picture. If this is true, then it is also fair to conclude that where the work does reproduce geographical details, they represent what was of interest to Constantine, and not just what his informants chose to tell him. They reproduce, to some extent, the pattern of priorities that we saw in the *DT*. Several ethnographic chapters include lists of towns, both inhabited and abandoned. Mountains are unavoidably mentioned in connection with Dalmatia and the Slavs of the Peloponnese, but otherwise they figure much less prominently than coasts and rivers. The northern Black Sea littoral and the Dalmatian islands are described in some detail, and with attention to their importance for naval communications. The rivers Danube and Dnieper are also described in terms of communication, including details of journey times. Otherwise, the river systems of central and eastern Europe serve to mark the boundaries between peoples and to define the habitat of nomadic populations. Rivers again appear as boundary markers in the Caucasian chapters, where the mountains are again conspicuous by their absence, as too is Lake Van.

In general, the descriptions do not have much to say about land use and agricultural production, and trading activity is implied rather than described. Exceptional is the notice on the Georgian town of Ardanaoutzin, describing the defense, strategic value, and layout of the settlement along with its rich agricultural hinterland and commercial network, which produces an "enormous customs revenue" (DAI:216–217).

---

[33] See Preface to the *Life* in Bekker 1838:212.

Like the *DT*, the *DAI* pays attention to great ancient monuments of the past, in an area where they must have been much more scarce than in Asia Minor. Pride of place goes to Diocletian's palace at Split, which is indeed the basis for the whole historical narrative of the Dalmatian section (DAI:122–123). Chapter 40 signals three "ancient landmarks" of the former Danube frontier; going upstream, these are Trajan's bridge at Trajan's Gate, "the tower of the holy and great Constantine" at Belgrade, and the city of Sirmium. Chapter 37, on the Pechenegs, mentions six deserted cities on the Dniester, and adds: "Among these buildings of the ancient cities are found some distinctive traces of churches, and crosses hewn out of porous stone, whence some preserve a tradition that once on a time Romans had settlements there" (DAI:168–9). It is tempting to infer that the ancient monuments are mentioned in order to justify an imperial interest in the area.

A similar thought is prompted by the close attention to the hagiography of Dalmatia, which also recalls the *DT*. Chapter 29 lists the resting places of no less than seven saints, all of them venerated in Constantinople.

While these reminiscences of *DT* are specific to certain chapters of the *DAI*, there are two that pervade the text as a whole and may be seen as the defining characteristics of Constantine VII's vision of the historical geography of empire. One is the primary focus on peoples rather than territories, or peoples as the identifiers of the territories they occupy. The importance of ethnicity to Constantine is clear not only from the disproportionate size of the ethnographic section (22 out of 53 chapters), but also from the ethnocentric content of several other chapters: Chapters 1–13 on steppe diplomacy and Chapters 49–50 on the Peloponnesian Slavs. Even Chapters 51–53, on internal "reforms," treat certain groups of provincials almost as separate national entities: the Greeks of the Mani, the Mardaites of Attaleia, and of course the people of Cherson. It is particularly instructive to look at two passages where ethnicity is used, in one case to provide a false historical explanation, and in another case to justify a specious argument. In Chapter 47, Justinian II is said to look after the interests of Cyprus because he was a Cypriot. In Chapter 13, Constantine instructs his son to reject dynastic marriage proposals from northern peoples by telling them that inter-racial breeding is wrong: "For each nation has different customs and divergent laws and institutions, and should consolidate those things that are proper to it, and should form and develop out of the same nation the associations for the fusion of its life. For just as each animal mates with its own tribe, so it is right that each nation also should marry and cohabit not with those of other race and tongue but of the same tribe and speech" (DAI:74–75).

Additionally, a reading of the *DAI* amply confirms the Constantinople-centered vision of imperial geography that we saw in the *DT*. In every section,

Constantinople is the constant viewpoint and point of reference. This is always implicit, and in many passages it is made graphically explicit. Chapter 9 describes the river route taken by the Rus when they come to trade in Constantinople. When they come to the first set of rapids on the Dnieper, the channel at this point is said to be as narrow as the polo-ground of the imperial palace (DAI:58–59), while down-river they pass through a ford "as wide as the Hippodrome" (DAI:60–61). In Chapter 13, where the scene shifts to Constantinople, Constantine insists that the importunate requests of ambassadors from the northern nations are to be rebutted by invoking dread curses that Constantine the Great had inscribed on the altar of Hagia Sophia. In Chapter 21, the short notice, derived from Theophanes, of the Arab siege of Constantinople, is supplemented with the information that "the mosque of the Saracens in the imperial praetorium" was built at the request of the Arab commander, Masalmah (DAI:22–23). In Chapter 29, on Dalmatia, the city of Salona is said to be half as large as Constantinople (DAI:122–123), and the church of St Anastasia in Zadar is said to be a basilica resembling the Constantinopolitan church of the Chalkoprateia (DAI:138–139). The "Caucasian" chapters, 43–46, record not only the dispatch of imperial agents to the Armenian and Georgian principalities, but also the frequent visits of the princes and their relatives to Constantinople, where they were royally entertained and given imperial court titles, and the princely family of Taron even received, for a time, a sumptuous urban residence.[34] One of the two chapters in Section 4 is an excerpt from the canons of a church council, which, as the title specifies, was held in the "domed hall" of the imperial palace. Finally, Section 5 turns the spotlight squarely on Constantinople by including, under the category of administrative "reforms," in Chapters 50 and 51, the details of several recent appointments to court dignities and offices, mostly ceremonial. The long Chapter 51 is almost entirely about the staffing of the ceremonial galleys and barges by which the emperors from the time of Basil I onward traveled around the Sea of Marmara. These journeys took the emperors, mainly for recreation, as far as Nicomedia (Izmit) to the east, Region (Küçük Çekmece) to the west, and Pythia (Yalova), Prousa (Bursa), and Bithynian Mt Olympos (Uludağ) to the south. It is very likely that this was as far as any emperor after Basil I travelled outside Constantinople. In other words, this was the extent of the imperial geography that Constantine VII experienced for himself.

On a quick reading, these narratives of palatine procedure sit oddly with the adjacent notices on changes in provincial organization and military logistics, let alone the wider coverage of peoples and territories. We may feel that they are frivolous digressions in a work of historical geography; they seem

[34] DAI:190–191; Magdalino 2007:46–47.

more appropriate to Constantine's compendium on court protocol, the *De cerimoniis*.[35] Yet, fundamentally, these narratives complete the geographical picture of the *DAI*. Quite apart from their unstated, and I believe undoubted, political agenda, they fully conform to the optics of imperial power space that inform the work as a whole. They are not misfiled, and Constantine tells us so in the heading to the section, which, he says, will treat μὴ μόνον περὶ τῶν ἐν τῇ καθ'ἡμᾶς πολιτείᾳ, ἀλλὰ καὶ περὶ πάσης τῆς τῶν Ῥωμαίων ἀρχῆς κατά τινας χρόνους καινοτομηθέντων. However, we construe *politeia*—whether as "city" or "state"—it clearly represents a discrete entity within the boundaries of the empire of the *themata*. These boundaries were Constantine's virtual horizon; the limits of his real horizon, and of "our *politeia*," did not stretch beyond the Sea of Marmara. It is all the more remarkable, then, that he produced a work of historical geography which is still a fundamental source for the early medieval history of Serbia, Croatia, Hungary, and the Ukraine; and that these areas, which were never properly part of the medieval Byzantine Empire, were largely put on the historical map by tenth-century Byzantine imperialism.

[35] Reiske 1829–1830, vol. I; Vogt 1935–1940.

Abbreviations

PG   Migne, J.P., ed. 1857-1866. *Patrologiae cursus completus, series graeca*, 161 vols. Paris.

DAI Moravcsik, G., ed., and Jenkins, R. J. H., trans. 1967. *Constantine Porphyrogenitus, De Administrando Imperio*. Washington, DC.

DT   Pertusi, A., ed. 1952. *Costantino Porfirogenito, De thematibus*. Rome, Città del Vaticano.

Primary Sources

Bekker, I. 1838. *Theophanes Continuatus, Ioannes Cameniata, Symeon Magister, Georgius Monachus*. Bonn.

Billerbeck, M., et al., eds. 2006. *Stephani Byzantii Ethnica, I (Α-Γ)*. Berlin and New York.

Dennis, G. T., ed. and trans. 1985. *Three Byzantine Military Treatises*. Washington, DC.

———. and trans. 2010. *The Taktika of Leo VI*. Washington, DC.

Dewing, H. B., ed. and trans. 1914–1940. *Procopius*, 7 vols. Cambridge, MA.

Honigmann, E., ed. 1939. *Le Synekdèmos d'Hiéroklès et l'opuscule géographique de Georges de Chypre*. Brussels.

McGeer, E. 1995. ed. and trans. *Sowing the Dragon's Teeth: Byzantine Warfare in the Tenth Century*. Washington, DC.

Meineke, A., ed. 1849. *Stephani Byzantii Ethnicorum quae supersunt*. Bonn.

Migne, J.P., ed. 1857–1866. *Patrologiae cursus completus, series graeca*, 161 vols. Paris.

Moravcsik, G., ed., and Jenkins, R. J. H., trans. 1967. *Constantine Porphyrogenitus, De Administrando Imperio*. Washington, D.C.

Pertusi, A., ed. 1952. *Costantino Porfirogenito, De thematibus*. Rome, Città del Vaticano.

Piccirillo, M. and Alliata, E., eds. 1999. *The Madaba Map Centenary 1897-1997*. Jerusalem.

Reiske, J. J., ed. 1829–1830. *Constantini Porphyrogeniti imperatoris de cerimoniis aulae byzantinae*, 2 vols. Bonn.

Seeck, O., ed. 1876. *Notitia Dignitatum*. Berlin.

Sullivan, D. F., ed. and trans. 2000. *Siegecraft: Two Tenth-Century Instructional Manuals by "Heron of Byzantium"*. Washington, D.C.

Vogt, A., ed. 1935–1940. *Constantin VII Porphyrogénète, Le Livre des Cérémonies*, text (2 vols) and commentary (2 vols). Paris.

Wilkinson, J., with Hill, J. and Ryan, W. F., eds. 1988. *Jerusalem Pilgrimage 1099-1185.* London.

Wolska-Conus, W., ed. 1968-1973, *Cosmas Indicopleustès, Topographie chrétienne*, 3 vols, Sources chrétiennes 141, 159, 197. Paris.

Secondary Sources

Bowersock, G. W. 2006. *Mosaics as History: The Near East from Late Antiquity to Islam,* Cambridge, MA, and London.

Crow, J., Bardill, J. and Bayliss, R. 2008. *The Water Supply of Constantinople.* London,

Kazakou, M., Skoulas, V. 2008. *Egeria: Mediterranean Medieval Places of Pilgrimage.* Athens.

Haldon, J. 1999. *Warfare, State and Society in the Byzantine World, 565-1204.* London.

Haldon, J. with Lacey, A. and Hewes, C. 2006. "Greek Fire Revisited: Recent and Current Research," in E. Jeffreys (ed.), *Byzantine Style, Religion and Civilization. In Honour of Sir Steven Runciman.* Cambridge, 290-325.

Howard-Johnston, J. 2000. "The De Administrando Imperio: A Re-examination of the Text and a Re-evaluation of its Evidence about the Rus," in M. Kazanski, A. Nercessian, C. Zuckermann (eds.), *Les centres proto-urbains russes entre Scandinavie, Byzance et Orient.* Paris, 301-336.

Hunger, H. 1978. *Die hochsprachliche profane Literatur der Byzantiner*, 2 vols. Munich.

Jenkins, R. J. H. 1962. *De Adminstrando Imperio*, II, Commentary. London.

Laiou, A., Morrisson, C. 2007. *The Byzantine Economy.* Cambridge.

Lefort, J. et al. 1991. *Géométries du fisc byzantin.* Paris.

Lounges, T. 1990. Κωνσταντίνου Πορφυρογεννήτου *De administrando imperio (*πρὸς τὸν ἴδιον υἱὸν ʹΡωμαίων): μία μέθοδος ἀνάγνωσης. Thessaloniki.

Macrides, R., ed. 2002. *Travel in the Byzantine World.* Aldershot.

Magdalino, P. 1998. "Paphlagonians in Byzantine High Society," in S. Lampakes (ed.), *Byzantine Asia Minor (6th-12th cent.).* Athens, 141-50.

——. 2007. *Studies on the History and Topography of Byzantine Constantinople.* Aldershot.

Malamut, E. 1993. *Sur la route des saints byzantins.* Paris.

Messis, Ch. 2011. "Littérature, voyage et politique au XIIe siècle: *l'Ekphrasis des lieux saints* de Jean 'Phokas'," *Byzantinoslavica* 59/3 Supplementum: 126-146.

Mondrain, B. 2002. "La lecture du De administrando imperio à Byzance au cours des siècles," *Travaux et Mémoires (Mélanges en l'honneur de Gilbert Dagron)*, 14:485-498.

Mullett, M. 1996. "Originality and Byzantine Letter-Writing: the Case of Exile," in A.R. Littlewood (ed.), *Originality in Byzantine Literature, Art and Music.* Oxford, 39-58.

Signes Codoñer, J. 2004. "Los eslavos en las fuentes bizantinas de los siglos IX–X: el De administrando imperio de Constantino Porfirogéneto," *'Ilu. Rivista de Ciencias de las Religiones,* 13:115–131.

Sode, C. 1994. "Untersuchungen zu De administrando imperio Kaiser Konstantins VII. Porphyrogenitus," *Poikila Byzantina,* 13:149–260. Bonn.

Talbert, R. J. A. 2010. *Rome's World: The Peutinger Map Reconsidered.* Cambridge.

von Falkenhausen, V. 1989. "Italy in Byzantine Literature of the Tenth Century," in A. Markopoulos (ed.), Κωνσταντίνος Ζ' ὁ Πορφυρογέννητος καὶ ἡ ἐποχή του. Athens, 25–38.

Whitby, M. 1985. "Justinian's Bridge over the Sangarius and the Date of Procopius' de Aedificiis," *Journal of Hellenic Studies,* 105:129–148.

Wolska-Conus, W. 1962. *La topographie chrétienne de Cosmas Indicopleustès: théologie et sciences au VIe siècle.* Paris.

2

"Asia and Europe Commonly Called East and West"

Constantinople and Geographical Imagination in Byzantium

Dimiter Angelov

WRITING IN THE YEARS shortly before the fall of Constantinople to the Ottomans, Ioannes Kanavoutzes, a Greek teacher living in Genoese Phokaia in Asia Minor, addressed Palamede Gattilusio (1431–1455), the Genoese lord of Samothrace and Ainos, with a treatise on the ancient history of the island of Samothrace. In a creative act of inventing tradition, Kanavoutzes explained to his Latin patron that his island had once been an important link in the chain of events that led to the foundation of Rome by Greek settlers. Kanavoutzes' story, based on the *Roman Antiquities* of Dionysios of Halikarnassos, has its twists and turns, mentioning several mythical waves of Greek migration towards the Italian peninsula. When referring to the immigrants from Arcadia who sailed eastwards along the European coast of the Aegean Sea on their way to found Troy (so Aeneas, Rome's Trojan founder, became a Greek by blood) and stopped over temporarily in Samothrace, Kanavoutzes embarked on a short geographical excursus. He explained to his Genoese patron the division of the world into three continents and remarked that "the two parts of the world, namely Asia and Europe, are commonly called East and West." [1] As for Africa, it was "considered the East because it lies close to the South where the sun always dwells."

---

[1] Lehnerdt 1904:39–40, esp. 39:23–25: λέγεται δὲ κοινῶς τὰ μὲν δύο μέρη τῆς γῆς ἤγουν ἡ Ἀσία καὶ ἡ Εὐρώπη ἀνατολὴ καὶ δύσις. Regrettably little is known about Ioannes Kanavoutzes. He titles himself *magistros* and makes it apparent that he knew Greek and Latin. Ciriaco d'Ancona calls him "the teacher (*magister*) from Phokaia." Kanavoutzes was interested in history and astronomy. He completed before 1434–1435 a calculation of the length of the day for the latitude of Phokaia and was Ciriaco d'Ancona's guide in Sardis in 1444. In the letter where Ciriaco mentions "Kanavoutzes the teacher from Phokaia," he urged his correspondent Andreolo Giustiniani-Banca, who was on Genoese Chios, to ask a different Kanavoutzes (Crytes Canabuzios), presumably a relative of our

Kanavoutzes' insistence on the Greek identity of the Trojans is an aspect of his agenda that does not concern us here. Suffice it to say that the Trojan ancestry of the fifteenth-century Italians was discussed by contemporary humanists, while parallels were drawn during the same period between the Trojans and the rising Ottomans, so Kanavoutzes' account may have been a calculated, if somewhat forced, riposte to rival foundation myths.[2] Kanavoutzes' sense of Greek pride and identity is characteristic of the last centuries of Byzantine history. What is of particular interest is Kanavoutzes' global mental map and the two-partite division of the world into the "East" and the "West." In his interpretation, the East consisted of the continents of Asia as well as Africa, while the West was synonymous with Europe. The following discussion aims to demonstrate that this interpretation, which Kanavoutzes reports as commonly held in his time, was based on a centuries-long and characteristically Byzantine construction of geographical space. This construction of global geography assumed that the imperial city of Constantinople was a sort of Byzantine Greenwich and the focal point of spatial reference for determining the cardinal directions. As we will see, Byzantium had a distinctive, Constantinople-centered system of arranging the ordering of space within and beyond the confines of the empire.

The geographical notions investigated here can be better understood if they are examined from the contextual viewpoint of the multiple currents of geographical thought and imagination in Byzantium. What I mean by geographical thought and imagination is the large, diverse, and rich body of concepts and ideas describing, arranging, and mapping mentally the inhabited world, known or imagined by the Byzantines. A systematic study of macro-spatial concepts and ideas conceived of in Byzantium, or in specific periods of Byzantine history, is still a desideratum. Such a study would have to consider not only specialized geographical texts and travelogues, which are, as Paul Magdalino notes in this volume, relatively rare in Byzantium in comparison with ancient and other medieval civilizations, but it would have to undertake the massive task of scrutinizing historical, literary, hagiographical, and educational works shedding light on the geographical thought-world of Byzantine authors and audiences. Account would need to be taken of specific periods and literary genres and circles (e.g. secular versus monastic milieus, Constantinopolitan versus provincial authors). As is well known, the division of the world into three continents (Europe, Asia, and Africa) was first elaborated by the ancient Greek

---

Ioannes Kanavoutzes, to interpret an ancient Greek inscription. Ioannes Kanavoutzes may have owned a manuscript of George Gemistos Plethon. See Diller 1970:271–275. Bodnar 2003:28–29 and 411–412, has corrected the older interpretation (as in Diller 1972:257–258) that Ciriaco met Kanavoutzes at Foglia Vecchia in 1446. Cf. Trapp et al. 1976–1996:no. 10871.

2   Hankins 1995:139, 141; Kafadar 1995:90; Bisaha 2004:58, 90–92.

geographers and was carried over into the Greek and Latin Middle Ages. Initially defined as geographical terms, the continents evolved over time into cultural concepts. In the fourteenth- and fifteenth-century Latin West, and particularly in Renaissance Italy, "Europe" established itself as a meta-geographical notion expressing the sense of cultural and religious identity of the politically divided world of Latin Christendom vis-à-vis the rising Ottoman Empire and, to a lesser degree, the schismatic Christian East.[3] From this time onwards, Europe became an important concept in the construction of Western identity until the present day. The similarities and differences in the understanding of the continents in Byzantium shed light on its cultural environment and political experience of empire. The comparison is all the more interesting and justified in light of the circumstance that Byzantium and the medieval Latin West were sibling Christian civilizations that inherited, albeit through different paths and each to a different extent, the works of ancient geography.

The Multiple Geographical Traditions of the Byzantines

Classifying the currents of geographical thinking and imagination in Byzantium is a challenging task. What can be offered here is an introductory and by necessity incomplete discussion, not a fully developed typology. I would like to draw specific attention to three different kinds of geographical thought which are distinct in terms of their origin and perspective: first, academic geography based on the ancient tradition; second, political geography reflecting current administrative practice; and third, popular geography. To these three types, one may add at least one more variant that will not be treated here: the hagio-geography of pilgrimage and its network of saints' shrines dispersed throughout the territory of the empire and beyond, with Jerusalem being a natural focal point. Travel accounts to the Holy Land, starting with the earliest surviving one authored by Epiphanios Hagiopolites, and other texts pertaining to pilgrimage, display a sense of geographical orientation rivaling the centrality of the imperial metropolis.[4] An important subject left aside is the relationship between geography and ethnography, two closely related fields since Greco-Roman antiquity. As the ancients, the Byzantines too tended to associate territories with the peoples inhabiting them.[5] Despite being partial and preliminary, the typology worked out here provides useful background for discussing a rather

---

[3] Hay 1957:73–116; De Rougemont 1966:55–75.
[4] Kazhdan 1993; Külzer 1994; Külzer 2002; Wilkinson 2002: 19–20, 207–215.
[5] Maas 2007.

different mode of spatiality in Byzantium, one issuing from and oriented toward Constantinople. This mode of spatiality sometimes informed and permeated political and popular geography. Therefore, rather than seeing it as a distinct type of geographical or literary tradition, one is more justified to approach it as a pervasive system of spatial orientation. The Constantinopolitan spatial perspective is particularly significant as it marks a convergence between empire and imagined geography.

As a school discipline, geography lay at the margins of the educational curricula in Byzantium. The school tradition of geography, which one may call academic geography, was based entirely on ancient geographical works and was a powerful vehicle for the transmission of ancient place names and ethnography to Byzantium's classically educated literary elite. Geographical handbooks, epitomes, and commentaries serving educational purposes were based on the Roman geographers Strabo (d. ca. AD 64), Claudius Ptolemy (d. AD 168), and Dionysios Periegetes (second century AD). Many of these school texts have long been known, although they have been little studied, after their publication a century and a half ago by Karl Müller in the second volume of his *Geographici graeci minores*. A few of the prominent works of academic geography deserve mention here. The learned patriarch Photios (terms in office 858–867 and 877–886) has been credited with the authorship of the so-called *Chrēstomatheiai*, an abridgement of all 17 books of Strabo's *Geography*, and with scholia on Strabo, probably in the latter case with the significant subsequent input of Arethas of Caesarea.[6] The philosopher and teacher Michael Psellos (1018–after 1081) promoted the study of Strabo and was responsible, along with members of his educational circle, for the production of excerpts and epitomes.[7] The ninth century also saw the production of epitomes of the *Geography* of Ptolemy, a fundamental work of ancient cartography that assigned latitudes and longitudes to places in the known world and included detailed maps of the Roman provinces.[8] The earliest Byzantine manuscripts of the entire *Geography* of Ptolemy containing maps were connected to the activities of the teacher, scholar, and diplomat Maximos Planoudes in the second half of the thirteenth century.[9]

---

[6] Diller 1954:43–47; Wilson 1996:87–88.

[7] Lasserre 1959; Pontikos 1992:LIX–LX.

[8] A brief epitome of Ptolemy's *Geography* (published in Müller 1861 II:488–493) has been dated to the sixth or the ninth century AD. See Hunger 1978 I:512, n. 23. Another epitome, the *Compendium of Geography in Epitome (Hupotupōsis geōgraphias en epitomē)* (Müller 1861 II:494–509), which combines information from Strabo and Ptolemy, has also been assigned to the ninth century. Diller (1954:49–50) attributed the work to a student of Photios.

[9] Diller 1940.

The versified *Description of the Earth* by the Alexandrian geographer Dionysios Periegetes held a particularly high educational appeal. The brevity of this text in comparison with the works of Strabo and Claudius Ptolemy is probably the main reason for its abiding popularity. A Byzantine paraphrase in prose ensured additional facility of school usage, and in the twelfth century Eustathios of Thessaloniki produced a lengthy and much copied commentary for one of his students, Ioannes Doukas, pointing to correspondences and disagreements between Dionysios Periegetes and other antique geographers.[10] The abridgement of Dionysios Periegetes by the thirteenth-century scholar and monk Nikephoros Blemmydes, entitled *Synopsis of Geography*, may have, however, been forged by a Greek scribe working in Venice during the sixteenth century.[11]

Why did the school tradition of geography rely so closely on ancient works? For one reason, this tradition followed the pattern of Byzantine philosophical study in general, which was mostly scholastic and in the form of commentaries. While geography fell outside the late antique and Byzantine divisions of philosophy and did not form part of the advanced philosophical curriculum (the *quadrivium*), it was nonetheless considered akin to philosophy. Strabo opened his work by arguing that geography was relevant to philosophy, politics, the art of war, geometry, and astronomy.[12] The rise of interest in ancient geography in Byzantium tended to coincide with periods when the study of philosophy flourished. Some of the Byzantine geographers who composed epitomes and commentaries, such as Psellos, are well-known philosophers. An indirect stimulus for the study of ancient geographical works in Byzantium was the need to make sense of place names and ethnonyms encountered in the reading of both classical texts and the Bible. Familiarity with ancient geography was thus an auxiliary craft to the reading of ancient and early Christian literature. A result of the incessant educational interest in ancient geography and ethnography was the notorious preference by high-style Byzantine authors for using the antique names of places and peoples. The composition of glossaries of old and new geographical names was an understandable necessity and a characteristically Byzantine phenomenon.[13]

Imperialism and the interest in ancient geography could cross paths. Upsurges in the study of geography occurred in periods of Byzantium's territorial expansion and involved high imperial functionaries. While the emperor Justinian I (AD 527–565) was embarking on an ambitious project of territorial reconquest, the Constantinopolitan teacher (grammarian) Stephanos composed

---

[10] Müller 1861 II:201–406, 411–425; Diller 1975:187–207.
[11] Müller 1861 II:458–468; Brodersen 1995.
[12] Strabo, *Geography*, I.1.1; I.1.20; the Byzantine *Chrēstomatheiai* in Müller 1861 II:530.
[13] Diller 1973.

a large geographical and ethnographical lexicon, the *Ethnika*, which sums up important aspects of ancient geographical knowledge. One modern scholar has compared the *Ethnika* to a handbook for United Nations officials visiting little known places in the Third World.[14] The similarity vanishes on closer scrutiny, however, because the *Ethnika* lacks an immediate applicability to Justinian's imperialism and cannot be considered a true imperial handbook. Rather, Stephanos assumed that his readership already had a good knowledge of contemporary geography in and outside the empire and chose to focus instead on etymologies, multiple meanings of geographic terms, and curiosities. A more obvious correlation between the study of ancient geography and imperialism is discernible in the second half of the ninth and the tenth century, a time of renewed military and diplomatic offensive of the empire. Photios, whose work on Strabo has been noted, was a top imperial bureaucrat holding the title of *prōtoasēkrētis* (head of the imperial chancery) prior to his appointment to the patriarchate. He was closely involved in planning Byzantium's missionary activity in central Europe, with long-term consequences for the history of the Slavs. A similar link between the study of ancient geography and imperial foreign policy may be assumed in the case of Eustathios of Thessaloniki's commentary on Dionysios Periegetes, which was addressed to Ioannes Doukas, a future holder of the office of *epi tōn deēseōn* (master of petitions) and the son of Emperor Manuel I's (1143–1180) powerful minister Andronikos Kamateros, who formulated the emperor's religious policy toward the Armenian and the Roman church. It is possible that Andronikos Kamateros was grooming his son John for a similar diplomatic role when he asked Eustathios to prepare his geographical commentary.[15]

The geographical thought-world and writing of the Byzantines was inevitably affected by the language and practices of the imperial administration. The territorial divisions and subdivisions of the empire and the Church introduced new geographical terms. The driving force for this kind of geography, which one may term political geography, was not learned tradition or popular imagination, but practical considerations and the reasoning of lay and ecclesiastical bureaucrats at times of administrative restructuring. Political geography approached the territory of the empire as the matrix for mapping space. It often contradicted academic geography and could be at odds even with earlier administrative nomenclature. The Byzantine theme of Macedonia created in the late eighth century, with its main city being Adrianople, was located at the heart of the old Roman province of Thrace.[16] The theme of Macedonia had nothing to do with the region of Macedonia as described by Strabo or Claudius Ptolemy, or with the

[14] Hunger 1978 1:530–531.
[15] Karlin-Hayter 1972:259–265; Magdalino 1993:259–260; Diller 1975:182.
[16] Treadgold 1988:92–93n114.

Roman province and the early Byzantine diocese of Macedonia with its main city being Thessaloniki; rather, the name of the theme appears to have derived from the withdrawal of troops from Macedonia and their stationing in Thrace during the period of the Slavic invasions. Self-contained works of political geography have survived in the form of descriptions or simple lists of administrative territorial units. The sixth-century list by Hierokles lays out the provinces of the early Byzantine Empire with their main cities, while numerous and constantly revised lists of bishoprics rank in a hierarchical order the episcopal sees under the authority of the patriarch of Constantinople.[17] The tenth-century work *On the Themes* by the emperor Constantine VII Porphyrogenitus belongs partly to the category of political geography, although it is notable for its historical and antiquarian rather than practical content.[18]

Geographical thought in Byzantium was also a living tradition of the people, a tradition that can be termed popular geography. The popular element varied. Geographical notions were engendered by the imagination of the common people and entered popular parlance. Entire geographical works may be classified within this tradition because their strong scriptural basis reflects not only piety and devotion, but also ignorance or neglect of academic geography. The coinage of new geographical terms was often a matter of popular usage. The visible features in a locality could give rise to a new geographical name: the designation "Morea" for the Peloponnese, attested already in the ninth- or tenth-century scholia on Strabo, means literally a mulberry tree.[19] The name may derive from the diffusion of mulberry trees used for silk production in certain areas of the Peloponnese rather than from the shape of the peninsula reminding one of a mulberry leaf.[20] The Greek word *zygos* —meaning "yoke" in classical Greek and also "mountain" in Byzantine demotic usage—became a favorable designation for mountains because of their perceived yoke-like shape. The twelfth-century epic romance of *Digenis Akritis* calls the Anti-Taurus mountain range in Asia Minor Zygos.[21] Zygos became also a name for the Balkan Mountains called Haimos in antiquity. In the twelfth century, Anna Komnene designates mountains in different areas in the Balkans as "Zygos," including the Balkan mountain range in present-day Bulgaria and the Kapaonik Mountain further west in today's Serbia that marked the Byzantine frontier with Dalmatia.[22] On one occasion she calls the mountain "somehow known locally as Zygos." This

---

[17] Honigmann 1939; Darrouzès 1981.
[18] See Magdalino in this volume.
[19] Diller 1954:38.
[20] Jacoby 1991–92:454n9.
[21] Grottaferrata 5, line 260, Escorial, line 262, in Jeffreys 1998:150, 258.
[22] Anna Komnene (Comnena), *Alexiad,* 9,1,1; 9.4.2–5; 10,2,6; 10,3,1 in Reinsch and Kambylis I 2001:258, 266–267, 286, 287; Stephenson 2000:125, 148–150, 291.

snippet of information in the work of an elite author such as Anna Komnene provides unique insight into a local geographical usage. The local usage entered the vocabulary of Constantinopolitan court orators writing in high Attic Greek. In the second half of the twelfth century, they identified the Bulgarians who rebelled against imperial rule as "the people of the Zygos," and thus imputed a spatial identity to the provincial population in a way strikingly similar to the modern use of the word "Balkan."[23] In the early thirteenth century, a learned Byzantine legal author engaged in a humorous word play and referred to the Bulgarians as "the people inhabiting the land of Zygos who have raised their necks against the authority of the Rhōmaioi and have shaken off shamelessly its yoke (zygos)."[24]

The Christian holy scriptures were understandably an inspiration for popular geography. Hence the idea, commonly found in homilies, of a terrestrial paradise, the land of Eden with its four rivers which lay in the East;[25] and likewise the belief in the existence of the people of Gog and Magog,[26] whom a legend popular in Byzantium held that Alexander locked up behind the Caspian Gates in the East until their anticipated release by Antichrist in the end of days.[27] A biblical perspective marked the imagined geography of prophetic and eschatological writing. It also influenced the sixth-century *Christian Topography* composed by an unknown Alexandrian author and attributed subsequently to the monk Kosmas Indikopleustes (the "Sailor to India"), a fascinating work pandering, as has always been seen, to popular imagination by locating the land of Eden and describing the exotic animals of India.[28] The *Christian Topography* vehemently attacked the pagan Ptolemaic tradition of geography, proposing instead a flat world surrounded by oceans.

The three currents of geographical imagination traced above—academic, political, and popular—were distinct in terms of origin and perspective, but were capable of influencing one another. In addition, each of them could carry discordant interpretations. The geographical term "Hellas" provides a good example of mutual cross-fertilization and the lack of uniformity in each tradition. Ancient geographers did not agree on the boundaries of Hellas. Strabo described Hellas as a peninsula, or rather a series of overlapping ones, which consisted of the Peloponnese and central Greece.[29] Claudius Ptolemy and Dionysios Periegetes, on the other hand, regarded Hellas solely as central Greece

---

[23] Regel and Novosadskii 1892–1917:277.8–13; Van Dieten 1972:106.18–19.
[24] Prinzing 2002:423, no. 146.17–22.
[25] Genesis 2:8–14.
[26] Revelation 20:7–8.
[27] Alexander 1985:185–192; Stoneman 1991:185–187.
[28] Anastos 1946; Wolska 1962:1–11.
[29] Strabo, *Geography*, VIII.1.3; the Byzantine *Chrēstomathiai* in Müller 1861 II:580–581.

without the Peloponnese.[30] In the entry on Hellas in his *Ethnika*, the sixth-century geographer Stephanos mentioned no territorial entity, but instead explained the etymology of Hellas as deriving from an ancient town under the same name in Thessaly and referred to the existence of another town called "Hellas" in Coele-Syria.

The different localization of Hellas in the works of the ancient and Byzantine geographers was matched by a similar confusion at the level of political geography. The sixth-century list of provinces by Hierokles understands Hellas as a different name for the late Roman province of Achaia that encompassed the Peloponnese and Central Greece.[31] In the late seventh century, at a time of administrative reorganization forced by the Avaro-Slavic invasions in the Balkans, a theme of Hellas was created, which seems initially to have included parts of central Greece, the Aegean Islands, and the Peloponnese, where the empire still maintained a degree of central control. In other words, the theme of Hellas was designed to correspond to the boundaries of the late Roman province of Achaia, or Hellas. At the end of the eighth century, however, the theme of Hellas was restricted to east-central Greece, while a new theme of the Peloponnese was created. The two themes of Hellas and Peloponnese were occasionally combined between the tenth century and the fateful year of 1204, when the crusaders imposed their political dominance over the area and put an end to the administrative territorial unit called Hellas.[32]

The late period of Byzantine history saw the revival of an ancient philosophical view of the location of Hellas, which contradicted both the tradition of academic geography and defunct administrative vocabulary. In his *Politics* Aristotle notes that Hellas lies at the midpoint between East and West, North and South, a reason for the Hellenes to possess the best mixture of the climatically predetermined characteristics of the easterners and westerners.[33] The philosopher and emperor Theodore II Laskaris (b. 1221–1222, r. 1254–1258) was influenced by this interpretation. In a polemical work against a Latin religious opponent, he praised at length the land of the Greeks (called Ἑλληνίς or γῆ τῶν Ἑλλήνων) for its central location in the world, which contributed to the perfectly balanced character of the Hellenes.[34] In a similar fashion, the statesman and scholar Theodore Metochites (1270–1332) backed up his point about the superiority of the Hellenic character by referring to the geographical

---

[30] Claudius Ptolemy, *Geography*, III.15, VIII 12.16–23; Dionysios Periegetes, vs. 398–402 in Müller 1861 II:127; Eustathios of Thessaloniki in Müller 1861 II:290–291.

[31] Hierokles, *Synekdēmos*, 643.6, in Honigmann, 1939:16.

[32] Koder and Hild 1975:56–60; Gregory 1991; Živković 1999.

[33] Aristotle, *Politics*, 1327b20–36.

[34] Krikonis 1988:138–140.

location of the Hellenes in the middle of the inhabited world.[35] The idea of the centrality of Hellas, as revived in late Byzantium, had the potential of becoming a strong rival to the centrality of Constantinople, but its elite circulation appears to have prevented such a development.

That the three traditions of geographical thought and imagination were not fully capsulated currents is seen in the case of popular geography, which was not confined to the illiterate or the poorly educated. The *Christian Topography* aroused the interest of elite audiences. In the ninth century, when the learned Photios ridiculed the geographical knowledge of the *Christian Topography*, a richly illustrated manuscript (Vaticanus gr. 699) was produced and was followed by two other middle Byzantine ones, a circumstance that suggests elite patronage.[36] In the thirteenth century, the *Christian Topography* was known to the emperor Theodore II Laskaris, a highly educated man, who nonetheless cracked an indecent joke in one of his rhetorical works by comparing the vocal consternation that his words could elicit in his amazed audience to the mating and loud birth pangs of the Indian buffalo (*taurelaphos*), one of the exotic animals described in the *Christian Topography*.[37] Thus, in the thirteenth as in the ninth century, the *Christian Topography* continued to attract an elite readership. Furthermore, geographical terms of popular origin entered over time the vocabulary of the imperial chancery and attained official usage. One of the earliest mentions of the word *Rhōmania*, which signified the territory of the Byzantine Empire, is in the sixth-century *Chronicle* of Malalas composed in low-register Greek. Middle Byzantine authors writing in high style used the word with increasing frequency, and eventually it found its way into imperial charters of the twelfth century.[38] The popular usage of the word *Rhōmania* continued, however, to be a living tradition, a circumstance that makes modern interpretations of its precise geographical meaning difficult. For example, a region in northern Thrace disputed by Byzantium and the Bulgarian kingdom in the thirteenth and fourteenth centuries was known locally as *Rhōmania*.[39]

Constantinople and Geographical Imagination

The city of Constantinople plays a different role in each of the three traditions of geographical thought. Constantinople is almost invisible in epitomes and

---

[35] Müller and Kiessling 1821:758.
[36] Brubaker 2006.
[37] Tartaglia 2000:87.28–35.
[38] Wolff 1948:5–8.
[39] George Pachymeres, in Failler 1999 IV:491.20; Malingoudis 1971:57.

textbooks in the tradition of academic geography; in the rare cases when it appears there, it is named Byzantion in a classicizing fashion and no mention is made of it being the imperial metropolis. By contrast, Constantinople is omnipresent in the works of political geography and influenced deeply popular geographical imagination. In contrast to academic, political, and popular geography, where one can easily identify works representing each current, no self-contained geographical work or treatise had as its subject "the world as viewed from Constantinople." Rather, Constantinople's long shadow was cast in the form of a pervasive set of spatial notions based on centrality and dominance of the imperial metropolis. Furthermore, and to a large degree again in contrast to academic, political, and popular geography, geographical notions originating from Constantinople were often "global" in character and tended to evaluate rather than describe space. Constantinopolitan geographical thinking had as its starting point the idea that Constantinople was an imperial metropolis surpassing in location, status, and worth all territories of the civilized world (*oikoumenē*), both within and outside the power of the emperor. Constantinople was considered a central and hegemonic city dominating over other cities and over a vast geographical space.

The role of Constantinople in imagined geography was partly a consequence of the ways in which claims to empire and imperialism were constructed and expressed in Byzantium. The main carriers of the claims to imperial universalism were two figures of power at the top of the state and Church hierarchies, and one city: the emperor, the patriarch, and the city of Constantinople itself. This trio operated in confluence and agreement, while each of its members maintained its own distinct voice and sphere of claims. The emperor projected the public image of a divinely-sanctioned world ruler and earthly imitator of Christ, the heavenly king. The patriarch of Constantinople, titled as "ecumenical" since the sixth century, manifested his own universalist ambitions by initiating missionary activities beyond the empire's borders and by projecting an image steeped in imperial associations. The city of Constantinople was intimately connected to the imperial identity of Byzantium. Known since the late fourth century as "the New Rome," Constantinople inherited the Roman tradition of being seen as a city-turned-empire. The imperial symbolism of Constantinople gained added importance due to the absence in Byzantium of a developed conceptual vocabulary of empire as a state formation and the carryover of Greek philosophical terminology based on the polis.[40] The architectural landscape of Constantinople, with its imposing monuments and statues (some transported from Rome, Greece, and Egypt) as well as the Great

---

[40]   Magdalino 1991:193–197.

Palace of the emperors, infused the city with a tangible aura of being the center of a world power.[41] The opportunities for career and patronage were greater in Constantinople than elsewhere in the empire. Most of the political and literary elite of Byzantium was the creation of Constantinople's environment of power and assumed a Constantinopolitan identity, which is well attested in the twelfth and the thirteenth centuries.[42]

The location of Constantinople at the border of Europe and Asia led to comments about the city's global geographical position. The most fertile breeding ground for the literary expression of these geographical constructs was the tradition of the praises of the city. Erwin Fenster, the modern scholar who studied this rich literary tradition embedded in historical, rhetorical and hagiographical works, has demonstrated the early establishment of a standard repertory of themes and imagery about Constantinople.[43] Relatively soon after its foundation, Constantinople was perceived as occupying a central location in the inhabited world. The fourth-century Athenian rhetorician Himerios exclaimed: "You are the beginning of Europe and you are also its end; you have been allotted the same fate with regard to Asia."[44] In the fourth century, the orator Themistius and the church father Gregory of Nazianzos described Constantinople as "the eye" of the *oikoumenē*, an expression that would become a rhetorical commonplace about Constantinople.[45] The concept of the eye of the *oikoumenē* was understood not simply in terms of passive observation; it meant engagement with the surrounding world. For ancient and Byzantine philosophy considered vision to be a process by which the eye sent and received signals— hence the ancient, medieval, and still common Mediterranean belief in "the evil eye."[46] The characterization of Constantinople as the eye of the *oikoumenē* thus conveyed the idea of the ability of the imperial city to maintain contact and interact with the civilized world. Alongside "eye of the *oikoumenē*," other metaphors came to express the central world position of Constantinople within a century or two after its foundation, among them: "the navel of the earth," "midpoint of the *oikoumenē*," and "heart of the earth."[47]

---

[41] Bassett 2004.

[42] Magdalino 1984:65; Magdalino 1991:289–290; Van Dieten 1975 I:593.

[43] Fenster 1968.

[44] Himerios, Oration 41, in Colonna 1951:170.44–47; Fenster 1968:38.

[45] Themistius, Oration 6, in Schenkl 1965:124.4–9; Gregory of Nazianzos, Oration 42, in Migne, PG, vol. 36:469C. Themistius asked rhetorically: "Is it not, if the whole earth is considered to be one body, its second eye, even its heart and its navel, or whatever of the parts one might say is the more important?"— translated by Heather and Moncur 2001:197.

[46] Magdalino 2005:109.

[47] Fenster 1968:30, 102, 133, 141, 146, 189, 198, 205, 212, 287.

The hegemony of Constantinople over other cities was also noted and considered reason for pride. Since at least the sixth century, Constantinople was praised as "the queen of cities," an image exuding authority, precedence, and imperial status.[48] Beyond the literary praises of Constantinople, two sixth-century laws of Justinian I (*Novellae* 46 and 90) make use of the phrase "Constantinople and the outer territories" (αἱ ἔξω χῶραι). The expression makes a telling distinction between the Constantinopolitans and the provincials, presenting the latter as outsiders, and voices clearly the notion of an imperial core and a periphery.[49] Byzantine law and literature continued to make use of the catchy phrase long after the sixth century: for example, the monk Theodore Stoudites in the ninth century;[50] the tenth-century legal collection *Basilika*;[51] and Ioannes Apokaukos in the thirteenth century.[52] In the twelfth century, the canonist Theodore Balsamon mused that the rule of law could not be enforced effectively in the outer territories, much in contrast to the situation in Constantinople, and could not suppress local customs and traditions.[53]

The spatial constructs based on Constantinople's location were no empty rhetoric, but functioned, as we just saw, in legal contexts and were the building blocks of an ideology of empire expressed in highest-level public discourse. Court oratory under the Palaiologoi (1261–1453), the imperial dynasty that ruled the Byzantine Empire in the last two centuries of its existence, provides an example of how the image of Constantinople's centrality and hegemonic position in the world functioned ideologically. The period of the rule of the Palaiologan family began with the euphoria of the Byzantine recovery of Constantinople after more than half a century of Latin domination. The only two self-contained prose encomia on Constantinople from the entire Byzantine period—both of which present the city in exultant terms as a grand imperial metropolis—are the work of early Palaiologan authors, Theodore Metochites and George Karbones. The spirit of glorifying Constantinople permeated the orations in praise of the Palaiologan emperors, the most solemn and refined form of public oratory in Byzantium. While imperial orations of the earlier period had little to say about the city and articulated, during the twelfth century, claims to imperial universalism by commenting on imperial victories, Constantinople became ubiquitous

---

[48] Fenster 1968:93, 120, 135, 188, 205.
[49] Kroll and Schöll 1895:282.30, 453.14–16.
[50] Fatouros 1992 I:194.29.
[51] XXI.1.54 in Scheltema, van der Wal and Holwerda 1953–1988.
[52] Papadopoulos-Kerameus 1909–1910:17.7–8. A similar phrase is found in Emperor Michael VIII's privileges granted to Venice in 1277, after the Byzantine recapture of Constantinople in 1261: ἔν τε τῇ Κωνσταντινουπόλει καὶ ταῖς ἄλλαις χώραις τῆς βασιλείας ἡμῶν (Miklosich and Müller III 1865:89.24).
[53] Magdalino 1991:185–188.

in Palaiologan court oratory.[54] One imperial panegyrist of the Palaiologoi described Constantinople as "the eye of Asia, the head of Europe, a metropolis for people in every land, wherever Hellenes and barbarians reside—a metropolis which draws and binds together the ends of the West and the East."[55] George Karbones noted in his encomium on Constantinople that all other cities on earth were Constantinople's slaves because "it is a law of nature that the weaker serve the stronger" and described at length an imaginary quarrel between the personifications of Asia and Europe who contested the ownership of the city.[56] In the first half of the fifteenth century, when the territory of Byzantium consisted of Constantinople and a few disjointed possessions in Thrace, Macedonia, the Aegean, and the Peloponnese, the emperor's panegyrists at the court, such as the future Cardinal Isidore, praised the city for having once ruled over the entire continents of Europe and Asia and compared the relationship between the current emperor and other rulers to the innate superiority of Constantinople over other cities.[57] Thus, while the "empire" increasingly resembled a city-state encircled by the Ottomans, the imperial symbolism of the city persisted and was even magnified in court rhetoric.

Constantinople contributed to a characteristically Byzantine understanding of the location of the East and the West. The Byzantines, it must be noted, were neither unique nor the first to think of their empire as lying along an East-West axis. The Romans sometimes imagined their empire as consisting of an eastern and a western part.[58] In fact, in the fourth century AD, Rome was still a legitimate point of reference for a two-partite division of imperial space into East and West. The large praetorian prefecture of the Orient (*Anatolē*) created in the fourth century included, alongside the dioceses of the Orient, Pontos, and Asia, also the diocese of Thrace, which lay west of Constantinople. Clearly, Rome was capable of determining where the Orient should be localized. In the same vein, Gregory of Nazianzos called Constantinople in his funerary oration on St. Basil of Ceasarea "the city presiding over the East" (τὴν προκαθημένην τῆς Ἑῴας πόλιν).[59] It is remarkable, however, that in another oration the same Gregory of Nazianzos commented on the borderline position of Constantinople between the East and the West, praising Constantinople as "the node at the termination of the East and the West where extremities from every side converge."[60] In the fourth century, Rome and Constantinople were competing foci of

---

[54] Radošević 1993:156–161; Angelov 2007:102–105, 114, 418–419.
[55] Polemis 1992:31.35–32.2.
[56] Fenster 1968:345.26–346.6, 347.23–353.10.
[57] Lampros 1926 III:136–137, 152, 202–203.
[58] De Rougemont 1966:41.
[59] Gregory of Nazianzos, Oration 43, ch. 14, in PG, vol. 36:513A.
[60] Gregory of Nazianzos, Oration 42, ch. 10, in PG, vol. 36:469C; Fenster 1968:60.

global spatiality, and therefore it was possible for the same author to present Constantinople both as the chief city of the East and as a city straddling the East and the West.

By the tenth century, the point of reference determining the "East" had become firmly that of Constantinople. Rome ceased to be a locus of empire in the fifth century, and the late Roman administrative divisions disappeared in the seventh century with the emergence of a new territorial unit, the themes. As Konstantinos Amantos has shown in a seminal article, middle Byzantine authors tended to conceive of the East and the West as the land masses lying to the east and to the west of Constantinople; specific localization of the East and the West varied in individual works.[61] Further and more systematic research on semantics is likely to produce illuminating results. Particularly intriguing, for example, is the question of when and how the Greek word *Anatolē* became synonymous with Asia Minor. I would like to restrict myself here to just a few examples from the middle and late Byzantine periods. In his treatise *On the Themes*, the tenth-century emperor Constantine VII Porphyrogenitus explained that the theme of *Anatolikon* (literally the "Eastern theme") created in the seventh century bore this name not because it was located in the "upper and prime East where the sun rises," but because, "with respect to us living in Byzantion [i.e. Constantinople] and on European territory, it is the East." Constantine VII went on to stress the relativity of the cardinal directions. The perspective of the observer, he stated, could change the definition of the East: "The theme of Anatolikon is called the Middle West (*dutikon meson*) and Asia Minor (*Asia mikra*) by the people of Syrian Mesopotamia and of Great Asia, where the Indians, Egyptians and Ethiopians live."[62] (That Constantine placed the Egyptians and Ethiopians in Asia and not Africa may be explicable with the notion found in the works of the ancient geographers that the Nile River divided Asia from Africa.) Constantine VII underlined that his own perspective was a Constantinopolitan one, which justified for him the name of the "eastern" theme.

Approximately at the time when Constantine Porphyrogenitus was making this comment, the two supreme generals of the empire became the domestics of the schools (*domestikoi tōn scholōn*) of the East and of the West, who led the Byzantine mobile armies on campaigns in Asia Minor and the Balkans, respectively.[63] In the fourteenth century, the domestics of the Eastern and the Western themes were high fiscal officials responsible for collecting taxes from the Byzantine territories remaining in Asia Minor and the Balkans.[64] The axis of

---

[61]   Amantos 1936.
[62]   Pertusi 1952:60.1–7.
[63]   Oikonomides 1976:141–143.
[64]   Verpeaux 1966:188.

spatial orientation underlying this administrative jargon is an East-West one, and the point of reference is Constantinople. Beyond the language of the imperial bureaucracy, middle Byzantine historians speak of the East and the West as the two parts of the empire. The ninth-century chronicler Theophanes the Confessor refers to the two military fronts of the empire as the East and the West.[65] On rarer occasions, the two sections of the empire were called Asia and Europe, as in the work of the eleventh-century historian Michael Attaleiates.[66] In the twelfth century, Anna Komnene remarks that in ancient times the Roman Empire spanned all cardinal directions (South, East, North, and West) and approached the limits of the inhabited world.[67] However, as she switches from the past to the present and describes the current imperial frontiers, she revealingly refers to only two cardinal directions, the East and West: at the time of the accession of Alexios I Komnenos (1081–1118), Anna's much-praised father, the East-West frontier had been merely the Bosporus and the city of Adrianople, but subsequently Alexios succeeded in extending the empire to the Tigris and the Euphrates in the East and the Adriatic Sea in the West.

The fall of Constantinople to the Latins in 1204 did not weaken the territorial understanding of the concepts of East and West; on the contrary, the view was as pronounced in the first half of the thirteenth century as it was ever before. Thirteenth-century literati and churchmen used the geographical language of the East and the West in order to construct a spatial identity for the newly-formed, rival Byzantine successor states of Nicaea and Epiros-Thessaloniki: "emperor of the East" and "paradise of the Church in the East" in reference to Nicaea; "western bishops" in reference to the Greek bishops in the state of Epiros-Thessaloniki; "the union of the East and West" in reference to resolution of the brief schism (1228–1233) between the churches of the two principalities.[68] Even literary works composed in Slavonic in Bulgaria during the first half of the thirteenth century share the same understanding of the notions of East and West by referring to the emperor in Nicaea as the "eastern tsar" and to their own bishops as "western bishops."[69] It is evident that after the collapse of the empire in 1204, both Greek and non-Greek speakers in the former

---

[65] De Boor 1883 I:356.7–8.

[66] Pérez Martín 2002:25.13–18.

[67] Anna Komnene (Comnena), *Alexiad*, 6.11.3, in Reinsch and Kambylis I 2001:193. When Anna refers to the pillars of Dionysus "somewhere near the frontiers of India" as the eastern frontier of the ancient Roman empire, she is deriving her information from Dionysios Periegetes (Müller 1861 II:143, vs. 622–626). She would have, therefore, read this author in the course of her education.

[68] Lampros 1880 II:149, 353–354; Prinzing 1983:35.41–42; Loenertz 1970:464.4–19, 497.382–383, 499.438, 500.448.

[69] Angelov 2011:111–113.

Byzantine provinces understood the East and the West in a similar fashion. This development demonstrates the successful dissemination into the provinces of geographical language originally couched from a Constantinopolitan perspective.

Remarkably, the geographical language of the East and the West helped to construct self-referential statements of identity in the aftermath of 1204. In letters addressed to the patriarch of Constantinople in Nicaean exile, the bishops of the short-lived state of Epiros-Thessaloniki prayed "God to deem us, the western people (*hoi dutikoi*), worthy of your holy prayers" and identified themselves as the "the western congregation of hierarchs under you."[70] The emperor Theodore II Laskaris referred to his arrival at the Balkans from Asia Minor in the winter of 1255 as a crossing into "the western fields" and called the territory of the empire of Nicaea in Asia Minor "the holy land, my mother, the East (*Anatolē*)."[71] While the rival states of Nicaea and Epiros-Thessaloniki each claimed the political traditions of the Byzantine Empire as their own, they were in the process of acquiring local spatial identities based on pre-1204 notions of the East and the West. This innovative process ended abruptly with the reconquest of Constantinople by Nicaea in 1261 and the restoration of the old seat of the empire. Interestingly, a spatial identity based on the Constantinopolitan notion of the East persisted in the empire of Trebizond, a Byzantine splinter state formed in 1204 on the northeastern Black Sea shore of Asia Minor, which persisted until its conquest in 1461 by the Ottomans. Sometime between 1282 and 1360, the emperor of Trebizond assumed the title "emperor and *autokratōr* of the entire East [*pasēs Anatolēs*], the Iberians, and *Perateia* [the overseas territories in the Crimea]."[72] The "East" mentioned in the title of the emperors of Trebizond was defined vis-à-vis Constantinople, the restored capital of a Byzantine state.

In the middle and late Byzantine periods, the East and the West came to mean not only the current, or former, territories of the empire in Asia Minor and the Balkans, but also the continents of Asia and Europe. As Constantinople was considered to be marking the boundary between Europe and Asia, it should come as no surprise that a Constantinopolitan viewpoint came to identify the continents with the two cardinal directions. There is a stark contrast between this contemporary usage and the classicizing tradition of academic geography. First, the ancient geographers and their Byzantine epitomists were interested in delineating the land border between Europe and Asia further east from Constantinople, setting it usually along the Tanais (Don) or Phasis (Rioni) Rivers (e.g. Strabo, *Geography* XI.1). When the border between the two continents

[70]   Prinzing 2002:370, no. 112:58–60; Loenertz 1970:464.5–6.
[71]   Festa 1898:246.43–44, 281.74.
[72]   Oikonomides 1978.

was set nearer Constantinople, it was the Hellespont, not the Bosporos, that was mentioned as the boundary.[73] Constantinople, thus, did not determine the border between the continents in the classicizing geographical tradition. Furthermore, Byzantine academic geography did not view the East and the West as territorial or administrative concepts, but merely as orientating directions. The ninth-century *Compendium of Geography in Epitome* specifies that "Europe is the continent extending to the West and the North, Africa, the continent directed toward the South and the West, and Asia, the continent facing solely the East."[74] This description reflects the ancient geographical theory that Asia was far bigger than the other continents, and therefore it would have to face solely the East, while the other two continents were described through a combination of two cardinal directions.

The cardinal directions played a different role in global geographical imagination shaped in Constantinople. By the twelfth century, an explicit identification was made between the continents of Asia and Europe and the two cardinal directions. The *Ecloga Basilicorum*, a twelfth-century legal collection, refers to a ship arriving at Constantinople "from Asia, that is, the East."[75] Neilos Doxapatres, the twelfth-century Byzantine theologian and canonist exiled to the Norman court in Palermo, remarks in his geographical work on the hierarchy of the Church addressed to the king of Sicily Roger II that "the entire inhabited world is divided into three parts, Asia, that is, the East (*Anatolē*), Europe, that is, the West (*Dusis*), and Libya."[76] Unlike Kanavoutzes in the fifteenth century, Doxapatres divides the world into three rather than two parts corresponding to the three continents, yet just like Kanavoutzes, Doxapatres understands the East and the West as territorial concepts. Elsewhere in his geographical treatise, Doxapatres consistently uses the two cardinal directions as synonyms of the two main continents, calling Asia "the East" and Europe "the West."[77] In the late Byzantine period, a list of old and new geographical names dating to the fourteenth century explained the term "Europe" as meaning "the entire West." This identification of Europe with the West is accompanied in the same list by the statement that "Asia" refers to the city of Ephesos, which was indeed the see of a metropolitan bishop who titled himself as "metropolitan of Asia."[78] The practice is related to the early Byzantine diocesan structure of the Church, which tended to follow the contemporary provincial divisions. Thus, the

---

[73] Dionysios Periegetes, vs. 799–800, in Müller 1861 II:154, 420.
[74] Müller 1861 II:495.
[75] *Ecloga Basilicorum*, VII, 3,1 in Burgmann 1988:251.22.
[76] PG, vol. 132:1084B.
[77] PG, vol. 132:1085D, 1092BC.
[78] Diller 1973:32–33 [List C].

diocese of Asia with capital Ephesos became a metropolitan bishopric; the province of Europe in the diocese of Thrace became the metropolitan bishopric "of Europe" based in Herakleia Thrakikē.[79] The fourteenth-century list speaks with the voice of different geographical traditions and demonstrates once again the complexity of the geographical thought-world of the Byzantines.

We have now arrived close to the period of the literary activity of Ioannes Kanavoutzes with which this discussion began. When Kanavoutzes—a man who lived outside Constantinople and had weak ties, if any at all, with the imperial metropolis—referred to Asia and Africa as the East and Europe as the West, he was operating in a geographical frame of mind created in the imperial metropolis. His understanding of the continents had little to do with academic or political geography and reflected a long tradition of an imperial, Constantinople-based system of spatial orientation. By Kanavoutzes' times, the geographical notions created in the metropolis were detached from the milieu of Constantinople and had taken on a life of their own. It did not matter whether one resided in Constantinople: Kanavoutzes, after all, lived in a former Byzantine city held by the Genoese. Nor did it matter whether Constantinople was the seat of the Byzantine emperor: the Latin conquest of Constantinople in 1204 did not uproot the preexistent territorial understanding of the East and the West. In a similar way, the fall of Constantinople to the Ottomans did not put to an end, among Greek speakers at least, to the older Byzantine view. The sixteenth-century ecclesiastical author Damaskenos Stoudites notes in a sermon published in his homiletic collection, the *Thesauros*: "The entire world is divided into three parts—Asia, that is, the East (*Anatolē*), Europe, that is, the West (*Dusis*), and Libya."[80] Printed in Venice in 1558 and soon thereafter translated into Slavonic by an Athnonite monk, the *Thēsauros* of Damaskenos inspired a popular, pseudo-scientific literature of edification and entertainment among the Bulgarians and the Serbs.[81] The Byzantine background should be taken into consideration in any study of the imagined geographies of the Greeks and the Balkan Slavs living in the Ottoman Empire.

The Byzantine notions of Asia as the East and Europe as the West may seem remarkably close to the discourses of modernity. The similarity is superficial, however. As defined from the viewpoint of Constantinople, the notions had a narrowly territorial significance in Byzantium and rarely contributed to the construction of political identity. The most prominent exception after late antiquity is the thirteenth century, when the concepts of the East and the West (but notably not the continents) helped to create the spatial self-awareness of

---

[79] Neilos Doxapatres in PG, vol. 132:1092BC.
[80] Damaskenos Stoudites, Oration 20 on Saint Nicholas, in Deledemou 1943:426.
[81] Petkanova 1965.

new political formations in the Byzantine world, at a time when the imperial metropolis lay in the hands of a foreign power. This innovative development took place in the former provinces and was cut short by the Byzantine recovery of Constantinople in 1261.

Produced through the lens of Constantinople, the Byzantine understanding of Asia as the East and Europe as the West is highly idiosyncratic and does not lend itself to Orientalist Saidian interpretation, for it is not concerned with otherness. The Byzantine usage is worlds apart from the literary representation of Asia and the East in ancient Greek literature analyzed by Said in the premodern section of *Orientalism*.[82] Aeschylus employs in the *Persians* the word "Asia" as a metonymy for the hostile Persians. Herodotus presents the war between the Hellenes and the Persians as a conflict between Europe and Asia. Herodotus' *Histories* were known, copied, excerpted, and occasionally admired among highly-educated Byzantines.[83] Byzantine authors, such as the fourteenth-century scholar and polymath Theodore Metochites, sometimes rehashed the classical Greek view that Asiatics were by nature receptive to despotic rule. In one of his essays on historical subjects, Metochites observed that the European Hellenes and "many peoples in Europe" had traditionally been less prone to accepting despotic rule without resistance.[84] Yet this is a rarest interpretation by a Byzantine author. The general pattern was for the continents of Asia and Europe not to serve as foci of oppositional conceptions of *us* versus *them*. In the rare cases when the cardinal directions became such foci, they did not produce durable cultural concepts of identity and self-definition. It is telling that in the fifteenth century Ioannes Kanavoutzes did not associate either the continents or the cardinal directions with the foundation myths of Troy or Rome, but embarked on his global geographical description for the sake of edification and as a digression.

Let us consider as one final example the historical memoirs of the emperor John VI Kantakouzenos (ca. 1292–1382; r. 1341–1354), which are profoundly classicizing in their language, literary echoes (especially ones from Thucydides), and ethnographic vocabulary, such as the designation of the Turks as "Persians" and their rulers as "satraps."[85] Kantakouzenos generally speaks of Asia as a place of arrival or departure.[86] He calls Umur Beg (r. 1334–1348), the emir of Aydin, the "strongest of the satraps in Asia" and presents Süleyman, the son of the Ottoman ruler Orhan (r. 1326–1362), as "one of the satraps in Asia" (the Greek

[82] Said 1994:55–58.
[83] Rapp 2008:129–132.
[84] Müller and Kiessling 1821:674–676.
[85] Kazhdan 1980.
[86] Schopen II 1831:385.8–11; 407.12; 409.18; 416.3; 596.24.

expression is κατὰ τὴν Ἀσίαν).[87] In a reported speech dating to 1354, after the fall of Gallipoli to the Ottomans, Kantakouzenos puts in his own mouth the words: "we are forced to fight not only in Thrace, but also against all the barbarians in Asia" (κατὰ τὴν Ἀσίαν).[88] The preposition used here is "in," not "of," Asia, which in itself presupposes location rather than imputation of spatial identity. The impression is reinforced by the circumstance that Kantakouzenos does not consider "Europe" to be a term of identity and polar opposite of "Asia," the continent with which he associates the barbarians. In a speech addressed to papal ambassadors, Kantakouzenos states that in the past the polity of the Romans had ruled successfully over both Asia and Europe, thus conveying the conventional notion of Byzantium as an empire spread on two continents.[89]

The territorial understanding of Asia and Europe contrasts to the Renaissance view of the continents as cultural categories, a view that gained prominence at the very time Kantakouzenos was composing his historical memoirs. The poet Petrarch (1304–1374), Kantakouzenos' contemporary, compared the crusade planned by the French King Philip VI (r. 1328–1350) to the conflict between the East and the West at the time of the Persian Wars.[90] In an exhortation addressed in 1452 to Pope Nicholas VI, the Greek émigré and Italian humanist George of Trebizond (1395–ca. 1472–1473) described Constantinople and Greece as an integral part of Europe pitted against barbarian Asia. The geographical and cultural perspective of George of Trebizond was that of Renaissance Italy, not Byzantine Constantinople.[91] A view similar to that of George of Trebizond appears in the works of the chancellor of Florence Poggio Bracciolini (1380–1459). But it was Aeneas Silvius Piccolomini (1405–1464), elected pope under the name Pius II (1458–1464), who elaborated—in greater detail and with rhetorical fervor—the concept of Europe as a synonym of Latin Christendom defined in opposition to the expanding "Asiatic" Ottoman Empire. Piccolomini has been credited with coining the adjective "European" as cultural self-designation.[92] This semantic development was shaped by the special cultural and historical environment of fifteenth-century Italy: the humanist adoration of the ancient classics which contained instances of binary opposition of the East versus the West; the spatial perspective of authors who lived on the Italian peninsula far removed from the boundaries of Europe and Asia; and the rising Ottoman threat.

---

[87] Schopen II 1831:55:19–20; 476:13.
[88] Schopen III 1832:298:13–14.
[89] Schopen III 1832:60:15–16.
[90] Bisaha 2002; 2004:51.
[91] Bisaha 2004:115–116.
[92] Hay 1957:83–87; Bisaha 2004:83–87.

The view of the continents as bywords for two different civilizations was generally alien to the worldviews found in Byzantium. The notions of Asia as the East and Europe as the West became common knowledge over time, yet these notions appear not to have functioned as polar binaries of identity. The reason lies not simply in the territorial extent of Byzantium, which, with the exception of the early thirteenth century and the last century of the empire's history, always straddled parts of the two continents. Another reason, I suggest, was the important role of Constantinople in determining the meaning of the continents. In its capacity as the metropolis of New Rome situated at the border of Europe and Asia, Constantinople was identified through, and indeed with, the continents: a city of Europe and Asia; an imperial city dominating over the cities of Europe and Asia. Conversely, Constantinople shaped the understanding of the two continents and the cardinal directions that came to describe them. The ideological and political pull of the imperial metropolis proved too powerful to permit the semantic evolution of the notions of East and West into cultural dichotomies.

Abbreviations

PG   Migne, J.P., ed. 1857–1866. *Patrologiae cursus completus, series graeca,* 161 vols. Paris.

Works Cited

Alexander, P.J. 1985. *The Byzantine Apocalyptic Tradition.* Berkeley.

Amantos, K. 1936. "Άνατολὴ καὶ Δύσις." *Hellenika* 9:23–26.

Anatsos, M. 1946. "The Alexandrian Origin of the Christian Topography of Cosmas Indicopleustes." *Dumbarton Oaks Papers* 3:73–80.

Angelov, D. 2007. *Imperial Ideology and Political Thought in Byzantium (1204–1330).* Cambridge.

——. 2011. "Prosopography of the Byzantine World (1204–1261) in the Light of Bulgarian Sources." *Identities and Allegiances in the Eastern Mediterranean after 1204* (eds. J. Herrin and G. Saint-Guillain) 101–120. Aldershot.

Bassett, S. 2004. *The Urban Image of Late Antique Constantinople.* Cambridge.

Bisaha, N. 2002. "Petrarch's Vision of the Muslim and the Byzantine East." *Speculum* 76:284–314.

Bisaha, N. 2004. *Creating East and West: Renaissance Humanists and the Ottoman Turks.* Philadelphia.

Bodnar, E.W., ed. and trans. 2003. *Cyriac of Ancona: Later Travels.* Cambridge, MA.

Brodersen, K. 1995. "Die geographischen Schriften des Nikephoros Blemmydes." *Rom und der griechische Osten. Festschrift für Hatto H. Schmitt* (eds. Ch. Schubert and K. Brodersen) 43–50. Stuttgart.

Brubaker, L. 2006. "The Christian Topography (Vat. gr. 699) Revisited: Images, Texts and Conflict in Ninth-Century Byzantium." *Byzantine Style, Religion and Civilization: In Honour of Sir Steven Runciman* (ed. E. Jeffreys) 3–24. Cambridge.

Burgmann, L., ed. 1988. *Ecloga Basilicorum.* Frankfurt am Main.

Colonna, A., ed. 1951. *Himerii declamationes et orationes cum deperditarum fragmentis.* Rome.

Darrouzès, J., ed. 1981. *Notitiae episcopatuum Ecclesiae Constantinopolitanae.* Paris.

De Boor, C., ed. 1883–1885. *Theophanis chronographia,* I, II. Leipzig.

Deledemou, E., ed. 1943. Θησαυρὸς Δαμασκηνοῦ τοῦ ὑποδιακόνου καὶ Στουδίτου. New York.

De Rougemont, D. 1966. *The Idea of Europe,* trans. N. Guterman, New York and London.

Diller, A. 1940. "The Oldest Manuscripts of Ptolemaic Maps." *Transactions and Proceedings of the American Philological Association* 71:62–67.

———. 1954. "The Scholia on Strabo." *Traditio* 10:29–50.

———. 1970. "Joannes Canabutzes." *Byzantion* 40:271–275.

———. 1972. "Joannes Canabutzes and Michael Chrysococces." *Byzantion* 42:257–258.

———. 1973. "Byzantine Lists of Old and New Geographical Names." *Byzantinische Zeitschrift* 63:27–40.

———. 1975. *The Textual Tradition of Strabo's Geography.* Amsterdam.

Failler, A., ed. 1984, 1999. *Georges Pachymérès, Relations historiques,* I, II, III, IV. Paris.

Fenster, E. 1968. *Laudes Constantinopolitanae.* Munich.

Festa, N., ed. 1898. *Theodori Ducae Lascaris epistulae CCXVII.* Florence.

Gregory, T. 1991. "Hellas." *Oxford Dictionary of Byzantium,* II (ed. A. P. Kazhdan) 911. Oxford.

Hankins, J. 1995. "Renaissance Crusaders: Humanist Crusade Literature in the Age of Mehmed II." *Dumbarton Oaks Papers* 49:111–207.

Hay, D. 1957. *Europe: The Emergence of an Idea.* Edinburgh.

Heather, P., Moncur, D., trans. 2001. *Politics, Philosophy and Empire in the Fourth Century: Select Orations of Themistius.* Liverpool.

Honigmann, E., ed. 1939. *Le Synekdèmos d'Hiéroklès et l'opuscule géographique de Georges de Chypre.* Brussels.

Hunger, H. 1978. *Die hochsprachliche profane Literatur der Byzantiner,* I and II. Munich.

Jacoby, D. 1991–1992. "Silk in Western Byzantium: Trade before the Fourth Crusade." *Byzantinische Zeitschrift* 84/85:452–500.

Jeffreys, E., ed. and trans. 1998. *Digenis Akritis: The Grottaferrata and Escorial Versions*. Cambridge.

Kafadar, C. 1995. *Between Two Worlds: the Construction of the Ottoman State*. Berkeley.

Karlin-Hayter, P. 1972. "Jean Doukas." *Byzantion* 42:259–265.

Kazhdan, A. 1980. "*L'Histoire* de Cantacuzène en tant qu'oeuvre littéraire." *Byzantion* 50:279–335.

——. 1991. "Epiphanios Hagiopolites." *Oxford Dictionary of Byzantium*, I (ed. A. P. Kazhdan) 714. Oxford.

Koder, J. and Hild, F. 1975. *Tabula imperii Byzantini, 1, Hellas und Thessalia*. Vienna.

Krikonis, Ch., ed. 1988. Θεοδώρου Β΄ Λασκάρεως περὶ χριστιανικῆς θεολογίας λόγοι. Thessaloniki.

Kroll, W. and Schöll, R. 1895. *Novellae (Corpus iuris civilis, III)*. Berlin.

Külzer, A. 1994. *Peregrinatio graeca in Terram Sanctam: Studien zu Pilgerführern und Reisebeschreibungen über Syrien, Palästina und den Sinai aus byzantinischer und metabyzantinischer Zeit*. Frankfurt am Main.

——. 2002. "Byzantine and Early Post-Byzantine Pilgrimage to the Holy Land to Mount Sinai." *Travel in the Byzantine World* (ed. R. Macrides) 149–161. Aldershot.

Lampros, S., ed. 1912–1923, 1912–1924, 1926, 1930. Παλαιολόγεια καὶ Πελοποννησιακά, I, II, III, IV. Athens.

——. 1879, 1880. Μιχαὴλ Ἀκομινάτου τοῦ Χωνιάτου τὰ σωζόμενα, I, II. Athens.

Lasserre, F. 1959. "Étude sur les extraits médiévaux de Strabon, suivie d'un traité inédit de Michel Psellus." *L'Antiquité classique* 28:32–79.

Lehnerdt, M., ed. 1904. *Ioannes Canabutzes*. Leipzig.

Loenertz, R.-J., ed. 1970. "Lettre de Georges Bardanès, métropolite de Corcyre, au patriarche oecuménique Germain II." *Byzantina et Franco-Graeca*, I:467–501. Rome.

Maas, M. 2007. "Strabo and Procopius: Classical Geography for a Christian Empire." *From Rome to Constantinople: Studies in Honour of Averil Cameron* (eds. H. Amirav and R. B. ter Haar Romeny) 67–83. Leuven.

Magdalino, P. 1984. "Byzantine Snobbery." *The Byzantine Aristocracy, IX to XIII Centuries* (ed. M. Angold) 58–78. Oxford.

——. 1991. "Constantinople and the ἔξω χῶραι in the Time of Balsamon." *Byzantium in the Twelfth Century: Canon Law, State and Society* (ed. N. Oikonomides) 179–197. Athens.

——. 1993. *The Empire of Manuel I Komnenos, 1143–1180*. Cambridge.

———. 2005. "Ο οφθαλμός της οικουμένης και ο οφθαλμός της γής. Η Κωνσταντινούπολη ως οικουμενική πρωτεύουσα." *Byzantium as Oecumene* (ed. E. Chrysos) 107–123. Athens.

Malingoudis, P., ed. 1971. *Die mittelalterlichen kyrillischen Inschriften des Hämus-Halbinsel*. Thessaloniki.

Miklosich, F and Müller, J., ed. 1860, 1862, 1865, 1871, 1887, 1890. *Acta et diplomata graeca medii aevi*, I, II, III, IV, V, VI. Vienna.

Migne, J.P., ed. 1857–1866. *Patrologiae cursus completus, series graeca*, 161 vols. Paris.

Müller, G., ed. 1855, 1861. *Geographi graeci minores*, I, II. Paris.

Müller, C. and Kiessling, Th., ed. 1821. *Theodori Metochitae Miscellanea philosophica et historica*. Leipzig.

Oikonomides, N. 1976. "L'évolution de l'organisation administrative de l'empire byzantin au XIe siècle." *Travaux et mémoires* 6:125–152.

———. 1978. "The Chancery of the Grand Komnenoi: Imperial Tradition and Political Reality." Ἀρχεῖον Πόντου 35:299–332.

Papadopoulos-Kerameus, A., ed. 1909–1910. "Συνοδικὰ γράμματα Ἰωάννου τοῦ Ἀποκαύκου, μητροπολίτου Ναυπάκτου." *Byzantis* 1:3–31.

Pérez Martin, I., ed. 2002. *Miguel Ataliates, Historia*. Madrid.

Pertusi, A., ed. 1952. *Costantino Porfirogenito, De Thematibus*. Vatican City.

Petkanova, D. 1965. *Damaskinite v bŭlgarskata literatura*. Sofia.

Polemis, I., ed. 1992. Ὁ λόγιος Νικόλαος Λαμπηνὸς καὶ τὸ ἐγκώμιον αὐτοῦ εἰς τὸν Ἀνδρόνικον Β΄ Παλαιολόγον. Athens.

Pontikos, I.N., ed. 1992. *Anonymi Miscellanea Philosophica: A Miscellany in the Tradition of Michael Psellos (Codex Baroccianus Graecus 131)*. Athens.

Prinzing, G., ed. 1983. "Die Antigraphe des Patriarchen Germanos II. an Erzbischof Demetrios Chomatenos von Ohrid und die Korrespondenz zum nikäisch-epirotischen Konflikt 1212–1233." *Rivista di studi bizantini e slavi* 3, 21–64.

———. 2002. *Demetrii Chomateni Ponemata diaphora*. Berlin.

Radošević, N. 1993. "L'Oecuménè byzantine dans les discours impériaux du XIe et XIIe siècle." *Byzantinoslavica* 54:156–161.

Rapp, C. 2008. "Hellenic Identity, *Romanitas* and Christianity in Byzantium." *Hellenisms: Culture, Identity, and Ethnicity from Antiquity to Modernity* (ed. K. Zacharia) 127–147. Aldershot.

Regel, V. and Novosadskii, V., ed. 1892–1917. *Fontes Rerum Byzantinarum. Rhetorum saeculi XII orationes politicae*. St. Petersburg.

Reinsch, D. and Kambylis, A., eds. 2001. *Annae Comnenae Alexias*, I and II. Berlin.

Said, E. 1979. *Orientalism*. New York. 1994. Second edition.

Scheltema, H.J., van der Wal, N. and Holwerda, D., eds. 1953–1988. *Basilicorum libri LX,* 17 vols. Groningen.

Schenkl, H., Downey, G. and Norman. A.F., eds. 1965, 1970, 1975. *Themistii orationes quae supersunt*, I, II, III. Leipzig.

Schopen, L., ed. 1831-32. *Ioannis Cantacuzeni eximperatoris historiarum libri IV*, I, II and III. Bonn.

Stephenson, P. 2000. *Byzantium's Balkan Frontier: A Political Study of the Northern Balkans, 900–1204*. Cambridge.

Stoneman, R., trans. 1991. *The Alexander Romance*. London.

Tartaglia, L., ed. 2000. *Theodori Ducae Lascaris Opuscula rhetorica*. Munich.

Todorova, M. 1997. *Imagining the Balkans*. Oxford.

Trapp, E. et al. 1976–1996. *Prosopographisches Lexikon der Palaiologenzeit*. 12 vols. Vienna.

Treadgold, W. 1988. *The Byzantine Revival, 780–842*. Stanford.

Van Dieten, J.-L., ed. 1972. *Nicetae Choniatae Orationes et epistulae*. Berlin.

———. 1975. *Nicetae Choniatae Historia*, I and II. Berlin.

Verpeaux, J., ed. and trans. 1966. *Pseudo-Kodinos: Traité des Offices*. Paris.

Wilkinson, J. trans. 2002. *Jerusalem Pilgrims before the Crusades*. Warminster. Second edition.

Wilson, N.G. 1996. *Scholars of Byzantium*. London. Revised edition.

Wolff, R.L. 1948. "Romania: The Latin Empire of Constantinople." *Speculum* 23:1–34.

Wolska, W, 1962. *La Topographie chrétienne de Cosmas Indicopleustès: théologie et science au VIe siècle*. Paris.

Živković, T. 1999. "The Date of Creation of the Theme of Peloponnese." *Symmeikta* 13:141–155.

3

Cartography and the Ottoman Imperial Project in the Sixteenth Century

Pınar Emiralioğlu

IN THE SIXTEENTH CENTURY, Ottoman encounters with the Habsburg Empire in the West and the Safavids in the East turned violent as the Ottomans fought these rival empires on the battlefields. During this period, Ottoman ruling elites articulated the imperial claims of the Ottoman dynasty to universal leadership by representing the Ottoman sultans as the new world conquerors. Travelers, historians, sea captains, cartographers, poets, and astrologers assisted in this enterprise by creating a distinct body of geographical literature. Although it is well known that rulers in medieval and early modern Europe commissioned geographical works to project their royal or imperial aspirations,[1] the rich collection of surviving Ottoman geographical accounts has never before received the same analytical treatment, presumably because the Ottomans did not participate in the so-called "Age of Exploration." While recent studies demonstrate that Ottomans not only participated in, but helped to define, a variety of early modern diplomatic, economic, and religio-political trends, including to some extent European activities in the Indian Ocean,[2] Ottoman geographical works have been analyzed only rarely by historians for their value as tools of imperial propaganda.[3]

Through an examination of sixteenth-century *portolan* charts, atlases, and *isolario* in Ottoman-Turkish, this chapter demonstrates a heightened sensitivity to geographical knowledge about the Mediterranean in the period. It claims that this development was intimately related to the articulation of the Ottoman

---

[1] Harley 1988; Buisseret 1992.

[2] Casale 2010; Subrahmanyan 1997.

[3] Karamustafa 1992; Soucek 1992; Jardine and Brotton 2000; Pinto 2001; Ebel 2002; Goffman 2002; Hagen 2003; MacLean 2005; Birchwood and Dimmock 2005; Emiralioğlu 2006; Ágoston 2007:75–103.

claims to universal imperial sovereignty that had to be broadcast to the political and religious rivals in both East and West. By depicting the geographical and political features of the Mediterranean, Ottoman geographers portrayed the Ottoman Empire as ruling the whole world. They recast available geographical knowledge and promoted the imperial magnificence of the Ottoman sultans. They projected the Ottoman Empire as the center of the universe over which they ruled.

Selim I and the Formation of Ottoman Imperial Ideology

The beginnings of the Ottoman claims to universality coincided with the reign of Selim I. Shorty after ascending the Ottoman throne in 1512, Sultan Selim embarked upon one of the most difficult military campaigns in Ottoman history against the Savafi sufi brotherhood and their Turcmen supporters, whose rapid territorial expansion in the East threatened Ottoman power. In 1501, Shah Ismail, their young and charismatic leader, declared Tabriz his capital and eventually gained nominal control of Ardabil, Yazd, Kashan, Hamadan, Isfahan, Shiraz, Diyar Bakr, and Baghdad.[4] Ismail placed further pressure on the Ottomans by introducing a religious dimension to the conflict because he declared Twelver Shi'ism the official religion of his realm.[5] In his poetry, Ismail referred to himself as Faridun, Khusraw, Rustam, Alexander, Jesus, and he also claimed to be the *Mahdi*, the Expected One, who would emerge from concealment and reform the world drastically.[6] Safavid military power and Shia proselytizing activities thus constituted a two-pronged attack against Ottoman sovereignty in Eastern Anatolia.

Selim's armies defeated Shah Ismail at the Battle of Chaldıran in 1514 and then immediately launched his next campaign against the Mamluks of Egypt and Syria. After capturing Aleppo and Damascus in 1516, Selim I ordered immediate preparations for the invasion of Egypt and was able to enter Cairo in 1517. The Islamic holy lands of Mecca and Medina now fell under the jurisdiction of the Ottoman sovereign following his defeat of the Mamluk sultan. For the first time in the empire's history, the Ottoman sultan was in command of a predominantly Muslim population and the trade routes connecting the eastern Mediterranean to Anatolia and Central Asia.

---

[4]   Minorsky 1940–1942:1006a–1053a; Aubin 1959:37–81; Aubin 1970:235–244; Aubin 1988:1–130; Newman 2006:13–25; Mitchel 2009:19–58.
[5]   Uluçay 1953:53–90; Uluçay 1954:117–142; Uluçay 1955:187–200; Tekindağ 1967–1968:54–59; Uğur 1985; Çıpa 2007:14–71.
[6]   Arjomand 1984:109.

Selim's conquests had important implications for the evolution of Ottoman imperial ideology.[7] Despite his military successes against Muslim rivals and the resulting territorial conquests, the sultan needed to legitimize his wars against other Muslim powers in the eyes of Ottoman soldiers, subjects, and neighboring Muslim rulers. The well-established tradition of frontier warfare known as the *ghaza*, which the Ottomans used to legitimate their campaigns against Christian states in the past, no longer sufficed. The Ottoman response to the Safavid challenge required a new political and cultural discourse in Constantinople. After conquering Egypt and Syria, Selim assumed the role of the champion of Islam against 'heretics' and 'infidels'—in other words, Safavids and Mamluks—whose intransigence hindered the Ottoman struggle against the Christian enemies of the empire.[8] In response to Shah Ismail's embodiment of important Mediterranean religious and political figures, the Ottoman sultan and his ruling elites began to refer to Selim as "the protector of the two holy cities and the pilgrimage routes, and of all Muslims of the world," the *Mahdi* (the guided one),[9] and *sahib-kıran -ı heft iklim* (master of the auspicious conjunction in seven climes), pertaining to his universal persona.[10] Thus began the transformation of the sultan from a temporal political ruler into the embodiment of an idealized universal sovereign.

Selim's Early Examples of Ottoman Cartography of the Mediterranean

Selim's conquests extended Ottoman control to the major trade ports of the eastern Mediterranean, including Alexandria and Tripoli, from which vital Egyptian grain now flowed. Their defense was indispensable for the success of Ottoman economic and political policies. Furthermore, the communication lines between Anatolia and Arab lands, in particular with the holy cities of Mecca and Medina, had to be kept open. As soon as he returned from his eastern campaign, Selim I strengthened the Ottoman navy by enlarging the shipyards in Kasımpaşa on the Golden Horn and by constructing a new arsenal for the

---

[7]   Agoston 2007:94.
[8]   Feridun Ahmed Beg 1858, I:386–395.
[9]   Celalzade Mustafa 1990:39–40.
[10] Chronicles, *gazavatnames* (accounts of military campaigns), *shahnames* (royal histories), and travel accounts portrayed Sultan Selim not only as the servant of the two holy Islamic cities of Mecca and Medina, but also as the *sahib-qıran* (master of the auspicious conjunction), a Turco-Muslim and Alexandrine world conqueror, and the *Mujaddid* (the Renewer). These titles were direct answers to Shah Ismail's claims to be Alexander, God, and Ali. Fleischer 1992:160–163; Subrahmanyam 1997:751–752. On Shah Ismail's usage of similar titles see: Minorsky 1940–1942; Subrahmanyam 1997:753.

Ottoman navy in Constantinople.[11] In 1519, Hayreddin Barbarossa (d. 1546), an influential corsair in the Mediterranean, offered his services to the Ottoman sultan.[12] These small but important engagements in the Mediterranean during the reign of Selim help to account for a new growing sense at the Ottoman court that the Mediterranean was central to the empire's new political ideology.

Selim's military campaigns meant that Ottoman sultans could take on the roles of world conqueror and universal sovereign. As bureaucrats, administrators, and the military actively consolidated this image, Ottoman cartographers provided the geographic knowledge to articulate and assist this imperial claim. Ottoman interest in cartography dated back to the reign of Mehmed II (r. 1451–1481), who actively collected and drew maps. Mehmed was also known to commission Byzantine and European geographers to translate the works of Ptolemy and to prepare atlases for him.[13] It was during the reign of Selim I, however, that Ottoman geographers started to organize and refine Ottoman involvement in geography and geographical understanding, and made the Ottoman Empire an active player in the transmission of geographical knowledge across the Mediterranean. They collated recent geographical knowledge and material from the travel accounts and maps circulating in the Mediterranean into traditional Muslim accounts of geography.

Perhaps the most influential of these geographers was Piri Reis (d. 1554), a sailor who joined forces with Ottoman naval captains during the reign of Bayezid II.[14] Piri Reis produced a world map in 1513, which he presented to Selim I after his conquest of Cairo, and assembled the notes for an *isolario* (island book).[15] The sultan rewarded Piri Reis by assigning him to the imperial sea captains corps in Alexandria.[16] Sadly, the eastern two-thirds of the map have been lost. The extant section depicts the Atlantic Ocean, the western coast of Europe, Africa, and the eastern coast of the New World. On this segment, there is a long legend where Piri Reis lists his sources: twenty *portolans* (sea charts), a world map, eight Arab and four Portuguese sailing charts, and a map by Columbus.[17] In his own words, Piri Reis "took into consideration the maps that have recently appeared of the seas of India and China that up to now nobody knew in the lands

---

[11]   Celalzade Mustafa 1990:45.
[12]   Bostan 2002–2003:64–66.
[13]   Babinger 1951:8–15; Babinger 1978:81; Karamustafa 1992:210; Brotton 1997:90; Pinto 2001:5.
[14]   Soucek 1993:308–309.
[15]   Babinger 1936:1070–1071; Kahle 1956:99–108; Adıvar 1991:74–78; Kreiser 1986, 2:607–609; Afetinan 1987; Soucek 1992:267; Soucek 1993:308–309.
[16]   Orhonlu 1967:35–45; Casale 2010:36.
[17]   Piri Reis 1513.

of Rum."[18] As the sections of the map depicting the Mediterranean, China, and the Indian Ocean are missing, we cannot evaluate Piri Reis' claims.

Today, the manuscript libraries in Istanbul hold copies of the *portolan* charts by al-Katibi from Tunis (1413–1414), the Majorcan cartographer Johannes de Villadestes (1428), and İbrahim al-Mursi (1461), as well as Pedro Reinel's world map (ca. 1519).[19] It is possible that Piri Reis drew on these and other maps. As a sea captain, he also had an easy access to other sea charts circulating in the Mediterranean. What is striking about his world map is that, by claiming to incorporate the latest knowledge and discoveries, the cartographer advances his own vision of what a good geographical work should encompass while also seeking imperial patronage. In the early sixteenth century, this was the practice of cartographers and mapmakers who catered to important political figures in Europe.[20] Henricus Martellus Germanus's world map (1488) and the Nuremberg merchant Martin Behaim's terrestrial globe (1492) are the earliest examples of this endeavor.[21]

Piri Reis's world map is drawn in the tradition of *portolan* charts and it is contemporaneous with the Cantino map (1502), the Pesaro map (ca. 1505–1508), and Vesconte Maggiolo's map (1516). These three maps were meant to please their patrons, and to relate the most recent information on the geography of the world. In this respect, though no different than his contemporaries, Piri Reis was a pioneer who contributed to the development of geography as a distinct genre in the Ottoman Empire. Though he presented his work to the sultan as a prestigious patron, his maps also sought to serve a larger cause—to buttress the emerging Ottoman imperial ideology, which anticipated the sultan's universal sovereignty. Piri Reis's world map, in presenting the Ottoman domains and beyond, sought to depict the borders of the known world over which the sultan's imperial authority would radiate.

Süleyman the Magnificent and the Ottoman "Grand" Project

After the death of Selim in 1520, his son Süleyman ascended the throne. Süleyman I inherited an empire that encompassed lands extending from the Arabian Peninsula in the east, to the Balkans in the west, and to Egypt in the south. He assumed a host of imperial titles, including that of the "sultan of seven climes," a direct and geographical reference to the universal sovereignty

[18] Piri Reis 1526, 1:3a.
[19] Soucek 1992:264–266; İhsanoğlu 2000:3–4.
[20] Fernandez-Armesto 2007:754–758.
[21] Woodward 1987:316.

of the Ottoman sultans. Süleyman had to prove himself as a successful ruler by continuing Selim's conquests and by consolidating the imperial claims for universal sovereignty that had evolved so rapidly during his ambitious father's reign. About the same time that Süleyman ascended to the Ottoman throne, Europe witnessed the rise of Charles V who wished to fulfill both the Spanish and the Austrian/Germanic aspirations to a universal monarchy. His dignitaries presented him as the messianic 'Last World Emperor.'[22] In 1519, Charles added Austria to his domains, which already included Spain, Naples, the Netherlands, and the New World. The same year he was elected Holy Roman Emperor. Süleyman and Charles, each ambitious and intelligent, soon became famous rivals. Their armies fought on two fronts—in Hungary, where Ottoman military campaigns challenged Charles's European domains and culminated in the 1529 seige of Vienna[23] and in the Mediterranean—while their palaces saw advisors and intellectuals articulating competing imperial discourses.

Under the leadership of Süleyman's grand vizier, İbrahim Pasha, both the military campaigns and the political discourse conveyed one clear message: Sultan Süleyman was challenging the authority of both the Pope and the Holy Roman Emperor. The sultan was the expected Last Emperor, a universal ruler who would unite all mankind under a single rule and single religion before the Day of Judgment.[24] While Charles V and his advisors had made similar univer-salist claims, Süleyman had one great advantage: he laid claim to the Byzantine legacy and to being the legitimate heir to the Roman Empire as emperor of Constantinople, the New Rome. In accordance with the apocalyptic expecta-tions of his age, the tenth century of the Muslim Era, Süleyman also proclaimed that he would disseminate justice around the world as the messianic ruler.[25]

It is not a coincidence that during the first half of Süleyman's reign, most Ottoman military campaigns challenged Charles's domains in Europe. In this period, the Ottoman-Habsburg rivalry focused in particular on control of Hungary.[26] Ottomans entered Budin (Buda) in 1526 and claimed Hungary as an Ottoman vassal state. As Charles V's forces sacked Rome in 1527, Süleyman I was planning his second campaign to Hungary. His long siege of Vienna, the royal capital of the Habsburgs, ended in failure in 1529, but his armies entered Hungary again in 1532. Though this campaign also ended in failure, İbrahim Pasha carefully scripted Süleyman's triumphal entries into Nish and Belgrade, as spectacles designed for western observers and European diplomats present

---

[22]   Peirce 1993:25; Peter Burke 1999:411–418, 426–433; Ágoston 2007:97–98.
[23]   Fodor 1991:271–345; Gökbilgin 2001:12–16.
[24]   Necipoğlu 1993:175–225; Fleischer 1992; Turan 2007.
[25]   Fleischer 1992:159–165.
[26]   Fodor 1991:271–345; Gökbilgin 2001:12–16.

in those cities. In these massive processions, Süleyman carried a tall helmet, fashioned with gems and constructed out of four superimposed crowns, with a tiara at the top. Commissioned by İbrahim Pasha, the priceless helmet imitated not only the crown that Charles V wore during his 1530 coronation in Bologna, but also the papal tiara.[27] Ottoman sultans had not worn or carried crowns before, nor did they do so after: the symbolic meaning of the object was clear. Messianic ambitions aside, the campaigns in Hungary were unsuccessful, and İbrahim Pasha, their mastermind, came under criticism after a 1533 treaty left western and northern Hungary in Habsburg control.

Süleyman's Mediterranean and Ottoman Canonical Cartography

Following the unsuccessful siege of Vienna, the Ottoman-Habsburg rivalry entered a new phase in the Mediterranean exemplified by conflicts between Andrea Doria, the Genoese admiral of a Habsburg armada, and Hayreddin Barbarossa, the *kaptan-ı derya* (naval captain) of the Ottoman fleet. They challenged each other in particular around the Aegean Sea and North Africa. Süleyman's campaigns during the first half of his reign, and in particular his rivalry with Charles V over Hungary and the Mediterranean, spurred the production of geographic and cartographic works in the Ottoman Empire that highlighted the importance of this region for the Ottoman imperial claims for universal sovereignty.

During this period, Ottoman geographers created an independent body of geographical literature that was accessible to palace dignitaries and the sultan. The maps that the sultan had at his disposal in the sixteenth century were the works of various individuals. In the Ottoman Empire, there was no official cartographer. There was no school of navigation in Constantinople similar to the *Casa de la Contratación* (House of Trade) established in 1503 in Seville to regulate all commerce and navigation to the New World and to the Indies. The House of Trade recruited skilled cartographers and sea pilots to draw maps of the Habsburg possessions in the New World and to train navigators, growing into an important center for cartographic production in Europe.[28]

Piri Reis was as close to an official cartographer as we can find in the Ottoman Empire.[29] His *Kitab-ı Bahriye (Book of the Sea Lore)* best exemplifies the heightened importance of the Mediterranean in Ottoman geographical consciousness.

---

[27] Necipoğlu 1993:401–427; Ágoston 2007:101.
[28] Parker 1998:59–63; Kagan 2000:55–63; Padrón 2004:40; Portundo 2009:95–102.
[29] Soucek 1994:134–135.

Piri Reis had initially completed his *isolario* in 1521. Later on, commissioned by İbrahim Pasha, he prepared an expanded version of the work for the Sultan Süleyman.[30] Piri Reis completed his revisions and presented the *Book of the Sealore* to Süleyman I after his 1522 conquest in Rhodes and while he prepared for his first campaign to Hungary. Written during a period of consolidation of the claims to universal sovereignty, Piri Reis's *isolario* focuses exclusively on the history and geography of the Mediterranean and represents the Mediterranean archipelago with great accuracy and detail.[31] This first Ottoman Turkish *isolario* offers a more detailed and up-to-date account of the Mediterranean than his contemporaries prepared in Europe.[32] The book contains Piri Reis's own observations and experiences as a sailor, his descriptions of landmarks and of facilities offered by each port, and his practical sailing suggestions supplemented by brief accounts of local history and mythology. Like his contemporary, the Portuguese cartographer Valentin Fernandes, whose *isolario, De insulis et peregrinatione Lusitanorum*, focuses exclusively on the Atlantic islands, Piri Reis's *Book of the Sealore* is written in the vernacular and thus marks a turning point in the development of Ottoman Turkish as a technical language for mariners.[33] The book circulated widely among the palace circles from the sixteenth century onward.[34]

Although Piri Reis compiled the initial edition of the *Book of the Sealore* as a sailor's guidebook, in the second edition he improved the work by adding colorful charts depicting the Mediterranean islands and ports. He extended the narratives of local anecdotes and practices, his activities in the region, and excerpts from naval battles. He also wrote a new and a lengthy introduction in rhyming verse, in which, after a long passage on the mariner's life, Piri Reis conveys his knowledge on topics ranging from the classifications of sea storms, to techniques of mapmaking and compass navigation, to the history of Portuguese discoveries in the Indian Ocean and Columbus's discovery of the New World. Although Piri Reis had already described the discoveries of Columbus in

---

[30] Piri Reis 1526:3a.

[31] Tolias 2007:268–269.

[32] Soucek 1992:262; Tolias 2007:269–270.

[33] Tolias 2007:270.

[34] Even today, there are 45 extant copies of the work. There are 5658 manuscript maps in the known copies of the work. Nine of these copies are located in British, Italian, French, Austrian, and German libraries. The rest are listed in the catalogues of different libraries and museums in Istanbul. Among the 45 manuscripts of the work, two of them include text only, and three of them consist of maps only. The copy that is located at the Süleymaniye Library in Istanbul under the catalogue number Ayasofya 2612 was donated to the library by Mahmud I (r. 1730–1754) and is attested to be the most complete copy (Esiner 1996:20–22). Among the extant manuscript copies, about two-dozen are from the sixteenth century, and, with a few exceptions, these copies found their way to the Ottoman palace library (İhsanoğlu 2000:23–25).

the New World in the text surrounding his 1513 world map,[35] in this new work he discusses in some detail Portuguese activities in the Indian Ocean and the Red Sea and their effects on the trade, as well as the difficulties of sailing in the Indian Ocean.[36] He devotes the rest of his work to the Mediterranean. As early as the reign of Mehmed II, the Ottoman rulers claimed to be the Roman Caesars. During the first half of Süleyman's reign, unification of the *Mare Nostrum* and extension of Ottoman control over the Mediterranean became the *sine qua non* of Ottoman claims for world conquest. Piri Reis's work, prepared during a crucial time in this enterprise, articulated these Ottoman assertions and aided their realization by offering detailed geographical and historical knowledge.

In the *Book of the Sealore,* the description of the entire Mediterranean is divided into 214 sections, each accompanied by one or two maps illustrating different Mediterranean islands and port cities. In this section, Piri Reis changes his writing style from verse to prose. He explains his reason for this change in style as follows: "The reason for shifting to prose here is that so far in this book, we have explained the matters regarding compass, map, and the situation of the winds and shallows completely in verse. But we described the Mediterranean in prose. Had we done it in verse, it would have taken very long. When you use this book at nights or at places of difficulty, verbosity is not proper."[37] This passage clearly shows that Piri Reis's main goal was to produce a guidebook for the seaman. However, by presenting the sultan with a work on a region that occupies a central position in the imperial claims for world conquest, he also hoped to gain his favor. Piri Reis was a talented and an ambitious cartographer.

The *Book of the Sealore* focuses in particular on the regions that Piri Reis deemed important for his patron: the eastern Mediterranean and the North African coast. Although he portrays important islands and port cities of the central and western Mediterranean, such as Malta, Corsica, Sardinia, and Gibraltar, in separate chapters, these sections are devoid of historical or anthropological information. For the eastern Mediterranean and the North African coast, which Piri Reis knows best, the author provides short episodes from recent history and discusses various geographical features.[38] The chapters on Egypt, the Nile, Damascus, and Alexandria, in particular, include minute details about geography and useful hints about how to navigate complex waters. Similarly, his chapters on Djerba, Tunis, and Tripoli are remarkably rich in details regarding castles, harbors, the recent history of the region, and local customs.[39]

[35] Piri Reis 1513.
[36] Casale 2010:37.
[37] Piri Reis 1526:43a.
[38] Soucek 1992:262.
[39] Piri Reis 1526:333a–336b.

Piri Reis was obviously driven by the desire to create an instructive and impressive work on the Mediterranean for his patron. The way that he prioritizes North Africa and the eastern Mediterranean also speaks to their importance for the Ottoman world order. His chapters on these regions are far more detailed than anything found in contemporary Italian or Catalan *portolans* or *isolarii*.[40] Indeed, Piri Reis's *isolario* presents unique firsthand knowledge of the geography of the Mediterranean. But perhaps more importantly, Piri Reis's particular geographical focus served a political purpose more than a cartographical one: to remind the Ottoman sultan of his role as world conqueror and to affirm the importance of the Mediterranean to Ottoman imperial aspirations. Written originally on the eve of Süleyman's conquest of Rhodes in 1522, Piri Reis's *Book of the Sealore* reminds the Ottoman sultan of past victories and assures him of future success.

After the *Book of the Sealore*, Piri Reis compiled another cartographic work, a world map drawn in *portolan* style. Today, only the northwest corner of this map from 1528 survives. In 1547, Piri Reis was appointed Admiral of the Fleet of Egypt and India and commanded expeditions against the Portuguese in the Red Sea. After a failure in a campaign in Hormuz in 1552–1553, he was executed in Cairo.

Second Half of the Sixteenth Century: A Somber Image and Sober Policy

By the 1540s, it was clear that neither Charles V nor Süleyman I could establish universal rulership. The military confrontation in Hungary ended in stalemate, and Charles V withdrew to a monastery in 1556. The aging Süleyman, meanwhile, stopped participating in imperial campaigns and royal processions except for the Friday prayers. He delegated most of his power to the imperial bureaucrats and withdrew to his own quarters in the palace.[41] Although Ottoman campaigns into Central Europe did not bring a major victory after the 1540s, Ottomans still reigned supreme in the Mediterranean. If Süleyman was to be considered a true successor to the Roman emperors, he had to control the *Mare Nostrum*. Hayreddin Barbarossa had erased the bad memories of the loss of Tunis with a victory at Preveze in 1539 against the Venetians. After this incident, which brought the whole of the Peloponnese and the Dalmatian coast under Ottoman control, the Ottoman fleet was in nominal control of the eastern and central Mediterranean. Then, in 1565, the Ottomans faced their greatest

---

[40] Soucek 1992:272–279.
[41] Fleischer 1986:135–142; Necipoğlu 1991:29–30.

challenge in the Mediterranean when they failed to conquer the strategic island of Malta.[42] European visual, musical, and verbal depictions depicted the event as a victory of Christianity in southern Europe against the Muslim Empire.[43]

During this period, in order to increase pressure on the Safavids, the Ottomans also attempted to secure a foothold in the Red Sea that would serve as an *entrepôt* into the Indian Ocean. When Süleyman ascended the Ottoman throne, the Portuguese had already established commercial and political networks in the Indian Ocean. In a report addressing İbrahim Pasha in 1525, the Ottoman captain Selman Reis warned the grand vizier about Portuguese control over the spice trade in the Indian Ocean and the threat to the holy cities of Mecca and Medina and even to Egypt. Selman Reis urged the grand vizier to take measures as soon as possible.[44] As the Portuguese successfully blockaded Muslim shipping in the Red Sea, the Ottoman fleet prepared war galleys in Suez.[45] Around the same time, the possibility of opening a canal between the Nile and the Red Sea port of Tor was also discussed in the Ottoman court.[46] Although the canal never materialized, Ottoman captains struggled against the Portuguese in the Red Sea in the next decades and attempted to penetrate into the Indian Ocean both by military and diplomatic means. The Ottomans took control of Aden in 1538 but failed in the siege of Diu the same year. In 1552, their attempts to conquer Hormuz, which since 1543 had been a Portuguese base used primarily to ship Iranian silk to their possessions in India, also failed.[47]

After these incidents, Ottoman attempts to establish a foothold in the Indian Ocean slowed and eventually vanished. As the imperial campaigns fizzled on both fronts, the aging Süleyman I faced a series of personal setbacks. The sultan felt compelled by rumors and military defeats to order the executions of his beloved grand vizier İbrahim Pasha and later his son Mustafa. Shaken by these events, the sultan began to espouse a somber imperial image and employed a far less personal icon of rulership: the imperial law. During this period, the *Şeyhülislam* (chief jurist consult) Ebussu'ud Efendi (1490–1574) and the chancellor Celalzade Mustafa (1490–1567) systematically codified, compiled, and reconciled the *kanun* (imperial law) with Islamic Law.[48] In other words, the imperial law was reformulated and became the embodiment of impersonal rule and the sign of the sultan's impersonal authority.[49]

---

[42] Cassola 1994:325–355.
[43] Cassola 1994:83–89.
[44] Kurtoğlu 1935:67–73; Özbaran 1978:81–88; Casale 2010:36–40.
[45] Özbaran 1994:94.
[46] Casale 2010:48–49.
[47] Newman 2006:61.
[48] Fleischer 1992:166–170; Imber 1997.
[49] Fleischer 1986:191–252.

The historian, mathematician, and geographer Matrakçı Nasuh (d. 1564) provided an excellent example of the centrality of imperial law to the sultan's universal authority in his work the *Beyan-ı Menazil*, the diary of Süleyman's Iraq campaign between 1533 and 1536. Only one manuscript copy of this work has survived; it is located in the Istanbul University Library.[50] Matrakçı entered the palace service as a *devshirme* and was a product of Ottoman schooling and administration. He became a protégé of Rüstem Pasha, the grand vizier to Sultan Süleyman during the second half of his reign.[51] Matrakçı, who composed the *Beyan-ı Menazil* during the actual journey and later illustrated it with 130 miniature depictions of the major stations *en route*, presents the Ottoman sultan as the dispenser of justice within and beyond the Ottoman realm. When describing the Ottoman entrance to Tabriz, the geographer writes: "After the victorious troops who were in that region [Tabriz] set their aims on reaching eternal success with reverence and honor and respect and consideration, with the appearance of the sultanic and imperial throne and the starlike arrival of the Rumis, they held the court of justice because the celestial-sphere-adorning court of the Sulaiman of the time was necessary for that land."[52] Matrakçı Nasuh reminds his readers on several occasions that the sultan brought security and justice to Anatolia and beyond. Whenever he reached an important station along his campaign route, the author recounts, the sultan set up his *divan-ı adalet* (court of justice). In several miniatures, Matrakçı even depicts the sultan's tent, the physical symbol of his justice, and where the imperial court was held, surrounded by smaller tents of his retinue.[53] In his depictions and narrative, Matrakçı highlighted the importance of imperial law for the universal claims of the Ottoman sultan.

In 1566, Süleyman I died under the walls of the fortress of Szigetvar during his last campaign to Hungary. His grand vizier Sokullu Mehmed Pasha continued the siege and conquered the town, but under the reigns of Süleyman's successors Selim II (r. 1566–1574) and Murad III (r. 1574–1595) Ottoman military campaigns slowed down. The Ottoman conquest of Cyprus in 1570, followed by the Ottoman defeat at Battle of Lepanto in 1571, led to a stalemate in the Mediterranean.

The reign of Murad III, in particular, was a period of acute political and financial crises for the Ottomans as the empire was forced to fight wars on two fronts. The Ottomans were in intermittent conflict with the Safavids from 1579 to 1639 in Iraq while in Hungary, a long and costly war with the Habsburgs raged

---

[50] Matrakçı Nasuh, *Beyan-ı Menazil-i Sefer-i Irakeyn-i Sultan Süleyman Han*, Istanbul University Library, TY. 5964.
[51] Selen 1943; Taeschner 1956:53–55; Johnston 1971:159–166; Orbay 2001; Ebel 2002:222–225.
[52] Matrakçı Nasuh 1533–1536:28b–29a.
[53] Matrakçı Nasuh 1533–1536:13b–14a, 15b, 20b, 24b, 25a, 26b, 29b, 31a, 72a, 73a, 74a, 74b.

between 1593 and 1606.[54] Facing financial crisis, the Ottoman state levied new taxes on peasants, borrowed money from internal moneylenders, and debased the silver coinage. Irate over lost wages, the janissary corps revolted in the capital. Contemporary historians in the Ottoman capital noted these events as a sign of decline.[55]

The *realpolitik* in this period prompted urgent and practical solutions from the Ottoman dignitaries. As Murad III continued the claims of his predecessors to universal sovereignty, the Ottoman court proposed unconventional and creative answers to address the rising Shi'i power beyond its eastern frontier. Safavid economic, military and political achievements under Shah Abbas I (r. 587–1629) seriously challenged the Ottoman presence and legitimacy in the East.[56] The chroniclers of the Safavid court in Isfahan articulated the Safavid supremacy vis-à-vis the two Sunni powers: the Ottomans in Anatolia and Iraq and Uzbeks in Transoxiana. In their works, Safavid literati associated the Safavid dynasty with Tamerlane (d. 1405) in an effort to consolidate their authority in Central Asia.[57] Istanbul responded to these Safavid claims and attempted to influence the changing conditions in Central Asia. A decade earlier, in 1568–1569, Sokullu Mehmed Pasha, the grand vizier to Selim II (r. 1566–1574) had promoted a project to increase the Ottoman presence in the region by opening a canal between the Don and Volga rivers. The project aimed at creating easier connections from the Ottoman lands to Central Asia. Although the plan failed to gain the sultan's approval, it was one of the earliest attempts to consolidate Ottoman control over the trade routes and establish better connections with the Muslim rulers in the region.[58] Negotiating political and economic alliances with the Central Asian Muslim rulers against the Safavids was the Ottomans' only option.

During the peak of the conflict with the Safavids in the 1580s, the Ottomans continued to assume a pious Sunni Muslim image vis-à-vis their Shi'i Muslim neighbors, the Safavids. Contemporary accounts picked up this thread, portraying the Ottoman sultans more and more as pious rulers. In 1582, at the fifty-day imperial circumcision festival, Murad III made a public display of his piety with the circumcision of his sons and thousands of orphans and *devshirme* recruits as well as conversions of the members of the Safavid embassy to Sunni Islam.[59] He commissioned chroniclers and miniaturists to depict and describe

---

54 Imber 2005:101–102.
55 Kafadar 1993:37–48; Necipoğlu 2005:256–257.
56 Krstic 2009:35–63.
57 Newman 2006:50–73.
58 Casale 2010:135–136.
59 Terzioğlu 1995:85–86.

these ceremonies and to articulate his piety.[60] Concomitantly, Ottoman literati highlighted the prestige and political legitimacy of the dynasties of Chingiz Khanid descent in Central Asia more than before. For instance, the renowned historian, Mustafa Ali (d. 1600) compares the universal empires of Tamerlane and Chingiz Khan to that of the Ottomans in his monumental world history, the *Künhü'l-Ahbar* (*Essence of History*) written between 1591 and 1599.[61] Mustafa Ali and several other contemporary historians from the same period prepared works for the Ottoman sultan where they attached great importance to Uzbeks and Crimean khans due to their Chingizid descent.[62] The Ottomans could never claim to descend from Chingiz Khan; however, they made use of their only plausible connection to Central Asia extensively in this period. In 1593–1594, the court historian Talikizade delineated twenty qualities of the Ottoman dynasty that assured their supremacy in the Islamic world. One of these qualities, Talikizade asserts, is the Ottoman dynasty's descent from the Central Asian Turkic ruler Oghuz Khan.[63] These references to the Ottoman lineage going back to Chingiz Khan indicate the Ottoman awareness of shifting economic and political networks at the end of the sixteenth century. The Ottoman sultans were no longer the Roman emperors but rather pious Sunni-Muslims who tried to bolster their connections to Central Asia.

Boundaries of the Ottoman World and Ottoman Cartography in the Second Half of the Sixteenth Century

In 1534, the French cosmographer Orance Fine (d. 1555) prepared a woodcut heart-shaped world map. This map integrated the latest geographical discoveries in the New World in a conventional way and represented the world in a unified form with no political or religious borders.[64] What is striking about this map is that in 1559, a world map based on Fine's 1534 woodcut was also prepared in Ottoman Turkish. The map, entitled *The Representation of the Whole World Designed in its Entirety*, was prepared in Venice by Hacı Ahmed of Tunis. Today we know that Hacı Ahmed was a fictitious character and that the compiler of the text was neither an educated Tunisian nor an Ottoman.[65] Unfortunately no copies of the map survive from the sixteenth century. The woodblocks remained

---

[60] Terzioğlu 1995; Woodhead 2005:85–98.
[61] Fleischer 1986:277.
[62] Fleischer 1986:277.
[63] Necipoğlu 2005:30.
[64] Mangani 1998:59–82; Cosgrove 2001:113, 133; Lestringrant and Pelletier 2007:1464–1468.
[65] Ménage 1958:299–311.

in the Venetian archives and only in 1795 were twenty-four impressions made.[66] Despite the misspellings and grammatical mistakes in the text, the language and the correct honorifics used for the Ottoman sultan make it plausible that the map was prepared with the Ottoman market in mind.[67] Recent research in the Venetian archives showed that Prince Selim, the future Sultan Selim II and son of Süleyman I, ordered world maps from the workshops in Venice in the early 1550s just before the succession struggle started. All three sons of Süleyman I were most probably interested in Venetian cartographical productions as symbols of prestige and power during their struggle for the Ottoman throne.[68] The Hacı Ahmed Map and the story of its production is an example of how European cartographers sought the patronage of the Ottoman princes and sultans for their latest works.

In the 1560s, a time when the Ottoman struggle against the Spanish Habsburgs intensified, we see a flurry of world maps, navigation charts, and *portolan* atlases circulating in the Ottoman court in Constantinople. The earliest of these atlases, *Walters Sea Atlas* (ca. 1560), features seven *portolan* charts and a world map based on European cartographic concepts.[69] The atlas was probably prepared in Italy for a readership in the Ottoman Empire.[70] Although we cannot identify the cartographer or the client of the atlas, the elaborate illustrations on the charts suggest a wealthy and prestigious customer, possibly a member of the Ottoman dynasty.[71]

On the eve of the Lepanto defeat and Cyprus conquest, we see two more *portolan* atlases produced in Europe for an Ottoman patron. The atlas of Ali Macar Reis, which is today preserved at the Topkapı Palace Library, dates from 1567.[72] A work of eighteen pages, the atlas consists of six nautical charts and a world map prepared in the style of the contemporary Italian schools of Ottomano Freducci and Battista Agnese.[73] Ali Macar Reis, supposedly an Ottoman sea captain of Hungarian origin, drew the maps of the atlas. It has been suggested that the atlas was actually prepared in Italy and that the place names, which were left blank, were filled in later by Ali Macar Reis.[74] The world map in the atlas is a copy of the large Gastaldi world map of 1561.[75]

---

[66] Manners 2007:21–22.
[67] Ménage 1958:299–311; Brotton 2000:35–48.
[68] Arbel 2002:21–30.
[69] Goodrich 1986:25–50.
[70] Soucek 1971:17–27.
[71] Goodrich 1986:25–50.
[72] Ali Macar Reis 1567.
[73] Soucek 1992:280.
[74] Soucek 1971:18–19.
[75] Goodrich 1984:99.

The *Atlas-ı Hümayun* (Imperial Atlas) (ca. 1570) is the last and the largest of the atlases prepared in Ottoman for an Ottoman patron in this period. Reminiscent of the Ali Macar Reis Atlas and the *Walters Sea Atlas*, it is a combination of eight *portolan* charts and a world map. There are differing opinions regarding whether the atlas was produced in an Ottoman or an Italian workshop.[76] Another chart that represents Ottoman interest in the cartographical productions in this period is the *Aegean Sea Chart* by Mehmed Reis of Menemen. This *portolan* chart dates from 1590–1591. It is still uncertain whether Mehmed Reis is a fictional character or not. Like Hacı Ahmed, we do not have other references to Mehmed Reis in any other document from the period.[77] Mehmed Reis's chart encompasses the eastern Mediterranean in great detail, covering the Aegean archipelago and circumnavigating the Peloponnese from Durazzo (Albania) to the Dardanelles and the Sea of Marmara as far as Constantinople. It also charts the Mediterranean coast of Asia Minor until the Gulf of Alexandretta.

The three Ottoman atlases from the sixteenth century are strikingly similar in style and coverage to the atlases prepared and diffused in European centers. They were produced in one of the cities along the Mediterranean for a wealthy patron. The structure of these atlases directly reflects Ottoman imperial aspirations to world power even at a time when imperial conquests had begun to slow down. The charts in these atlases depict the Mediterranean more than any other area of the world. Less attention is paid to the more distant regions of the British Isles, the Atlantic Ocean, or the Indian Ocean. Except for the *Walters Sea Atlas*, which contains a chart of the Indian Ocean, the remaining atlases do not provide any record of explorations across the Atlantic and into the Indian Ocean. The presentation of a world atlas structured to emphasize the Mediterranean in this period may be interpreted as a way to reaffirm and reiterate to the highest echelons of the Ottoman court the centrality of the Mediterranean. In a post-Süleymanic era, the Mediterranean was still the space where the imperial claims for universal sovereignty should be validated and consolidated.

---

[76] Goodrich 1985:83–101; Soucek 1971:17–27.
[77] Vedovato 1951:49; Brice, Imber, and Lorch 1977; Brice and Imber 1978:528–529.

Primary Sources

Ali Macar Reis. 1567. *Atlas TKS*. Hazine 644. Istanbul.

Atlas-ı Hümayun (Imperial Atlas). Istanbul Archeology Museum 1621. Istanbul.

Hacı Ahmed. *Mappamundi*, Bodleian, March, nr. 454.

Feridun Ahmed Beg. 1858. *Münşeatü's-Selatin*, 2 vols. Istanbul.

Kahle, Paul. 1926. *Piri Reis: Bahrije, Das türkisches Segelhandbuch für das Mittelandische Meer von Jahre 1521*. Berlin.

Matrakçı Nasuh. 1533–1536. *Beyan-ı Menazil-i Sefer-i Irakeyn-i Sultan Süleyman Han*, Istanbul University Library, TY. 5964. Istanbul.

Menemenli Mehmed Reis. *Portolan Chart*. Ms. Venedig, Museo Correr, Port 22.

Piri Reis. 1513. *Mappamundi TKS*. Revan Köşkü 1633 mük. Istanbul.

Piri Reis. 1526. *Kitab-ı Bahriye*, Süleymaniye Ayasofya 2612. Istanbul.

Walters Sea Atlas. Walters Art Museum W 660.

Yurdaydın, Hüseyin. 1976. *Matrakçı Nasuh: Beyan-ı Menazil-i Sefer-i Irakeyn-i Sultan Süleyman Han*. Ankara.

Secondary Sources

Adıvar, A. A. 1991. *Osmanlı Türklerinde İlim* ed. 4. Istanbul.

Afetinan, A. 1987. *Piri Reis'in Hayatı ve Eserleri: Amerika'nın En Eski Haritaları*. 2nd ed. Ankara.

Ágoston, G. 2007. "Information, Ideology, and Limits of Imperial Policy: Ottoman Grand Strategy in the Context of Ottoman-Habsburg Rivalry." In Aksan and Goffman 2007:75–103.

Aksan, V. and D. Goffman, eds. 2007. *Early Modern Ottomans: Remapping the Empire*. New York.

Arbel, B. 2002. "Maps of the World for Ottoman Princes? Further Evidence and Questions Concerning 'The Mappamundo of Hajji Ahmed.'" *Imago Mundi* 54:21–30.

Arjomand, S. A. 1984. *The Shadow of God and the Hidden Imam: Religion, Political Order and Societal Change in Shi'ite Iran from the Beginning to 1890*. Chicago.

Arnold, T. 2006. *The Renaissance at War*. New York.

Astengo, C. 2007. "The Renaissance Chart Tradition in the Mediterranean." In Woodward 2007: 174–262.

Aubin, J. 1959. "Études Safavides. I. Shah Isma'il et les notables de l'Iraq persan." *JESHO* 2:37–81.

——. 1970. "La politique religieuse de Safavids." In *Le Shi'isme imamate*, ed. T. Fahd, 235–244. Paris.

——. 1988. "L'avenèment des Safavides reconsidérè (Études Safavides. III)." *Moyen Orient et Ocean Indien* 5:1–130.

Babinger, F. 1936. "Piri Muhyi'l-Din Re'is." In *Encyclopedia of Islam*, ed. M. Th. Houtsma, 1070-1071. Leiden.

——. 1951. "An Italian Map of the Balkans, Presumably Owned by Mehmed II, The Conqueror (1452–53)." *Imago Mundi* 8:8–15.

——. 1978. *Mehmed the Conqueror and His Time.* ed. W.C. Hickman, trans. R. Manheim. Princeton.

Bacqué-Grammont, J.L. and van Dunzel, E. 1987. *Comité International d'études pré-Ottomanes et Ottomanes, VIth Symposium, 1-4 July 1984.* Istanbul.

Birchwood, M. and Dimmock, M. 2005. *Cultural Encounters Between East and West, 1453-1699.* Cambridge.

Brice, W., C. Imber, and R. Lorch. 1977. *The Aegean Sea-Chart of Mehmed Reis Ibn Menemenli, A.D. 1590/1.* Manchester.

Brice, W. and C. Imber. 1978. "Turkish Charts in the 'Portolan' Style." *Geographical Journal* 144 (1978):528–529.

Brotton, J. 1997. *Trading Territories: Mapping the Early Modern World.* Ithaca.

——. 2000. "Printing the World." In Frasca-Spada and Jardine 2000: 35–48.

Buisseret, D., ed. 1992. *Monarchs, Ministers, and Maps: The Emergence of Cartography as a Tool of Government in Early Modern Europe.* Chicago.

Burke, P. 1999. "Presenting and Re-presenting Charles V." In Soly 1999: 393-476.

Casale, G. 2010. *The Ottoman Age of Exploration.* Oxford.

Cassola, A. 1994. *The 1565 Ottoman Malta Campaign Register.* Malta.

Celalzade M. 1990. *Me'asir-i Selim Hani: Selim-name* (Ahmet Uğur and Mustafa Çuhadar). Ankara.

Çıpa, H. E. 2007. *The Centrality of the Periphery: The Rise of Power of Selim I, 1487-1512.* PhD diss. Harvard University.

Cosgrove, D. 2001. *Apollo's Eye: A Cartographic Genealogy of the Earth in the Western Imagination.* Baltimore.

Ebel, K. 2002. *City Views, Imperial Visions: Cartography and the Visual Culture of Urban Space in the Ottoman Empire, 1453-1603.* PhD diss., University of Texas at Austin.

Emiralioğlu, P. 2006. *Cognizance of the Ottoman World: Visual and Textual Representations in the Sixteenth-Century Ottoman Empire (1514-1596).* PhD diss., University of Chicago.

Fernandez-Armesto, F. 2007. "Maps and Exploration in the Sixteenth and Early Seventeenth Centuries." In Woodward 2007: 738-757.

Fleischer, C. H. 1986. *Bureaucrat and Intellectual in the Ottoman Empire: The Historian Mustafa Ali (1541-1600).* Princeton.

———. 1992. "The Lawgiver as Messiah: The Making of the Imperial Image in the Reign of Süleyman." In Veinstein 1992: 159–177.

Fodor, P. 1991. "Ottoman Policy towards Hungary." *Acta Orientalia Academiae Scientiarum Hungaricae* 45:271–345.

Frasca-Spada, M. and Jardine, N., eds. 2000. *Books and Sciences in History.* Cambridge.

Goffman, D. 2002. *The Ottoman Empire and Early Modern World.* New York.

Gökbilgin, T. 2001. "Kanuni Sultan Süleyman'ın Macaristan ve Avrupa Siyasetinin Sebep ve Amilleri, Geçirdiği Safhalar." *Kanuni Armağanı.* Ankara.

Goodrich, T. 1986. "The Earliest Ottoman Maritime Atlas — The Walters Deniz Atlasi." *Archivum Ottomanicum* 11:25–50.

———. 1985. "Atlas-i Humayun: A Sixteenth Century Ottoman Maritime Atlas Discovered in 1984." *Archivum Ottomanicum* 10:83–101.

———. 1984. "Some Unpublished Sixteenth Century Ottoman Maps." In Bacqué-Grammont and Emeri van Dunzel 1987:99–103.

Hagen, G. 2003. *Ein Osmanischer Geograph bei der Arbeit Entstehung und Gedankenwelt von Katib Celebis Cihannüma.* Berlin.

Harley, J. B. 1988. "Silences and Secrecy, the Hidden Agenda of Cartography in Early Modern Europe." *Imago Mundi* 40:57–76.

Harley, J. B. and D. Woodward, eds. 1992. *The History of Cartography,* vol. 2, book 1: *Cartography in the Traditional Islamic and South Asian Societies.* Chicago.

———, eds. 1987. *The History of Cartography,* vol. 1: *Cartography in Prehistoric, Ancient and Medieval Europe and the Mediterranean.* Chicago.

İhsanoğlu, E. ed. 2000. *Osmanlı Coğrafya Litertatürü Tarihi.* Istanbul.

Imber, C. 1997. *Ebu's-Su'ud: The Islamic Legal Tradition.* Stanford.

Inalcik, H. and Kafadar, C., eds. 1993. *Sülayman the Second and his Time.* Istanbul.

———. 2005. "Frozen Legitimacy." In Karateke, H. and Reinkowski, M.: 99–111.

Jardine, L. and J. Brotton. 2000. *Global Interests: Renaissance Art between East and West.* Ithaca.

Johnston, N. J. 1971. "The Urban World of the Matrakci Manuscript." *Near Eastern Studies Journal* 30/3:159–166.

Kafadar, C. 1993. "The Myth of Golden Age: Ottoman Historical Consciousness in the Post Süleymanic Era." In İnalcık and Kafadar 1993: 117–137.

Kafesçioğlu, Ç. 2009. *Constantinopolis/Istanbul: Cultural Encounter, Imperial Vision, and the Construction of the Ottoman Capital (Buildings, Landscapes, and Societies).* University Park, PA.

Kagan, R. 2000. *Urban Images of the Hispanic World, 1493-1793.* New Haven.

Kahle, P. 1956. "Piri Reis, the Turkish Sailor and Cartographer." *The Journal of the Pakistan Historical Society* 4:99–108.

Karamustafa, A. 1992. "Introduction to Ottoman Cartography." In Harley and Woodward 1992:205–208.

———. 1992. "Military, Administrative, and Scholarly Maps and Plans." In Harley and Woodward 1992:209–227.

Karateke, H. and Reinkowski, M., eds. 2005. *Legitimizing the Order: The Ottoman Rhetoric of State Power*. Leiden.

Kleinschmidt, H. 2004. *Charles V: The World Emperor*. Phoenix Mill, UK.

Kreiser, K. 1986. "Piri Reis." In Kretschmer, Dörflinger, and Wawrik: 607–609.

Kretschmer, I., Dörflinger, J. and Wawrik, R., eds. 1986. *Lexicon zur Geschicte der Kartographie*, 2nd. ed. Vienna.

Krstic, T. 2009. "Illuminated by the Light of Islam and the Glory of the Ottoman Sultanate: Self-Narratives of Conversion to Islam in the Age of Confessionalization." *Comparative Studies in Society and History* 51/1:35–63.

Kurtoğlu, F. 1935. "Amiral Selman Reis Layihasi." *Deniz Mecmuasi* 47/335:67–73.

Lestringant, F and Pelletier, M. 2007. "Maps and Descriptions of the World in Sixteenth-Century France." In Woodward 2007:1463–1480.

MacLean, G. 2005. *Re-Orienting the Renaissance: Cultural Exchanges with the East*. New York.

Mangani, G. 1998. "Abraham Ortelius and the Hermetic Meaning of the Cordiform Projection." *Imago Mundi* 50:59–82.

Manners, I. 2007. *European Cartographers and the Ottoman World 1500-1750: Maps From the Collection of O.J. Sopranos*. Chicago.

Ménage, V. L. 1958. "The Map of Haji Ahmed and Its Makers," *BSOAS* 21:299–311.

Meserve, M. 2008. *Empires of Islam in Renaissance Historical Thought*. Cambridge, MA.

Minorsky, V. 1940–1942. "The Poetry of Shah İsma'il I." *BSOAS* 10:1006a–1053a.

Mitchel, C. P. 2009. *The Practice of Politics: Power, Religion, and Rhetoric*. New York.

Necipoğlu, G. 1991. *Architecture, Ceremonial, and Power: The Topkapı Palace in the Fifteenth and Sixteenth Centuries*. New York.

Newman, A. J. 2006. *Safavid Iran: Rebirth of a Persian Empire*. New York.

Orbay, I. 2001. "Istanbul Viewed: The Representation of the City in Ottoman Maps of the Sixteenth and Seventeenth Centuries." PhD diss., MIT.

Orhonlu, C. 1967. "Hint Kaptanlığı ve Piri Reis." *Belleten* 34/234:35–45.

Özbaran, S. 1978. "A Turkish Report in the Red Sea and the Portuguese in the Indian Ocean (1525)." *Arabian Studies* 4:81–88.

———. 1994. *The Ottoman Response to European Expansion: Studies on Ottoman-Portuguese Relations in the Indian Ocean and Ottoman Administration in the Arab Lands during the Sixteenth Century*. Istanbul.

Özen, M.E. 1998. *Piri Reis and His Charts*. Istanbul.

Padrón, R. 2004. *The Spacious Word: Cartography, Literature, and Empire in Early Modern Spain*. Chicago.

Parker, G. 1998. *The Grand Strategy of Philip II*. New Haven.

Peirce, L. 1993. *The Imperial Harem: Women and Sovereignty in the Ottoman Empire*. Oxford.

Pinto, K. C. 2001. *Ways of Seeing: Scenarios of the World in the Medieval Islamic Cartographic Imagination*. PhD diss., Columbia University.

Portundo, M. M. 2009. *Secret Science: Spanish Cosmography and the New World*. Chicago.

Selen, H. H. 1943. "16. Yüzyılda Yapilmiş Anadolu Atlası." *İkinci Türk Tarih Kongresi, İstanbul, 20-25 Eylul 1937, Kongreye Sunulan Bildiriler*. Istanbul.

Setton, K. M. 1984. *The Papacy and the Levant (1204-1571)*, vol. 3. Philadelphia.

Soly, Hugo. ed. 1999. *Charles V, 1500-1558, and His Time*. Antwerp.

Soucek, S. 1971. "The 'Ali Macar Reis Atlas' and the Deniz Kitabı: Their Place in the Genre of Portolan Charts and Atlases." *Imago Mundi* 25:17-27.

——. 1973. "Tunisia in the Kitab-i Bahriye by Piri Reis." *Archivum Ottomanicum* 5:129-297.

——. 1992. "Islamic Charting in the Mediterranean." In Harley and Woodward 1992:263-287.

——. 1994. "Piri Reis and Ottoman Discovery of the Great Discoveries." *Studia Islamica* 79:121-142.

——. 1996. *Piri Reis and Turkish Mapmaking after Columbus: The Khalili Portolan Atlas*. London.

Subrahmanyam, S. 1997. "Connected Histories — Notes towards a Reconfiguration of Early Modern Eurasia." *Modern Asian Studies* 31-33:735-762.

Taeschner, F. 1956. "The Itinerary of the First Persian Campaign of Sultan Süleyman, 1534-36, According to Nasuh al-Matraki." *Imago Mundi* 13:53-55.

Tekindağ, Ş. 1967/68. "Şah Kulu Baba Tekeli İsyanı." *Belgelerle Türk Tarihi Dergisi* 3:34-39, 4:54-59.

Terzioğlu, D. 1995. "The Imperial Circumcision Festival of 1582: An Interpretation," *Muqarnas* 12:84-100.

Tolias, G. 2007. "*Isolarii*, Fifteenth to Seventeenth Century." In Woodward 2007: 265-267.

Turan, E. 2007. *The Sultan's Favorite: Ibrahim Paşa and the Making of the Ottoman Universal Sovereignty in the Reign of Sultan Süleyman, 1516-1526*. PhD diss., University of Chicago.

Uğur, A. 1985. *The Reign of Selim I in the Light of Selim-Name Literature*. Berlin.

Uluçay, Ç. 1953, 1954, 1955. "Yavuz Sultan Selim Nasıl Padişah Oldu?." *Tarih Dergisi* 9:53-90, 10:117-142, 11:187-200.

Vatin, N. 2004. *Rodos Şövalyeleri ve Osmanlılar: soğu Akdeniz'de savaş diplomasi ve korsanlık: 1480-1522.* (Trans. T. Altınova). Istanbul.

Vedovato, M. 1951. "The Nautical Chart of Mohammed Raus, 1590." *Imago Mundi* 8:49.

Veinstein, G., ed. 1992. *Soliman le Magnifique et son temps.* Paris.

Woodhead, C. 2005. "Murad III and the Historians of Ottoman Imperial Authority in late 16th-Century Historiography." Karateke and Reinkowski: 85–98.

Woodward, D., ed, 2007. *The History of Cartography,* vol. 3: *Cartography in the European Renaissance.* Chicago.

———. 1987. "Medieval Mappaemundi." In Harley and Woodward 1987:286–370.

Yates, F. A. 1985. *Astrea: The Imperial Theme in the Sixteenth Century.* London.

4

Ferīdūn Beg's *Münşe'ātü 's-Selāṭīn* ('Correspondence of Sultans') and Late Sixteenth-Century Ottoman Views of the Political World

Dimitris Kastritsis

THE QUESTION of Ottoman political geography has yet to be addressed in any depth. The place of the science of geography in the Ottoman Empire has received some attention in recent years, as has the cultural meaning of the geographical term "lands of *Rūm*," broadly signifying the former Byzantine territories where the Ottoman venture began, the core regions of Ottoman civilization.[1] What is missing, however, is an examination of the place of geographical space in the ideology of empire, the study of which has thus far been confined to the examination of court ceremonial and more explicit political discourse.[2] Put differently, we may have some idea why an author like the seventeenth-century polymath Kātib Çelebi wrote about geography the way he did, or how the Ottomans represented their relations with other powers in court ceremonial, processions, and illustrated manuscripts; but what is mostly lacking is an examination of how the Ottomans conceived of political geography, of the position of their own empire within a larger world made up of other state actors, and how this relates to the real political situation at any given time. It is that gap that the present chapter begins to address, if only to a very limited degree.

Given the state of the field and the near total absence of a secondary literature dealing directly with the problem at hand, the aims of this contribution are necessarily modest. Far from constituting a comprehensive examination of the development of Ottoman geographical consciousness across several centuries, what follows is but a tentative glimpse at a particular period in the empire's

---

[1]   Hagen 2003; Hagen 2000; Kafadar 2007; Faroqhi 2004:179–210.
[2]   Karateke et al, 2005; Necipoğlu, 1991; Yılmaz, 2005.

history, as reflected in the 1848 edition of Ferīdūn Beg's chancery manual, entitled *Münşe'ātü 's-Selāṭīn* (*'Correspondence of Sultans'*). Needless to say, a detailed examination of Ferīdūn's *Münşe'āt* would be an enormous task. The original work contained at least 528 documents spanning the period from the rise of Islam to the time of its completion (982 / 1574–1575). Any serious study of the *Münşe'āt* would entail a comparison of the known manuscripts with the printed editions of 1848 and 1858, which pose considerable problems.[3] Perhaps one day there will be such a study. Until then, there is no reason not to make use of the existing editions, provided that it is understood that they reflect widely divergent manuscripts, which remain to be properly studied. As we will see, our edition even includes accretions from the early seventeenth century—specifically, a list of titles which is itself of considerable interest.

The work in question has been chosen for several reasons. First of all, its production coincides with the vizierate of Ṣoḳollu Meḥmed Paşa, who undoubtedly played an important role in its seeing the light of day. The *Münşe'āt*'s compiler Ferīdūn Beg was Ṣoḳollu's private secretary and close confidant. One of the greatest statesmen in Ottoman history, Ṣoḳollu is known for his imperial vision at a time when the empire was more outward-looking than in any period prior to the nineteenth century. Effectively ruling the empire from his appointment as grand vizier by Sultan Süleymān I in 1565 until his murder by a petitioner dressed as a dervish in 1579, his vision was founded on trade, logistics, and diplomacy rather than on military expansion. The conquest of Cyprus and destruction of the Ottoman fleet at Lepanto were brought about by the scheming of his enemies, Ṣoḳollu's achievement at that juncture consisting rather in the rebuilding of the destroyed fleet in record time. The most famous examples of his geopolitical vision are the abortive Suez and Don-Volga canal projects and a military alliance with the Sultan of Aceh against the Portuguese; even more important, however, are his numerous buildings and pious foundations, many of them situated on major trade routes.[4]

A consummate diplomat, Ṣoḳollu was a lifelong friend of the Venetian bailo Marcantonio Barbaro even at times of war, and had dealings with all the great powers of his time: Iran, Russia, Austria, Poland, France, and England, to give but a few examples. It is therefore fitting to examine the *Münşe'āt* as part of his vision and try to understand it in that context. The choice and chronological organization of the material provides insight into how the Ottoman state under Ṣoḳollu wanted to represent its relations with other countries—in other words,

---

[3] Ferīdūn 1848; Ferīdūn 1858; Mordtmann 1983. Both editions of Ferīdūn are rare. The later one contains more documents; however, I have been unable to consult it for the purposes of this chapter and have used the first instead.

[4] Veinstein 1997, which contains a useful bibliography.

it gives us an idealized picture of Ottoman diplomacy, rather than an accurate record of the day-to-day dealings of the Ottoman chancery with foreign powers. However, a hierarchical list of titles appended to the beginning of the work several decades after its completion may perhaps come closer to providing insight into those day-to-day dealings, since it appears to have been intended as a practical guide. While it did not form part of the original work, and refers to a period several decades later in the empire's history, it is interesting in its own right, and provides a useful contrast to the compilation made by Ferīdūn. It will therefore be discussed in some detail in the middle part of the present chapter.

First, however, a note on methodology is in order. Some may view the choice to focus on Ṣoḳollu Meḥmed Paşa and his circle as indicative of an outdated and flawed "great men" paradigm of history. Surely the study of Ottoman views of political geography should form part of a larger discussion of political culture, which transcends the influence of any single individual? While there can be little doubt that the formation and transformation of Ottoman political ideology over time should be attributed to a great many groups and individuals, most likely to remain forever obscure and anonymous, the period under examination is exceptional in that it is possible to identify a distinct political vision with a particular individual and his network of patronage, which extended from diplomacy to trade and the arts. For example, apart from the architecture already mentioned, it is known that Ṣoḳollu was behind a project of systematic visual representation of the Ottoman sultans down to his own time, for which he instructed artists to study western portraiture.[5] Surprisingly, however, the *Münşe'ātü 's-Selāṭīn* has not been examined in the same light. The work in question is familiar to most Ottomanists as a collection of potential primary sources, rather than as a literary work in its own right produced by the circles around Ṣoḳollu at the time of the grand vizier's greatest power and influence (1575). While the authenticity of the documents contained in the *Münşe'āt* is a frequent subject of scholarly discussion—those attributed to the first Ottoman sultans ʿOẟmān and Orḫan are known to be forgeries[6]—the compilation has yet to be examined as a whole for what it can tell us about Ottoman conceptions of diplomacy and political geography when it was made.

Such an examination is certainly worthwhile, for as we will see, Ferīdūn's compilation reflects Ṣoḳollu's imperial vision, a vision that aimed to create an orderly taxonomy of the Ottoman dynasty. In this way, it forms an interesting parallel to the sultanic portraits just mentioned. It appears that by selecting (and in some cases, creating) documents and incorporating them into a book, Ferīdūn intended to express an imperial vision of the Ottoman Empire and its

[5] Topkapı Museum 2000.
[6] Mordtmann 1983.

diplomatic dealings with the outside world. A further indication that the work was identified with Ṣoḳollu's vision is its poor reception: the book was compiled under Sultan Selīm II, who was a strong supporter of Ṣoḳollu, but upon Selīm's death had to be presented to his heir Murād III, who was under the influence of Ṣoḳollu's enemies at the court.[7]

Ṣoḳollu Meḥmed Paşa's Foreign Policy and Imperial Vision

Before turning to an examination of the chancery manual and the list of titles subsequently appended to it, both of which shed light on Ottoman views of the larger political world at the end of the sixteenth century, it is a good idea to discuss first what is already known about Ṣoḳollu's foreign policy and the imperial vision that it reveals. Several historians have studied Ottoman foreign relations at this time, most recently Giancarlo Casale, whose work has provided valuable insight into Ṣoḳollu's vision of a "soft empire" in the Indian Ocean.[8] Like his powerful predecessor Rüstem Paşa, who was also a vizier of Sultan Süleymān I and with whose legacy he self-consciously competed, Ṣoḳollu perceived the Ottoman Empire's greatness as founded on its ability to control trade. Since much of this trade came from the Indian Ocean, the result was intense competition with Portugal, the other great trading power in the region. As Casale has made clear, Ṣoḳollu Meḥmed Paşa's strategy was "to expand Ottoman influence not through direct military intervention, but rather through the development of ideological, commercial, and diplomatic ties with the various Muslim communities of the region."[9]

An essential ideological element underlying those ties was the Ottomans' position as the leading Sunnī power in the world. This position was founded on the Ottoman record of conquest of new territory for Islam, as well as on possession of the main Muslim pilgrimage sites of Mecca and Medina, which gave the Ottoman sultan the right to use the title "Servitor of the Two Holy Shrines" (*Ḫādımu 'l-Ḥarameyni 'ş-Şerīfeyn*). With this right, however, came the obligation to protect the annual Hajj pilgrimage, which took place along some of the same routes as international trade. In fact, the Hajj was as much a trading expedition as a religious pilgrimage, as it involved numerous caravans. In the area of foreign policy, the need for the Ottomans to ensure the smooth functioning

---

[7] Ibid.

[8] Casale 2007; Casale 2010. Although primarily concerned with events in the 1580s, Casale 2007:276–282 contains a useful overview of Ṣoḳollu's policy of "soft empire" in the 1560s and 70s and its implications.

[9] Casale 2007:277.

of the Hajj meant defensive alliances against predatory infidel powers like the Russians and Portuguese, while within its borders it involved large works of infrastructure. It is in this context that we must view the numerous pious complexes constructed by Ṣoḳollu along the main Ottoman imperial axis, which stretched from the Hungarian borderlands in the northwest, via the Balkans, Istanbul, Central Anatolia, and Syria, to Mecca in the southeast. Many of these complexes were built by the great architect Sinān, who recognized Ṣoḳollu as one of his greatest patrons. In fact, the choice to build along this axis echoed the preferences of Sultan Süleymān himself, and was apparently calculated to raise the reputation of Ṣoḳollu as a patron of architecture above that of Rüstem Paşa, whose numerous endowments are situated in regions nearer to the capital.[10]

Thus we see that Muslim sacred geography formed a crucial element in the Ottoman imperial worldview during this time. Fulfilling the requirements of the Ottoman role as protector of the Hajj was a prerequisite for Ṣoḳollu's policy in the Indian Ocean, to which we now turn. In that part of the world, with the exception of the Sultan of Aceh in Indonesia, who requested military aid against the Portuguese in exchange for accepting Ottoman suzerainty, the situation that generally prevailed was a more informal one, in which close ties with Istanbul were encouraged among the local leadership. Because of the Hajj, Muslim trading elites in places like Gujarat, Calicut, and Ceylon began to look to Istanbul as a kind of metropole. Family connections were established, "Rūmī" traders and commercial factors made their appearance, and Ṣoḳollu encouraged and financed certain pro-Ottoman religious organizations, which in return recited the Friday sermon (*khuṭba*) in the Ottoman sultan's name. Ṣoḳollu's policy resulted in the recognition of the sultan in Istanbul as leader of the Sunnī Muslim world in the entire Indian Ocean region, so that for a time even the Mughals of India were forced to acknowledge his claims.[11]

But the Indian Ocean was only one area in which the Ottomans were operating during this time. Others were Europe, the Mediterranean, and the Caspian region. As already mentioned, Ṣoḳollu was a strong supporter of two visionary canal projects of great geopolitical significance, both eventually realized by others: the Suez canal connecting the Mediterranean and Red seas, and the Don-Volga canal linking the Caspian to the Black Sea. The first was never begun, because the vizier's main rival in the Ottoman court, Lala Muṣṭafā Paşa, was governor of Egypt when Ṣoḳollu and his ally Ḳoca Sinān Paşa proposed it in the late 1560s. (In fact, Ḳoca Sinān made another effort after Ṣoḳollu's death.[12]) However, the second project was actually begun as part of the Ottoman

---

[10] Necipoğlu 2005:345, 578–579.
[11] Casale 2007:277.
[12] See Casale 2007:285.

Astrakhan campaign of 1569, only to be abandoned due to weather, Russian attacks on the workmen, and lack of support from the Ottomans' main vassal in the area, the Crimean Khan. It would be attempted again by Peter the Great and finally completed after the Second World War. The Don-Volga canal project provides a good illustration of the intersection of politics, trade, and ideology in the context of the late sixteenth-century Ottoman Empire. Its ostensible purpose was to facilitate the movement of Hajj pilgrims from Central Asia through territory that had recently fallen into the hands of the infidel Russians; however, its success would have also led to the reconquest of the recently fallen vassal territories of Kazan and Astrakhan, thus strengthening the Ottoman hold over Shirvan, Georgia, and Karabagh and opening a second front against Iran. After the failure of the plan, in a manner typical of his overall diplomatic approach, Şoḳollu was able to patch up Ottoman-Russian relations.[13]

After the Indian Ocean and Caucasus regions, let us turn briefly to the situation in Europe and the Mediterranean. The period of Şoḳollu's grand vizierate is best known in Ottoman-European relations as that of the Battle of Lepanto (1571), long viewed as a decisive victory for the West at a time when the Ottoman navy seemed invincible in the Eastern Mediterranean. But however great the Ottoman defeat may have been from a military point of view, its larger historical significance is still hotly disputed. While it is true that the Ottoman fleet was utterly destroyed at Lepanto, the empire was nevertheless able to hold on to Cyprus, whose recent acquisition was the direct cause of the battle.[14] Moreover, as already mentioned, Şoḳollu was able to rebuild the destroyed navy in a few months time, boasting according to one chronicler that "the Ottoman state is so powerful, if an order was issued to cast anchors from silver, to make rigging from silk, and to cut the sails from satin, it could be carried out for the entire fleet."[15] Finally, it has even been suggested that the defeat may have been engineered by Şoḳollu in order to eliminate his enemies, since he presented himself from the beginning as opposed to the entire Cyprus campaign.[16]

If we look at the situation in purely territorial terms, in Şoḳollu Meḥmed Paşa's first decade as grand vizier, the Ottomans may have failed to capture Malta, but succeeded in adding Cyprus and Tunis to their Mediterranean domains. In this way, they turned Crete into a lone Venetian outpost in the eastern Mediterranean awaiting eventual conquest in the mid-seventeenth century. Like the Black Sea before it, the eastern half of the Mediterranean (with the exception of the Adriatic, which Venice referred to as its "gulf") thus

[13]   Veinstein 1997.
[14]   Hess 1972; Pedani 2005.
[15]   Hess 1972:54. The chronicler in question is Peçevī.
[16]   Pedani 2005:31.

became an Ottoman lake. As for the western half, after 1570 it was apparently abandoned to the Ottomans' Christian enemies and the Muslim privateers of the Maghreb (the "Barbary pirates") over whom the Ottomans began to practice a policy of limited control.[17]

In Central Europe, the Ottomans' greatest rivals were of course the Habsburgs, with whose Austrian territories they shared a long and contested border. Earlier in the 16th century, Charles V's claims to universal empire, publicized by a ceremony in which the Pope had crowned him Holy Roman Emperor, had caused Sultan Süleymān I to retaliate with his own propaganda campaign involving a priceless helmet-crown fashioned in Venice.[18] This crown, which was designed for a purely western audience, is a good example of the Ottomans' versatility in adopting the imperial symbolism of their enemies. Since the disaster of 1402, when they were crushed by the Central Asian empire-builder Timur, they had been at least as acutely aware of their neighbors to the East, where more Persian and Central Asian ideas of kingship prevailed. In that connection, it should be noted that Ṣoḳollu's career is closely related to the rise of illustrated manuscripts celebrating the exploits of the Ottoman dynasty in the verbal and visual language of the Persian *Shāhnāma*. Ṣoḳollu was the main patron of the great *şehnāmeci* Seyyid Lokman.[19] At the same time, Ṣoḳollu strengthened the Ottoman alliance with France—the capitulations of 1569 were apparently the first to be ratified, and Ferīdūn Beg, the author of our chancery manual, was also behind the translation from French to Turkish of a history of the kings of France. This is probably connected to the Ottoman portraiture project, which follows a similar format.[20] Other European countries with which the Ottoman Empire became involved at this time include Poland and England.[21]

The *Münşe'ātü 's-Selāṭīn*: The List of Titles and Forms of Address

After this brief overview of Ṣoḳollu Meḥmed Paşa's foreign policy and imperial vision, it is time to turn to the text that forms the main object of this examination. As already discussed, the 1848 edition of the *Münşe'ātü 's-Selāṭīn* consulted for the present chapter begins with a detailed list of diplomatic titulature, apparently intended to serve as a guide for scribes engaged in correspondence with foreign rulers, but also with various high-ranking members of the Ottoman

---

[17] Pedani 2005:28; Hess 1978:74–87.
[18] Necipoğlu 1989.
[19] Fetvacı 2005:83–134.
[20] Fetvacı 2005:107–108.
[21] Veinstein 1997; Mordtmann 1983.

ruling class. From the rulers addressed, some of whom are mentioned by name, it is clear that this section was added several decades after Ferīdūn Beg completed his compilation. There is mention of Shah ʿAbbās I of Iran (1587–1629) and the Ottoman sultans Meḥmed III (1595–1603) and Aḥmed I (1603–1617), suggesting that the list was made shortly after the turn of the seventeenth century. Needless to say, by then the political world in which the Ottoman chancery was operating had changed considerably. Be that as it may, it is still worth taking a look at this very interesting list, which provides rare insight into the functioning of the Ottoman chancery in the field of foreign affairs.

As we would expect, the list begins with the Ottoman sultans, who are called "Pādiṣāhs of Islam." There are sixteen long sets of titles used to address them. It should be noted that each of these is more than just a disjointed compilation, but follows an internal rhetorical logic, sometimes employing metaphors such as a garden or the celestial spheres. Furthermore, it is striking how many of the titles are derived from the Shāhnāma: as we have seen, by this time comparing the Ottoman sultan to a hero of the Shāhnāma was a standard form of representation. However, there may also be echoes here of the long Ottoman-Safavid war of 1578–1590. In any case, for the purposes of the present investigation, let us focus instead on imagery of a more geographical nature. First of all, there is the well-known title first used by Meḥmed the Conqueror, "Sultan of the Two Continents and the Two Seas" (*Sulṭānü 'l-berreyn ve 'l-baḥreyn*). This is of course an allusion to the location of the Ottoman capital, specifically the Topkapı palace built by Meḥmed on its acropolis, at the key intersection where Asia meets Europe, and where the Bosphorus (and by extension the Black Sea) meets the Sea of Marmara (and by extension the Mediterranean). Another title is "Great Khan of the Two Easts and of the Two Wests" (*Ḥāḳānu 'l-maṣrıḳeyn ve'lmaġribeyn*), which seems at least superficially similar to the previous one. In fact it is of an altogether different nature, for it is derived from an expression used for God in the Qurʾān, "Lord of the Two Easts and Lord of the Two Wests" (*Rabbu 'l-maṣriqayni wa rabbu 'l-maghribayn*, Qurʾān 55:17). The resemblance is obviously an intentional one, for like other rulers before them, the Ottoman sultans called themselves "Shadow of God on Earth" (*ẓıllu 'llāh fī 'l-arż*), another title appearing on our list. However it may perhaps be taken literally as well to mean Anatolia and the Arab east (the two easts) and the Balkans and North Africa (the two wests). Finally, as we saw earlier, the Ottoman sultan's control of Mecca and Medina is recognized in his most prestigious title of all from an Islamic point of view, "Servitor of the Two Holy Shrines" (*Ḥādımu 'l-ḥarameyni'ş-şerīfeyn*).[22]

---

[22] Ferīdūn 1848:2–4.

After enumerating the titles of the Ottoman sultans, the list moves on to those of other rulers. From the order in which these are given, as well as from their content, it is possible to discern an official hierarchy in foreign relations as reflected in diplomatic protocol. As we would expect, first come the Sharīfs of Mecca, to whom respect is owed because of their supreme place in Islamic sacred geography. However, they are followed by others whose position is connected to a very different worldview: the Khans of the Crimea. While the Crimean Khans had been vassals of the Ottomans since 1475, and began sending a hostage to the Ottoman palace around 1530, it is important to bear in mind that their pedigree (unlike that of the Ottomans) was beyond question in the northern tier of the Islamic world: they were members of the Giray family, rulers of the Golden Horde descended from Chingis Khan. As we have seen in the Don-Volga canal affair, the Khans of the Crimea were active in strategically important territory bordering on hostile non-Muslim states, their position in such a borderland giving them the power to act with a high degree of independence.[23]

Next in the list come other Muslim allies of the Ottomans: the Uzbek sultans, whose ruler ʿAbdullāh Khan (d. 1598) is mentioned by name, and the emirs of the Kurds and Gujarat. It is worth pointing out that one of the titles of the Uzbek sultan, whose alliance with the Ottomans resulted from having as common enemy the Shīʿī Safavids of Iran, makes explicit reference to the fact that like the Ottomans, he rules over people who follow the Sunnī Ḥanafī school of Islam. Then there is a brief mention of the ruler of Morocco (*Ḥākim-i Fās*), over whose territory as we have seen the Ottomans ceased to make claim, but with whom they made alliances against the Portuguese and Habsburgs. After them come some generic titles useful for addressing princes (*elḳāb-ı evlād-ı selāṭīn*) and sultans, and only then do we finally find the Persian shahs (*Şāhān-ı ʿAcem*), the Safavid rulers of Iran.

For the Ottomans, the Safavid Shahs were of course enemies and schismatics. Although they are mentioned late, no fewer than ten sets of titles are given for addressing them, and quite elaborate ones at that. This suggests that the list we are discussing served at least two parallel purposes: to provide a diplomatic hierarchy of the rulers with whose courts the Ottoman chancery was dealing, and to give more practical instructions on the diplomatic protocol for addressing them. While these goals are to some extent complementary, the need to satisfy them both leads at times to a contradiction, for it was natural for the chancery to need to correspond more frequently with enemies on the empire's border such as the Safavid Shah than with distant friends like the Emīr of Gujarat. In other words, there was a conflict between the ideology of

---

[23] Ferīdūn 1848:4–6; İnalcık 1983.

diplomacy and its day-to-day practice. This conflict is also apparent in the case of Christian rulers, to whom we will turn in a moment. Specifically in the case of the Safavids, however, it seems that it was necessary to show awareness and respect appropriate for a powerful enemy ruling over the heartlands of Irano-Islamic civilization, while avoiding any religious references. This was achieved through the use of literary language evoking the Persian classics, especially the Shāhnāma.[24]

Following the Safavid Shahs, the list turns to the ruling class of the Ottoman Empire itself. In order of presentation, these are viziers, governors (*mīrmīrān*), top bureaucrats (*āsitāne defterdārı, nişāncı*), the sultan's favorites, and tribal leaders. Of these, specific mention is made only to the *emīrs* of the Roma people of Ḳırḳ Kilise, modern Kırklareli (*ümerā'-yı Çengāne-yi Ḳırḳ Kilise*) for whom it is stated that it is inappropriate to use more than two titles—perhaps a case of proto-racism. They are followed by more officials, listed only roughly in order of importance: in brief these are the head scribe (*re'īsülküttāb*) and other members of the central bureaucracy, provincial governors (*emīr, sancaḳbeyi*), eunuchs (*ḳapu ağaları*), ship captains, castle wardens, mutes, judges and other men of religion, descendants of the Prophet (*sādāt*), and the head physician of the court (ibid., 9–12).

Only after finishing with all these people does the list finally turn to the rulers of non-Muslim countries. In the order given, these are as follows: the Austrian Emperor (*Nemçe İmparatorı*) as addressed by the grand vizier; the Austrian chief minister (*Nemçe vezīri*); the King of France (given the title *pādişāh*, presumably because he was an Ottoman ally); the Austrian, Polish, and Hungarian kings (*ḳrāl*); collective titles for addressing several Christian rulers at once (*cemʿ ile ʿunvān*); Venetian admirals (*deryā cenerali*); the Doge of Venice; the king of the Imeretians (*Açık Baş*); the kings of Guria and Imeretia when addressed together; the queen mothers of Christian kings (interesting at a time when Ottoman queen mothers had begun to wield a great deal of power); the voyvodas of Moldova and Wallachia; Wallachian boyars and monks; the Grand Hetman of Poland; the minister of the King of Poland; the Hetman of the Cossacks (specifically, the Zaporizhian Cossacks); and finally, the leaders of the Three Nations of Transylvania (*unio trium nationum*, a political entity consisting of Hungarians, Saxons, and free Szeklers) (ibid., 12–13).

What is interesting in the list of Christian rulers is the contrast between the multitude of different people and parties being addressed and the brevity of their titles. Not only do these rulers, with whom the Ottomans were obviously negotiating on a regular basis, come at the end of the list, but the entire

[24] Ferīdūn 1848:6–9.

catalogue of their titles takes up no more space than that of the Safavid Shahs. The Safavids may have been the Ottomans' enemies, but despite being Shīʿī they were part of a shared Islamicate civilization (to use Marshall Hodgson's term) and ruled over a territory that occupied a central position in that civilization's cultural geography. It would thus appear that by the early seventeenth century, when the list was apparently compiled, the Ottoman chancery was self-consciously subscribing to such a worldview.

Whether the diplomatic protocol it reflects is indicative of the regard in which various strata of Ottoman society held the inhabitants of central and western Europe is, of course, impossible to determine entirely from the source in question. Preliminary research into the reception of European world maps in Ottoman ruling circles around this time appears to support the idea of a shift from an openness to such maps to a more traditionalist Islamocentric view of the world, but it is too early to make generalizations.[25] It is worth pointing out, however, that in the field of artistic patronage there were at least two such backlashes against western influence, which reached its height during the reign of Meḥmed II (1451–1481) and then again in the first two decades of the reign of Süleymān I (1520–1566). As we have seen, Ṣoḳollu Meḥmed Paşa had a wide worldview and is known to have appreciated western art; but even during the apogee of his career, there were limits to how explicitly such a worldview could be expressed, especially in an area as conservative as diplomatic protocol. In any case, it is probably a good idea to distinguish between the reality of diplomatic and cultural interaction with a region such as Europe, and ideological topoi to which scribes and authors felt obligated to pay lip service.

The *Münşe'ātü 's-Selāṭīn*

Let us turn now to the body of Ferīdūn's chancery manual to see what it can tell us about Ottoman conceptions of political geography. As is typical, the work begins with a lengthy and elaborate introduction praising God and the sultan and explaining the circumstances of its composition (ibid., 14–23). It is impossible to assess its significance in any detail here; suffice it to say that it refers to Ferīdūn's presence at the siege of Szigetvar, which is described in more detail in his chronicle, *Nüzhetü 'l-Esrāri 'l-Aḫbār*, as well as to the fact that Murād III

---

[25] See the ongoing work of Giancarlo Casale, who has been studying the so-called map of Hajji Ahmed from the point of view of its possible authors and intended audience. An article by him on the subject is forthcoming in the proceedings of a workshop held at the University of Indiana on October 30, 2009; the volume will be entitled *Editing the Past, Fashioning the Future: Historiography of the Ottoman Empire* (ed. Erdem Çıpa and Emine Fetvacı).

used Ferīdūn's boat to cross from Mudanya to Istanbul upon his accession.[26] Reference is also made to Ottoman campaigns in Arabia, Yemen, and elsewhere, suggesting that a more detailed study of this part of the work might be of considerable value, especially in conjunction with other narrative sources from the same period. Introductions such as the one in question are usually ignored by historians, except as a source for specific factual information on the life of the author and circumstances of composition.

After the introduction, the chancery manual turns to its main purpose, the presentation of letters exchanged between rulers. Since the point of view is an Islamic one, it is natural that the first ruler to make an appearance should be the Prophet Muḥammad, followed by his immediate successors to the leadership of the early Muslim community, the four Rightly Guided Caliphs. Since the authenticity of such documents is highly questionable, they have so far failed to attract scholarly attention; this is unfortunate, for they form an integral part of the overall work, where they fulfill an important rhetorical function. By choosing to begin with Muḥammad and the Rightly Guided Caliphs, Ferīdūn Beg is able to present the Ottoman sultans, whose correspondence forms the bulk of the work, as successors to the Prophet Muḥammad in their leadership of the Islamic community (i.e. as Caliphs). Moreover, by his choice of the succession to Muḥammad, he makes it clear that the manual is the work of a Sunnī serving Sunnīs: Muḥammad is succeeded by the Rightly Guided Caliphs and not by a series of imams. Finally, the geographic location of the rulers with whom these early Muslim leaders correspond is also of great significance, for these are areas in which the Ottomans too were active around Ferīdūn's time. This point will be developed further in a moment; first, let us turn to the documents.

The first letter is from the Prophet to the Byzantine Emperor, "the Caesar of Rūm" (*Ḳayṣar-ı Rūm*), and is followed by one to the early Muslim community as a whole. Then comes a letter to Ḥarith ibn Abū Shamra, a ruler whose land was conquered after he tore up the Prophet's letters inviting him to become a Muslim. After that, there is one to the Persian King (*Kesrā*, Khosrow) and one to the king of the Abyssinians. Then there is a letter to the Coptic governor of Egypt (*Muḳawḳis*) and the Persian governor of Bahrein, al-Mundhir ibn Sāwī.[27] Many other places and personages of early Islamic history are mentioned: for instance, there is a letter to the people of al-Adhraḥ, a town under Roman rule in Syria, which submitted to the Prophet and paid the *jizya* after receiving a letter from him with an ultimatum. The letters attributed to the Prophet are

---

[26] Mordtmann 1983; Vatin 2010.
[27] Ferīdūn 1848:31–33.

followed by several by the Caliphs Abū Bakr, ʿUmar, ʿUthmān, and ʿAlī, as well as one each belonging to ʿĀʾisha and Ḥusayn (ibid., 34–47).

As was already discussed, it would be a mistake to dismiss all this out of hand as nothing more than a standard exercise in religious piety. The majority of the documents in question pertain to military expansion, an expansion that enlarged the domains of Islam to encompass much of the ancient Roman and Near Eastern world. It is, of course, a historical fact that enormous conquests were made in the first decades of Islam; but in light of what has just been said about Ottoman politics at the time of Ṣokollu Meḥmed Paşa, it is also probable that when reading the Prophet's correspondence with the rulers of places like Iran, Abyssinia, and Bahrein, Ferīdūn's readers would have drawn a connection between those early years of Islam and their own time. The places mentioned were ones in which the Ottomans themselves were active in the late sixteenth century, so that such documents would justify their activity, since the Ottomans were widely seen by their contemporaries as the pre-eminent Sunnī Muslim power in the world.

In fact, what follows in the *Münṣe'āt* is an attempt to show the Ottomans in precisely that light. Not bothering with the Abbasids and other intervening dynasties, the compiler jumps ahead to the Seljuks, the Turkish dynasty that briefly reunited the Middle East under Sunni rule in the mid-eleventh century, and which was also largely responsible for the Islamization of Anatolia. Since the fifteenth century, Ottoman chroniclers had attempted to legitimize the ruling dynasty by means of stories involving a transfer of power in the early fourteenth century from the moribund Seljuk state of Rūm to the Ottomans.[28] The Ottomans supposedly became Seljuk vassals when a symbolic white banner and drum were sent to them by the Seljuk Sultan ʿAlāeddīn—the same objects sent by Meḥmed the Conqueror to the Crimean Khan to assert his own power as overlord.[29] Thanks to Ferīdūn, these would no longer be simple stories in chronicles: a long document is provided whereby the Seljuk Sultan grants ʿOsmān I the right to rule Söğüt and the region around it in his name, followed by one sent to accompany the famous banner and drum. ʿOsmān's replies are also provided.[30]

Turning now to the documents attributed to ʿOsmān's successor Orḫan, it is interesting to note that most of these pertain to the Ottoman conquests being made during his reign. They are *fetḥnāmes*, namely letters announcing victory to other rulers. Among these rulers are not only those of the neighboring Anatolian emirates (the *beyliks*) but also "the Persian Shah (*ʿAcem Şāhı*) Ḥasan the Jalayirid." Another Persian Shah is presented as corresponding with

[28] Imber 1987:13–15.
[29] Kafadar 1995:147.
[30] Ferīdūn 1848:48–60.

Sultan Murād I.[31] The use of the title ʿAcem Şāhı would inevitably have evoked the Safavids in the minds of sixteenth-century Ottoman readers, creating the impression that already from the early fourteenth century, the Ottoman Sultan had dealings with Iran. Although the term used is not the geographic Īrān but rather the more ethnic ʿAcem (meaning "Persian"), the impression created is similar: that of a foreign ruler governing a foreign land, one not geographically part of the Ottoman Empire, but with a long history of its own, an ancient and prestigious part of the Islamic world. While it may seem obvious in our day to derive the title of a ruler from the country or people being ruled, it is important to remember that in the premodern period this was not necessarily the case. Indeed, for the Ottomans it was often the other way around: in the fourteenth and fifteenth centuries, they called some of the territories with which they came into contact after their rulers (e.g. Serbia was called Laz-ili, "the land of Lazar," after the Serbian king of that name).

In the age of Şoḳollu's global empire, however, the world was a much bigger place. As we follow Ferīdūn's manual through the reigns of Murād I and subsequent sultans all the way to Süleymān the Magnificent, we witness the military expansion of the Ottoman state. The vast majority of the documents pertain to that expansion, which can be observed through letters announcing important conquests to foreign rulers (feth-nāme, iʿlān-nāme), documents of congratulation from such rulers (tebrīk-nāme) and the like. Through such a presentation, conquest and diplomacy appear to go hand in hand, and the Ottoman Sultan's world supremacy seems founded upon the recognition of his conquests by other important Muslim sovereigns. Even in cases where the Ottoman Sultan's actions do not meet with the approval of a foreign ruler, the inclusion in the Münşeʾāt of the Ottoman response to such challenges serves the purpose of refuting them. Take for example the exchange between the Ottoman Sultan Meḥmed I and the Timurid ruler Shāhrukh:

> [Shahrukh] To the great sultan, master of the kings among nations, killer of the infidels and subduer of the wicked, him who exerts efforts [mujāhid] in the path of God, the one and only orderer of the world and religion [niẓāmuʾl-mulk va ʾd-dīn] Sultan Mehmed (sic), may God perpetuate his rule and prolong him in his royal beneficence. When this [letter] arrives, let it be known that it has attained our lofty ears that Süleyman Beg and Musa Beg and İsa Beg were in a state of dispute and contention with him, and that following the Ottoman custom [töre-i ʿOsmānī] he has freed each one of them from the commotion of this

---

[31] Ferīdūn 1848:73, 91.

world [Quranic excerpt omitted here] But according to Ilkhanid custom [*töre-i ilḫānī*], this manner of action among dearly beloved brothers is deemed unacceptable, since a few days' worth of dominion has no permanency, that such actions be perpetrated on its account.

[Mehmed]   As for the counsel that was given on the matter of the brothers of the Age [*iḫwān-i zamān*], we are obedient [*farmānbarīm*]. However, from the first hints of the rise of the dawn of the Ottoman state [*Dawlat-i ʿOsmāniyye*]—may God have mercy on their ancestors and perpetuate their successors!—[the Ottoman sultans] resolved to take on the problems of the day mostly guided by experience. And there is no doubt that the totality of political power [*salṭanat*] does not admit division. In the words of the author of the Gulistān [i.e. *Saʿdī*], which are strung together like pearls—may God the King the Merciful pardon his sins!—"Ten dervishes can huddle together on a carpet, but two kings don't fit in the same clime." Given this situation, security depends upon the peculiar fact that the enemies of religion and the state all around are constantly awaiting the smallest opportunity [to strike]. While the strength or collapse of worldly possessions does not depend on politics but divine predestination, nevertheless, if the neighboring rulers were Muslim princes of high lineage, there would be no reason to worry. Heaven forbid that the base infidels should obtain an opportunity! For as his Highness [Shahrukh] is aware, in the incident involving my deceased ancestor [Yıldırım Bayezid], many lands that had been won to Islam such as Selanik [Thessaloniki] and other places were lost from the hands of the Muslims [couplet omitted here] And that is the reason why in these matters of the sultanate and succession they [the Ottomans] have chosen to separate themselves from the rest of the world. And the best is that which is preferred by God.

Ferīdūn 1848:150–151;
translation from Kastritsis 2007:203–205

Leaving aside the question of whether or not this correspondence is authentic, which it probably is, its inclusion by Ferīdūn in his manual had several advantages for the compiler's effort to produce a consistent and flattering picture of the House of ʿOsmān. First of all, it justified bloody Ottoman succession practices, which by the sixteenth century were institutionalized, but still not fully accepted. Perhaps more importantly, though, it reminded readers that as early as 1416 a distant foreign ruler of the status of Shāhrukh, who at this time considered Mehmed I as his vassal, recognized Ottoman accomplishments in conquering new territory from the infidels.[32] The question of the degree to which the Ottomans viewed and presented themselves as warriors of the faith (*ġāzī*) before the conquest of Constantinople in 1453 may still be a contested one,[33] but no one doubts that by Ferīdūn's time, this attribute had become a central part of Ottoman claims to political legitimacy.

The correspondence between Meḥmed I and Shāhrukh is just one example of how documents in Ferīdūn's *Münşeʾāt* can be considered as part of a coherent project of imperial legitimation. Surely there are many more, which should ideally be studied in a systematic manner across the entire work. However, as stated from the outset, the present discussion is by necessity based on no more than an impressionistic overview of the *Münşeʾātü 's-Selāṭīn*. Its goals are modest, and are mostly limited to suggesting possible avenues by which the work may be approached as a whole. One way to advance this agenda is by briefly considering a coherent set of documents contained in the larger compilation in order to illustrate the sort of questions, rich in political implications, that arise from the study of Ferīdūn's manual as a complete literary work rather than a mere treasure trove of documents.

Let us briefly focus then on the reign of Sultan Selīm I (1512–1520).[34] Selīm's reign has the advantage of being short enough to examine in its entirety, but of central importance to the *Münşeʾāt*'s overall presentation of the Ottomans as a dynasty destined to take the leading role in a larger community of Muslim states. The sultan in question played a crucial role in that process, for it was he who defeated not only the schismatic Safavids, but also the Mamluks, who had until then been the Servitors of the Holy Shrines, but were unable to live up to their role as leaders of the Islamic community, because they could not confront the Portuguese in the Red Sea without Ottoman assistance. By replacing them, Selīm expanded Ottoman territory to include the holy shrines of Mecca, Medina, and Jerusalem, and many of the other central lands of Islam.

The documents from Selīm's reign begin with one from his brother and rival Ḳorḳud, followed by one to the ruler of Samarkand. After these comes the lengthy correspondence between Selīm and the Safavid Shah Ismāʿīl leading up to the Battle of Çaldıran (1514). The documents following this event are *fethnāmes* announcing that great victory to the following: prince Süleymān, the future sultan; the Crimean Khan; various local rulers of eastern Anatolia (*ümerāʾ-yı şarḳ*) and the Kurds; and the local nobility (*aʿyān*) of Tabriz. Then there is a letter to the Ottoman general assigned the task of conquering that city, and one showing

---

[32] Kastritsis 2007:4, 202–220.
[33] Imber 1987; Lowry 2003.
[34] What follows is based mostly on the book's table of contents (Ferīdūn 1848:xxi–xxiv). When the actual documents are discussed, the pages numbers can also be found from this table.

goodwill to the population of "the eastern province" (*vilāyet-i şarḳ*). After these come more *fethnāmes*: to the ruler of Luristan (a part of Iran not under Safavid rule); to a certain Kurdish ruler; and to various other allies in the area. Finally, there is a *fethnāme* to the Ḳāḍī of Edirne (*Edrene ḥākimi*). The inclusion of the former Ottoman capitals of Edirne and Bursa in such lists is a pattern that is also repeated elsewhere in the collection, which suggests a special reverence for those towns. By including them, Ferīdūn seems to be suggesting that despite their status as world rulers, the Ottomans never forgot where they came from.

These letters are followed not by more correspondence but by campaign diaries. The inclusion of such material is of great interest, for it provides further proof that Ferīdūn's compilation was never intended as a practical chancery manual at all, but rather as a type of history writing. The first campaign diary is a detailed list with dates of all Selīm's stops (*menzil*, pl. *menāzil*) on his way to and from the Battle of Çaldıran, taking up twelve large pages in the printed edition. This section is followed by a similar diary for the sultan's travel from Amasya to Kemah, whose conquest along with the territory of Dulkadır is announced to the future Sultan Süleymān in a *fethnāme*. This letter provides continuity and allows Ferīdūn to return to the presentation of correspondence. But it is worth dwelling here for a moment more on the campaign diaries. It should be borne in mind that in the Ottoman context, the genre in question reached its apogee in the richly illustrated manuscript of Maṭrāḳçı Naṣūḥ, which depicts Sultan Süleymān's stops on his campaign of the so-called "two Iraqs" (*al-ʿIrāḳeyn*, namely Iraq and Iran) in an innovative manner emphasizing towns and public buildings.[35] In our chancery manual, there are several more campaign diaries; one of these relates to Selīm's campaign against Egypt at the end of his reign. But first come documents similar to the ones already discussed: further correspondence with Shah Ismāʿīl and the Mamluk Sultan Qansūh al-Ghawri, who is about to give up his empire and life to the Ottoman Sultan; *fethnāmes* for Kemah and Egypt sent to the Tatar Khan, the Shirvānshāh (who appears frequently throughout the manual), the rulers of Gīlān and Māzandarān (all governing non-Safavid regions of Iran), and the Ḳāḍī of Edirne; and finally, congratulations to Selīm from the *pādişāh* of India and the Ḳāḍī of Bursa.

To conclude this brief survey, what if anything can be deduced about the Ottoman view of the world in the late sixteenth century from this brief examination of Ferīdūn Beg's *Münşeʾātü 's-Selāṭīn*? Needless to say, this chapter provides little more than a glimpse into what might await the brave researcher willing to take on the monumental task of studying the work as a whole. The main point to retain is that the mere fact of the creation of such a compilation at this particular

---

[35] Maṭrāḳçı Naṣūḥ 1976; Faroqhi 2004:196–197.

juncture in Ottoman history is significant in and of itself. Ṣoḳollu Meḥmed Paşa was perhaps the greatest diplomat in Ottoman history, and we have seen that he had a very large view of a world he hoped to dominate not through war, but through diplomacy, trade, and logistics. The documents in Ferīdūn's manual (whether authentic or not) present an image of the Ottoman sultans as Muslim rulers involved in territorial expansion and correspondence with other Muslim rulers—hence its title *Münşeʾātü 's-Selāṭīn*, "Correspondence of Sultans." Although in reality the Ottomans at the time probably corresponded at least as much with non-Muslim rulers as they did with Muslim ones, such "infidel" rulers are mentioned much less frequently—and needless to say, the Ottoman Sultan did not share his victories with non-Muslim rulers by means of *fetḥnāmes*.

Throughout the present article, Ferīdūn's work has been called a chancery manual, in accordance with the standard terminology of the field and the genre to which the work in question purports to belong. However, its contents are not an accurate description of the day-to-day workings of the Ottoman chancery in the field of foreign affairs. These workings are probably better represented by the list of titles and forms of address discussed in the middle part of this chapter, which was appended to the volume a few decades later. Instead, the *Münşeʾāt* should be viewed first and foremost as another piece of imperial image making, like the sultan's portraits and magnificently illustrated Shāhnāma-type works produced at approximately the same time. As we have seen, the image that Ferīdūn's work tries to convey is that of an Ottoman dynasty whose legitimacy derives from its conquests in the non-Muslim world, its succession to the Seljuks of Rūm, and its leadership of the Islamic community, which effectively makes the Ottoman Sultan a successor to the Prophet Muḥammad himself.

Reading Ferīdūn's *Münşeʾāt*, one gets the sense of an Ottoman progression from humble beginnings to world supremacy and empire. However, in line with Ṣoḳollu Meḥmed Paşa's vision, the empire in question is a "soft" one, and the Ottoman Sultan a first among equals, conquering enemies, but also corresponding with his peers. Such an image was useful to Ṣoḳollu in promoting his Ottoman influence in the Middle East and Indian Ocean, and as it happens, is also a fairly Islamic one. But perhaps one of the most remarkable aspects of Ṣoḳollu Meḥmed Paşa's regime was the ability to promote multiple visions across multiple media, experimenting with imperial image making in a way that strikes us at times as surprisingly modern. After all, his vision was wide enough to encompass alongside the *Münşeʾāt* a work on the Kings of France. If we compare Ṣoḳollu to the other two great grand viziers of Sultan Süleymān I, the European-oriented İbrāhīm Paşa and the trade-oriented Rüstem Paşa, we see that he has attributes of both. As for Ferīdūn, he was Ṣoḳollu's closest confidant, so it is natural that his *Münşeʾāt* should be seen as part of the same vision.

Abbreviations

Ferīdūn 1848.
Ferīdūn. 1848 (–1857). *Mecmūʿa-yı münşeʾāt-ı Ferīdūn Bey*. Istanbul.

Works Cited

Topkapı Museum. 2000. *The Sultan's Portrait: Picturing the House of Osman*. Istanbul.
Casale, G. 2007. "Global Politics in the 1580s: One Canal, Twenty Thousand Cannibals, and an Ottoman Plot to Rule the World." *Journal of World History* 18:267–296.
Casale, G. 2010. *The Ottoman Age of Exploration*. Oxford.
Faroqhi, S. 2004. *The Ottoman Empire and the World Around It*. London. 179–210.
Ferīdūn. 1848 (–1857). *Mecmūʿa-yı münşeʾāt-ı Ferīdūn Bey*. Istanbul.
——. 1858. *Mecmūʿa-yı münşeʾāt al-Selāṭīn*. Istanbul.
Fetvacı, E. 2005. "Viziers to Eunuchs: Transitions in Ottoman Manuscript Patronage, 1566–1617." PhD dissertation, Harvard University.
Hagen, G. 2000. "Some Considerations on the Study of Ottoman Geographical Writings." *Archivum Ottomanicum* 18:183–193.
——. 2003. *Ein osmanischer Geograph bei der Arbeit: Entstehung und Gedankenwelt von Kātib Čelebis Ğihānnümā*. Berlin.
Hess, A. 1972. "The Battle of Lepanto and its Place in Mediterranean History." *Past and Present* 57:53–73.
——. 1978. *The Forgotten Frontier: A History of the Sixteenth-Century Ibero-African Frontier*. Chicago.
Imber, C. 1987. "The Ottoman Dynastic Myth." *Turcica* 19:7–27.
Imber, C., Kiyotaki, K. and Murphey, R., eds. 2005. *Frontiers of Ottoman Studies: State, Province, and the West* vol. 2. London.
İnalcık, H. 1983. "Girāy." *Encyclopedia of Islam*, Second edition. Leiden.
Kafadar, C. 1995. *Between Two Worlds: The Construction of the Ottoman State*. Berkeley.
——. 2007. "A Rome of One's Own: Reflections on Cultural Geography and Identity in the Lands of Rum." *Muqarnas* 24:7–25.
Karateke, H., and Reinkowski, M., eds. 2005. *Legitimizing the Order: the Ottoman Rhetoric of State Power*. Leiden.
Kastritsis, D. 2007. *The Sons of Bayezid: Empire Building and Representation in the Ottoman Civil War of 1402-13*. Leiden.
Lowry, H. 2003. *The Nature of the Early Ottoman State*. Albany.
Maṭrākçı Nasūh 1976. *Beyān-ı menāzil-i sefer-i ʿIrākeyn-i Sulṭān Süleymān Hān* (ed. Hüseyin G. Yurdaydın). Ankara.

Mordtmann, J.H. 1983. "Ferīdūn Beg." *Encyclopaedia of Islam*, Second edition vol. 2. Leiden.

Necipoğlu, G. 1989. "Süleyman the Magnificent and the Representation of Power in the Context of Ottoman-Habsburg-Papal Rivalry." *The Art Bulletin* 71:401–427.

———. 1991. *Architecture, Ceremonial, and Power: The Topkapi Palace in the Fifteenth and Sixteenth Centuries*. Cambridge, MA.

———. 2005. *The Age of Sinan: Architectural Culture in the Ottoman Empire*. London.

Pedani, M.P. 2005. "Some Remarks Upon the Ottoman Geo-Political Vision of the Mediterranean in the Period of the Cyprus War (1570–1573)." In Imber, Kiyotaki and Murphey 2005:23-53.

Vatin, N. 2010. Ferîdûn Bey, les plaisants secrets de la campagne de Szigetvár: édition, traduction et commentaire des folios 1 à 147 du Nüzhetü-l-esrâri-l-ahbâr der sefer-i Sigetvâr (ms. H 1339 de la Bibliothèque du Musée de Topkapı Sarayı). Vienna.

Veinstein, G. 1997. "Ṣoḳollu Meḥmed Paşa." *Encyclopaedia of Islam*, Second edition vol. 9. Leiden.

Yılmaz, H. 2005. "The Sultan and the Sultanate: Envisioning Rulership in the Age of Süleymān the Lawgiver (1520–1566)." PhD dissertation, Harvard University.

5

Imperial Geography and War

The Ottoman Case

Antonis Anastasopoulos

PREMODERN EMPIRES in southeastern Europe and western Asia, with the Ottomans being the last in a succession of empires that controlled territories in both regions,[1] were big territorial entities, and as such more diverse in terms of physical and human geography than the modern nation-states. Physical geography, which will be the focus of this chapter, is an important factor that affected imperial government in a number of ways. For instance, the distance of a province from the seat of power, as well as its accessibility, could affect the level of imperial control over it; divisions could emerge within the ruling elite on the basis of its members' geographical backgrounds; the expansion or defense of the imperial territory depended on geographical and other environmental factors; etc. Geography also was a means through which the administration conceptualized the realm: one may consider, for instance, in the case of the Ottoman Empire, the division by geographical region of some types of registers of the central administration, such as the *ahkâm defterleri*, or the concurrent appointment of two officials (such as the *Rumeli* and *Anadolu kazaskers*) at the same post, one for the European and another for the Asian territories as divided by sea from the Black Sea down to the Mediterranean.[2]

Furthermore, territorial expansion is often intrinsically woven in the fabric of empires, especially if they claim to be world empires. Since war is the basic method for achieving expansion, the aim of my chapter is to use the Ottoman Empire as a case study for discussing war from the point of view of imperial geography, or, in other words, for exploring how war connects with geography

---

[1] Nowadays, the Ottoman Empire is described as "early modern" rather than "pre-modern"; my selection of term here does not negate the usefulness of studying the Ottoman Empire as an early modern state.

[2] Cf. Brummett 2007:47–49.

in the imperial context. The concept of "geography" as I use it in this chapter, revolves around "space," by which I mean the natural, but also the human, environment (terrain, climatic conditions, cultures, etc.). However, space is also associated with other notions, such as "distance," "time," and "movement," and I will also take these into consideration. As for the concept of "empire," what I am principally interested in is the exercise of power and the political relationship between the imperial center and the territories over which it rules. Finally, what I conceptualize as "imperial geography" is how geography is politicized, so to speak, within an empire, or the interweaving of imperial politics with geography. This includes, on the one hand, how diverse regions become a territorial political entity that is perceived by the imperial government as being composed of a center and a number of provinces, and on the other hand, the impact that geographical factors can have on imperial authority in terms of policy- and decision-making and implementation, as well as political control.

In chronological terms, I will cover the long period from the early centuries of the Ottoman Empire until the proclamation, in 1839, of the *Tanzimat*. This event marks a break in Ottoman history, since it is the official declaration by the sultan of the decision of the government that the "traditional," premodern, Ottoman institutional framework had to be altered, so that the empire could adjust to the requirements of West-dominated modernity and be "elevated" to the status of a respected modern state within the European state system. However, I will more particularly refer to the sixteenth, seventeenth, and eighteenth centuries.

To give a few examples of questions that can be formulated on the basis of my introductory remarks, how did geography affect the conduct of war by the Ottoman Empire, and in what ways was it important? How did the empire mobilize men and collect animals, munitions, and provisions from its extensive and heterogeneous territories in times of war? What were the political implications of the fact that during war the leadership of the empire did or was expected to leave the imperial capital and move to the war front? What were the consequences of territorial expansion or contraction through war in political, social, and economic terms? I do not claim to be able to make categorical statements for or provide comprehensive answers to all these questions; rather I will make suggestions and hopefully demonstrate that the joint examination of the concepts of "war," "geography," and "empire" may throw light on certain aspects of imperial rule, such as methods of government, coordination of forces, use of resources, and center-periphery relations.

The most obvious geographical aspects of war are, on the one hand, that it is intended to result (and very often eventually does result) in territorial gains for the winners and losses for the defeated, and on the other hand, that it is a localized phenomenon. The latter aspect refers to the fact that war usually concerns (in reality or in the minds of those who plan and carry it out) specific regions as war zones, or lands to conquer or defend, even though it indirectly affects a much wider area than the one where military action takes place. But obviously there are many more aspects to the interrelationship between empire, geography, and war. First of all, war forces the state to mobilize troops, and collect wartime taxes, provisions, ammunitions, and animals from its provinces. Second, the state needs to march the troops and their animals over long distances and varied geographical settings. Third, in imperial campaigns the head of the empire or a high-standing official (in the Ottoman case, often the sultan, or his deputy, the grand vizier) has to lead the troops, which means that he has to abandon his peacetime governmental routine and place of residence in the capital. Fourth, war is an instance when the imperial authority seeks and has to reaffirm the loyalty of its subjects from all over the empire, which is particularly important especially when regular or urgent war needs require good timing or impose strict deadlines; as such, war is an instance when the various ethnic and religious groups across the imperial domains have to be convinced or forced to coordinate their efforts, under the command of the state, for the benefit of the empire.

In the words of John A. Hall and G. John Ikenberry, "the state's most important institution is that of the means of violence and coercion."[3] War is an institutionalized form of violence *par excellence*, and one that is usually justified and glorified through the invocation of higher ideals and the projection of role models, although, when stripped of its embellishments, it can clearly be described as what Charles Tilly had provocatively called a form of "organized crime."[4] Furthermore, war was one of the relatively few fields (especially in comparison with the modern state) in which the premodern state, including empires, was active; the Ottomans did not deviate from this norm.

Empires, in particular, as a specific type of state with universalist claims, come into being and exist through expansion, and expansion is closely linked to conquest; in this respect, the formation, and sometimes the institutions and the elites of empires rest on war.[5] With a (generous) touch of sensationalism, we may claim that the history of the Ottoman Empire is interwoven with war. The first mention of the Ottomans in a Byzantine source (Pachymeres) is the battle of Bapheus in Bithynia (northwestern Anatolia). For centuries, the empire was dreaded by Christian Europe for its formidable military might to which it

---

[3] Hall and Ikenberry 1989:1–2.
[4] Tilly 1985.
[5] For the association of empires with universalism, militarism, violence, and conquest, see, for instance, Howe 2002:13–18.

owed its expansion, and it was time and again suggested that the Ottomans could only be defeated by a coalition of powers, and not by a single state.[6] Over its long history, the empire was involved in many successful and unsuccessful campaigns, land and sea battles, sieges, and raids against many different enemies, and quite a few among the wars in which it was engaged left their mark on the power, prestige, and reputation of the sultans who were associated with them. Poor performance in war in the course of the eighteenth century alarmed the Ottoman leadership as to the need for reforms, and it was military reform that inaugurated the wider Westernizing institutional reforms of the nineteenth century. Finally, the end of the empire came about as a result of its participation and defeat in the First World War.[7]

The official image of the ideal sultan, as the head of state, was for long that of a warrior who personally led his troops to battle,[8] while the state personnel, both military and civilian, were collectively described as the *askeri* (the military), which reflects their original identity and purpose. Thus, for instance, the Ottoman provincial administration was a by-product of (or largely coincided with) the mechanism through which the state raised its provincial troops.[9] Moreover, territorial expansion was crucial for the increase of the resources of the state, and, subsequently, of the posts and income that it could allocate to its officials.

On the whole, the army was an important institution of the Ottoman state and one that in many respects (from recruitment to the timely payment of the soldiers' wages to checking the political influence of the military) required a considerable amount of attention and energy from the state leadership, regardless of whether the empire was at peace or at war. The Ottoman army was an unequivocally Islamic army, which officially was motivated by faith in Islam, and waged holy war (*gaza, jihad*) on the infidels and the heretics. This exclusivist ideology did not allow much space for admitting in large numbers the many non-Muslim subjects of the empire to the army. Even though until the seventeenth century the janissary infantry was manned principally through the recruitment of Christians, those were forcibly converted to Islam before they could join this corps. The Christian *sipahi*s of particularly the early Ottoman centuries gradually became extinct, and overall non-Muslim participation in

---

[6] Valensi 2000:25; Marsigli 1732:II 199.

[7] Maps that show the stages of expansion and dismemberment of empires, while also indicating the sites of major battles, campaign routes, and raids, are an expression of the association that is generally made between territorial changes and war (for the Ottoman Empire, see Pitcher 1972; İnalcık 1973:24–25; İnalcık with Quataert 1994:xxxiv; Kennedy 2002:47b, 48; cf. Ebel 2008:6, who makes a similar comment).

[8] Imber 2002:118–120; but for the eighteenth century, see Zilfi, 1993.

[9] Imber 2002:177–215.

the Ottoman army gradually became rather marginal, and usually concerned men in auxiliary capacities.[10]

Even though the Ottoman state was in principle a military state, the Ottoman society was not meant to be a militarized society. The state aimed at controlling the access of the tax-paying non-*askeri* population, the *reaya* (the flock), to guns;[11] and because of the Islamic character of the state, the prohibition to bear weapons applied even more strictly to the non-Muslims, the *zimmis*. However, in actual practice, the distinction between *askeri* and *reaya* was often not as clear-cut as the state would have had it be: for instance, the *reaya* subjects of the sultan were formally called up and provided military services to the state throughout Ottoman history, and from the end of the sixteenth century onwards, especially through the increasing infiltration of the janissary ranks by *reaya*, being *askeri* gradually ceased to automatically signal true elite and military status. Moreover, Ottoman archival sources suggest that, in spite of the state's ban on the ownership of weapons by the *reaya*, this was a widespread phenomenon,[12] even among the non-Muslims.[13]

Ottoman Imperial Geography and War

War is not a mere series of military engagements, but a complex phenomenon that can be and has been analyzed from many different perspectives. If viewed from a spatial angle, the impact of geographical factors on waging war cannot be overlooked. Furthermore, there is a strong political side to war, since it is associated with the goals and interests of states, including power and prestige. My intention here is to examine the interaction and interrelation of the geographical and the political aspects of war in the context of the Ottoman imperial polity. One may consider, for instance, the fortresses, the gunpowder and munitions factories, and the post-stations that formed networks that extended all over the Ottoman Empire, all the way from the imperial center to the frontier.[14] These can be treated as mere infrastructure that was technically necessary for the successful waging of war, but at the same time they were markers of imperial presence that were spread over long distances and varied territories, and suggested sovereignty and efficacy. Frontier fortresses in particular were

[10] Cf. Marsigli 1732:I 85–86, 101–102, 145; Stein 2007:89–93; Sfyroeras 1968. For French soldiers who fought for the Ottomans in the course of the 1593-1606 war against the Habsburgs, see Finkel 1988:107–109.
[11] İnalcık 1975:195–196.
[12] İnalcık 1975:195–198; but for firearms, see Jennings 1980.
[13] See, for instance, Pylia 2001:91–92; Stathis 2007.
[14] Heywood 1980; Heywood 1996; Ágoston 2005; Stein 2007.

statements of sovereignty which, on the one hand, guaranteed the security of the population in the interior, and on the other hand, served as a warning or threat to external enemies; their aim was predominantly defensive, but they were also used as bases for raids and attacks, or campaigns, against the enemy territory. Thus, they were outposts that communicated the center's authority over lands hundreds of miles away from it.

During its long history, the Ottoman Empire was engaged in many land and naval military campaigns, some of which to destinations very far away from the seat of power and the "core" provinces of the empire (i.e. central and western Anatolia and the southern and central Balkans): Egypt, Iran, Hungary, Vienna, Malta, India, and many more. (A catalog of raids also includes such places as the environs of Venice and the coasts of France and Spain.) Military campaigns are by definition related to movement, and thus space and geography. This relationship is apparent in all the stages of a campaign, even in its beginning: the official starting point of an imperial campaign changed depending on its destination (usually, Üsküdar, on the Asian coast opposite Istanbul, when campaigning in Asia, and Edirne, in Thrace, when campaigning in Europe). To reach its eventual destination and confront the enemy, the army often had to march very long distances over diverse geographical and climatic zones,[15] which took weeks or months.[16] This posed serious problems in particular to the provincial timariot *sipahi* corps, as its members were remunerated through the collection of largely agrarian taxes, and ideally wished to be back to their base districts at the specific time when these taxes, especially the tithe, had to be collected. This could prove impossible when they had to fight hundreds or thousands of miles away from their homes, or when wars dragged on for two consecutive campaigning seasons and they were made to spend the winter near the front.[17]

Because the campaign season started in spring and ended in autumn (due to the technology available at the time), it was not unusual for the Ottoman army to be forced to lift sieges and discontinue campaigns because otherwise it would be impossible to overcome distance and bad weather and road conditions in order to return to its base. The most famous example is perhaps the lifting of the siege of Vienna by Süleyman the Magnificent in mid-October 1529, as winter was kicking in.[18] However, in order to better understand the importance of geography and weather, it may suffice to point out that, whereas winter, rain, and snow were a threat for Süleyman in central Europe, thirteen

---

[15] On its part, the fleet sailed extremely long distances only in the sixteenth century, but even sailing the eastern Mediterranean or the Black Sea was not a negligible feat.

[16] Finkel 1988:66; Murphey 1999:65–67.

[17] Veinstein 1983; Finkel 1988:56, 309.

[18] Finkel 2006:124–125.

years earlier, in 1516, in a very different geographic setting, winter and rain were not a problem when his father, Selim I, decided to campaign from Syria against the Mamluks of Egypt. The march southwards started on December 15, and in this case the rain facilitated rather than obstructed the march of the army through the desert.[19] It was, therefore, important for the marching army to correctly assess the terrain and the weather conditions, but also to maintain a pace that would be quick enough to allow it to reach the front in time and yet would not exhaust the soldiers and the animals before getting there. It also had to be taken into account that the army would need to march back home or to its winter quarters at the end of the season and/or the campaign.[20] Good planning and an effective leadership apart, the terrain, the weather conditions, the feeding capacity, and the human geography of the land were factors with a crucial contribution to this. Moreover, the selection of where to set camp also was very important, which again highlights the centrality of geographical and environmental factors. Count Luigi Ferdinando Marsigli (1658–1730), a military man himself and an eyewitness observer of Ottoman military practice, noted that a camp should absolutely have access to water, forage, and wood, and be safe from enemy attacks.[21]

Marsigli distinguished three phases in the march of the Ottoman army. The first phase was the gathering of the troops from all over the empire at the location that had been arranged by the central authorities to be their meeting point; but he was quick to point out that he did not consider this a proper military march, since the troops did not arrive there in a disciplined manner. The second phase was the solemn parade of the military forces before the commander of the army, whether the sultan or another high-standing official. The last phase was, in Marsigli's view, the real march, and included the movement of troops from one place where they had camped to the next or to the location where they were expected to meet the enemy; there were four categories that moved or had to be carried in the context of this march: infantry, cavalry, artillery, and baggage. Geography, time, and thus correct scheduling, were important in all three phases; for instance, Marsigli noted that when a campaign to Hungary was organized, the troops who came from farthest away (he specified this as "Egypt and Asia") had to depart first from their places of origin and move faster than troops who came from places nearer the meeting point. Furthermore, he

---

[19] Emecen 2009:411–412.
[20] Cf. Forster and Daniell 1881:I 219.
[21] Marsigli:II 72.The Ottoman imperial camp had its own micro-geography reflecting the hierarchical position of and the military value attributed to the various officers and units of which the army was composed, with the tent of the army commander positioned at the center. Likewise, the spatial arrangements of the Ottoman battle formation reflected the relative value of the various units, with the most expendable military forces placed at the front (Marsigli:II 72f.).

indicated the standard itineraries of troops to the meeting point, depending on where they had started from, which can help us visualize the simultaneous movement of troops from different locations across the empire to a common destination in the context of what must have amounted to an operation of gigantic proportions.[22] In fact, the imperial camp and the troops that belonged to it were a mobile population that was intended not only to fight but also to convey the message of imperial power and unity to the subjects of the sultan as it crossed the empire. However, on the other hand, disciplining the army during war is a serious challenge for every state. Apart from Marsigli's first phase described above, deserters, gangs of armed men who tried to benefit from the confusion of war, and disorderly troops that returned from a lost battle or an unsuccessful campaign turned the image of a glorious imperial army on its head; their behavior left a negative mark on the human geography of the lands that they crossed, as the reports of the Venetian consuls of Salonica in the second half of the eighteenth century suggest.[23]

The movement of troops is inconceivable without maps, or reconnaissance and preparation of the terrain so that it becomes passable or fordable (in the case of rivers).[24] The Ottomans were generally interested in mapmaking, with the works of people like Piri Reis (sixteenth century) and Ebubekir Dimişki (seventeenth century) being among the best-known examples. However, the use of geographical works and maps outside the palace and elite circles has not been positively ascertained, while maps were not always produced with a view to serving practical needs in the way that modern maps do.[25] Even though concrete information about the actual use of maps and sea charts during campaigns is almost nonexistent, there is evidence that suggests that maps and geographical works were used for practical military purposes. For instance, the grand vizier Kara Mustafa Pasha ordered a description of Hungary and Germany from Willem and Joan Blaeus's *Atlas Maior* ahead of departing for the campaign against Vienna in 1683.[26] There are also maps on silk, which appeared in the late eighteenth century and had military use.[27] In addition, Ottoman campaign journals contain notes about rivers, streams, and irrigation canals.[28] Furthermore, the imperial elite could use the maps as succinct and easy to grasp depictions of the empire, as well as of imperial political projects that were to be achieved

---

[22] Marsigli 1732: II 105–117; cf. Káldy-Nagy 1977:174–183.

[23] Mertzios 1947:404–418; cf. Faroqhi 2004:115; Finkel 1988:49.

[24] See, for instance, Emecen 2009:412.

[25] Hagen 2000:191–192; Hagen 2006b:534–535.

[26] Hagen 2000:192; Hagen 2006a:233.

[27] Goodrich 1993:127.

[28] Murphey 1999:67. For more on Ottoman maps and their military use, see Soucek 2008; Brummett 2007:esp. 46–47, 50–54; Hagen 2006a:227–233; Faroqhi 2004:179–180; Marsigli 1732:I 97–98.

through war, and as such maps were brought to the attention of the monarch. For instance, it has been proposed that a map of Kiev and its vicinity was part of a proposal to the sultan to organize a campaign against it and conquer it, and that a map of Malta belonged to a report that was submitted to the sultan regarding the progress of the Ottoman campaign against this Mediterranean island in 1565.[29]

The Ottomans also used advance forces to scout enemy territory and prepare the terrain.[30] The technology of the day sometimes made delays in the march of the army unavoidable, particularly when bridges had to be built over rivers. However, as might be expected, within the Ottoman territory, the imperial campaigns followed specific, fixed, and thus familiar, routes.[31] Basically, on a wider scale, the combination of various geographical and environmental factors, in conjunction with the technology available at the time, determined to a great extent the realistic limits of Ottoman military expansion.

Stripped of its military context, the march of the army may be treated as a form of geographical exploration, in terms of both natural and human geography, as soldiers move to new regions, come across new landscapes, and become acquainted with new cultures. The sixteenth-century illustrated works of Matrakçı Nasuh can be seen as the end product of such an exploration: the author had eyewitness experience of a considerable proportion of the urban and rural landscapes that are included in his works, as he participated himself in at least two imperial campaigns. It should also be noted that Matrakçı's works were prepared for an elite readership and constituted, as majestic depictions of the empire's territories, a celebration of imperial grandeur and military success, but were at the same time intended for practical use.[32] Another example of an illustrated work that was presented to the sultan is the *Şeca'atname* by Asafi Dal Mehmed Çelebi, which celebrates the military leadership of Özdemiroğlu Osman Pasha on the eastern front in 1578–1585. In this work, the author describes, for instance, the oil pits in Baku,[33] while the 77 miniatures depict towns, castles, forts, and landscapes.

Keep in mind, however, that geography was not crucial in war only in relation to the march of troops. There were also two other important political aspects to it. One is the geographical distribution of the military forces in peacetime, and the other is how the state recruited men and collected animals, provisions, and munitions for its military campaigns.

---

[29] Karamustafa 1992:210–213.
[30] Káldy-Nagy 1977:171–173; Finkel 1988:65; Murphey 1999:23–24, 66–68, 109, 126, 191.
[31] Finkel 1988:63–66.
[32] Yurdaydın 1991; Rogers 1992:235f.; Yurdaydın 2003; Brummett 2007:50–54 and n77; Ebel 2008.
[33] Özcan 2007:LXXIX, 242–243.

In terms of the geographical distribution of forces in peacetime, the military forces of the Ottomans were scattered across the realm, but a distinction was maintained between central and provincial troops. The central standing army, namely, the janissaries, and the horsemen and other corps of the Porte, differed from the rest of the army in a number of characteristics that we do not need to analyze here. For our purposes, it suffices to note that, in their great mass, they were stationed where the sultan was based, which was Istanbul from the mid-fifteenth century onwards. On the other hand, the majority of the troops came from the periphery (principally, the marches in the early period and the provinces in later times). The provincial governors, that is, state appointees, were the commanders of only some of these forces, while others were led by individuals who did not directly or fully depend on sultanic appointment for their power. These included the so-called lords of the frontiers (*uç begleri*) in the fourteenth and fifteenth centuries, and the Muslim provincial notables (*ayan*) in the eighteenth and early nineteenth centuries.[34]

The janissaries constitute an interesting case in the context of this discussion, because the establishment of janissary garrisons outside Istanbul and the great rise in their numbers from the late sixteenth century onwards meant that eventually even they, the central troops *par excellence*, were distributed across the empire. Formally, the imperial troops that were stationed in the provinces represented central state authority and symbolized the presence of the state in the lives of its subjects. But, in reality, distance hindered effective control of the troops from the center and prevented the constant reaffirmation of their bond with it, which led to their gradual integration into and identification with the local communities where they lived; the infiltration of the ranks of the janissaries by the *reaya*, as noted above, but also the participation of the janissaries in the local urban guilds, were aspects of this phenomenon.[35] Thus, geographical expansion resulted in the breach of the official dichotomy of society between the *askeri* and the *reaya*. For its part, the central state insisted on maintaining the separation between central and provincial troops even when the janissary regiments were established in greater numbers in the provinces. Thus, an official distinction was introduced between imperial (*dergâh-ı âli*) and local (*yerli*) janissaries, that is, between those regiments based in the provinces which, in principle, were sent from Istanbul and those that, again in principle, were staffed locally.

In other words, the distinction between central and provincial troops suggests that the location where the various troops were stationed was not a

---

[34] On the military organization of the Ottomans, see Murphey 1999, Imber 2002:252–317, Aksan 2007. On the role of the *ayan* during war, see, for instance, Nagata 1999.

[35] Raymond 1991; Greene 2000:33–44.

mere matter of geographical positioning, but bore political connotations and implications mainly in terms of the power relations between the center and the periphery, but also in terms of the relation of the troops to the ruler. Thus, the creation of the janissary corps is generally attributed by historians to the need of the sultans to have a personal army as a counterweight to the troops of the lords of the frontiers, who were not always ready to submit unquestioningly to the will of the sultan. In other words, it happened at a time when the distinction between a geographical and political center and a periphery, as well as between a superior central authority and subordinate lords and officials, was coming into being.[36] In a way, this balance of power between the center and the provinces followed the opposite direction in later times, most markedly at around the turn of the nineteenth century, when some powerful *ayan* were able to question the absolute authority of the sultan in the areas that they controlled.[37] Part of this ability rested on their capacity to raise and maintain troops.

Coming now to the second issue suggested above, war made necessary the raising of men, animals, funds, and provisions from a vast area, which practically required the involvement of the Ottoman population at large in the war effort.[38] This operation—which was huge and complicated, considering the size of both the army and the empire—had two aspects. One was technical (in that it was administrative and organizational), and centered on forward planning with a view to getting the troops to gather at the right time, at the right place, in the right number and composition, with the right quantities of provisions and ammunitions, and the right number of animals of various sorts (such as horses, camels, and water buffaloes). In major campaigns, the size of the imperial camp reached tens of thousands of men, that is, the equivalent of a major city by the standards of that era, and it should not be overlooked that such a number of men also needed tens of thousands of animals to go along.[39] The case of the district of Karaferye, in the southern Balkans, in the course of the 1768–1774 war between the Ottoman Empire and Russia, can give us an idea of the expectations of the state from its provinces during war in the second half of the eighteenth century. Karaferye was not near the actual war zones, but was dramatically affected by the war. The district was required to dispatch soldiers and auxiliary troops (for whom local notables acted as commanders, or guarantors towards the state regarding their reliability and discipline), as well as oxcarts, water buffaloes, and camels, and also to deliver provisions (such as flour and sacks for the baking,

---

[36] Kafadar 1995:111–113, 138–150; Finkel 2006:75.
[37] Moutaftchieva 2005; Yaycıoğlu 2008:192–293.
[38] On raising and paying the troops and provisioning the army, see the useful analyses of Finkel 1988, Murphey 1999:esp. 85–103, and Aksan 2007:esp. 67–75, 142–151.
[39] Forster and Daniell 1881:I 219.

storage, and transportation of hardtack) either for the army in the war front, or for troops and officials passing through the district (who required considerable quantities of foodstuff, firewood, packhorses, etc.). Obviously, all of these demands placed a heavy financial burden on the local population. Around half of the entries of the surviving registers of the local court of justice from this period are related to the war. It is also interesting to note that it took weeks, or even months, for an imperial decree to reach the Karaferye court of law, which doubled as the administrative center of the district. This meant that, if orders for war were to be in the hands of their recipients around the empire in time, they had to be issued well ahead of the actual beginning of the provincial troops' campaign season in March—and sometimes as early as the end of the previous September.[40]

The other aspect of recruitment and provisioning was political: attaining the recruitment and provisions goals that the state set in its many decrees was not simply a matter of good organizational and administrative skills, but also of testing and proving the taxpaying population's loyalty and obedience to the empire. Wars are major "imperial projects,"[41] and the subjects of the empire have to cooperate with the central authorities if they are to be, at least organizationally, successful. For instance, one may find many Ottoman decrees that demand the immediate execution of orders that were being sent for the second time, because their recipients had failed to carry them out the first time that they were issued. Such documents suggest that the state was not always able to impose its will on its population, and that there was considerable space for negotiation, as the massive use of coercion across the empire in order to force the loyalty of the population was both technically impossible and counterproductive (if only for the fear of generating reaction by the population subjected to it).[42] A sultanic decree of 1772 provides some evidence on the weakness of the center towards its provinces. The state had previously ordered the local *ayan* and the wealthy inhabitants of Karaferye to finance the dispatch of 300 foot soldiers to the imperial army. However, as the local Christians complained in a petition that they submitted to the central authorities, the *ayan* collected the money for these troops from them, contrary to what the sultan had stipulated.[43] Then the *ayan* were ordered to return the money to the Christians, and were warned that if it had not been for the war, they would have been severely punished

---

[40] Anastasopoulos 1999:142–161.
[41] I borrow the term "imperial project" from Sinopoli 2001:197.
[42] Aksan 2007:47; Anastasopoulos 1999:157–158; cf. Finkel 1988:51.
[43] Cf. Mertzios 1947:419.

(as would the local judge for tolerating their illegal behavior).[44] My argument is that distance and the vastness of the Ottoman territories were factors that facilitated such oppressive acts, but also any other (malicious or benign) act of disobedience, and thus increased the bargaining potential of the imperial subjects vis-à-vis the state. Furthermore, war conditions made the latter more lenient towards such phenomena of disregard for its orders, since priority was given to obtaining the necessary men and provisions. Besides, the fact that each year Istanbul received very many petitions from very many districts about oppression meant that the state could not possibly deal proactively with each single one of them, and largely hoped that the issuing of a decree and possibly the dispatch of an envoy would suffice to secure the desired solution.

The bargaining limits of the state were tested by the combination of geography with war in another respect, as well. Difficult terrains and harsh campaigning conditions were important agents that could give rise to unrest among the soldiery, and possibly result in rebellion, and destabilization of the position of even the sultan. There are many cases that demonstrate that the army leadership needed to be flexible and able to find the fine balance between imposing discipline through coercion and negotiating with the mass of the army.[45] Maybe the best-known case involves the problems that Selim I had with his troops during and after the successful campaign against the Safavids and the battle of Chaldiran in 1514. The janissaries first mutinied on the way to Chaldiran, and a few months later refused to spend the winter in Karabakh, too far away from their base, with a view to a new campaign. The reason for the two mutinies was that the troops had experienced a very long march (some maybe up to 1,500 miles) under difficult environmental conditions, harsh terrains (which included barren lands devoid of grass and water), and lack of provisions. The conditions were aggravated by the scorched-earth tactics of the Safavids and their avoiding battle until the Ottoman army was exhausted and led to a location, like Chaldiran, that presumably was thought to be advantageous to the Safavids. Despite being nicknamed "the Grim" (Yavuz) and being notorious for his violent disposition, Selim was forced in the first case to placate the mutineers and talk them into continuing the march, and in the second to accede to their demands, retreat to Ottoman territory, and cancel the campaign.[46]

---

[44] Vasdravelles 1954:200–202. The original entry can be found in Karaferye Sicil vol. 93/page 353/ entry 2 (evail-i Ramazan 1186 / 26 November–5 December 1772). The Ottoman judicial registers (*sicil*) of Karaferye are kept at the Imathia branch of the General State Archives of Greece in Veroia.

[45] See, for instance, Finkel 1988:12–13.

[46] Shaw 1976:81; Uğur 1985:104, 126–127, 245–246, 248–249, 251–253, 272, 274; Murphey 1999:134–135; Varlık 1993:193–194; Emecen 2009:409–410, 413.

Another cause of disobedience and rebellion as an expression of the political repercussions of war was territorial losses as a consequence of military defeat. For instance, the English ambassador in Istanbul reported that, during the revolt against Mustafa II in 1703, one of the accusations that the rebels voiced against the sultan was that he had lost territory to the infidel Christians by accepting to negotiate and sign peace treaties with them to this end, which rendered him unworthy of keeping his throne.[47] Besides, defeat in war and the loss of territories had at that same time an impact on Ottoman mentality and attitude towards war, expressed, for instance, in the hesitation of one section of the governing elite to embroil the empire in further wars. This is apparent particularly in the early decades of the eighteenth century, following defeat in the war of 1684–1699. And, of course, territorial losses resulted in movements of populations (refugees and settlers), cultural changes, and social unrest.

Finally, a political side effect of a different kind was produced by the fact that the Ottoman sultan was expected to lead the troops to battle in person. Thus, as a consequence of war, the locus of central decision-making had to be moved from the capital to the front, while, at the same time, a prince, who normally served as a governor in a provincial district, was summoned to the capital in order to substitute for his father, the sultan.[48] The displacement of the seat of authority was reflected in the imperial decrees (*fermans*), which during war did not bear Istanbul as the place of their issuing but the location where the imperial camp was. In the seventeenth century and later, this practice persisted, even though usually the sultans no longer led the troops to battle. Thus, decrees coming from the imperial camp still were *fermans* issued in the name of the sovereign. But, in this way, a curious dichotomy came into being: as a physical presence the sultan was in Istanbul (or elsewhere, such as Edirne, the preferred city of various sultans), but as the head of state he symbolically was wherever the imperial camp and his troops were.[49] Generally speaking, at this later period, the sultan often only reviewed his troops and maybe symbolically led them out of the walls of Istanbul,[50] or, maybe he led the army up to a safe point mid-way between the capital and the war front, as did Mehmed IV, who waited in Belgrade, while his grand vizier Kara Mustafa besieged Vienna in 1683.[51]

---

[47] Abou-El-Haj 1984:22, 71–72; cf. Faroqhi 2004:117. It has to be pointed out, nevertheless, that the fact that this claim is only reported through a Western source may justifiably give rise to doubts about its accuracy.

[48] For the case of Selim I and prince Süleyman, see Uğur 1985:236, 244.

[49] See, for instance, Vasdravelles 1954:41–42; Anastasopoulos 1999:144–145; cf. Kolovos 2004:300 and n18.

[50] Zilfi 1993:185.

[51] Finkel 2006:284–287.

Conclusion

In an era when, in the words of Tilly, "any state that failed to put considerable effort into war making was likely to disappear,"[52] an extensive territory with abundant human, natural, and financial resources gave its ruler advantage over his competitors.[53] On the other hand, being efficient at extracting resources from a vast territory without possessing an extensive, competent, and well-staffed administrative apparatus, and with the technological limitations of the premodern or the early modern era, was a challenging problem for the central state authorities not only of the Ottoman Empire, but of every empire of its time.

Geography, distance, terrain, climate, and weather, were all factors that played a part in the success or failure of military campaigns, and made their appearance in all the phases of the war effort: preparation, troop provisioning, speed and ease of army movement, battle engagement or siege, and return home. Nevertheless, geography was not merely a natural agent, but had an important secondary political dimension: the distant (in psychological, but for many provinces also in physical terms) center of power, which during war formally had moved from the capital to the imperial camp near or beyond the frontiers, issued decrees through which it made demands, often urgent ones, in trying to address needs that arose from the progress of war. In this respect, geography—much more dramatically in times of war than in peacetime—was one of the factors which put to the test the capacity of the empire to show itself to be administratively and militarily efficient, and also to obtain its subjects' obedience to and/or acquiescence with its commands. To put it in different terms, war was about logistics, but it also was about power and prestige. A well-run war suggested a well-run empire; and geography was a factor that had an impact on both war and imperial administration.

---

[52] Tilly 1985:184.
[53] On the admiration of the Venetian ambassadors in Istanbul for the resources and riches available to the Ottoman sultans, see Valensi 2000:35–40.

Works Cited

Abou-El-Haj, R. A. 1984. *The 1703 Rebellion and the Structure of Ottoman Politics.* Leiden.

Ágoston, G. 2005. *Guns for the Sultan: Military Power and the Weapons Industry in the Ottoman Empire.* Cambridge.

Aksan, V. H. 2007. *Ottoman Wars, 1700-1807: An Empire Besieged.* Harlow, England.

Aksan, V. H., and Goffman, D., eds. 2007. The *Early Modern Ottomans: Remapping the Empire.* Cambridge.

Alcock, S. E., D'Altroy, T. N., Morrison, K. D., and Sinopoli, C. M., eds. 2001. *Empires: Perspectives from Archaeology and History.* Cambridge.

Anastasopoulos, A. 1999. *Imperial Institutions and Local Communities: Ottoman Karaferye, 1758-1774.* Unpublished Ph.D. dissertation. Cambridge.

Anastasopoulos, A. and Kolovos, E., eds. 2007. *Ottoman Rule and the Balkans, 1760-1850: Conflict, Transformation, Adaptation. Proceedings of an International Conference Held in Rethymno, Greece, 13-14 December 2003.* Rethymno.

Brummett, P. 2007. "Imagining the Early Modern Ottoman Space, from World History to Piri Reis." In Aksan and Goffman 2007:15–58.

Dankoff, R. 2006. *An Ottoman Mentality: The World of Evliya Çelebi.* Leiden.

Ebel, K. A. 2008. "Representations of the Frontier in Ottoman Town Views of the Sixteenth Century." *Imago Mundi* 60:1–22.

Emecen, F. 2009. "Selim I." *Türkiye Diyanet Vakfı İslâm Ansiklopedisi,* vol. 36:407–414. Istanbul.

Evans, P. B., Rueschemeyer, D., and Skocpol, T., eds. 1985. *Bringing the State Back In.* Cambridge.

Faroqhi, S. 2004. *The Ottoman Empire and the World Around It.* London.

Finkel, C. 1988. *The Administration of Warfare: The Ottoman Military Campaigns in Hungary, 1593-1606.* Vienna.

——. 2006. *Osman's Dream: The Story of the Ottoman Empire, 1300-1923.* New York.

Forster, C. T. and Daniell, F. H. B. 1881. *The Life and Letters of Ogier Ghiselin de Busbecq.* 2 vols. London.

Goodrich, T. D. 1993. "Old Maps in the Library of Topkapi Palace in Istanbul." *Imago Mundi* 45:120–133.

Greene, M. 2000. *A Shared World: Christians and Muslims in the Early Modern Mediterranean.* Princeton.

Hagen, G. 2000. "Some Considerations on the Study of Ottoman Geographical Writings." *Archivum Ottomanicum* 18:183–193.

——. 2006a. "Afterword: Ottoman Understandings of the World in the Seventeenth Century." In Dankoff 2006:215–256.

——. 2006b. "Kâtib Çelebi and Sipâhîzâde." In Kaçar and Durukal 2006:525–542.

Hall, J. A., and Ikenberry, G. J. 1989. *The State*. Minneapolis.

Harley, J. B. and Woodward, D., eds. 1992. *The History of Cartography*. Volume Two, Book One. *Cartography in the Traditional Islamic and South Asian Societies*. Chicago.

Heywood, C. 1980. "The Ottoman *Menzilhane* and *Ulak* System in Rumeli in the Eighteenth Century." In Okyar and İnalcık 1980:179–186.

———. 1996. "The Via Egnatia in the Ottoman Period: The *Menzilhānes* of the *Sol Kol* in the Late 17th/Early 18th Century." In Zachariadou 1996:129–144.

Howe, S. 2002. *Empire: A Very Short Introduction*. Oxford.

Imber, C. 2002. *The Ottoman Empire, 1300-1650: The Structure of Power*. Houndmills.

İnalcık, H. 1973. *The Ottoman Empire: The Classical Age, 1300-1600* (trans. N. Itzkowitz, and C. Imber). London.

———. 1975. "The Socio-Political Effects of the Diffusion of Fire-arms in the Middle East." In Parry and Yapp 1975:195–217.

İnalcık, H., with Quataert, D., eds. 1994. *An Economic and Social History of the Ottoman Empire, 1300-1914*. Cambridge.

Jennings, R. C. 1980. "Firearms, Bandits, and Gun-control: Some Evidence on Ottoman Policy Towards Firearms in the Possession of *Reaya*, from Judicial Records of Kayseri, 1600–1627." *Archivum Ottomanicum* 6:339–358.

Kaçar, M., and Durukal, Z., eds. 2006. *Essays in Honour of Ekmeleddin İhsanoğlu*. vol. 1: *Societies, Cultures, Sciences: A Collection of Articles*. Istanbul.

Kafadar, C. 1995. *Between Two Worlds: The Construction of the Ottoman State*. Berkeley.

Káldy-Nagy, G. 1977. "The First Centuries of the Ottoman Military Organization." *Acta Orientalia Academiae Scientiarum Hungaricae* 31:147–183.

Karamustafa, A. T. 1992. "Military, Administrative, and Scholarly Maps and Plans." In Harley and Woodward 1992:209–227.

Kennedy, H. 2002. *An Historical Atlas of Islam / Atlas historique de l'Islam*. Leiden.

Kolovos, I. 2004. "A *Biti* of 1439 from the Archives of the Monastery of Xeropotamou (Mount Athos)." *Hilandarski Zbornik* 11:295–306.

Marsigli, L. 1732. *Stato militare dell'Impèrio ottomano / L'état militaire de l'Empire ottoman*. 2 parts. The Hague.

Mertzios, K. D. 1947. *Μνημεία μακεδονικής ιστορίας*. Salonica.

Moutaftchieva, V. 2005. *L'anarchie dans les Balkans à la fin du XVIIIe siècle*. Istanbul.

Murphey, R. 1999. *Ottoman Warfare, 1500-1700*. London.

Nagata, Y. 1999. *Muhsin-zâde Mehmed Paşa ve Âyânlık Müessesesi*. Izmir.

Okyar, O., and İnalcık, H., eds. 1980. *Türkiye'nin Sosyal ve Ekonomik Tarihi (1071-1920): Birinci Uluslararası Türkiye'nin Sosyal ve Ekonomik Tarihi Kongresi Tebliğleri / Social and Economic History of Turkey (1071-1920): Papers Presented to the First International Congress on the Social and Economic History of Turkey*. Ankara.

Özcan, A., ed. 2007. *Âsafî Dal Mehmed Çelebi (Bey, Paşa). Şecâ'atnâme. Özdemiroğlu Osman Paşa'nın Şark Seferleri (1578-1585).* Istanbul.

Parry, V. J. and Yapp, M.E., eds. 1975. *War, Technology and Society in the Middle East.* London.

Pitcher, D. E. 1972. *An Historical Geography of the Ottoman Empire from Earliest Times to the End of the Sixteenth Century.* Leiden.

Pylia, M. 2001. "Λειτουργίες και αυτονομία των κοινοτήτων της Πελοποννήσου κατά τη Δεύτερη Τουρκοκρατία (1715-1821)." *Μνήμων* 23:67-98.

Raymond, A. 1991. "Soldiers in Trade: The Case of Ottoman Cairo." *British Journal of Middle Eastern Studies* 18:16-37.

Rogers, J. M. 1992. "Itineraries and Town Views in Ottoman Histories." In Harley and Woodward 1992:228-255.

Sfyroeras, V. 1968. *Τα ελληνικά πληρώματα του τουρκικού στόλου.* Athens.

Shaw, S. J. 1976. *History of the Ottoman Empire and Modern Turkey.* Volume I. *Empire of the Gazis. The Rise and Decline of the Ottoman Empire, 1280-1808.* Cambridge.

Sinopoli, C. M. 2001. "Imperial Integration and Imperial Subjects." In Alcock et al. 2001:195-200.

Soucek, S. 2008a. "Ottoman Cartography." In Soucek 2008b:225-238.

———. 2008b. *Studies in Ottoman Naval History and Maritime Geography.* Istanbul.

Stathis, P. 2007. "From Klephts and *Armatoloi* to Revolutionaries." In Anastasopoulos and Kolovos 2007:167-179.

Stein, M. L. 2007. *Guarding the Frontier: Ottoman Border Forts and Garrisons in Europe.* London.

Tilly, C. 1985. "War Making and State Making as Organized Crime." In Evans, Rueschemeyer, and Skocpol 1985:169-191.

Uğur, A. 1985. *The Reign of Sultan Selīm I in the Light of the Selīm - nāme Literature.* Berlin.

Valensi, L. 2000. *Βενετία και Υψηλή Πύλη: η γένεση του δεσπότη (Venise et la Sublime Porte. La naissance du despote, 1987, trans. A. Karra).* Athens.

Varlık, M. Ç. 2009. "Çaldıran Savaşı." In *Türkiye Diyanet Vakfı İslâm Ansiklopedisi.* Vol. 8:193-195.

Vasdravelles, I. K., ed. 1954. *Ιστορικά αρχεία Μακεδονίας. Β΄. Αρχείον Βεροίας - Ναούσης, 1598-1886.* Salonica.

Veinstein, G. 1983. "L'hivernage en campagne talon d'Achille du système militaire ottoman classique. A propos des *Sipāhī* de Roumélie en 1559-1560." *Studia Islamica* 58:109-148.

Yaycıoğlu, A. 2008. *The Provincial Challenge: Regionalism, Crisis, and Integration in the Late Ottoman Empire (1792-1812).* Unpublished Ph.D. dissertation, Harvard University.

Yurdaydın, H. G. 1991 "Maṭrakči." *The Encyclopaedia of Islam.* New edition. Vol. 6:843–844. Leiden.

——. 2003 "Matrakçı Nasuh." *Türkiye Diyanet Vakfı İslâm Ansiklopedisi* vol. 28:143–145. Ankara.

Zachariadou, E., ed. 1996. *The Via Egnatia under Ottoman Rule (1380-1699). Halcyon Days in Crete II. A Symposium Held in Rethymnon, 9-11 January 1994.* Rethymnon.

Zilfi, M. C. 1993. "A Medrese for the Palace: Ottoman Dynastic Legitimation in the Eighteenth Century." *Journal of the American Oriental Society* 113:184–191.

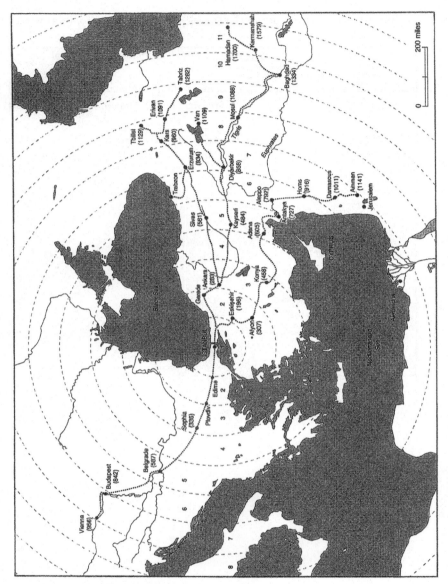

Figure 1: Distance of potential battlefields from Istanbul.
Source: Rhoads Murphey, *Ottoman Warfare, 1500–1700*.
London: UCL Press, 1999, xiv.

Figure 2: Tiflis and its environs: illustration from the chapter of the *Şecâ'atnâme* about the conquest of Tiflis by Özdemiroğlu Osman Pasha in the late sixteenth century.
Source: Abdülkadir Özcan (ed.), Âsafî Dal Mehmed Çelebi (Bey, Paşa). *Şecâ'atnâme. Özdemiroğlu Osman Paşa'nın Şark Seferleri* (1578–1585). Istanbul: Çamlica, 2007, 35 (folio 18r.). The original manuscript is kept at the Library of the University of Istanbul (T.Y., No. 6043).

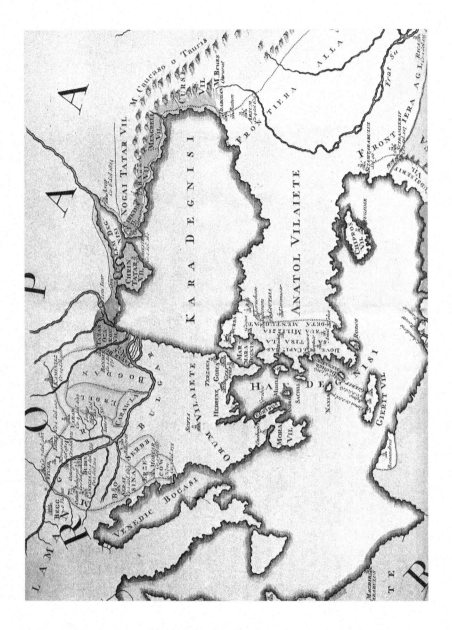

Figure 3: Map (detail) of the Ottoman Empire that indicates janissary garrisons in frontier fortresses around 1680 (Co: company; So.: soldiers). The map has been drawn on the basis of a map by Ebubekir Dimişki.
Source: Luigi Marsigli, *L'état militaire de l'Empire ottoman*. The Hague-Amsterdam, 1732 (reprint: Graz: Akadem. Druck- u. Verlagsanst., 1972).

6

Ambiguities of Sovereignty

Property Rights and Spectacles of Statehood in Tanzimat Izmir

Sibel Zandi-Sayek

THE RELATIONSHIP BETWEEN modern state power and geographic space, as evidenced in monumental constructions, institutional buildings, public works, and spectacles, as well as surveys, cadastres, and other mapping technologies, has received scholarly attention across disciplines.[1] While these studies have significantly underscored the importance of material spaces and practices to modern statehood—be it imperial, colonial, or national—they have generally approached the state as a self-contained territorial and political unit informed by a Westphalian notion of sovereignty. Accordingly, a single state is imagined to possess and exercise exclusive jurisdiction over affairs within its neatly demarcated territory. I would argue that such conceptualizations overlook a host of more ambiguous situations whereby multiple states claim the right to govern the same spaces, artifacts, and subjects, or a given state seeks to reinforce its claim to sovereignty through practices within the territory of another state. Despite recent calls in the fields of international relations, law, and politics for "unbundling territoriality"[2] to better elucidate the interplay of modern state power and space, the bulk of existing scholarship relies on the assumption that territory and power are neatly coterminous.

Using the late Ottoman Empire as a case study and probing specific urban practices and performances in the nineteenth-century seaport of Izmir/ Smyrna, this chapter complicates such assumptions, exposing how multiple jurisdictions operated within the same imperial, sovereign setting. I examine a formative moment in the history of the Ottoman Empire just before the

---

[1]   See, for example, Çelik 2008; Harris 2003; Scott 1998; Vale 1992; Anderson 1983.
[2]   Anderson 1996; Agnew 1994; Ruggie 1993.

paradigm of nation-state territoriality, which we now take for granted, crystallized and gained general acceptance. I focus on two arenas of state action in Izmir: property rights, particularly those applying to non-Ottoman subjects; and celebrations of national holidays in which both the Ottoman and various European states asserted their sovereignty vis-à-vis one another and the Smyrniot audience. Although seemingly unrelated, both the control of property and the monitoring of ceremonial functions converged on the management of urban space, offering valuable lenses to investigate how fundamental aspects of modern state power were negotiated in everyday life. Moreover, together they allow us to span two distinct yet interrelated scales at which modern sovereignty is constituted: exclusive and legitimate control over a designated territory, and international recognition of this control. In particular, I probe how the Ottoman and various European states competed to carve out their own spheres of influence in the city; how territorial and non-territorial conceptions of authority, inherent in the Ottoman configuration of power, interpenetrated and reshaped each other; and how these partial and untidy processes played out in everyday urban spaces and practices. Through a historically specific case, this chapter expands our understanding of modern geographic space beyond that of a uniformly governed terrain, revealing the multiple and often contradictory territorialities and sovereignties that could be interwoven in it.

The largest Ottoman port for international trade and arguably the most cosmopolitan city outside Istanbul, nineteenth-century Izmir offers a particularly opportune site for this study. As with other multinational and dynastic polities, in the Ottoman Empire, legal pluralism and differential legal statuses—accorded on the basis of subjecthood, religion, or social rank—were the norm. Hence, Ottoman and various European jurisdictions existed alongside one another, governing matters related to their respective subjects. In some cases, these jurisdictions intersected and partially overlapped, sometimes even converging on the same person, or applying to parts of the same dispute. For example, while extraterritorial jurisdictions governed civil and contractual matters pertaining to foreign residents such as marriage and inheritance, Ottoman territorial jurisdictions controlled all questions related to their property transactions and security without exception. Such intersections and overlaps were characteristic of many cities across the eastern Mediterranean. But in a highly diverse and vibrant commercial center like Izmir—home to varied religious, ethnic, and national communities, and commanding the attention of several European nations vying for influence—they produced an exceptionally dynamic set of exchanges. While local actors maneuvered between different judicial spheres, sometimes taking advantage of poorly defined jurisdictions,

Ottoman state officials and European consuls frequently disagreed and occasionally clashed about their respective spheres of sovereignty.

The decades between the 1840s and the 1880s are most revealing in this respect, as both the reformist Ottoman state and European powers were simultaneously refashioning themselves into modern sovereignties. On the one hand, Ottoman bureaucrats embarked on a series of reforms, the Tanzimat, to enhance state control over the empire's territory and assets and forge a cohesive polity that transcended ethnic or religious affiliations; censuses, income registers, and cadastral surveys that tracked population distribution and resources; new Nationality laws that fixed the parameters according to which people were officially considered to be Ottoman citizens; and the lavish and more overarching character given to Ottoman imperial feasts and state ceremonials were some of the most salient manifestations of this process in Izmir. On the other hand, foreign powers competed with one another to expand their influence within the empire, while simultaneously trying to maintain the region's stability within the context of the so-called Eastern Question. To broaden their economic and political sway in the empire, they tacitly permitted their legations to extend consular protections and immunities to various local groups. Indeed, the tremendous increase in the number of foreign subjects in Izmir—from about 10,000 in the 1840s to 50,000 in the late 1880s, while the total population only rose from an estimated 60,000 to 200,000[3]—attests as much to massive immigration from beyond the Ottoman borders as to mounting numbers of Ottoman subjects, especially non-Muslims, who placed themselves under the protection of an interested European power to gain immunity from certain tax liabilities and local police control. Consular legations also asserted their presence in Izmir's festive life. They engaged in increasingly elaborate diplomatic maneuvers and organized more ostentatious celebrations of their national holidays that drew enthusiastic crowds to the streets. In short, while Tanzimat statesmen territorialized their authority more systematically, European legations pushed back by expanding their long-standing extraterritorial agreements (or capitulations) within the empire, both parties seeking to enforce their respective jurisdictions in uncompromising and exclusionary ways.

Nowhere were these competing processes more evident than in the struggles over the control and meaning of property and festive practices in Izmir. As I show in the following pages, both the property of foreign subjects and diplomatic protocols were profoundly political arenas, contested sites through which the boundaries and scope of modern state power were constituted and

[3] Kütükoğlu 2000; Karpat 1985:122–123.

challenged. Seemingly innocuous local disputes over rights and ranks sometimes triggered international confrontations, while broader geopolitical dynamics periodically affected the status and rights of local subjects or the format of a parade or celebration. What foreign states could or could not do in Ottoman territory depended not only on how they leveraged their extraterritorial agreements, but also on everyday interactions and local politics on the ground. In other words, the delicate balance that characterized the period under consideration simultaneously hinged on geopolitical rivalries and on the particularities of local processes. The negotiations I explore in this chapter reveal an ever-shifting geography of power, calling for a more dynamic understanding of imperial space, in which state authority is contingent on whom and where one was.

Property and Entangled Sovereignties

In the Ottoman Empire, real property held by foreign subjects was governed by a variety of discrete regulations and pragmatic arrangements based on a mixture of territorial and extraterritorial laws.[4] Although foreigners in the empire did not have rightful access to freehold property until 1867, through a careful manipulation of existing laws, many of them did find ways of holding property.[5] In a highly commercialized city like Izmir, property was more than a shelter or a source of rental income; it comprised a substantial share of the assets of individuals and families, who used it as a vehicle for securing credit and as collateral to increase their financial resources for doing business. Smyrniots of all descriptions exchanged property frequently and engaged in legally binding transactions that involved property. And when formal laws got in the way, people found ways around them. They maneuvered the legal processes and navigated between different jurisdictional spheres to circumvent obstacles. Hence, according to British consular records, foreigners held over one-third of the taxable property in the mid 1850s[6]—a staggering proportion given the legal obstacles facing foreign subjects.

---

[4] I use real property in a broader sense to mean both freehold property (*mülk*) and various kinds of leasehold property (such as *gedik* and *vakıf*) that by the 1840s had become akin to freehold, permitting exchange, transfer, and inheritance. On the transformation of *gedik* property, see Akarlı 2004; Anastassiadou 1997. On *vakıf* property, see Barnes 1987.

[5] Foreigners held *mülk* in their name only on the rare occasion that they were equipped by a special order (*firman*) from the sultan. Collas 1864:80; Aliotti 1900:118–134.

[6] Taxable property included both *mülk* and *gedik* property. In 1854, the value of such property held by foreigners amounted to 82,250,821 piastres (PRO/FO 195/720, "Valuation," Blunt to Bulwer, August 2, 1862) while total taxable property in Izmir was assessed at 194,000,000 piasters (PRO/FO 195/447, "Report," Brant to de Redcliffe, July 20, 1854).

The prevailing method was to register the titles in the name of a third party who was an Ottoman subject and that the *kadı* court (*mahkeme*) recognized as the actual owner. In Izmir, this front person was usually a female relative of the foreigner—the wife or the mother-in-law. Given frequent intermarriage between foreign men and local Greek and Armenian women, many wives were already Ottoman subjects (or *rayahs*). If the woman who served as a front was not already an Ottoman subject, then she often agreed, for the purpose of conveyance, to be considered an Ottoman subject, which made her in the eyes of the *kadı* court a legitimate property owner and a registered proprietress.[7] When the front person was a business associate, the title deeds were supplemented with yet another contract, made before the consular court of the foreigner, in which the front person declared that he was not the rightful owner but had only lent his name to complete the required paperwork before the *kadı* court.[8]

In Izmir, as in cities like Alexandria, Istanbul, and Salonica, frequented for generations by foreign merchants, property holding under borrowed names became a widespread de facto practice.[9] This arrangement sufficiently reconciled legal norms with the local needs of a commercial society and profitably met the demands of all concerned parties, which may explain its frequent adoption as a favored tactic. For one, it allowed foreigners to invest their money without compromising their foreign status and the important personal and tax immunities that came with it. It also worked to the satisfaction of Ottoman officials as it retained real estate transactions within the laws of the empire, attracted investment, and generated revenues through transfer fees and construction permits. Moreover, it conformed to the formal tenets and procedures of the *kadı* court and maintained the superiority of this court in the overall hierarchy of the legal system.

Property transfers involving foreign subjects reveal how the seemingly discrete and disconnected jurisdictions of the *kadı* and consular courts were inevitably intertwined. In principle, territorial claims affecting ownership or use rights—such as acquisition, alienation, and various forms of leasing that determined or limited the extent of rights to a real property—were matters for the *kadı* court. They had to be carried out in conformity with the information

---

[7] On the rationale of third-party ownership, see CADN/FC 50, "Note," February 3, 1872; DUSCS "Memorial," July 20, 1872; Collas 1864:127–129; McCoan 1879, 2:195.

[8] Smyrnelis 2005:291.

[9] Van Dyck 1881:56. Different transfer strategies were used in different localities. For example, in Damascus a foreign lessee purchased a building through an indefinite lease of possession, under which the former proprietor could regain the property only on repayment of the money advanced to him (Reilly 1989:524).

recorded on the title deed.[10] In contrast, contractual obligations between foreign litigants, as in the use of real property as collateral or in cases of bankruptcy, were presumably within the jurisdiction of the consular court. Thus, property cases were usually divided between two courts—the consular court settling the personal obligation and the *kadı* court completing the actual transfer and registration. In practice, however, since territorial claims could also be part of larger contractual agreements, these judicial spheres frequently overlapped and sometimes conflicted.

Consular records provide some useful insight into the arbitration of property disputes between litigants bound by different legal rules. The necessity of coordinating the settlements pronounced at each court and forging convergence between different legal norms and procedures raised problems, often complicating the settlement of property cases.[11] At the same time, ambiguity about the division of labor between courts and imprecision in legal procedures, especially within and across consular courts, created opportunities for manipulation. Sometimes, consulates framed the issue so as to assume competence over all personal matters related to the case, leaving only the actual writing of the title deed to the *kadı* court. At others, they categorically refused to interfere with any aspect of the question—ultimately making property disputes a convenient instrument for reciprocal arm-twisting. This was the case with the Austrian court during the division of a large house and warehouse complex, known as *Frenkhane Fisher*, between the British heirs of J.K. Fisher and the Austrian heirs of Mrs. Kramer, widow of Fisher. The British plaintiff, C. Fisher, opposed the division requested by the *kadı* court, maintaining that the *molla*'s (senior judge's) jurisdiction "ceased when the question of ownership was decided by him," and that "division of property of whatever kind among European heirs should be made by their own authorities."[12] In contrast, the Austrian court, which generally played a more active role in similar cases, chose to declare itself incompetent and recognize the *molla*'s division, based on Islamic law, which dovetailed all too conveniently with the interest of its own subjects.

Gaps and blind spots in legal procedures also offered openings that allowed litigants to sway the case in their favor. A case in point was the ill-defined provision of having a *dragoman* (official interpreter) accompany the foreign litigant at the *kadı* court. Extraterritorial agreements called for the presence of

---

[10] Until the creation of a land registry in 1850s, title deeds for *mülk* were prepared at the *kadı* court in presence of the parties. Long-term leases for *vakıf* property were drafted by endowment administrators (*mütevelli*) and then delivered to the *kadı* court to complete the transaction.

[11] For example, while the *kadı* court had a more procedural cast of mind and sought to settle the case in a language compliant with the precepts of Islamic legal tradition, the consular court saw property in terms of granting or prohibiting absolute rights.

[12] PRO/FO 195/389, Fisher to Brant, April 30,1853.

a dragoman in cases with mixed litigants. Property suits, however, were based on the assumption that all parties to the litigation were Ottoman subjects. Hence the presence of a dragoman was a contradiction in terms. This was, at least, the perspective of Ottoman authorities in a suit brought in 1851 by an Armenian Ottoman subject, Hripsima, against Manoli Vapopoulo, a British subject, who refused to appear at court without the presence of his dragoman. A few days prior to declaring bankruptcy, Vapopoulo had his friend, a Greek Ottoman subject—under whose name he had formerly bought a warehouse—promise the property to an unsuspecting Hripsima who had already paid the purchase price. Meanwhile, unaware of this deal, the British consulate authorized Vapopoulo's creditors to seize his warehouse, making the same property subject to multiple claims.[13] Although the eventual settlement of the case remains unknown, Vapopoulo's insistence on bringing his dragoman was clearly a delaying tactic that postponed an unfavorable sentence for more than a year. Notwithstanding these complications and ongoing demand for more clear-cut procedures on the part of consuls—especially when third-party ownership raised vexing problems for foreign subjects—the rewards seem to have far exceeded potential frustrations, enticing people to invest in property, hence creating sufficiently stable and lasting, albeit constantly negotiated, arrangements that acquired the legitimacy and authority of bylaws.

Against this fluid background, in the 1860s, property ownership and inheritance rights took on an undeniably political significance as the Tanzimat regime sought to bring within the remit of Ottoman jurisdictions all individuals whose extraterritorial immunities undercut tax revenues and impeded local police action. At the Congress of Paris in 1856, where the Ottoman Empire was finally inducted to the Concert of Europe, Âli Pasha, minister of Foreign Affairs and zealous advocate of modernization reforms, declared that such privileges were incompatible with the norms of modern sovereignty and European public law and constituted an "intractable obstacle to any kind of improvement."[14] In a memorandum he sent in 1860, Âli Pasha announced to foreign legations that the Ottoman government categorically refused to recognize new protégés, asking such individuals either to leave the country within three months or to accept being treated as Ottoman subjects. He also required such individuals to sell their property prior to their departure and underlined that hereafter

---

[13] PRO/FO 195/389, Âli Pasha to Canning, December 10, 1851 and Brant to Canning, December 18, 1852.

[14] Transcript of the Congress of Paris in PRO/FO 78/1787, enclosed in Erskine to Russell, November 12, 1862.

they would be denied the right to inherit from their Ottoman parents.[15] While these drastic measures were impossible to implement in full, they ushered in a series of crucial provisions that linked real property to Ottoman sovereignty in unprecedented ways.

In Izmir, Âli Pasha's pronouncement stirred, most immediately, the question of third-party tenure, especially the widespread practice of using foreign female fronts. Ottoman authorities took an uncompromising stance and began to treat all proprietresses as bona fide Ottoman subjects. This procedure, wittingly or not, shielded foreign women from liability in the consular court, creating undeniable hurdles for these courts, when, for example, they had to issue a property repossession order in the case of the male relative's bankruptcy.[16] In tandem, the central government introduced more stringent identity checks for property transfers and sales. Those who wished to purchase property had first to obtain from their religious leader a certificate (*ilm-u haber*) that established their Ottoman subjecthood and their membership in that particular ethno-religious community (or *millet*). Following successive official orders sent from Istanbul in 1862, the measure was enforced unequivocally, tightening the screw on property registration in Izmir. Thereafter, all real estate purchase and sale contracts effected through private agreement or before a foreign authority—such as a consul—would be considered null and void.[17]

Within a matter of weeks, the measure suspended the registration of scores of transactions, making it clear to foreign subjects and protégés that their hold on property was at the mercy of the Ottoman state. It also categorically closed a vital loophole in Izmir's property market, cutting deeply into the interests of a significant portion of the population. In response, affected property owners forcefully argued their case in the local press to ensure the Porte heard their claims, insisting that the measure would inevitably lead to the collapse of the real estate market in the empire's second city. The consuls implored their respective governments to intervene on behalf of their subjects. They claimed that the Porte was acting arbitrarily by halting a practice that it had "admitted and acknowledged for nearly two hundred years," thus, in effect, denouncing the clear-cut procedures they had been demanding all along.[18] As Etienne Pisani, dragoman of the British embassy in Istanbul, declared, however, the Ottoman government had never knowingly admitted or sanctioned property ownership by foreign parties. The many foreign women who held property

---

[15] Pélissié du Rausas 1902, 2:36–40. The memorandum had repercussions across the empire. For its impact in Aleppo and Damascus, see Rafeq 2000.

[16] See the cases collected in PRO/FO 78/1787, 1861–1863.

[17] *L'Impartial*, July 14, 1862, enclosed in PRO/FO 78/1902, Lee to Russell, July 26, 1862.

[18] PRO/FO 195/720, Blunt to Bulwer, August 2, 1862.

in their own names were "allowed to hold it under the fiction that they are subjects of the Porte."[19] By abstaining from using their surnames in the title deeds, foreign-born women had willingly confounded themselves with their Ottoman-born counterparts, further sustaining this legal fiction.[20] Moreover, the Tanzimat regime countered Izmir's affected property owners' attacks by mobilizing Istanbul's foreign language press. James Carlile McCoan, founder and editor of the semi-official weekly, the *Levant Herald*, commended the measure for rectifying a fraudulent practice and doing away with large numbers of "sham protected subjects," blaming instead European subjects and protégés.[21]

Beyond its impact on Smyrniot proprietors, the measure changed the terms of the debate. Not only was a long-held property tenure practice recast as a legal fiction and an evasion of the law, but more importantly, it was also presented as a legitimate act of sovereignty by a modern state over its internationally recognized territories. Before long the issue escalated into an international crisis, forcing foreign missions to address what they had already been seeing as a difficult and complex question.[22] Eventually, in 1867, following long-drawn-out negotiations between the Porte, which wanted to sap extraterritorial jurisdictions, and foreign governments, which refused to relinquish them, an imperial decree recognized foreigners' right to own land in their own names on the condition that they submitted to Ottoman laws and accepted to be considered as Ottoman subjects in all matters concerning land and property.[23] In other words, foreign owners would give up their privileges and comply with Ottoman territorial jurisdictions except for the immunities attached to their person and their movable goods.

Although granting foreign subjects the privilege of owning real estate may seem to be yet another concession to foreign powers, the conditions within which this decree was issued suggest that it was proactive. For the Ottoman government, the decree was a tactical move that unmistakably asserted its territorial sovereignty. As mentioned earlier, prior to 1867 foreign subjects could not officially own property, although in practice they did. By explicitly granting them this right, however, the decree brought foreign property owners and their property under greater state control. Compliance with police regulations, tax obligations, and Ottoman laws (article 2) now became uniformly enforceable on foreign subjects—albeit for issues pertaining primarily to their property. The

---

[19] PRO/FO 78/1787, Pisani to Bulwer, November 5, 1861.

[20] PRO/FO 78/1787, Bulwer to Hornby, November 13, 1861; CADN/FC 50, "Note," 1872.

[21] *Levant Herald*, July 16, 1862.

[22] PRO/FO 78/1787, Bulwer, de Moustier, Prokesch-Oster, and Sohanov to Âli Pasha February 15, 1862.

[23] Aristarchi Bey 1873, 1:19–25. The 1867 decree applied throughout the empire, with the exception of the province of Hicaz.

decree also explicitly denied property rights to native-born Ottoman subjects who had acquired foreign naturalization (article 1). The Ottoman government had already been making concomitant efforts at checking consular protections and regulating dubious identity claims through a series of measures and countermeasures. The first of these came in 1863 as a result of international negotiations and brought strict limitations over the protégé status. Henceforth protections would only be granted with the approval of Ottoman authorities; they would no longer protect the entire household or be inherited. Rather, the benefits would be limited to a specific individual for the duration of his appointment. The new measure restricted further expansion of the protégé status, although it grandfathered those who had acquired it prior to the 1863 decree, resulting in two classes of protégés: permanent and temporary.[24] Most significantly, the 1863 measure triggered a considerable surge in the number of Ottoman subjects pursuing foreign naturalizations.[25]

Given these changes, the 1867 decree also constituted a strategic first step in deterring Ottoman subjects from acquiring foreign nationalities. While it brought foreigners on a more even footing with Ottoman subjects by granting them ownership rights in return for certain citizenship duties, it also categorically deprived Ottoman subjects who renounced their nationality in favor of another country from sharing similar benefits. In 1869, the Ottoman government went further and issued the Ottoman Nationality Law (*Tabiyet-i Osmaniye Kanunu*), which denied Ottoman subjects the possibility of renouncing their subjecthood without government authorization. The law also permitted the government to rescind Ottoman subjecthood from anyone who acquired foreign naturalization without prior official consent, thereby limiting their inheritance and ownership rights.[26]

Meanwhile, European nations made explicit claims over those they considered their own subjects. In signing the terms of the 1867 protocol—a process which took up to seven years for some signatory states—each foreign government ensured that except for questions of property and land, the protocol did not undermine their rights and control over their subjects.[27] Eventually, although the protocol did not entirely eradicate frictions and concerned parties often interpreted its provisions differently, it nevertheless placed Izmir's foreigners in a curious legal position. By virtue of the property they owned, they became

---

[24] Pélissié du Rausas 1902; Steen de Jehay 1906; Brown 1914:93–95.

[25] Testa et al. 1864, 7:542–545.

[26] Testa et al. 1864, 7:526–527.

[27] Susa 1933:83–84n39. Britain, France, Austria, and the Netherlands signed the protocol by 1869, followed reluctantly by Russia, Greece, and Italy, who had the largest numbers of *protégés*, and eventually by Prussia and the United States in 1874.

Ottoman subjects and were made to conform to the resulting obligations. Yet these new ownership rights and duties did not undo their foreign nationality. For other matters related to their person and movables, they retained their foreign privileges and immunities and, by extension, the rights and duties they held towards their respective governments. In short, they became part-Ottoman and part-foreign subjects, or in the language of Istanbul's French-language press, "*sujets Ottomans étrangers*"-that is, foreign Ottoman subjects, as opposed to foreign subjects.[28]

This hybrid category, through which both Ottoman and various foreign states made claims, is telling in a number of ways. First, it articulated a new relationship between property and modern sovereignty. Accordingly, property was not only a source of socio-economic power for its possessor or a source of revenue for the state. It was also a strategic instrument through which the Ottoman state sought to extend its power onto groups that formerly eluded its jurisdiction. Second, and perhaps more importantly, this elaborately negotiated category points to the difficulty of arriving at the kinds of clear-cut demarcations that modern state rule demands. Through most of the nineteenth century, the Ottoman regime remained remarkably resilient, accommodating multiple claims—even over the same assets and individuals and despite the obvious asymmetry of power, in which foreign states were chipping away at its sovereignty and seeking to assert themselves within its own territories.

Diplomacy and the Staging of Sovereignties

Property was not the only arena in which competing state powers were played out in everyday urban interactions. In the mid-nineteenth century, as the world's geopolitical realignment was in flux, diplomatic conduct and its repertoire of visual and material expressions were the means through which states preserved legitimacy and asserted their claims for recognition in the international arena. Flags and banners, uniforms and military parades, gun salutes and honor guards standing at attention acquired a new prominence in many parts of the world.[29] By moving international politics from the documentary to the spectacular, they gave a concrete character to diplomatic activity. As evidenced in official records and local newspapers, these tools were also deployed in Istanbul and major Ottoman urban centers to honor the national anniversaries or the birthday of the sovereigns of friendly nations and commemorate the sultan's birthday and accession day.

---

[28] *La Turquie,* June 6, 1871.
[29] Cannadine 2001; Goodman 2000; Anderson 1983; Smith 1987.

In Izmir, where 16 different countries—Britain, France, the Austro-Hungarian Empire, Russia, Greece, Italy, Germany, the Netherlands, Belgium, Denmark, Samos, Spain, Portugal, Persia, the United States, and Sweden and Norway—had official representation in the late 1870s, national days (*yevm-i mahsus*) were regularly observed through a range of formal and informal events. Foreign colonies held special religious services and dinners at their consulates, and set up street parties and theatrical performances to display national loyalties. In addition to social events, they performed diplomatic protocols appropriate to the size and prestige of the local colony. Generally, official celebrations began in the morning hours with an exchange of the royal 21-gun salute—the standard show of military power used in rendering the highest honors to sovereign states. Next, consulates hoisted their flags and received greetings from local Ottoman government officials, foreign consuls, their staff, and military commanders, all in their elaborate official uniforms. These symbolic enactments made state sovereignty and national community visible both within the borders of another sovereign country and in relation to other sovereign entities.

Although, in 1815, the Congress of Vienna prescribed consular dress codes and standard rules for diplomatic ceremonies to prevent the frequent controversies that occurred over the rank and precedence of states, rivalry for prestige and authority remained integral to diplomatic exchange in many parts of the nineteenth-century world. In Izmir, where all European powers had representation but none had managed to establish dominance, opportunistic appropriations of honors were not uncommon. Contending nations pulled rank and used diplomatic events to assert their superiority over one another. Given these competitions and increasing ceremonial regulations, ostensibly minor symbolic transactions could be magnified as expressions of national pride and rivalry. The importance attached to national flags during diplomatic ceremonies was a case in point. National flags had long been visible expressions of international presence in Izmir. They were flown over foreign ships at harbor, consulates, designated religious institutions, and similar buildings under foreign protection. These emblems, however, were also powerful tools to jockey for power and visibility in a multinational city. That France and Austria relentlessly flew their flags over two contiguous sections of the same Franciscan complex, the former over the Archbishop's House and the latter atop the adjacent Church of St. Mary, is a good illustration of the competing claims these states made over the protection of the complex—and by implication over the Catholics of the empire.[30] In a low-rise cityscape that visitors and foreign dignitaries approached primarily from the water, flags were meant to be seen from afar. Like minarets and church

[30] CADN/FC 46, Mure de Pélanne to Moustier, September 6, 1862.

towers, they organized the skyline and they stood against it as prominent statements of power. [Figure 4]

In the course of the second half of the nineteenth century, raising the national flag during diplomatic events became an essential device of political communication. Precisely because they lent themselves to quick changes, flag displays were effective indicators of the fluctuations in international politics as they happened. For example, on the coronation of Napoleon III in 1852, which was officially celebrated in Izmir, all consulates, with the exception of those of Austria, Prussia, Russia, and the United States, were reported to have raised their flags to honor France—although the Austrian and Prussian consuls presented personal regrets for having to refrain on the grounds that France had not yet accredited the ministers of their governments in Paris.[31] Similarly, in the years following the reunification of a large part of the Italian peninsula by King Victor-Emmanuel, only the consulates of governments that recognized the new Italian Kingdom hoisted their flag on the King's birthday.[32] And when the Spanish consulate did not raise its flag on Queen Victoria's birthday, the British consul refused to give his Spanish colleague the customary honors presented to diplomatic representatives when he came on the British ship in harbor.[33] The sheer number of consular and newspaper reports on this matter reveal the extent to which flags and corresponding honors were the means of choice for broadcasting adversarial or friendly messages between states on third-party soil.

Diplomatic enactments also provided occasions for foreign missions to enlist the sympathies of local populations and for local expatriates to express their allegiances to their home countries. On the birth of a male heir to the French throne in 1856, the French ship at harbor, the batteries on shore, and the Ottoman station-ship exchanged a rare 101 imperial gun salute and all consulates hoisted their flags. A detachment of French, Ottoman, and British squads marched in line through the streets, presenting an extravagant military feast, while the French consulate, illuminated for two nights, offered a glowing spectacle. Moreover, the consular gate and vestibule were decked with the French, Ottoman, and British flags and banners, shaped like trophies and topped with the imperial eagle. "Through the streets leading to the College and from the consulate to the French Church, one heard only good wishes and congratulations for the illustrious offspring of the great emperor," rejoiced the reporter to the *Journal de Constantinople, L'Écho de l'Orient* (March 31, 1856). Such spectacular and sensory celebrations became increasingly more common in the later part

---

[31]   CADN/FC 44, Pichon to Lavalette, December 22, 1852.
[32]   *Journal de Constantinople*, March 23, 1864.
[33]   PRO/FO 195/1075, May 27, 1876.

of the nineteenth century, coinciding with parallel developments in Europe. Feasts in honor of the Duchess of Edinburgh's visit to Izmir in 1876, the jubilee of Queen Victoria in 1887, and Bastille Day celebrations from the early 1880s onward were reported in great detail and with great pride to the respective Foreign Offices of home governments, particularly on account of the crowds they drew and the good order and respect they instilled. Such patriotic enactments not only linked foreign colonies to their home countries, helping cultivate a "will to nationhood,"[34] they also created opportunities for foreign governments to extend their cultural influence in foreign lands.

To be sure, Ottoman statesmen were not indifferent to such displays on their land. In a world that was increasingly organized around the principles of modern diplomacy, they were quick to adopt new procedures in line with European norms and use them to claim diplomatic equivalence and reciprocity. They also banned diplomatic shows and military displays that could potentially undercut Ottoman sovereignty and make them look inferior on their own turf. For example, in 1859 central authorities notified provincial governors that the celebrations of allied sovereigns were limited to one day per year, either on their onomastic or coronation day. In the hoisting of flags, gun salutes, and other military honors in ceremonial occasions, the government prescribed the use of international codes, which considered all sovereign states equal. Accordingly, gun salutes had to be reciprocated either with an equal salute from sea or a similar salute from land in the absence of Ottoman vessels of less than 10 canons in harbor.[35]

Similarly, an 1870 circular abolished the ostentatious custom of displaying military honors to new consuls arriving at an Ottoman port city. Instead, it required the raising of national flags over the consulate in question and the local citadel, in conformity with contemporary European practice.[36] Furthermore, new regulations enacted in the following years streamlined the ceremonial honors accorded to ambassadors and diplomatic agents in light of the stipulations of the Congress of Vienna, although such actions drew vehement protests from heads of foreign missions who maintained that the Ottoman Empire had not been a signatory in the Congress of Vienna.[37] Whether or not these procedures could be entirely implemented in Izmir, they illustrate the extent to

---

[34] Renan 1882.
[35] Aristarchi Bey 1873, 4:22–44. These and similar instructions were sent to all diplomatic missions and consulates. See e.g. PRO/FO 195/720, December 2, 1862; CADN/FC 46, February 28, 1863. On maritime international codes, see Testa 1886:113–121.
[36] Young 1905, 3:42n1.
[37] Young 1905, 3:42.

which Ottoman statesmen turned the new tools of diplomatic conduct to their advantage.

On occasion, diplomatic controversies erupted over the propriety of displaying national flags on local institutions—despite general rules that limited these displays to embassies and consulates. In 1862, for example, the display of the Austrian flag on the building of the Armenian Mekhitarist mission in the neighboring town of Aydın became a bone of contention between local authorities, foreign representatives, and the local mission. The deputy governor (*kaymakam*) prohibited the mission from using a foreign flag, as was ordinarily done in Izmir. Although the mission received Austrian support, the governor argued that the practice was unacceptable since both the missionaries and the congregation consisted of Ottoman subjects.[38] In assuming a direct correlation between a state's national flag and the allegiances of the body of citizens on its territories, local officials shrewdly used the logic of modern territorial sovereignty against Austria to counter its efforts at staking claims over Ottoman subjects.

Admittedly, Izmir's particular situation afforded more latitude for ceremonial innovation and expression. The semi-official press frequently decried the conspicuous breach of international norms in the city. "In every country of the world the national flag is privileged over foreign flags. In Turkey, it is different," scathingly noted the Izmir correspondent to the *Journal de Constantinople*. "Foreign flags are favored at the expense of the national one" (July 21, 1860). Nevertheless, the risk of diplomatic friction and local authorities' stance towards a specific event placed explicit and implicit limits on how such events should be performed in Izmir.

In conjunction with efforts at countering diplomatic displays in their territories, Ottoman officials introduced their own protocols that both affirmed the empire's sovereignty over its domestic constituencies and asserted its rightful place within the emerging international system. During Abdülmecid's reign (1839–1861), the central government encouraged celebrations of imperial power on occasions such as the anniversaries of the sultan's accession to the throne (*cülus-u humayun*) and birthday (*veladet-i padişah*).[39] These celebrations were not new, but they acquired a new dimension as public events observed on an annual basis throughout the empire. While previously they structured the rhythms of courtly life in Istanbul, in the course of the second half of the nineteenth century they gradually spilled out to other provinces to organize time and space across the empire.

---

[38] CADN/FC 46, September 6, 1862.
[39] Karateke 2004; Deringil 1998.

In Izmir, imperial events and most remarkably the visits of two consecutive sultans to the city—Abdülmecid in 1850 and Abdülaziz in 1863—eclipsed all other displays in size and scope. Diplomatic events were played out in clearly demarcated areas of the city, primarily along Frank Street where most consulates and foreign commercial establishments were located and along the harbor where foreign ships anchored. [Figure 5] In contrast, imperial celebrations took over the entire city to convey a sense of all-inclusiveness and Ottoman dominance at home. Street decorations and nighttime illumination overrode everyday divisions and boundaries, reinforcing the appearance of a unified people. On these occasions, every government building and consulate put out flags and illuminations. The residences of the Greek and Armenian Patriarchs and Jewish Rabbi and the mansions of local notables and merchants across communities were adorned and similarly illuminated, as were the lavishly decked vessels at harbor. Major thoroughfares such as Frank Street and *Kemeraltı* Street (the ring road around the bazaar) also had their shops and houses festooned with myrtle and evergreens.[40]

Imperial celebrations went beyond temporarily appropriating the city's existing public spaces to convey a message. They brought about permanent changes in the urban fabric. The arrival of Sultan Abdülmecid, for example, prompted the governor to repave all major streets and add an ornamental iron balustrade to the Caravan Bridge—the gateway to the city from its hinterland.[41] Moreover, until the late 1860s, there was no formally designed space for state performances in Izmir. The governor's house consisted of an old timber-framed mansion adjacent to the bazaar area—the *Kâtipzade konağı*, built in 1804. On official days, most large-scale social events such as balls and receptions had to be carried out on board ships, as the size and condition of existing outdoor spaces and building stock could no longer sustain the pomp and circumstance that these festivities required.[42] The construction of a new government palace (or *Konak*) between 1868 and 1871, and the creation of a formal outdoor space around it, added to the prestige of state institutions and made the area more fit for stately and splendid ceremonial exercises. [Figure 6] In the following years, the displays created on imperial celebrations acquired a more sumptuous character. On one occasion, it was reported that specially made braziers, reading *Maşallah* (a word of praise, literally "God willed it") when lit, were placed on every alley and thoroughfare; that fireworks were kept up from sunset till midnight; and that sightseers in small boats glided back and forth to admire the

[40] Gardey 1865:230–235.
[41] CADN/FC 43, Pichon to Aupick, June 28, 1850.
[42] *Levant Herald*, July 5, 1865.

continuous line of illumination overlooking the harbor.[43] After most consulates moved from Frank Street to Izmir's new quay, completed in the late 1870s, on festive days the waterfront was turned into a protocol strip. Framed on one side by the consulates raising their flags and on the other by steamers of different nations anchored at the harbor and flying colorful bunting, the area became a festive showcase. [Figure 7]

Most importantly, imperial events provided opportunities for the Ottoman state to demand the reciprocation of diplomatic honors parallel to the ones it offered foreign states with diplomatic representation on its lands. After the governor announced an upcoming feast, consuls and the consular offices had to conform to a set repertoire of requirements. For example, they had to decorate and illuminate the consulate for the duration of the festivities. They had to hoist their flag to reciprocate Ottoman gun salutes fired several times throughout the day. Consuls and their staff also had to take part in person in the official ceremonies. In the morning hours, they were the first group to present their congratulations to the governor. Their participation in ceremonial uniform (*büyük üniforma*) and in the company of their dragomans was integral to the new Ottoman ceremonial conventions.

Ceremonial uniforms and illuminations were considerable expenses that reveal the extent of the demands the Ottoman government placed on foreign legations. Ottoman ceremonial codes prescribed full uniforms and medals to be worn during all diplomatic visits. Ceremonial uniforms represented the status and authority of the bearer and indicated the level of honor accorded to the receiving party. Indeed, when the American consular uniform was revoked in 1853 to be replaced with the simple dress of the citizen, the consul of Izmir objected to the United States Secretary of State. Highlighting the profound political meaning attributed to uniforms in Izmir, he insisted that: "This regulation cannot be put in practice without some inconvenience particularly in the intercourse between the consulate and the local authorities, as they generally attach more importance to external distinctions than to anything else."[44] Similarly, illuminations of consular buildings constituted an imposition that required the consulates to demand additional funds from their home country. The repeated requests by the consulates from their home offices indicate not only the ability of the Ottoman government to enforce diplomatic reciprocity beyond the limits of its capital, but also attest to Izmir's increasing prominence as an arena for displays of international diplomacy.

---

[43] *Levant Herald*, July 9, 1873.
[44] DUSCS, Offley to secretary of state, August 5, 1853.

Conclusion

The practices I examine in this chapter signal incipient shifts in Ottoman rule, from a permeable, imperial territorial regime, based on accommodative practices, to a modern territoriality premised on more exclusionary practices. Historically, the Ottoman state had used extraterritorial exemptions and similar group-based privileges to attract diverse peoples to live and work within the empire, benefitting, in turn, from their economic activities. But these exemptions were becoming increasingly disruptive for the centralizing Ottoman state and were undermining its position within the emerging international state system. Hence the 1867 protocol—signed with foreign powers and formally recognizing non-Ottoman subjects' property rights—demanded, in exchange, subjections to Ottoman laws in all matters related to real estate, seeking to bring a highly differentiated group more evenly under state jurisdiction. Similarly, the Tanzimat government formalized and placed restrictions on diplomatic displays, aligning them with international norms to shore up its legitimacy in the domestic and international spheres.

While Izmir offers a telling case study, the challenges of implementing modern forms of territoriality were by no means unique to the Ottoman setting. Claiming exclusive control over a physical terrain and over the people living, conducting business, and investing in it, standardizing citizenship and property rights, and regulating ceremonial conduct are telltale signs of states territorializing their sovereignty. The struggles detailed in this chapter echo, if not replicate, processes elsewhere in the nineteenth-century world, and especially those in multinational empires. More importantly, however, the measures and tensions that are at the core of this chapter demonstrate how modern territoriality was intimately and reciprocally bound up with the city's material resources and assets. To begin with, state sovereignty is neither experienced nor implemented in the abstract. Rather, it is enacted through the world of artifacts by granting certain people rights to or placing constraints on their access to certain resources and spaces. Moreover, the particularities of sovereignty depend not only on geopolitical considerations and interstate negotiations but also on the specificity of place and space. On-the-ground resistance and opportunistic actions trickle up to inform the issues that states may, in turn, take up and fight over. In sum, as the foregoing pages have shown, the nature of sovereignty, its boundaries, policies, and zones of contention are inherently fluid and negotiated through everyday spaces and transactions.

Abbreviations

CADN/FC   Centre des Archives Diplomatiques de Nantes, Fonds Constantinople, Séries D, Correspondance Consulaire: Smyrne.

DUSCS   Despatches from United States Consuls in Smyrna. National Archives Microfilm Publication, Washington, DC.

PRO/FO   Public Record Office, Foreign Office, From Smyrna. National Archives, Kew.

Works Cited

Agnew, J. 1994. "The Territorial Trap: The Geographical Assumptions of International Relations Theory." *Review of International Political Economy* 1, no. 1 (Spring):53–80.

Akarlı, E. 2004. "Gedik: A Bundle of Rights and Obligations for Istanbul Artisans and Traders, 1750–1840." In Pottage and Mundy 2004:166–200.

Aliotti, A. 1900. *Des Français en Turquie; Spécialement au point de vue de la proprieté immobilière et du régime successoral.* Paris.

Anastassiadou, M. 1997. *Salonique, 1830–1912.* Leiden.

Anderson, B. 1983. *Imagined Communities: Reflections on the Origin and Spread of Nationalism.* London.

Anderson, J. 1996. "The Shifting Stage of Politics: New Medieval and Postmodern Territorialities?" *Environment and Planning D: Society and Space* 14, no. 2: 133–153.

Aristarchi Bey, G. 1873. *Législation ottomane ou Recueil des lois, règlements, ordonnances, traités, capitulations et autres documents officiels de l' empire ottoman.* 7 vols. Constantinople.

Barnes, J. R. 1987. *An Introduction to Religious Foundations in the Ottoman Empire.* Leiden.

Brown, P. 1914. *Foreigners in Turkey: Their Juridical Status.* Princeton.

CADN/FC. 1848–1877. Vols 43–50. Nantes.

———. 1872. "Note de la commission pour la défense de la propriété, en réponse à la circulaire de S.E. Server pacha, ministre des affaires étrangères de la Sublime-Porte, relative à l'impôt foncier à Smyrne." v. 50 (3 February):1–13.

Cannadine, D. 2001. *Ornamentalism: How the British Saw Their Empire.* Oxford.

Collas, M. B. C. 1864. *La Turquie en 1864.* Paris.

Çelik, Z. 2008. *Empire, Architecture, and the City: French-Ottoman Encounters, 1830–1914.* Seattle.

Deringil, S. 1998. *The Well-Protected Domains: Ideology and the Legitimation of Power in the Ottoman Empire, 1876–1909.* London.

DUSCS. 1853. Washington, DC.

———. 1872. "Memorial to the Honorable Hamilton Fish, Secretary of State of the United States of America from the American Residents at Smyrna, Turkey." (20 July): 1–30. Washington, DC.

Gardey, L. 1865. *Voyage du Sultan Abd-ul-Aziz de Stamboul au Caire*. Paris.

Goodman, B. 2000. "Improvisations on a Semicolonial Theme, or, How to Read a Celebration of Transnational Urban Community." *The Journal of Asian Studies* 59, no. 4 (November): 889–926.

Journal de Constantinople. 1856–1865. Constantinople.

Journal de Constantinople, l'Écho de l'Orient. 1846–1856. Constantinople.

Karateke, H. T. 2004. *Padişahım çok yaşa!: Osmanlı devletinin son yüz yılında merasimler*. İstanbul.

Karpat, K. 1985. *Ottoman Population, 1830–1914: Demographic and Social Characteristics*. Madison, WI.

Kütükoğlu, M. 2000. "Izmir şehri nüfusu üzerine bazı tesbitler." In *İzmir Tarihinden Kesitler*, 11–33. İzmir.

Levant Herald. 1860-1890. Constantinople.

McCoan, J. C. 1879. *Our New Protectorate: Turkey in Asia: Its Geography, Races, Resources, and Government*. London.

Owen, R., ed. 2000. *New Perspectives on Property and Land in the Middle East*. Cambridge, MA.

Pélissié du Rausas, G. 1902. *Le régime des capitulations dans l'empire Ottoman*. 2 vols. Paris.

Pottage, A. and Mundy, M. 2004. *Law, Anthropology and the Constitution of the Social: Making Persons and Things*. New York.

PRO/FO. 1852–76. Vols. 78/1787, 1902; 195/389, 447, 720, 1075. Kew.

PRO/FO, 195/447, "Report of July 13, 1854 meeting," Brant to de Redcliffe, July 20, 1854. Kew.

PRO/FO 195/720 "Valuation of property held by foreigners in Smyrna," Blunt to Bulwer, August 2, 1862. Kew.

Rafeq, A.-K. 2000. "Ownership of Real Property by Foreigners in Syria." In Owen, ed.:175–239.

Reilly, J. A. 1989. "Status Groups and Propertyholding in the Damascus Hinterland, 1828–1880." *IJMES* 21, no. 4 (November): 517–539.

Renan, E. 1882. *Qu'est-ce qu'une nation? Conférence faite en Sorbonne, le 11 mars 1882*. Paris.

Ruggie, J. G. 1993. "Territoriality and Beyond: Problematizing Modernity in International Relations." *International Organization* 47, no. 1 (Winter): 139–174.

Scott, J. C. 1998. *Seeing Like a State: How Certain Schemes to Improve the Human Condition Have Failed.* New Haven.

Smith, A. D. 1987. *The Ethnic Origins of Nations.* Oxford.

Smyrnelis, M.-C. 2005. *Une société hors de soi: Identités et relations sociales à Smyrne au XVIIIème et XIXème siècles.* Paris.

Steen de Jehay, F. M. J. G. van. 1906. *De la situation légale des sujets ottomans non-musulmans.* Bruxelles.

Susa, N. 1933. *The Capitulatory Régime of Turkey: Its History, Origin, and Nature.* Baltimore.

Testa, C. 1886. *Le droit public international maritime.* Paris.

Testa, I., Testa A., and Testa L. 1864. *Recueil des traités de la porte ottomane avec les puissances étrangères, depuis le premier traité conclu en 1536, entre Suléyman I et François I jusqu'à nos jours.* 11 vols. Paris.

La Turquie. 1866–1890. Constantinople.

Vale, L. J. 1992. *Architecture, Power, and National Identity.* New Haven.

Van Dyck, E. 1881. *Report on the Capitulations of the Ottoman Empire.* Washington.

Young, G. 1905. *Corps de droit ottoman: Recueil des codes, lois, règlements, ordonnances et actes les plus importants du droit intérieur, et d'études sur le droit coutumier de l'empire ottoman.* Oxford.

The Port of Smyrna.

Figure 4: View of flags from the shore, ca. 1850. Flags were an important aspect of Izmir's panorama. On special occasions, foreign flags were hoisted on consular buildings, while the Ottoman flag crowned the citadel on Mount Pagus, the commanding hill rising behind the city.
From William Harrison De Puy. *People's Cyclopedia of Universal Knowledge.*
New York: Phillips and Hunt, 1883.

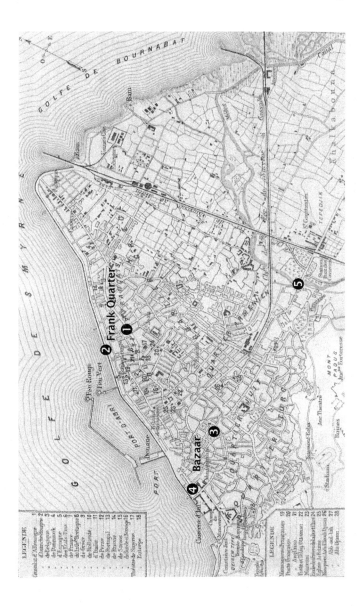

Figure 5: Map of Izmir, based on a map of the city by Demetrios Georgiades, 1880s.
From Demetrios Georgiades. *Smyrne et l'Asie Mineure au point de vue économique et commercial* (Paris: Chaix, 1885).
Legend: 1. Frank Street; 2. Quay; 3. Kemeraltı Street; 4. Konak; 5. Caravan Bridge.

Figure 6: Postcard: View of Konak Square, showing the governor's palace and the military barracks to the right. The clock tower was added in 1901 to mark the twenty-fifth anniversary of Abdülhamid's accession to the throne.
Courtesy of the Suna & İnan Kıraç Research Institute for Mediterranean Civilizations.

Figure 7: Postcard: View of the quay during ceremonies for the accession to the throne, 1909.
Courtesy of the Suna & İnan Kıraç Research Institute for Mediterranean Civilizations.

7

Ottoman Arabs in Istanbul, 1860-1914

Perceptions of Empire, Experiences of the
Metropole through the Writings of
Aḥmad Fāris al-Shidyāq, Muḥammad Rashīd Riḍā,
and Jirjī Zaydān

Ilham Khuri-Makdisi

I T IS A WELL-KNOWN FACT that Arab intellectuals—Egyptians, Syrians, North Africans, and others—traveled to Europe and wrote about their impressions of European capitals throughout the long nineteenth century, and to a lesser degree earlier.[1] Much has been written on the "discovery" of Europe by people like Rifā'a al-Ṭahṭāwī, Khayr al-Dīn al-Tūnisī, Aḥmad Fāris al-Shidyāq, Francīs al-Marrāsh, and countless others, who wrote vivid, entertaining, instructive, perceptive, and stereotypical accounts on Europeans (especially French), European cities, and Western civilization. This encounter has been traditionally viewed as profoundly transformative for the individual traveler, and one that constituted a foundational moment in the shaping of Arab Modernity and decisively shaped the *nahda,* or the Arab intellectual Renaissance of the nineteenth century. More so, while there are definite differences between the authors' writings on Europe, the existing body of literature, as well as the presence and development of common tropes, themes, concepts, and stereotypes, make it possible to talk of these descriptions as constituting a genre.[2] It is equally well known that empires, and especially metropoles, have produced a body of knowledge on "the Other" in the empire's peripheries or beyond. While empires may differ

---

[1] For early modern North African travelers to Istanbul and their descriptions of the city, see Matar 2009.

[2] Yared 1996; Hourani 1962. See also the many publications recently produced by Dar al-Suwaydi, which are translations of travel narratives (*Riḥla*) from the Arabic, the overwhelming majority of which are travels to Europe.

quite substantially, and while early modern empires such as the Ottoman and the Austro-Hungarian Empires differed from British or French ones diachronically and synchronically, some historians have aptly applied some of the concepts and methodological approaches traditionally reserved to the study of European "maritime" empires—such as the notions of "othering" and orientalizing—onto the Ottoman Empire.[3]

However, what happens if we shift the question of "Imperial Geographies" 180 degrees? In the context of the long nineteenth century and within the Ottoman Empire, how did "provincial" Arabs experience and view Istanbul, the empire's metropole? What tropes appear in their writings? How do their experiences and perceptions of Istanbul compare with their contemporaries' (or their own) experiences and impressions of Paris or London? These are some of the questions that this chapter sets out to explore. A few preliminary remarks are in order: first, this is (to the best of my knowledge) uncharted territory. For all sorts of reasons, this topic has received scant attention among scholars of the Ottoman Empire. One of the reasons might well be the dearth of primary sources, a fact reflected in this chapter's focus on three authors and a close reading of their writings. Nonetheless, this seeming absence of sources does not necessarily mean that they do not exist; rather that, if they do, they remain obscure and most likely unpublished. Hence, one of this chapter's aims is to call for further research on the topic by suggesting possible theoretical and thematic questions based on a few sources. At the same time, we should keep in mind that this supposed lack of sources did not mean Arabs did not travel to Istanbul or reside there in the nineteenth century. Indeed, many reasons brought them to the Empire's capital from present-day Egypt, Syria, Lebanon, Iraq, North Africa, and the Arabian peninsula: trade; study, in both "traditional" madrasa institutions, as well as in "modern" schools and colleges, including the law school, military academies, and the school of medicine;[4] employment in the Ottoman administrative system or the receipt of State decorations; appealing for justice or clemency;[5] or self- or state-imposed exile (among other reasons).[6] However, while some of these visitors ended up residing in Istanbul for a few years, most of them did not write. Or when they wrote, they did not write about Istanbul specifically, but about the empire as a whole.

A second preliminary remark is that, while the sources available do not quite constitute an embarrassment of riches, it would be a grave injustice to underplay the importance of the three authors whose works are analyzed in

[3] Makdisi 2002; Kühn 2007.
[4] Haddad 1994; Mushtaq 1968; Tamari 2008.
[5] Fattah 1998.
[6] Tunsi 1967; Perkins 1994.

this chapter, and their place in the pantheon of Ottoman Arab authors of the long nineteenth century. To put it succinctly, Aḥmad Fāris al-Shidyāq (1804?–1887), Muḥammad Rashīd Riḍā (1865–1935), and Jirjī Zaydān (1860–1914) were seminal, highly influential thinkers, authors, and self-appointed reformists, whose writings and ideas were foundational and formative of the entire infrastructure of the *nahda* during the period under study. All three were the founders and (quasi-exclusive) writers of widely disseminated periodicals that were read in the four corners of the Arabic-speaking world and beyond, including India. More biographical information will be provided below, but suffice it here to underline one major difference among them: Shidyāq lived in Istanbul for a quarter of a century (1860–1884), and it was then that he wrote and published the articles on Istanbul discussed here; Riḍā stayed in Istanbul around 1909 for about a year, and he published his articles on the city in his periodical *al-Manār* a few months upon his return to Cairo; and Zaydān merely spent a few days there, also in 1909, and scribbled (rather undecipherable) notes in his notebooks, much of which was later turned into a historical/contemporary novel he published on the Young Turk Revolution (entitled *al-Inqilāb al-'uthmāni*, or *The Ottoman Revolution*). He first serialized this novel in his periodical *al-Hilāl* before publishing it as a book in 1911. Hence, the amount of time these authors spent in the city—and subsequently, the amount of deep knowledge they had of it—differed considerably from one author to another, and so did the amount of ink they devoted to writing on Istanbul. The reasons that brought them to Istanbul also varied considerably, and unsurprisingly shaped what they chose to see and comment upon during their stay in the empire's capital. Finally, one very quick word about comparisons: travel literature, or writing about a "foreign" place or even a second home, seems to be implicitly or explicitly, consciously or unconsciously, comparative. One of the major themes that permeate through this chapter is comparison: what is Istanbul being compared to? How does it fare in the comparison? How does the comparison change, from one author to another? And how might we be able to interpret this comparison?

Shidyāq as Urban Critic

There is perhaps no better place to begin an examination of all these questions than Shidyāq's articles on the city. A maverick intellectual, essayist, journalist, and linguist, a convert from Maronite Christianity to Protestantism and then to Islam, (Aḥmad) Fāris al-Shidyāq (1804?–1887) left his ancestral village in present-day Mount Lebanon and worked in Malta, Tunis, and Egypt, before settling in Istanbul, where he lived from 1860 until his death in 1887. While in

Istanbul, he issued *al-Jawā'ib* (1861–1884), one of the foremost periodicals of the era and the city's first Arabic periodical, and established a publishing house there in 1870.[7] Like many of his peers, and as one of the main figures and leaders of the *nahda*, Shidyāq was obsessed with and elaborated certain concepts that provided building blocks for the intellectual infrastructure *nahda* intellectuals were busy erecting.[8] Among these foundational blocks were civilization (*tamaddun*), to be contrasted with barbarism (*al-ḥāla al-hamajiyya*), as well as the twin concepts of ordering and order (*tartīb wa niẓām*). Another concept was equality, especially that between members of different religious communities. Indeed, the Tanzimat had ushered in a new era, with the sultanic decree proclaiming the equality of all subjects, Muslims and non-Muslims alike. More so, like virtually every other member of the *nahda*, and every other Ottoman intellectual (Arab or otherwise) of the second half of the nineteenth century, Shidyāq looked closely and keenly to Europe, of which he had firsthand knowledge, having visited and resided in a number of European cities before settling in Istanbul. However, as we shall see, there were fundamental differences between Shidyāq's attitudes and those of his contemporaries writing in the 1860s, and the attitudes of a later generation of intellectuals writing in the 1880s and onward.[9] If, in the 1860s, Ottoman intellectuals could and did still believe that their empire could reform and strengthen itself by adopting certain European ideas, after the 1880s, the specter of European domination through colonial expansion had become reality, and it became urgent to "catch up" with Europe in order to survive against its superior military and technological powers.

Istanbul in the 1860s:
Transformation and (Uneven) Modernization

The 1860s were a time of tremendous urban changes, especially for Istanbul. The city's population had exponentially increased since the 1840s, and would continue to do so throughout the nineteenth century.[10] Commercial treaties, signed in the late 1830s, privileged and increased European trade, and created a class of predominantly non-Muslim Ottoman and foreign merchants. New and imposing buildings associated with trade—e.g. banks, stores, and offices—

---

[7] On biographical information on Shidyāq, see Roper 1998:233–234.

[8] Khuri-Makdisi 2010.

[9] Most, if not all of the articles used here appeared in the 1860s. They were published in 1871 in the first volume of *Kanz al-Raghā'ib*, which was mostly a compilation of articles that had appeared in *al-Jawā'ib*.

[10] The population in Istanbul and the suburbs had jumped from 391,000 in 1844 to 851,000 in 1886, at which time it had more or less stabilized. Ottoman Muslims represented around 58% of the population in 1835, this number decreasing to 55% by the late nineteenth century. Çelik 1993:37.

and concentrated mostly in Galata, mushroomed. The city's infrastructure also developed considerably in specific neighborhoods after 1855, prompted by the official verdict that "the capital cities of all leading countries were built to perfection, whereas Istanbul still badly needed embellishment, regularization, road enlargement, street lighting, and improvement of building methods."[11] A municipal commission was formed soon after that, dividing the city into fourteen districts. The Sixth District, comprising Pera, Galata, and Tophane, was to be the experimental area for change. To be selected on the Sixth District council, one had to have lived there for more than ten years, and to own property within the district whose value was at least 100,000 kurush. The inhabitants of the Sixth District were mostly wealthy non-Muslim Levantines who were Ottoman subjects, or Europeans who had settled in Istanbul mainly for business purposes. Their presence was mostly concentrated in Pera. In 1858, the main street connecting Tophane to the main street in Pera (the Grande Route) was "leveled, widened, and provided with gas lighting." Similar improvements were made on the street connecting Tophane to Galata. Later, between 1865 and 1869, the main arteries of the city on both sides of the Golden Horn were cut, the areas surrounding the most important monuments were cleared, and extensive infrastructure was provided, which remains in service even today.[12] In 1868 a municipal code of regulations was adopted, applying the administrative organization introduced in Pera-Galata to the remaining fourteen districts of the city. While these changes were monumental, they seem to have been confined to a handful of neighborhoods—at least in the 1860s. Most of the city remained unaffected by these grandiose modernization projects, the interconnection between individual neighborhoods was not addressed, and most neighborhoods still maintained their privacy and functioned as self-sufficient units in the 1860s.

If the municipality emerged as a quintessential urban institution of the second half of the nineteenth century, so did the newspaper. Newspapers and periodicals, which appeared in a plethora of languages in Istanbul, followed with great interest urban matters and especially urban transformation. And their readership was high; by the end of the nineteenth century, "a substantial part of the citizenry of Istanbul, perhaps as many as 300,000 persons, read some sort of daily or weekly publication."[13]

In the context of such massive and visible urban projects, it is no surprise that Shidyāq covered urban matters in his periodical, weaving descriptions and comments on the city's streets, its inhabitants, zoning, provisioning, coffeehouses, places of leisure, consumption, and housing, and constantly shifting his

[11]   Ibid., 44.
[12]   Çelik 1993:44; Rosenthal 1980.
[13]   Karpat 1985:96.

zoom between the minutely micro and the massively macro. It is partly through Shidyāq's writings on the city that his genius as publicist, political essayist, and modernist novelist becomes apparent.

Shidyāq as Urban Reformist

For Shidyāq, one of the main duties of newspapers was to suggest practical and useful urban improvements within the larger realm of public interest. In his mind, nothing that pertained to public interest was beyond newspapers' scrutiny or was unworthy of their attention. More so, reform was not limited to the grand and the monumental: all aspects of life, daily governance, and public interest could and should be reformed. The changes Shidyāq suggested had the potential to impact the lives of vast numbers of Istanbul's inhabitants, not only Europeans and Ottoman subjects living in Pera and Galata, and not exclusively the upper classes. Strikingly, while the changes he suggested were quite radical, they did not make away with the many institutions and practices that had regulated the lives of Istanbulis for centuries. They were also universalizable: they could be applied to any city in the Ottoman Empire, without requiring tremendous funds or labor. Shidyāq envisioned and articulated a blueprint of urban reforms throughout the empire, which would first be implemented in the empire's capital.

One of Shidyāq's main criticisms of Istanbul specifically, and "Oriental cities" generally, revolved around the organization of their markets and shops, and specifically the concentration of one specific commercial activity or artisanal production on one street or in a single neighborhood. In his article "On Lacunae" ("On the organizing and ordering of cities and markets"), he advocated the model applied in "civilized countries" whose neighborhood markets catered to all of their shoppers' needs, arguing this benefitted both sellers and residents—the former by increasing their sales, and the latter by providing all necessary goods locally, hence eliminating the need to venture far. For such a change to be successfully implemented in Istanbul, "the owners of most of these shops, who are mostly Greeks/Orthodox Christians (*Rūm*) and Armenians,"and who "are like children ... need the *muḥtasib* to conduct this reform and impose on all sellers to carry all of life's necessities. It is simply unacceptable that somebody should have to walk an hour or two to ... get a piece of bread."[14] Here, as elsewhere, Shidyāq argued that the Ottomans could adapt from European cities some of their best features while maintaining institutions that had regulated

---

[14] "*Fi'l-Khalal (Fī tanẓīm aḥwāl al-mudun wa tartīb al-aswāq),*" in Shidyāq: 104–105.

life in Islamic urban societies for centuries, rather than constantly and solely relying on new (and "European") institutions such as the municipality.

The issue, for Shidyāq, was much larger than street organization and provisioning, and he was highly critical of newspaper owners in Istanbul, who did not bother to write on this matter, whereas their duty was to "reform/ fix lacunas/weaknesses, not merely to report news with no benefit."[15] At the heart of Shidyāq's concerns were the empire's subjects, and specifically men of the pen and journalists partaking in the debate on the empire's reform and modernization: "our era, under the rule of our great sultan is one of goodness and improvement, so it is our duty not to be silent ... and mention what needs to be improved/reformed; for the [sultan himself] wants comprehensive reform in his country, for all and every part of its affairs."[16] The author repeatedly mentioned and praised the press in Europe for underlining pertinent and improvable matters to its readership.

Another space in dire need of reform if not outright elimination was the coffeehouse. In most of his writings on Istanbul, Shidyāq launched a vituperative attack on this feature of urban life, describing it as a den for "the idle and the lazy" (*dhawiyy al-baṭāla wa'l-kasal min al-nās*). It was not so much the consumption of coffee in and of itself that exasperated him, but rather the loss of productivity associated with coffee shops and coffee-making. "In truth," he complained, "this coffee has become a major disaster (*maṣā'ib*) ... it requires one man to make it, another one to serve it, yet another one to serve tobacco sticks; this is three men who are not engaged in useful work ... For these unnecessary expenses are unknown to the foreigners." Coffee shops could be reformed, too: "Indeed, there are many coffeehouses (*mawāḍiʿ li'l- qahwa*) in European cities, but people go there to read newspapers (*jurnālāt*) and gather useful news, not for idle talk."[17] Until this was achieved, Shidyāq advocated imposing a heavy fine on these establishments in Istanbul, beginning in the Süleymaniye district, notorious for its high concentration of coffee depots/dens.[18] Shidyāq's attack on coffeehouses was not unusual: throughout the nineteenth and early twentieth centuries, various intellectuals, in Istanbul and in other parts of the Ottoman Empire, associated coffeehouses with idleness, but also hashish consumption (especially in Egypt), and occasionally sedition. In an era obsessed with "catching up with Europe," both masses and elites were exhorted to "roll up

---

15   Ibid., 106.
16   Shidyāq 2001:107.
17   *"Fi'l-farq mā bayna'l-sharq wa'l-gharb,"* in Shidyāq: 140–141.
18   *"Fi'l-Khalāl (Fī tanẓīm aḥwāl al-mudun wa tartīb al-aswāq),"* in Shidyāq: 105.

their sleeves" and get to work, rather than lazing around in coffeehouses, in order to develop city, nation, and empire.[19]

The Lure of Europe?
What We Should Learn from Europe

Many of Shidyāq's suggestions on urban transformation in Istanbul were prompted or followed by comparisons with European cities and institutions. Shidyāq had lived in Paris and visited London in the late 1840s and 1850s, and was visibly struck by the elaborate web of public transportation, notably public carriages (*qāfila/'araba*) that transported people long distances, for a very modest fee, and protected them "from rain and mud and summer heat." What a difference in Istanbul, he complained, where the walker had to contend with staircases, animals carrying heavy loads and blocking his path, and mud. Istanbulis were tired of walking, he complained, especially to Beyoğlu. The problem was one of poor planning (*sū' al-tadbīr*), but it could be easily remedied through the construction of a few roads for carriages. However, he did not cast the blame on the Ottoman state for the dire conditions of transportation in Istanbul, but rather on (interest) groups who were profiting from the existing situation and charged exorbitant fees: owners of individual carriages and individuals who rented out horses for the route connecting Hagia Sophia and Beyoğlu. State and municipal funds should be primarily funneled into building roads for carriages and launching public carriages: "road-works [for carriages] and the presence of these public carriages are among the greatest reasons for comfort, and are much more beneficial than public baths and coffeehouses which the idle frequent. It is surprising that Istanbul's inhabitants have accepted the usefulness of steamboats (*vapur*) ... but have not yet realized that of public carriages."[20]

If Shidyāq bluntly exposed individuals who profiteered from these lacunae, his harshest criticism was reserved toward "the European residents of Beyoğlu, and not Istanbul's residents. The municipal council of Beyoğlu should have established a public carriage and run it in some places, so as to incite people to ask for more."[21] This was the real meaning of civilization, Shidyāq argued: "once people familiarize themselves with this means of transportation and taste its comfort, then they will know the meaning of civilization (*tamaddun*)." Hence, Shidyāq suggested the path to real civilization, real progress, and real modernization lay elsewhere: what the municipal council of Beyoğlu, and what

---

[19] Khuri-Makdisi 2010:90.
[20] *"Fi'l-farq ma bayna'l-sharq wa'l-gharb,"* in Shidyāq: 142.
[21] Ibid., 142–143.

European residents in Istanbul were doing was at best superficial, and at worse, distracting and deterring from it. Examining public transportation, or, for instance, the multiplicity of goods and services offered in each neighborhood in Paris and London (contrary to Istanbul), Shidyāq underlined two major points. First, he asserted that such issues had direct and indirect repercussions on the city's population *as a whole* (not only on the inhabitants of distinct neighborhoods), and served the public good and public interest in more than one way. However, it is important to note that he did not use the terminology of class and did not argue for the necessity of providing services to the working classes per se. Affordable public transportation, as well as the existence of a more extensive transportation system, ultimately lowered the price of commodities, since they guaranteed their continuous flow: "this means that prices are actually moderate in Europe, contrary to what people here think. As for the provisioning of food and drinks in eastern lands ... it is not consistent ... partly because of ... the dearth of ships and railways ... In Europe, when people purchase something, they do not need to pay for its delivery cost, for a shopkeeper will send an item to somebody's house for free [using cheap, public transportation]."[22] Hence, being modern was about adopting technologies, practices, and policies that ultimately improved everybody's quality of life, not just that of the elites.

Shidyāq's second major point was that there was an entire political economy behind being modern and civilized, and behind having access to affordable objects. Noting that furniture is cheaper in London than elsewhere, he explained to his readers that "most furniture and fabrics found in the Islamic world is imported from there (*al-bilād al-ifranjiyya*), where it is machine-produced rather than handmade, so one machine does the work of one hundred hands." Purchasing modern goods was essentially neither modern nor civilized if the goods in question had been imported rather than locally manufactured. The Istanbulis, Shidyāq lamented, set their eyes on and purchased objects produced all over the world, whereas Londoners were content with what their country produced (of course, he omitted to mention that the British Empire's political economy rested on cheap labor and access to cheap resources from the colonies).[23] For Shidyāq, "civilization among the people without industries is much worse and pettier." People should first develop these industries and then indulge in consuming their products, or abandon their use, except for the absolutely necessary ones. Hence, for Shidyāq, the city's management, its modernization, and issues of urban change were all connected to larger and smaller problematics that needed to be revised and perhaps altered: consumerism and

---

[22] Ibid., 143.
[23] "*Fī usūl al-siyāsa wa ghayriha*," in Shidyāq: 152.

consumer choices, the empire's political economy and foreign trade, notions of the public good and of accessibility to services and goods. Thinking about the city and how to reform it triggered these larger questions and ultimately prompted Shidyāq to reflect upon what kind of empire currently existed, and what kind of empire might exist, if the right reforms were introduced.

The City of Everyday Life

Shidyāq's articles depicted Istanbul in the quotidian. It was predominantly the city of its inhabitants, rather than the dazzling metropole of an empire—and of inhabitants generally unmarked by religion or ethnicity, going about their neighborhood or beyond, busying themselves in unglamorous activities. None of the grandeur of the city was made manifest, no monuments commented upon or even deserving a mention. No frisson either, at crossing the Bosphorus or catching sight of one of the mosques at sunset. Istanbul is almost absent from its description, and Shidyāq might as well be writing about any city in the (Ottoman) world. His preoccupation was first and foremost with the mundane, the unspectacular and the non-glorious: people's commute and transportation, public spaces, coffeehouses, and neighborhood provisioning.

This "banalization" of Istanbul—as well as the emphasis on the non-picturesque—was certainly partly due to the fact that Shidyāq was a resident of the city, and not a visitor. It was also connected to the genre of writing, namely newspaper articles: as previously mentioned, newspapers (in Istanbul, in other parts of the Ottoman Empire, and in the four corners of the world generally) closely followed urban matters, including reporting on municipal activities, and provided ample details on rather prosaic topics. Shidyāq was writing as a local journalist, but what is interesting is that his readership was probably overwhelmingly non-local. It was predominantly people from the Arab provinces and beyond—in Syria, Egypt, North Africa, and elsewhere—who read his articles. Perhaps the banalization of Istanbul was connected to his readership: Shidyāq might have intended to "demystify" the capital of the empire to its provincial subjects, and treat it on par with the rest of the empire's cities, almost provincialize it in fact. He might also have been suggesting that all these questions facing Istanbul in the 1860s faced or would face other cities in the empire, and therefore that Istanbul was a good case-study, or a laboratory for analyzing these mechanisms of modern daily life.

Finally, there is something extremely modernist in Shidyāq's writings on Istanbul. I have here distilled some of his main arguments and themes, and have strung them together so as to extract his main arguments. His articles, however, are everything but linear: Shidyāq jumped from topic to topic, and would revisit a theme he had begun to explore at a latter stage of an article. Both author and reader are made to meander through the text, somewhat like a flaneur in the city. Many of the same themes appeared in different articles, each time strung together in a different order. Shidyāq's writings, with their conscious rejection of one single linear and dominant narrative of the city, are quite reminiscent of Walter Benjamin's thoughts on collections and writing about the city.[24]

Muḥammad Rashīd Riḍā's Trip to Istanbul: Strengthening the *umma* and the Empire, and Modernizing Islam

If Shidyāq allowed himself to meander through Istanbul, physically and textually, and invited his readers to explore various layers of the city while using a multiplicity of lenses, Muḥammad Rashīd Riḍā (1865–1935) gave his readers a very focused and linear reading of the city. One of the most influential thinkers of Islamic reformism in the modern period, Muḥammad Abduh's disciple and torch-bearer, and the founder of the influential periodical *al-Manār* (Cairo, 1898–1935), Riḍā spent a year in Istanbul in 1909, and upon his return to Cairo in 1910, published a handful of articles on his time there. Unsurprisingly, the reasons that took him to Istanbul completely informed and shaped his perception and experience of the city. Riḍā was a man on a mission, and a self-imposed one. He went to Istanbul after the revolution of 1908 (which deposed Sultan Abdülhamid and restored the Ottoman constitution, abolished since 1878), with the hope of convincing the Ottoman state to help found *Ma'had al-Da'wa wa'l-Irshād*, an institution whose purpose would be to train Muslims and prepare them for missionary work among Muslims who had fallen off the rightful path. In other words, the Istanbul Riḍā was interested in was the capital of the largest Muslim empire, the seat of the caliphate, and the most likely and legitimate place in which to establish a school geared toward defending the *umma* against European political, economic, and moral encroachments. It was also the capital of an empire whose recently deposed Sultan (Abdülhamid) had adopted a pan-Islamic policy. This, however, had not made Riḍā a supporter of Abdülhamid. In Riḍā's eyes, Islam had been weakened from the inside, through the tyranny of its political leaders (including Abdülhamid), and the population's divergence from the rightful path and their adoption of practices and beliefs that were anathema to the spirit and laws of Islam. At the same time, it was imperative to strengthen Islam by adapting it to the necessities of the times; indeed, for Riḍā and many other Muslim reformers at the time, there was no inherent

---

[24] Sewart 2003:32.

contradiction between Islam, on one hand, and progress and modernity, on the other. The necessities of modern times included a constitution, as well as newspapers, railways, and other elements of modern technology, all needed to connect the Muslim world with the rest of the world, and thus paving the way toward progress and civilization.[25] However, even before he set foot in Istanbul, Riḍā was quick to criticize a substantial segment of its population, on account that they were too westernized, or pretending and aspiring to be westernized (*mutafarnijīn*).[26]

Istanbul for Riḍā represented central Islamic orthodoxy, in an empire where the threat came not only from the West, but also from the empire's heterodox and troublesome borderlands. The school Riḍā wished to establish would graduate missionaries "[whose] most immediate usefulness is to send them to lands where ignorance became rampant and troubles increased, such as Yemen and Iraq and Anatolia, in order to preach and guide [Muslims] on the right path (*irshād*), and prevent sins and rebellions (*fitan*) ... and befriend and get acquainted with all sects/groups and elements (*tawā'if wa 'anāṣir*)."[27] Hence, Riḍā's project, rather than being merely compatible with that of a centralizing state, was in his mind necessary for its survival. It also went hand in hand with the metropole's civilizing mission of its ignorant subjects living at the edge of civilization. At the same time, Riḍā made it clear that reformist ulama should be in charge of such a project: "my aim is not for the Ottoman government to establish such an institute. Politics corrupts everything, like [Muḥammad Abduh] said. The aim is to have an association of reformist ulama" (ibid., 46). The government should assist them by exempting the school's students from military service, directing income generated by *waqfs* (charitable endowments) to it, and covering the teachers' salaries.

---

[25] On his return to Syria in 1908–1909, after an absence of eleven years (he himself was originally from a village near Tripoli, in present-day North Lebanon, and had emigrated to Cairo in 1897), Riḍā described Tripoli as being beyond the pale of civilization: "Tripoli is now as if it were isolated from the civilized world ... one of the signs of this is the lack of daily newspapers, and the non-arrival of newspapers from Beirut there, because it is not connected through railway." More interesting and somewhat surprising is Riḍā's argument that Tripoli lagged behind other cities (and specifically Beirut) because of the lack of interaction between its inhabitants and "people who are more civilized than them (*arqā minhum*), foreigners and Ottomans." Riḍā 1971:13.

[26] Riḍā seems to have had a pre-set opinion about Istanbul, or at least about its Muslim inhabitants. During his trip to Syria, he remarked that the Muslims of Beirut were "ready to accept all religious and civil reform ... and the reason for this, from what it seems to me, is that those who love reform were not raised in a European fashion that has distanced them from their religion and has disfigured the civilization of their Elders (*salafihim*) in their eyes, triggering in them the desire to break with everything old and desire all that is new, as is the case for many *mutafarnijīn* in Istanbul (Asitana) and Cairo and Tunis." Riḍā 1971:12.

[27] Riḍā 1971:47.

Istanbul, in Riḍā's articles, emerged as a set of personal landmarks or a network of connections: influential people he met, visited, and talked to, who could help him realize his vision. His account reads like a Who's Who of Istanbul: a web of its most influential ulama, officials, educators, notables, and bureaucrats. Beyond these reformers of the umma, Riḍā had little to say about the city itself, but what he did say, as well as what he omitted, is quite telling. First, while acknowledging the unbeatable location of the city, he hastily began to enumerate what the city lacked: "Besides mosques, one cannot find a single trace of the ancient buildings of the previous sultans ... and no modern structures except for caserns and military schools ... Sofia, Athens and Cairo are all more refined (*arqā*). Istanbul ... is one big military encampment/ barracks (*mu'askar*), with a continuous and visible presence of soldiers" (ibid., 53). While Riḍā might have disapproved of such overt military power, his prime concern lay elsewhere. The empire's leaders had to be capable of building it and developing its infrastructure without relying on the West: "not with loans from foreigners, with interest rates (*ribā*) that went against the sharī'a, placed the Empire under European control, and provided them with a pretext ... to intervene" (ibid.). Hence, Riḍā's concern was with the manner in which space was produced: what power relations, what economic and political asymmetries were inevitably tied to urban development, in an empire struggling to fend off European interests.

Turning his attention to the city's moral and intellectual infrastructure, Riḍā compared education and instruction (*'ilm wa adab*) in Istanbul with Egyptian and Syrian cities, and broached the subject by focusing on women. Education in Istanbul might be more widespread and comprehensive, he pointed out, and women were better educated and more refined, but this was (partly) the consequence of provincial over-taxation and corrupt rule, the metropole essentially siphoning off wealth from the provinces during Hamidian rule. In Istanbul, he mused, "one never catches a glance of an uncovered woman in a window or on a roof; and one does not hear loud voices in houses, in the markets or on the streets, the way one does in Cairo." Overall, women in Istanbul both privately and publicly behaved in a most appropriate and modest manner, providing they were educated (but not necessarily schooled) *à l'ancienne*, whereas the modern manners and the tremendous dangers of *tafarnuj* (Europeanization), threatened to corrupt Islamic households (ibid., 54). Riḍā saw the empire's capital as being made out of two irreconcilable cities: Istanbul on one hand, and Galata and Beyoğlu on the other. While the distance between them was minimal, they represented two different, virtually unbridgeable, worlds. Istanbul resembled Tripoli in its customs and habits, especially in dress and dinner habits, whereas Galata's residents dressed differently and stayed up late. Contrary to his expectations, he noted (perhaps with a tinge of disappointment?) that Istanbul was not more refined, more built, and more civilized than Syrian cities; it simply had more men and women educated in social manners (*al-ādāb al-ijtimāʿiyya*) than Syrian cities. However, its modern buildings and civilization were not more refined than Beirut's, nor were its older structures more distinguished than those of Damascus. Where Istanbul fared better in the comparison was, interestingly enough, in its commoners: Riḍā found Istanbul's commoners or its masses (*al-ʿāmma*) more polished than Cairo's. However, in wealth and buildings, or when it came to the city's elites, Cairo was superior, and Cairene women were virtually on par with their Istanbuli counterparts (ibid., 55).

Riḍā's attempts to establish his school in Istanbul ultimately failed, and in 1912, the school found an ephemeral home in Cairo, before it was shut down two years later.[28] It is not clear whether his articles on Istanbul, which were published upon his return to Cairo, were written after he had lost hope of establishing his school in Istanbul. They do suggest, though, that Istanbul, in Riḍā's eyes, was in a dangerous predicament: with a past barely visible and worth mentioning (perhaps a past that, as an Arab Muslim, he did not, or could no longer consider his own); a present mired in European dependency and loans (which went against Islamic principles); a metropole at best on par with provincial Arab towns, and inferior to Cairo; and an empire whose future remained uncertain and worrisome. What would the role of the military be? Would the center of the Muslim world tilt elsewhere, perhaps toward Cairo? Riḍā expressed no such desire: on the contrary, he (still) pitted himself, and the school he so wished to establish in Istanbul, as the much needed doctor whose services would cure the ailments of the *umma*, the Empire, and its metropole, and guarantee them a future.

Jirjī Zaydān:
Istanbul as seen through the Lens of an
Ottoman Tourist and Writer

It was during that very same year, 1909—"year One of the revolution"—that another Syrian spent a few days in Istanbul. Jirjī Zaydān (1860-1914) founder, owner, and main writer of *al-Hilāl*, a formative and authoritative periodical based in Cairo, spent a few days in Istanbul and jotted down his impressions of the city in his notebooks.[29] A (Christian) Beiruti in origin, who had moved to Egypt in 1882 and spent the rest of his life there, Zaydān never lost interest in or contact

---

[28] For more information on this institution, see Adams (2000):197-198, and Hamzah (2012), forthcoming.

[29] Zaydān's unpublished notebooks are in the archives of the American University of Beirut, in AA6 AUBites papers: Jirji Zaidan, Box 1.

with the rest of the empire, especially the province of Beirut. He remained a fervent Ottomanist, penning articles on the empire's "best of sultans" in *al-Hilāl*'s very first issues, and including Ottoman reformist officials in his biographical compilation of famous Easterners (*Tarājim mashāhīr al-Sharq*).[30] His letters to his son also showed him to be fiercely attached to his Ottoman identity. At the same time, though, and as Anne-Laure Dupont has argued in her magisterial study on Zaydān, "the Ottoman Empire was not Zaydān's major preoccupation. Naturally, it constituted his horizon, but it was a rather distant one. Ottoman news items [in *al-Hilāl*] were ... classified as 'Egyptian events', 'Syrian events', and 'External events.' The empire thus did not constitute a space in and of itself (*en soi*)."[31] However, like Rashīd Ridā, he made sure to visit Istanbul a few months after the Young Turk Revolution, which he had passionately supported. He also had started taking private lessons in Cairo in Ottoman Turkish right before his trip to Istanbul. By January 1909, he was able to read the metropole's Ottoman press.[32]

It is unclear exactly how many days Zaydān spent in Istanbul, or, for that matter, whether this was his first or only trip there.[33] It is also not clear whether his notes on Istanbul were ever published in article form. What was certainly published was his novel on the Young Turk Revolution (*al-Inqilāb al-'uthmānī*), which dwelt at great length on Abdülhamid's character and his secretive life. This combination of genres—the historical novel, the detective story/ political thriller, and the newsreel/journalistic—comes out quite vividly in the notes he took. Reading them, it seems that Zaydān already had in mind the many styles for which they would be used. Unlike Ridā or Ibrahim al-Muwaylihi's writings on Istanbul, both of which were focused and linear descriptions of the city, Zaydān's experience of the city, and specifically his selection of spaces and places he visited and commented about, were very varied.[34] Undoubtedly, this difference was partly due to Zaydān's writings being scattered, unpublished notes, rather than finished, published articles. However, the differences were due to other factors as well. For one, unlike Muwaylihi, Zaydān visited

---

[30]   Dupont 2009:542–626.

[31]   Dupont 2006:553; Philipp 1985; Philipp 1990.

[32]   Dupont 2006:579–580.

[33]   Two of his notebooks contain details of his trip to Istanbul. They are both undated. It is not clear whether they refer to one trip or two different trips. In one of the notebooks he writes that he left Istanbul on August 21, 1909.

[34]   Ibrahim al-Muwaylihi wrote a series of articles on Istanbul during Abdülhamid's rule, which I am not discussing in this chapter for lack of space. Initially serialized by the Cairene pro-British periodical, *al-Muqattam*, they were later collected and published as a book entitled *Mā Hunālik*. The book was recently translated into English as *Spies, Scandals, and Sultans: Istanbul in the Twilight of the Ottoman Empire*. 2008, (translated and introduced by Roger Allen). New York.

Istanbul after the revolution and had access to sites that were beyond the reach of Muwaylihi. More significantly, Istanbul, in Zaydān's notes, was simultaneously the imperial capital and the city of modest people and simple pleasures; it was also a historic city, that of the revolution of 1908 and of its heroes—a historical city—and a modern one. Zaydān was also sensitive to the fact that different ethnic and religious groups lived there, some of whom were concentrated in specific neighborhoods. Finally, while Zaydān was surely in Istanbul for work—most likely, to gather material for his novel and for some articles—he was not there with a tangible political project in mind. Unlike Riḍā, he clearly spent more time strolling around than establishing contacts with people and meeting influential figures, although he did meet fellow newspaper editors and some politicians. He was there for a few days, maybe a week, and was partly tourist and flaneur, partly reporter, and partly author in search of characters and a set for his novel.

Istanbul as the Stage of the 1908 Revolution and the End of the Ancient Regime

As a writer well attuned to his readers' desires, Zaydān started his notebook with information on Yıldız, Abdülhamid's palace and adjacent mosque. The autocratic and paranoid Abdülhamid had remained out of the public eye, and his subjects knew almost nothing about him.[35] After the Revolution, Abdülhamid's secluded world, which had been off-limits to his subjects, could be penetrable, and Zaydān recorded with frenzy every possible detail about the dethroned sultan's private space: the palace's conservatory, its colored glass and painted ceilings, even the curtains were described with painstaking detail, and accompanied with sketches and plans. The notes also provided ample details of the Hamidiye Mosque, which was part of the Yıldız palace complex, as well as of the women who prayed there.[36] While this was neither the only nor the most important mosque about which he wrote, this was the only one described with people praying in it. Perhaps this was Zaydān's way to illustrate how this quintessentially Hamidian space had been appropriated by the people he had oppressed.

For Zaydān, Istanbul was the stage for History with a capital H, namely the revolution of 1908. Muwaylihi's narrative had described a static, atemporal city, stuck in a web of tyranny, corruption, and intrigue, with no history to write of,

---

[35] It is also very likely that Zaydān had read al-Muwaylihi's descriptions of Abdülhamid's Istanbul on the pages of *al-Muqaṭṭam*, and that he was perhaps implicitly or subconsciously "responding" to al-Muwaylihi's account, by providing further information on Abdülhamid and his era.

[36] Zaydān, unpublished notebooks, n.d.

and no visible future in sight. Riḍā's writings on Istanbul made no mention of 1908—besides qualifying 1909 as "Year One"—and the city for him was first and foremost a node within Dar al-Islam, albeit a central one. Shidyāq's Istanbul was predominantly the city of the quotidian and the uneventful. Zaydān's Istanbul, however, was primarily the stage of the empire's revolutionary heroes, and most importantly of its thinkers: he included the names of the Committee of Union and Progress's members for 1906 and 1909, provided physical and psychological descriptions of them, and jotted down meetings he had with some of them. He also described the building housing the Majlis al-Mabʻuthān, the much-celebrated Council of Representatives/Delegates and one of the major achievements of the 1908 Revolution, and provided information on the Council's activities. Other historical events also made an appearance in Zaydān's fragmented notes, usually prompted by a site or a place: a monument, a building, a neighborhood. One neighborhood, for instance, "contains the remains of Russian soldiers who died in the war of 1877" (ibid.).

Like Shidyāq's articles, Zaydān's notes unraveled layer after layer of the city's history without hierarchy or linear progression. He interwove past, present, and future, the sacred and the profane, the grand and the humble, the quotidian and the eventful, stringing together snapshots of the city: that of "a bear and a monkey with their master"; Roberts College and the villages of Bebek and Istiniye; Eyüp, its main mosque and the footprint of the Prophet on one of the walls; the Patriarchate in Fener; reading rooms cum-coffeehouses ("qirāatkhāna, by which they mean coffeeshops"); the archeological museum and some of its artifacts such as the tomb of Alexander; the Süleymaniye mosque and the Mosque of Sultan Ahmed. The effect is somewhere between a guide-book and a peep-box. Interspersed among these scenes were women carrying loaves of bread, notes on how the residents of Istanbul announced their dead, lists of the most important Istanbul newspapers, description of house interiors and exteriors, ethnological information on various ethnic groups living in the city (dress, profession, and the like), and a quick description of the slave market (*sūq al-jawārī*). Zaydān did not only dwell on the picturesque, though. He recorded with interest and pride the various kinds of schools, including military schools, colleges of medicine, and teachers' colleges, and noted the various languages of instruction. Istanbul's modernity is given its due: Hayderpaşa, the railway station and the Istanbul-Baghdad railroad (he noted that the trains at Hayderpaşa ran on electricity); the city's paved streets, with imported stones ("similar to those imported to Egypt from Trieste"). While he included virtually the entire panoply of nineteenth-century modern institutions—the museum, the municipality, the newspaper, the train station—he intertwined them with pre-nineteenth-century spaces and practices: transportation carts, pulled by cows and buffalos, coexisting with the modern railway; the spring ('ayn) in Üsküdar, from which people still got their water and carried it in barrels to the city; the sumptuous interiors of westernized elites, who decorated their homes with European paintings (ṣuwar ifranjiyya) as well as oriental carpets. There was no value judgment, implicit or explicit, no hierarchy, and no dichotomy. However, functional Islamic institutions and figures, ulama, sufi lodges, and madrasas, remained glaringly absent from his tableaux vivants.

Zaydān depicted Istanbul as the city of its different communities, religious and ethnic. It was made up of a series of neighborhoods, many of which had a majority or dominant ethnic or religious resident group. Perhaps the liveliest and fullest description of a neighborhood was that of Kadiköy. Its inhabitants, predominantly Greek (Yunān)/Orthodox (Arwām)[37] and Armenian, Kadiköy was also home to a few Jews, and "if there were among them a Muslim, he would be a stranger" (gharīb). However, if various communities were mentioned, they hardly interacted in Zaydān's notes. Was he simply not interested in this issue? Or on the contrary, was it so evident to him that it was not worth noting down? Or was it that the interactions were less visible than signs of difference? Zaydān's scribbles are also somewhat reminiscent of Western narratives of Istanbul and "Oriental cities" generally, with their need to classify people according to their religion and ethnicity, based on outer signs of distinction (usually sartorial). Unsurprisingly, given Zaydān's own communal background, Istanbul appeared as the spiritual and communal metropole of Greek Orthodoxy: Hagia Sophia, which he described as both a mosque and a church, and dwelled on its Islamic references as well as on its Christian mosaics; the Patriarchate in Fener; the monastery in Halki and the school attached to it; and (briefly) the Bulgarian church. (He also wondered whether the mosque of Nurosmaniye had originally been a church.)

Difference and Distinction:
Istanbul, Cairo, and Paris in Zaydān's Writings

One way to read further into Zaydān's depiction of Istanbul is by analyzing his writings on other cities, and especially Paris, which he visited and about which he published a series of articles in 1912.[38] By looking at his writings on Paris, it becomes easier to identify what Zaydān omitted about Istanbul, while keeping in mind the uneven nature of the sources. Zaydān's trip to Paris, and

---

[37] Zaydān uses both terms, seemingly interchangeably.
[38] According to Dupont, these articles first appeared in al-Hilāl in installments, in Vol XXI (1912–1913), and were later posthumously published as a book in 1923. Dupont 2006:715.

to Europe generally, was explicitly didactic in a way his trip to Istanbul was not: Zaydān was in Paris to learn from the West and share his knowledge with his readers. He explained the origins of the Third Republic (1870), the French political system with various representative chambers and presidential elections, before delving into a description of the urban landscape. Making note of large boulevards, grand buildings, electric lights, and the large numbers of chic pedestrians donning the latest fashion, he noted that Cairo compared quite favorably to Paris—although he did concede that Paris had grander and more beautiful buildings—and concluded that "it is not arrogant to claim that the civilization of modern Cairo is a small picture of that of Paris."[39] On the other hand, he did not comment about or even jot down any mention of Istanbul's boulevards and grand "European" buildings, although there were quite a few of them. Like Shidyāq sixty years earlier, what most impressed him was Parisian public transportation: trams and buses. He was particularly taken by the fact that the drivers did not hassle riders for more money. He was not all praise, though: he clearly disapproved of the French state's banning of certain religious organizations and claimed that the French had become extremists in their anti-religious stance, and that the spread of religious doubt among the population had led to corruption.

One noticeable difference between his writings on Paris and Istanbul was the manner in which he wrote about "the masses." Whereas he very often included descriptions of commoners in his Istanbul notebooks, he did not conceive of them as constituting a class per se. In his articles on Paris, on the other hand, the *'āmma* (commoners) emerged as a separate category, with Zaydān tracing the emergence of the *'āmma* as a category in French history, and remarking that in France and other countries, the *'āmma* have caused massive changes and revolutions. As a consequence of their role in the French revolution, he wrote:

> The masses in France differ from ours quite substantively and in many ways: they are more and better educated and instructed (*arqā tarbiya wa awsa' ta'alluman*); all of them can read and write ... everybody reads newspapers, from shoe polishers to concierges ... They are interested in public issues and discuss politics ... and political parties ... the difference [from us] is that they know their rights ... since the French Revolution, France has witnessed the establishment of parties made up of the masses.
>
> Zaydān 2002: 44

---

[39] Ibid.

While this was presented as a positive development, Zaydān was nonetheless critical of what he deemed the over-empowerment of workers and the spread of strikes, which caused the greatest harm to the public, since they led to an increase in prices.[40] Aside from workers, Zaydān devoted a great deal of attention to women. Reminding his readership of Europe's negative treatment of women in premodern times, he hailed the considerable improvements that had been ushered in by "the light of modern civilization." European women had been liberated and allowed to work but this was partly due to their constituting a cheap labor force, he argued. While women worked in various realms—in shops, factories, mines, as servants, office employees, post office workers, and also as scientists and doctors—Zaydān criticized the "extreme freedom" that Parisian women had. In Paris, "they" have:

> sent the woman to the markets where she mingles with men ... and frequents them, while she is weak and sensitive! She became exposed to a great deal of corrupt behavior ... and men have seduced her with money ... she ended up wasting her life on the streets and alleys and her only source of income became [prostitution] ... In Cairo there is a small sample of this class known as (*filles de trottoir*) (*banāt al-raṣīf*), but in Paris, they number in the thousands: not a single garden or promenade or street is free of them, especially at night.
>
> Zaydān 2002:47

Zaydān did not blame women for prostituting themselves. Rather, he cast the blame on men, and the lure of higher earnings—and in fact, the whole economic and societal basis that allowed for the mingling of sexes—all of which left women with no choice but to prostitute themselves. It is the "letting loose of woman (*itlāq sirāḥ al-fatāt*) and making her equal to man, and putting her in charge of earning money like him, as well as the French government's official condoning of prostitution, that is to blame." He made the "classical argument" that women should be educated because they were created as mothers and educators of their children. However, it was "not natural" for women to work, and they should not do so, except out of sheer necessity and extreme duress.[41]

---

[40] In Zaydān's words, "Because of the industrial revolution ... and technological inventions, many members of the upper classes have become much wealthier, which has upset workers ... they have had to gather and protest and strike. What has helped them to do so is the spread of socialism (*al-ishtirākiyya*) and the deputies' need for the vote of the masses. And this has made the *umma* greedier and stronger, and they've multiplied their strikes until they've ... caused losses for owners, but it is the public that is mostly suffering, because of resulting increases in prices." Zaydān 2002:44.

[41] Ibid., 50.

Zaydān was not only (or perhaps even chiefly) concerned with the fate of Parisian women. The proliferation of prostitutes, especially in the Quartier Latin, threatened the well-being and morality of another group of people who mattered infinitely more to him: Egyptian students on governmental educational missions (*irsāliyyāt*). The Parisian street was thus a space of moral contamination for the Egyptians, and it could potentially affect all of Egypt (ibid., 48). Interestingly, he blamed the Egyptian government, as well as the families of those studying in Paris, for sending Egyptian boys to study in Paris, and thus exposing them to these dangers; other parts of France were a lot safer, he opined, and this is where students should be dispatched.

Women aside, though, Paris for Zaydān was clearly the capital of high civilization in ways Istanbul was not. At one point in these articles, he abandoned the seemingly objective lens through which he was noting difference and comparing East and West mostly in terms of buildings and infrastructure, and "acknowledged" the East's debt to France. Like others of his generation, he had internalized the Orientalist argument that Bonaparte's conquest of Egypt in 1798 had brought knowledge and progress to the East, and argued that "the seeds which he [Bonaparte] planted remained there until they were cultivated by men from the East who rose from their slumber/awoke (*nahaḍū*) ... the Syrians (sic), Egyptians, Turks and Persians, when they sought out and busied themselves with this civilization (*madaniyya*), were mostly being inspired by the French and followed the footsteps of the French nation. They learned its language, translated its body of knowledge, and imitated its literature and customs and habits." He also listed the most prominent French personalities who left their mark on Egypt culturally and scientifically: Dr. Clot Bey, and the founder of the Egyptian museum Mariette Pasha among others, and reminded his readers that "when the Turks rose/awoke (*nahḍa*) in Istanbul to embrace modern civilization, they mostly relied on translating modern literature (*al-adab*) from French: Rousseau, Montesquieu, Hugo and others" (ibid., 52).

Conclusion

To conclude, what do these findings say about Arab perceptions of Istanbul in the late-nineteenth and early-twentieth centuries? While keeping in mind that this is a first foray into this topic, and that more substantive research is needed, one preliminary conclusion is that Istanbul did not seem to enjoy the same kind of mystique and perhaps interest as Paris, London, or Cairo did in the eyes of some Arab intellectuals. Or more accurately, as the metropole of an empire, Istanbul represented a different kind of metropole to its provincial intellectuals than London or Paris represented to their colonial subjects. Indeed, similar examples of banalization or de-centering of empire can be seen in the neighboring Austro-Hungarian Empire, whose fate, like that of the Ottomans, hung in the balance in the early years of the twentieth century.[42] This suggests the need to rethink notions of empire/periphery and prompts a more nuanced analysis of the meaning of empires for the turn-of-the-century. Specifically, while taking into consideration the vastly uneven quality and quantity of available writings on Paris and Istanbul, the difference in Zaydān's writings on the two cities suggests that by the first decade of the twentieth century, Istanbul was no longer exemplary. It was still the capital of an oft-beloved empire, but there was very little to learn from it, and little that dazzled, coming from "the provinces." Riḍā even found Istanbul lacking, as compared to Cairo and even Beirut. Surely part of the "blasé" attitude of the two authors was due to their being Cairene. After all, the account of an Iraqi student from Baghdad, Ṭālib Mushtāq, who came to Istanbul in 1917 at the tender age of seventeen, reads very differently: Istanbul was the quintessentially modern city in his eyes, with its streetlights and its fancy buildings. Written and published half a century later, Mushtāq recalled how excited and happy he had been at the thought of seeing Istanbul, "the seat of the Caliphate and the beautiful city of hope and dreams. Istanbul was the ka'aba of ambitious men from Iraq: whoever wanted a desirable position would fill his suitcase with expensive gifts and head to Istanbul. Whoever wanted promotion or a raise would fill his pockets with tens of gold liras and head there; and among well-to-do families, whoever wanted to educate their children in high culture, would send them to Istanbul. Most would study law or, if they were from poor or modest families, attend military schools."[43] Surely many, if not most, other Arabs who came to Istanbul still felt like they were in the center of the world. However, discursively, at least for Riḍā and Zaydān, two influential intellectuals whose writings made a great impact on large numbers of reading Arabs, as the first decade of the twentieth century was coming to a close, Istanbul had been decentered.

---

[42] See the writings of Joseph Roth, a native of Brody, a provincial city in Galicia, who headed to Vienna in 1911 for his studies, and spent approximately a decade there. In the handful of letters that have been translated and published, Roth did not describe Vienna as the seat of an empire, nor as an exceptional and different place. Rather, he wrote about the familiar, about his neighborhood and its residents, and about the minutia of life. He was not dazzled by city lights nor by the grand imperial architecture. The institutions and spaces that (often hastily) figured in his letters were the university and cultural institutions, especially the theater and concert halls. For Paris, on the other hand, he reserved a very different treatment. Discovering it in 1925, an elated Roth ranked it as the world's capital, adding that: "whoever has not been to Paris is merely a half-human being and could not be considered a European. Here is the rule of liberty, of the mind (l'esprit)—in the noblest sense of the term—and of irony mixed with the most sublime of pathos." His empire no longer existed, but he had found the capital of the world, as well as his own private home. Roth, 2007:42–43.

[43] Mushtāq 1968–1969:36.

Works Cited

Adams, C. 2000. *Islam and Modernism in Egypt.* London and New York.

Atiyeh, G., ed. 1995. *The Book in the Islamic World: the Written Word and Communication in the Middle East.* Albany, NY.

Çelik, Z. 1993. *The Remaking of Istanbul: Portrait of an Ottoman City in the Nineteenth Century.* Berkeley.

Dupont, A-L. 2006. *Jurji Zaydān, 1861-1914: Écrivain réformiste et témoin de la renaissance arabe.* Damascus.

Fattah, H. 1998. "Representations of Self and Other in Two Iraqi Travelogues of the Ottoman Period." *International Journal of Middle Eastern Studies (IJMES)* 39, Feb.:51–76.

Grabovski, E. and Hardin, J., eds. 2003. *Literature in Vienna at the Turn of the Century: Continuities and Discontinuities around 1900 and 2000.* Rochester.

Haddad, M. 1994. "The Rise of Arab Nationalism Reconsidered." *IJMES* 26 May:201–222.

Hamzah, D. 2012. "From 'Ilm to Sihafa or the Politics of the Public Interest (Maslaha): Muhammad Rashid Rida and his journal al-Manar (1898-1935)." In Hamzah, D. Forthcoming 2012.

_____. Forthcoming 2012. *The Making of the Arab Intellectual: Empire, Public Sphere, and the Colonial Coordinates of Selfhood.* London.

Hourani, A. H. 1962. *Arabic Thought in the Liberal Age.* Cambridge and New York.

Karpat, K. 1985. *Ottoman Population 1830-1914: Demographic and Social Characteristics.* Madison.

Khayr al-din al-Tunsi. 1967. *The Surest Path: the Political Treatise of a Nineteenth-Century Muslim Statesman* (trans. L. Carl Brown). Cambridge, MA.

Khuri-Makdisi, I. 2010. *The Eastern Mediterranean and the Making of Global Radicalism 1860-1914.* Berkeley.

Kühn, T. 2007. "Shaping and Reshaping Colonial Ottomanism: Contesting Boundaries of Difference and Integration in Ottoman Yemen, 1872-1919." *Comparative Studies of South Asia, Africa and the Middle East* 27(2):315–331.

Makdisi, U. 2002. "Ottoman Orientalism." *The American Historical Review* 107.3 June, 2002:768–796.

Matar, N. 2009. *Europe through Arab Eyes 1578-1727.* New York.

Mushtāq, T. 1968-1969. *Awrāq Ayyāmī 1900-1958.* Beirut.

Muwaylihi, I. 2008. *Spies, Scandals, and Sultans: Istanbul in the Twilight of the Ottoman Empire* (trans and intro R. Allen). Lanham and New York.

Perkins, K. 1994. "The Masses Look Ardently to Istanbul: Tunisia, Islam, and the Ottoman Empire, 1837-1931." In Ruedy 1994:23–36.

Philipp, T. 1985. *Syrians in Egypt, 1725-1975.* Stuttgart.

Riḍā, M. R. 1971. *Riḥlat al-Imām Rashīd Riḍā* (ed. Y. Ibish). Beirut.

Roper, G. 1998. "Fāris al-Shidyāq and the Transition from Scribal to Print Culture in the Middle East." In Atiyeh 1995:209–222.

Rosenthal, S. 1980. *The Politics of Dependency: Urban Reform in Istanbul.* Westport, CT.

Roth, J. 2007. *Lettres choisies, 1911–1939* (trans. and ed. S. Pesnel). Paris.

Ruedy, J. ed. 1994. *Islamism and Secularism in North Africa.* New York, NY and Washington, DC.

Shidyāq, A. F. 2001. *Mukhtārāt min Āthār Aḥmad Fāris al-Shidyāq* (ed. Y. Khūrī and Y. Ibish). Beirut.

Stewart, J. 2003. "The Written City: Vienna 1900 and 2000." In Grabovski and Hardin 2003:27–50.

Tamari, S. 2008. "With God's Camel in Siberia: The Russian Exile of an Ottoman Officer from Jerusalem." *Jerusalem Quarterly* no. 35 (Aut 2008):31-50.

Yared, N. 1996. *Arab Travelers and Western Civilization.* London.

Zaydān, J. n.d. Unpublished notebooks, in the American University of Beirut Archives and Special Collections, Jafet Library, Beirut, Lebanon: AA6 AUBites papers: Jirji Zaidan, Box 1.

——. 1911. *Al-Inqilāb al-'Uthmānī.* Cairo.

——. 2002. *Al-Rihla ila Europa.* Beirut.

——. 1990. *The Autobiography of Jurji Zaidan: Including Four Letters to his Sons* (trans., ed. and intro. edited T. Philipp). Washington, DC.

8

Evading Athens

Versions of a Post-Imperial,
National Greek Landscape around 1830

Constanze Güthenke

On New Ground

In 1834, the German archaeologist Ludwig Ross, freshly minted overseer of Greek antiquities in the Peloponnese, described the arrival in Athens, Greece's freshly minted capital, of King Otho's bride Amalia as the first Queen of Greece:

> With the advent of Western civilization and its true benefits to Greece also came some of its obligatory nonsense. The Athenian authorities, whether it had occurred to themselves or whether it had been suggested to them, had decided to present the young queen upon arrival with a speech and the symbol of the city in the form of a living bird of Minerva, legs and wings bound with white and blue silk ribbons. No sooner had the queen set foot on Greek soil than she almost fell over the great number of olive branches strewn in her way, only to have to attend next to that poor little screech owl that by then was practically frightened to death.[1]

> Ross 1863:104–105

Geographies, imperial, national, or otherwise, rely on actual material ground, but what constituted Greek ground—its extent, borders and ownership—when Amalia stepped onto Greek soil, was an issue complex enough to make lesser people than a new queen stumble. An out of control owl, terrified and disoriented, rather than a gift of welcome that would be easy to hold on to acts here as

---

[1] All translations are my own.

placeholder of Athens, throwing the newly arrived, foreign queen even further off course. This episode underlines that the "geography" of Greece, the ordering, perception, and representation of Greek land, is deeply structured by reference to its ancient strata and the value derived from them. Ross leaves open whether this symbol of Athena, made real and causing havoc, is suggested as a token of Greece's ancient past by well-meaning Greeks themselves or by the Bavarian administrative corps charged with staging the royal welcome; but he knows that it is the lens of Western civilization that makes that attempt understandable in the first place.

Much has been written in the last two or three decades on Greek nation-building and its peculiarities; the interest in the structures of the modern nation, and the identities generated and unsettled by it alike, was itself in many ways catalyzed by a global situation in which the concept of nation emerged as an imaginatively engineered "challenge for a collection of territories recently emerged from colonial domination."[2] Much has also been written on the project of modernity as itself a "colonialist project,"[3] in a sense of state politics, as much as in a sense of self-colonization as an intellectual background with an effect on political and cultural production.[4] Almost any colonial situation is bound to be complex and diffuse in its thematic boundaries and its multiple local allegiances past and present; but the establishment of the Greek nation-state begs the question of just what kind of colonialism or post-colonialism is at issue here. Upon its ostensible liberation from Ottoman dominance, Greece was a country as yet ill-defined in its territorial extent, social makeup, and political organization. It was granted sovereign statehood, as opposed to semi-autonomous or otherwise special status, when it was recognized by the three Protecting Powers (England, France, and Russia) in the London Protocol of 1830. With statehood agreed upon, the form of governance chosen for the new state was a monarchy (and after 1843 a constitutional monarchy). The monarch eventually chosen, after what amounts to a game of diplomatic and royal Musical Chairs, was the underage prince Otto von Wittelsbach of the Bavarian royal family, who ruled Greece initially by way of a three-member regency from 1833 until his legal coming-of-age in 1835. The fact that his father, Ludwig I of Bavaria, was a known Philhellene and admirer of classical Greece in its modern Greek manifestation is less a significant biographical fact than it is representative of Hellenism as a shaping, and so to speak, a colonizing, factor well beyond Bavaria. It shows up the valuation of Greek antiquity as a link between past cultural excellence and a receptive modernity, and as a discourse with political, aesthetic, and

---

[2] Peckham 2001:x, quoting Macdonald 1995:272 on Indonesia.
[3] Thomas 1994, quoted by Peckham 2001:4.
[4] For example, Gourgouris 1996.

organizational effects for the new nation-state of Greece, as much as for its European observers.

The main stress in the historiography of the modern Greek nation-state has therefore been on its early place in the sequence of national movements in Europe, as well as on its relative and to an extent maybe unexpected success.[5] Making Greece a newly refined paradigmatic case in the study of nationalism, such as Beaton does in a recent volume, has merit. At the same time, it is also possible to view the early phase of nationhood in the light of the changes both within and away from an imperial situation in which the territory that would become Greece was located. Molly Greene, in her work on the Early Modern Eastern Mediterranean, has described well how a real sea change in the Mediterranean world may have had less to do with the breakup of the Roman Empire or the rise of Islam than with the Early Modern and Modern change from an ancient regime to a new regime of national empires. These new empires stretched much beyond the Mediterranean, but extended their influence into the Mediterranean: Britain, France, and Russia, in addition to the Ottomans.[6] In other words, much as the acknowledgement of Greece as a nation-state is a break with the Ottoman imperial system, it is also the moment of a reorientation within a continuing situation of national empires in the greater Mediterranean and Western European context. To treat the new Greek nation-state of the 1830s through the lens of imperial, rather than only national, geography may therefore help to throw its complex spatial understanding into new relief, and to unsettle the frame of analysis from the dominant nation-state model.

The moment of the queen's arrival, as wife of the new head of state, was one that promised an end in sight to the current provisionality. Moving the focus a little further away, it was also a moment that described the transition between the long-drawn-out and spatially very ambivalent War of Independence—its changing borders, changing locales of political influence, and changing seats of changing governments—on the one hand, and a politics of irredentism tightly bound up with the Eastern Question in the years to come, on the other hand. For the modern Greek case, it might have been appropriate and maybe more obvious for this present collection to hone in on imperial geographies in the context of Greece's own so-called Eastern Question from the middle of the nineteenth century onwards, after prime minister Ioannis Kolettis' famous formulation of the Megali Idea—the "Great Idea" that sees Greece as including the "unredeemed territories" of Asia Minor populated by ethnic Greeks—became a dominant part of political, and in some larger sense, social and cultural rhetoric.

---

[5] Beaton 2009.

[6] Greene 2000:3–12.

This formulation produced interaction with Western imperial powers and their literary models, too, that make geography a central focus.[7] Instead, I suggest a new look at the phase preceding that political and cultural expectation, a moment quite literally of transition and of indeterminacy when it comes to distributing roles of East and West, home and abroad, colonizer and colonized. Foregoing the usual focus on the disputed borders and margins of the Greek territory in its more obvious imperial context (and contact), I focus on the quite radical indeterminacy of what constitutes the homeland even *within* the putative borders of the new state, in the place where it seems most uncontroversial.

The conceptual challenge of experiencing a formerly imperial space, recently changed to a national territory with fluid boundaries, was a large one, and it manifested itself in bureaucratic as much as representational forms, in property law and distribution as much as in novels, themselves a new literary space.[8] The combination of both, in a quasi-new-historicist reading, will be the focus of this contribution, not least since representation is concerned with spatial thinking: if one thing is represented through another thing or word, a substitution or replacement opens space. I may be accused of using the terminology of literary representation in a deliberately figurative way itself, but I will attempt to show that it was in and by way of literary texts and their enabling structures that a geographical imagination of Greek territory was first articulated in the 1830s.

Amalia's arrival in Athens testifies to this complex net of Greek geographies, in space and in time. Her arrival on new territory as sovereign and foreigner expected to make her home there, rather than as colonial ruler, signals a particular moment in time and space and its particular tensions. In 1834, which is also roughly the date of composition of the two Greek novels I will discuss below, the newly founded nation-state is supposed to inhabit properly a capital, Athens, that links ancient tradition and cultural value with a new modernity, and that will be rebuilt to that design.[9] Contemporary accounts, such as that by Bettina von Savigny, who moved with her husband, the lawyer and administrator Konstantinos Schinas, first to Nafplio and then to Athens, describe a town of a few thousand inhabitants, exhausted and dilapidated by military conflict and the still very recent Ottoman occupation. Athens had little or no infrastructure, and certainly not enough space readily available for a large contingent of the military, as well as a Bavarian entourage and capital-builders to be accommodated.

---

[7]   Miliori 1998; Gotsi 2006.

[8]   Tziovas 2003, for further bibliography; for the provisionality and instability of the emerging national geography, see also the papers by Batsaki, Stavrakopoulou, and Zandi-Sayek in this volume.

[9]   See Bastea 2000:69–104, especially, for the architectural planning of the new capital.

The city had been chosen over Nafplio, the former capital, in a move not only inspired by classical precedent, but in the true conviction that its locality and spatial layout were wholesome and both historically and naturally promising, as opposed to Nafplio's unhealthy climate, in an environmental as much as a political sense.

In an unsigned report on the question of the seat of government, dating from May 1833 and written in German (undoubtedly by a German official from the Greek Ministry of the Interior), Athens is praised for: its cultural eminence and clear ability to feed a city in classical times; its access to a sea port linking it easily with the East (the alternative, the area of the Corinthian Isthmus, was in this argument only accessible from the sea by way of the Gulf of Corinth); its access by sea to building materials not otherwise available; and its ready space. Even though no national land was really available there (most of it was privately owned), and little actual building infrastructure was currently present, mosques and churches could readily be appropriated for public buildings, and inhabitants were allegedly willing to sell their property at an attractive rate to the arriving contingent.[10] An addendum to that document adds that Athens, as opposed to Nafplio or a place nearby, promises a much greater level of homogeneity and social stability.[11] If one reads further in the documents it becomes increasingly clear, however, that almost all members of the Greek administration were arguing strongly against Athens, among them Trikoupis, Mavrokordatos, and Kolettis (the last favoring Megara). Their arguments for a new Greek geography, in contrast, make much of the ideal situation of the isthmus that provides access to two gulfs (Corinthian and Saronic), the relative prosperity of agriculture in the area, and the availability of public land.[12] In the end, it was the Bavarian vision that would prevail: a geography of historical integration, circumscribing an almost utopian place where social and political fractiousness would be diffused by sheer force of tradition.

I have elsewhere focused on the cultural reasons for and aesthetic structures of representing Greek landscape in a way that deliberately risks and probably necessarily encourages failure.[13] As opposed to this analysis of Romantic representation from a philological and philosophical point of view, I would here like to pay more attention to the moment when the question of what is Greek ground was almost unanswerable also in a practical way. I examine this historical moment in dialogue with two Greek novels that deliberately choose a contemporary setting and make much of its space, against a background

[10] Papadopoulou-Symeonidou 1996:12–16.
[11] Ibid., 19–22.
[12] Ibid., 26–56
[13] Güthenke 2008.

of literal disaggregation, reconstruction and construction, and suspension of place. This is a reminder that the process of nation building was not only undercut discursively,[14] but that it also involved the refusal and inability to build on stable and defined ground in a fundamental way.

Panagiotis Soutsos' Leandros, and Alexandros Soutsos' The Exile of 1831

Two Greek novels are published at roughly that same point in time: Panagiotis Soutsos' *Leandros* (1834), the first of its kind within the new nation according to its author, a claim which also sheds light on the self-definition of the poets of his generation; and his brother Alexandros Soutsos' *The Exile of 1831*, published in 1835, but written at least as early as *Leandros*. Both novels deal with the story of a young idealist, whose love for his country and for a young woman are equally fervent; both protagonists witness their unavailable object of love either wither away or be destroyed; and both novels are deliberately contemporary. Leandros has precedence, as Soutsos acknowledges openly in the prologue, in Goethe and Foscolo, but he "is also a Greek, and he lives around 1833 and 1834."[15] *The Exile of 1831*, as the title suggests, which is after all more specific about a precise historical date than about the name of its generic hero, is a strange amalgam of romantic narrative with historical and political commentary.

Leandros is the epistolary novel of a young Greek who, born in Constantinople, but (through his involvement in the Greek insurrections) displaced throughout the Balkans, Europe, and Greece, has arrived in Athens. There he chances upon his childhood love Koralia, who is now married and a mother. Their love is resuscitated by the encounter, yet Koralia holds to her marital vows; the impossibility of their reunion and Leandros' suffering lead Leandros' friend to trick him into a journey through Greece, on an itinerary that includes memorial sites of classical as well as of recent political significance. His route commemorates the Greek War of Independence by explicit comparison with the desolate contemporary situation of chaos and corruption, and it mirrors the memories of the short past and prematurely failed future with Koralia. Leandros returns to Athens to find Koralia dying of her conflicting emotions and her moral steadfastness. After her death, Leandros, like a good Wertherian, commits suicide. The novel has clear debts to Goethe's *Sorrows of Young Werther* (1774) and Ugo Foscolo's Wertherian *The Last Letters of Jacopo Ortiz* (1801), both of which Soutsos knew (*Werther*, at least, in French translation) and unapologetically makes reference to in his

---

[14] Peckham 2001.
[15] P. Soutsos 1996:45.

prologue. And yet, the theme of the fulfillment of the past made impossible not just in the present but because of the present, and its interference in the romantic union, is also what distinguishes *Leandros* from his literary 'models.' Although the unsuccessful relationship and the suicide of the protagonist are the themes both of *Werther* and *Jacopo Ortiz*, the past is given less of a motivating and hampering role. Werther and Lotte are ostensibly kept apart by a social code; the story of *Jacopo Ortiz*, told around the fate of a dissident in the secessionist upper Italian provinces of the Napoleonic era, is already of a more openly political nature (here, too, it is the state of a non-unified country that mirrors the impossibility of a happy match); but none of the literary 'models' aligns the themes of intertwined erotic tension, territorial disorientation and political situatedness between East and West, ancient and modern, quite so explicitly as *Leandros* does.

The Exile of 1831 is the story of another unnamed Constantinopolitan whose political energies make him return from abroad to join the Greek revolution, and whose strong criticism of the policies of the first governor, Ioannis Kapodistrias, makes him fall foul of the government. His sympathies are with those demanding a constitution and with those rallying around local leaders to unseat Kapodistrias and his Westernized, self-interested administrators, especially after Kapodistrias' assassination in 1831 by the local leaders and brothers Mavromichali from the Mani area of the Peloponnese. His tale of exile, imprisonment, and revolution is interlinked with the pursuit of the adorable Aspasia, whose hand in marriage he first rejects for the sake of his best friend, who is in love with her also. This friend's early death (from unrequited love) should clear the way for a happy union, were it not for the demands of political action and an ambitious political and romantic rival who sabotages the Exile's every attempt to win Aspasia and her father, and who is in fact largely responsible for the main character's political persecution and exile. With new political success after Kapodistrias' death and the disintegration of his government, the Exile eventually wins back Aspasia (who appears to have fewer moral scruples and more practical wisdom than her literary sister in *Leandros*), only to see her poisoned by his frustrated rival. The Exile abandons the state of Greece to return to Constantinople, where he continues to live a life in isolation from society.

At first sight these novels look like generic Romantic pastiche, and even pastiche of the wilder kind, and this is largely how they have been evaluated until fairly recently.[16] In recent scholarship it has been more fully acknowledged (and here it should be said that prose fiction of the 1830s and 1840s in general has only recently become both better known and better studied), that

[16] Vayenas 1996; Tonnet 2002.

both of these novels make the process of traveling across space, the description of place, and the significance of space and place as national, political, and emotional, all central elements. Soutsos' *Leandros* especially has been reevaluated as a novel very openly acknowledging its claim as the self-styled first Greek novel in relation to nation-building, national identity, issues of national space, and Romantic aesthetics.[17] However, there has not been nearly as much attention paid to Soutsos' *Exile*, an even more incongruous and disaggregated novel, stylistically as much as generically. These novels are literally unsettled, very consciously addressing the question of what ground their characters move over. For Panagiotis Soutsos, the failure to secure a shared, lived-in space, becomes sublimated both onto a higher and a deeper level: into both religiosity and the substitution of the past for the present; and into a shying away from the form of the actual, current landscape. In Alexandros Soutsos' novel, there is a more stubborn attention to very contemporary detail, including that of place. But here too, there is failure: the whole story is a long-drawn-out sequence of missed encounters and opportunities, political as much as erotic, which fail on a spatial level as much as on an emotional one.

To illuminate the two brothers' narrative geographies, it is worth contextualizing them within contemporary attitudes to the national land, for want of a better term. Both wrote and in many ways centered their novels in Nafplio, even though they were published after the capital had been moved to Athens. The Soutsoi were of a politically very active family: one brother had been killed in the Battle of Dragatsani right at the beginning of the War of Independence, and a cousin, Dimitris, was a prominent judge in Nafplio. However, both brothers belonged to that peculiar first generation of Greek writers, concerned with what constituted a national literature, who were themselves just that little bit too young to have fought actively in the War of Independence themselves. Moreover, almost all came originally from outside the territory of the new state, sharing their origins in the well-connected, intellectual cultural world of the Phanariots, i.e. the Greek class holding high administrative office in the Ottoman Empire, clustered around Constantinople and the Danubian principalities in particular. Alexandros, born in 1803, and his younger brother Panagiotis, born in 1806, had first arrived in the new rump state of Greece in 1825, after being educated in Italy and then in Paris, to which they returned for some more time two years later.

---

[17] Tziovas 2009; Güthenke 2008:173–190; Calotychos 2004:111–121; Peckham 2001:22–25. In general, the political context and to an extent the outlook of both novels has only recently been commented upon more forcefully; see the introductions to their most recent editions, both 1996, by Alexandra Samouil and Nasos Vayenas, respectively.

The new kingdom was small. The territory of the Greek state in 1832 did not include more than the Peloponnese, Attica, and mainland Greece no further north than the imaginary line from the town of Arta, near Missolonghi, to the town of Volos, a little north of Euboea.[18] Nafplio was more thriving than the provincial and war-ravaged town of Athens, but still only a minor port city; both places in any case, and this is abundantly clear from the sources, were unprepared to accommodate the sizable foreign and then mainly Bavarian military and administrative contingents.[19] What was more, in the narrow circles of the newly forming society there was, in the 1830s, no structure of an established middle class nor of an established artistic profile integrated into or, for that matter, opposed to it. The social strata taking up the functions of the upper and middle classes were composed of foreigners, administrators, and functionaries, captains of the local bands and members of the local elites, with no small amount of animosities between them. The wealthy merchant communities that had gradually formed abroad in the late eighteenth century largely continued to stay abroad, and it took several more decades before the hierarchies of the upper and middle classes were filled and determined by new groups of merchants, manufacturers, bankers, and intellectuals. Bettina von Savigny again gives a perceptive and detailed description in her letters of the sheer spatial challenges of social life at Nafplio and then in Athens in 1833–1834, for Greeks and foreigners alike: the difficulty of finding furniture; the bartering over housing among new arrivals; the attempts of the Greek and Bavarian Administration to improve living conditions (for example, at Pronoia, the "new town" part of Nafplio); the sheer number of people to entertain; the confusion over what visiting etiquette was to be the rule; and the presence of visitors in the house at almost all times (hindered in Athens by the fact that available living space was so restricted that many had to move to locations out of town, making for longer ways and unexpected effects of social isolation). There are also her observations on the piecemeal character of the Greek houses she would see when paying social visits, sparsely and traditionally furnished, though proud to display a few valuable, but somewhat incongruous, objects, such as a gigantic gilded mirror, or an enormous mahogany chest of drawers.[20]

The confusion over both actual and social space was carried over into the figurative geography of professions and their respective place and role in a new society. The literary authors of new Greece, writing from a location that was provisional while ostensibly indicating continuity, and operating in the small, albeit international circles of Nafplio and later Athens, moved no less in a

[18] See Clogg 2002 for maps.
[19] Koliopoulos and Veremis 2002:195–99; Skopetea 1988:87–92; Petropoulos 1968.
[20] Savigny 2002:58–72.

somewhat ill-defined field of professional activity; here the challenge of delineating national ground was matched by the difficulty of delineating the shape
of the artist. This impasse of creating a new literature must have been acutely
felt: in Alexandros Soutsos' novel, the final and fateful poisoning of the heroine
is almost, but only almost, prevented by a moneyless writer of commissioned
verses, who is a lodger in the same house, and whose name, Phoibapollon, of
course is a pathetic and powerless inversion of the master of the Muses. This
Phoibapollon involuntarily brings about Aspasia's death, and indirectly the
withdrawal from society by one of its most ardent political activists, by over-
sleeping instead of revealing the murderous plan he has overheard in the night.
Soutsos' novel is in part deliberate satire, but it is not always easy to tell where
its boundaries with non-satire run. Alexandros Rizos Rangavis, another writer
of the Soutsos generation and background who went on to a career as writer,
translator, professor of archaeology, and diplomat, tells a similar story about
the expectations set by a classical past, however conceived, on a modern literary
landscape. In his extensive memoirs, he mentions how as an aspiring writer and
just arrived in Nafplio, he found himself advised by a local notable well-versed
in the expectations of philhellenic sentiment to go out and converse with the
ancient monuments so as to write, in this environment, on the recent heroes of
the War of Independence. Much as he tries, though, Rangavis admits that all his
honest efforts to make continuity and revolution converge on a common Greek
ground come to naught.[21] In other words, here we find the writer's unclear position expressed in relation to the actual space that is supposed to be the arena of
a national literature.

The Status of National Land

At the same time, the status of Greek territory and actual land policy was clearly
of interest to both brothers. In the closing reprise of the prologue to *Leandros*,
Panagiotis Soutsos addresses his target audience: the new generation, whose
duty it is to continue what his own generation has accomplished. In his phrasing,
the identity of his generation becomes multiple, and the roles of fighters, politicians, and poets deliberately indistinguishable:

> Youth of Greece! What you could have demanded from our own genera-
> tion has been done. We wonder-workers have built you a future, given
> you a homeland and freed the earth of your ancestors ...

> P. Soutsos 1996:47

---

[21] Rangavis 1892 i:273–275.

The blurring, however, continues beyond the margins of the text. With the direct address to the new generation, recounting the labors of his own, Soutsos uses material that he also employed almost verbatim in a speech delivered before King Otto, on the occasion of a memorial being erected in the Argolid, in January 1834.[22] Given the dating, as much as the role of the public poet that Soutsos implies here, it is futile to debate which manifestation of the sentiment came first: the material occasion, itself shaped by ideals, or the insertion into a literary product that deals in materiality. The overlap of functions, the uncertain footing of *Leandros*, as character and text, on shifting political and literary platforms, characterizes the genesis of this novel as a whole. What is more, sections of the novel, particularly the observations on the state of agriculture, industry, and the political life of Greece, were first serialized in November 1833 as travel letters in the periodical *Helios*, founded and edited by the two brothers. The sections were published under the title "My Wanderings" and signed "The Traveller." The fatal love story that makes *Leandros* comparable to the literary models the prologue invokes, was then only gradually imposed as the framework to turn social and geographical observation into narration.[23]

As a publication with a literary as much as a socio-political agenda, the journal offered a forum for social criticism and political ideas, particularly along the lines of Saint-Simonism, a utopian, Christian socialism attracting a considerable audience in France of the first half of the nineteenth century. Before elucidating its role and its link with a quasi-imperial geography and social vision of land use, a few more words are needed on the parameters of how land was treated and understood in the Greek context at this point of writing.

If it is difficult enough to establish borders, and with it identities, it was just as difficult, on a more local level, to establish a shape, nomenclature, and provenance for the ground under one's feet. To stay with the novels of the Soutsoi, what was the actual status of the land over which their characters roam, and where does the narrative, so deliberately contemporary, take place? Under Ottoman rule, land had been cultivated and owned in a multilayered way and on a fluid scale of public, semiprivate, and de facto private. (The notion of exclusively private ownership in Ottoman law was elusive: land could be de facto privately owned, yet could belong to a range of officials or foundations and ultimately to the sultan, who in turn held it in trust for God.)[24] In the period of at least the century before the Greek revolution, a *çiftlik* economy (monocultures on large estates to allow for large-scale production, especially of wheat and cotton) had been adopted in a few Greek provinces (mainly in the north

[22] Soutsos 1834:2; Güthenke 2008:177.
[23] Vayenas 1996:23–24.
[24] McGrew 1985:22–40.

and to an extent the western Peloponnese). However, this type of economy was by no means adopted by all provinces; the *çiftlik* economy was itself an effect of imperial economic politics beyond the Ottoman Empire, as Western Europe sought to import such goods in large quantities. The standard "experience" of Ottoman land regulations for the area that would become the Greek state, however, was a system of local tax farming, whereby local "big men" would advance payments to the Porte increasingly in need of cash revenue, to be reimbursed by the local taxpaying population in ways unsupervised by the Porte itself.[25] Within this system, an estate was tantamount to a claim, rather than to a piece of actual property, and it is this indirect, rather figurative sense of property ownership that is of interest to the scholar of literary texts thinking about attitudes to land and about semantic transfer implied in literary representation and figurative language. By the same token, Ottoman common law knew of a system of complicated strata of ownership or belonging, in that, for example, the produce of a piece of cultivated land could be the private property of the cultivator, while the soil in which the produce grew technically was not. In short, the prevailing experience of land tenure under Ottoman rule was one of nested, and often multiple, affiliations with the land, and of overlapping registers of belonging. Put differently, there was little precedent of exclusive, let alone collective, national ownership of, and natural or national entitlement to, ground—a good illustration of the legacy of imperial geographies for those of the new nation-state.

With the uprisings of 1821, and the confused political situation that followed for the next several years, the question of national land became pressing in more than an ideological sense. Areas were abandoned by Turkish landholders, especially in the Peloponnese (e.g. Tripolis); much cultivated land had been damaged; and, in addition, a substantial number of refugees, often clustered in communities, were seeking land to settle on, having arrived from areas of the Ottoman Empire that had been particularly badly hit in the uprisings (such as Hydra, Spetses, and Psara) and/or had suffered from reprisals (such as Chios).[26] As early as 1823, a freeze had been declared on the sale and legal categorization of land in territories shakily under Greek authority, a ruling that did not necessarily work in practice (much land changed hands along the lines of local power), but that allowed the use, or reuse of so-called "perishable

---

[25] Ibid.

[26] Only some resettlements or rather semi-authorized and semi-legalized settlements such as those of several Cretan communities near Nafplio, or of some Hydriots at Piraeus were more long-lasting. McGrew 1985:187–195.

land"—including vineyards, orchards, mills, inns, and urban property, such as shops—so as to keep revenue coming in.[27]

The government of Kapodistrias, at Nafplio, was the first to attempt a serious review of land holdings so as to decide further procedure, an undertaking that was not helped by the fact that reliable data, and land registers, had not been kept current during the preceding decades. This attempt was also cut short by Kapodistrias' assassination in 1831 and the ensuing civil unrest. The only other comparable attempt at charting the land of the new Greek state, though not so much interested in the same questions and certainly not established to harmonize its findings with the Administration and its outdated tax records, was the general geographical (plus archaeological, botanical, and zoological) survey of the Peloponnese (Morea) undertaken from 1829 to 1831 under the naturalist and geographer Colonel Bory de Saint-Vincent, on orders of the French government. The *Expédition scientifique de Morée* was modelled on the scientific charting of Egypt that had been part of Napoleon's imperial campaign there in 1798–1801, and it was carried out in the wake of a military contingent arriving under General Maison in 1828 to drive Ottoman troops out of the Peloponnese.[28] While the French expedition laid the groundwork for much topographical mapmaking of Greece in the nineteenth century, it did little to help the completion of land registers or answer questions of ownership as opposed to adding to the archaeological record.

As for the new nation-state, the Ottoman system of land cultivation and distribution stayed largely in place for the time being, as did the system of tax farming, with contracts auctioned off to locally powerful highest bidders, a system that ostensibly allowed the government to maintain badly needed revenue during an ongoing military campaign with an uncertain outcome. In addition, Greek governments from as early as 1823 had begun to promise land compensation to those fighting for independence and to those who had lost land during the revolution. Whether the land was the Greek authorities' to give was still another question. Both the Petersburg Protocol in 1824 and the London Treaty in 1827 (and finally in 1832) had envisioned that Greece would buy land from the Ottoman Empire and pay indemnities, and eventually (after 1832) Greece did pay compensation to the sultan, financed, like much else, by way of foreign loans. Those foreign loans, in turn, financially disadvantageous to Greece and often not officially authorized, for example in the British case, were staked on Greek national lands as guarantees, and Britain, fearing undue influence of other protecting powers, especially Russia, was keen to see any real

---

[27] McGrew 1985:53–79.
[28] Briffaud 1998; Sinarellis 1998; Godlewska 1999:149–192; Witmore and Shanks, forthcoming.

land distribution still avoided for a while.[29] The Kapodistrias government, in other words, found itself in a situation where national land was given out in promise with one hand, and kept in trust with the other, leaving the question of estates pending, and building up a legacy of unfulfilled obligations, with a great amount of land, in addition, uncharted, unaccounted for, and in legal and administrative limbo.

Upon Otto's appointment as king and the Regency administration's arrival in Greece in 1833, "the national estates were in total confusion."[30] Moreover, like the Kapodistrian government but with much larger reach, the Regency aimed for a complete overhaul of national administration based on Western European models (under the direction of Georg von Maurer). It redrew internal boundaries, replotted communities (*koinotites*) into demes as the basic administrative units (under new names and often indebted to ancient toponyms), and established a centralized government whose actual presence, on newly designated national territory, was maybe the biggest change from the experience of an imperial geography whose center was at the spatially remote Porte in Constantinople.

Eventually, Otto's administration would provide for a model of land donation, including a scale of preference for those entitled to acquire land. What seems paramount for grasping the conceptual challenge of experiencing and representing national space as part of a post-imperial geography is that here we find a historical and geographical context of cultural production, and a backdrop of literary narrative, where the ground is not only uncertain, but beset by multiple claims, and even a lack of knowledge of what, where, whose, and of what kind Greek land actually is. Many recent, and good, studies have focused on the border anxiety and "cartographic anxiety"[31] that had a large impact on the formation of Greek national identity (or identities, plural): expanding borders; the question of the extent of national territories; and the interferences that arise along borders and that are represented in material and figurative "mappings." What is neglected in this approach, however, is the level of absent certainty over knowing and experiencing the exact status of Greece even within what is or was agreed to be national territory. In other words, we may find that interior differentiation and multiplicities of spatial experience located away from the borders are no less significant, and just as dynamic, when it comes to imagining a national, post-imperial or para-imperial space.

Given the political involvement of the Soutsos brothers, these issues were not merely literary. Alexandros Soutsos had worked for a while as a surveyor for Kapodistrias' project to chart the national lands. It was only afterwards that

[29] McGrew 1985:41–52.
[30] Ibid., 79.
[31] Peckham 2001:38.

his disaffection with Kapodistrias' government made him into the full-time critic and satirist who, like his character the Exile of 1831, would have to face multiple lawsuits. Meanwhile, the social and political outlook promoted in the journal edited by the brothers owed much to the opinions also promoted by the followers of Saint-Simon, with which they had come into contact during their time in Paris, but also in Nafplio directly.[32] Several Saint-Simonists arrived in Greece in 1834, and under the premiership of Ioannis Kolettis, one of the most prominent local Saint-Simonists would have been Gustave d'Eichthal. A Jewish convert to Catholicism with extremely good family connections in Bavaria, Eichthal was appointed to a position at the Office of Public Economy in Nafplio from May 1834 to October 1835, part of the Ministry of the Interior that was truly gargantuan in the range of its dossier. There he was charged with promoting the industrialization and economic advancement of the state, and it was there that he dreamt up unsuccessful plans about the possible colonization of Greece in the literal sense first of all: the land cultivation and industrialization by foreigners and through foreign and Greek financial investment.[33]

The vision of Claude Henri de Rouvroy, Comte de Saint-Simon (1760–1825), and his followers, publicized widely through Saint-Simon's own writings and a number of print journals, had the objective to "improve the class of the most numerous and of the poorest." It rested strongly on the belief that a new Golden Age of industrialization would best and most speedily be brought about by the investment of financiers, industrialists, and enlightened rulers.[34] It is especially relevant for Greece, as well as other parts of the Mediterranean under Ottoman rule, that Saint-Simon and his followers put their hope for a test space explicitly in an area where East and West, and their relative values and virtues, could meet—in short where an enlightened despot would be free to impose new policies and experiment with new investments. Ottoman Egypt, Istanbul, and the newly liberated Greek state were attractive candidates.[35]

The rhetoric of the Saint-Simonists, like that of many other Romantic discourses, included a reliance on an organic model that was both historical and social: the worldview of Saint-Simonism saw a progressive development of humanity towards increasing rationalization, harmonized with art, science, and eventually industrialization, to benefit all of society. However, this also included the assumption of a natural inequality between "Africans" and "Asians," on the one hand, and "Europeans," on the other hand. Such a natural hierarchy is seen repeated on the level of the individual in society: here, Saint-Simonism

---

[32] Vayenas 1996:34–37.
[33] Eichthal 1836.
[34] Emerit 1975.
[35] Ibid.

postulates a (quasi-Platonic) dominance of the artist, scientist, and industrialist, each with their sphere of influence, a "clerisy of scientists and artists" to guide, and an industrial dynamic to catalyze and materialize social improvement.[36] This opinion is also reflected in the search for an appropriate position of the writer in the young Greek state. After the Comte de Saint-Simon's death in 1825, his social vision developed in different groups: the Parisian commune of Père Enfantin, for example, came to exaggerate the religious-mystical element of the sect, which compares with Panagiotis Soutsos' religious trajectory of his literary characters, their vision of religious sublimation as a spatial alternative, and his increasing focus on a Christian mysticism in later works; other followers (including Enfantin himself) expanded into grand-scale industrial projects at home and overseas, such as the Suez Canal Company, and the development of the French railway system.

The success of administrators with a Saint-Simonist bent in Greece was ultimately limited, as were other colonization schemes. The few actual efforts of either foreign or internal colonization and cultivation turned out to be short-lived, either because of the quick turnover of administrations and administrative personnel (Eichthal withdraws, ostensibly for health reasons, after little more than a year), or because actual settlements did not take hold.[37] It remains significant nonetheless that a socio-political vision of that stripe should coexist with a literary vision that tries to make the spatial discovery of the Greek land an enabling feature of a new national literature.

The Inner Geographies of the National Novel

How does all of this line up with the narrative of space and geography in the two novels? They both, I suggest, reflect a notion of "Greek territory" that is empty and overcrowded at the same time. It is empty in the sense of its openness to

---

[36] Leopold 1998.

[37] A case in point are the attempts to settle Bavarian troops of the royal entourage and their families in a more lasting fashion, which, with the medium-term exception of a Bavarian "colony" at Iraklion near Athens, seems to have fallen victim to clashing expectations, and unwillingness on all parts to find a workable solution. Seidl 1981, Machroth 1930, McGrew 1985:187–195. Colonization as a model certainly appears in contemporary writing, and usually with reference to the Peloponnese and specifically the fertile Argolid. But whether it is George Cochrane drawing up a detailed plan for Greek and foreign investment and new foreign military contingents (added to the national debt at substantial interest) to guard territory and agrarian progress; or whether it is Ludwig Steub who entertains a vision of clean, ruddy Swabians, ringing church bells, maidens dancing around maypoles, and new local wine of German provenance—in both, and other cases like them it is the travelogue that is the main forum for such thoughts, where they are embedded in a discourse of travel and its aesthetic. Cochrane 1837:323–353; Steub 1841:47–50.

development, progress, and freedom, waiting to be settled; but it is also empty in the sense of its being derelict, abandoned, or inhabited by the past to the extent that there is no space for the present. It is crowded in so far as it accurately reflects an urban culture marked by excess, in terms of numbers as much as in terms of ideal expectations. It is also crowded in that it signifies multiple levels of belonging, which may or may not add up to an ordered stratigraphy.

In terms of their topography, it is worth beginning with the fact that both narratives, albeit in different ways, evade Athens, the new center of (Western) government by the time both novels go to print. Much of the plot of *Leandros* may take place in Athens, but both of its main characters are foreigners to the town. Here the past and their pasts are suddenly in the foreground: just as Athens is the rediscovered place awaiting rebuilding, Leandros and Koralia rediscover each other there (they were childhood lovers) in a situation of displacement. Quite apart from the excavation of a personal and ultimately irretrievable past throughout the novel, there is also abundant direct reference to archaeological sites, a fact that provoked discussion at the time: would the great number of ruins in Athens (and elsewhere) mean that their space was lost to habitation and should be kept empty, or would there be a way of integrating ancient and modern in an architectural and urban planning sense?[38] Ruins, as "memorials" of the ancient past, serve as settings for a number of significant meetings between the protagonists, who oscillate between positive and negative interpretations of the scene, stressing the value of memory or the absence of past glory, depending on whether the predominant mood is one of hopefulness or despair. This is the place where the lovers are free and able to communicate their past, their present desire, and the impossibility of their future. Nature is on the one hand the ostensibly harmonious environment, which, as opposed to the restrictions of social space, allows the meetings of the protagonists to take place, if only for a time (Leandros and Koralia meet for long walks around Athens), and which also lets them experience their meeting of minds in the light of the material remains of ancient Greece and the natural, unchanged beauty of Greece present. Koralia is directly aligned with the past, both the individual past and the national past: in a night walk around the ancient sites of Athens, her ideal beauty is set next to the temples' ideal beauty. The impossibility of recreating the past is, however, the overriding (European) mode(l), quite literally when it comes to the works by Goethe and Foscolo, which Soutsos himself points to as his templates.[39] Other

---

[38] See Papadopoulou-Symeonidou 1996:44, with reference to Mavrokordatos; the same anxiety surrounded the question of the location for the royal palace and Schinkel's extravagant plans for integrating it on the main, extended plateau of the Acropolis.

[39] See also Güthenke 2008, more generally, on the structural expectation of failure to recover the past.

scenes of the novel use as foreground the absence of ancient grandeur, and in a vignette of Athens, Soutsos draws attention to what was then becoming the standard reference of such lack: the Parthenon marbles, having been taken away by Lord Elgin.[40]

Happiness, or any form of livable or representable experience, is impossible inside and outside the capital alike. It is the combination of Leandros' desire and Koralia's resistance, which eventually sets him, against his will, onto the path to roam the territory of the new state and the material traces of its ancient past. The itinerary, which takes up a good part of the book, doubles as a foil for the paradoxical emotions of its observer (rich with memory, or derelict, as was the case with Athens) and an educational survey for the benefit of the reader. It is the education of the reader, and the role of the writer, after all, on which Greece's competitiveness in relation to Europe depends. Outside Athens, and the force field of Koralia's presence, and in a territory that is more compatible with the tenets of admiration for unconfined Greek nature, Leandros engages in a repeated praise of the country life, once more far from society, that is presented as the home of freedom and innocence. Such praise may be reminiscent of the progress towards cultivation envisaged in the pages of the journal *Helios*. And yet, Leandros' rovings recall the itineraries of the Grand Tourists, the Greek travelers, as opposed to their European counterparts, as not just itinerant, but propelled onto a path of flight because they have, and quite literally, too, nowhere to settle.

The Exile of 1831 is equally frank about overlaying the educational topography of European visitors with a picture of flight paths necessitated by political dissent and displacement. Soutsos opens the novel with his main character surveying the panorama at Thermopylae, guided by an old local schoolteacher. His imaginary vision of Persians and Greeks readying for battle in an as yet empty and peaceful landscape contrasts sharply with the first "documentary" episode a little later that intersects the narrative by giving a summary of the recent military campaigns through the eyes and ears of a young farm boy sent by the Exile to Nafplio (to deliver, or rather fail to deliver, a letter to his beloved). Just as much as the Bavarian officials feared and suspected the political combustibility of Nafplio, the urban space of the Exile (much as its author would have disagreed with most of the Bavarians most of the time) is a place of confusion, ambition, overcrowding, and misdirected, despotic politics. This becomes clear throughout the novel where it is never urban space as such that enables visions of love, harmony, or belonging; instead, it is islands, the countryside, orchards, and even the short sea passage across the gulf of Nafplio, which the Exile has

[40] P. Soutsos 1996:78.

to make when he is arrested wrongfully and taken to the little prison island of Bourtzi. On the sea and away from the shore, between imprisonments figurative and real, his spirit soars. In this pattern, even Athens is glossed over, when the Exile stops there only for a brief moment of sublimity and awe, without Alexandros Soutsos going into any detail. Unlike his brother, it would appear, he willfully ignored the possibility of Athens as a political place altogether.

Alexandros Soutsos may appear to be spending less time on the description of antiquities,[41] but he is a careful reader of ancient texts nonetheless, utilizing them to the fullest when he undermines the sense of rightful Western or Greek "comfort" within any of the Greek territory. The opening scene, in which the moment before battle at Thermopylae is imagined, is not simply a commonplace invocation of the Persian wars as a foundational myth of Western historiography, as the transitional moment from myth to history.[42] Instead, Soutsos makes extended use of the complicated spatial model of cross-projection that is characteristic already of Aeschylus' tragedy *Persians*: here the basic situation is that of a Greek audience watching a play set entirely at the Persian court (though played by Greeks); the play, moreover, is unusual in that it stages an event directly linked to recent Athenian political history (the ultimately unsuccessful Persian campaign against Athens), rather than a mythological theme. It does so, moreover, at a point in time when Athens' own military aspirations put reflections on Persian *hybris* and warnings about failure in new perspective. Aeschylus stages the intimate experience of the Persian defeat in front of an Athenian audience at a time of Athens' rise to imperial power itself. In Soutsos' novel, reference to the Persians is abundant, here as well as in other places with regard to Salamis, Athens, and especially in the Exile's confrontation with Kapodistrias himself. Kapodistrias is likened to the Greek general Themistocles at Salamis (not a figure of Aeschylus' play), who enjoys the Athenians' support, though he will, so the historical implication goes, be changing his allegiance to the Persians once he has lost that goodwill.[43] Earlier on Kapodistrias is being compared to the Persian king Xerxes himself; another hint at Kapodistrias' risk of tyranny comes in the "Neronian ethos" he is charged with by the Exile; and in another comparison to a mishellene and foreign emperor.[44] The perspective Aeschylus offers is far from a simple celebration of victory, but instead a reminder of impermanence. The movable structure of superimposing and

---

[41] One of the few references to "ruins" are the very contemporary marble fragments left over from a monument to Kapodistrias, which fails to get built, and behind which an assassin sent to the Exile tries to hide.

[42] Lianeri 2007.

[43] A. Soutsos 1996:102.

[44] All three from A. Soutsos 1996:70.

inverting the roles of conquerer and conquered, both liable to be tripped up by lack of measure, tallies well with Soutsos' critical tone *vis-à-vis* the Kapodistrian administration holding on to European models.[45] It is also matched by the consistent portrayal of Nafplio and its society, at least those who find or seek to find favor with the government, as simultaneously Westernized and Orientalized. A good, representative example is the house of Aspasia's father, by the shore and, so the narrator informs us, dating from a time where the scene was not yet the built-up town it will soon become, with everyone trying to gain financial advantage, driving up house prices and building extensively. The father, gossip has it, had made his money supporting Ibrahim Pasha's Peloponnesian troops and allies (the ones General Maison, vanguard of the scientific expedition, was sent to drive out), while staying on the good side of the Kapodistrians. Despite having spent time in Marseille, however, he has not given up his "Asiatic" garb (including a shaved head and a dyed moustache). He is a landowner of despotic bent too, and it is only the prospect of having to provide a dowry that keeps him from accepting the Exile's rival as his son in law (at least until the rival manages to get the Exile condemned to death for insurrection). The father, the rival, and most Nafplians associated with them are therefore described as displaying a "fancy" that may be European in appearance but is stereotypically "oriental" in essence—just as the house has a large number of expensive furnishings, objects, and paintings showing typically Western idylls and picturesque landscapes, together with agricultural scenes, the house's owner lives comfortably in the style of the oriental despot.[46]

In this oscillation between who or what is East and West, colonizer and colonized, there is one more striking instance that brings into focus the ambivalence of cultivating new ground in a new state defined by ancient precedent and open to foreign intervention. This is the figure of speech, repeated in many contemporary poems, speeches, and articles, which hailed the new king Otto as a new Danaos, settling the Argolid. In mythology, Danaos, an Egyptian though with Greek divine ancestry (the usual pedigree of most Greek mythological figures, however foreign), seeks exile in Greece and eventually becomes a peaceful king of Argos. The Argolid, to which Nafplio belongs geographically, since antiquity had had a reputation for its fertility—and the figure of the semi-foreign ruler settling what is to become a Greek heartland is an attractive, and, more importantly, a flexible figure to think through the arrival of a Bavarian king expected to represent Greece. Panagiotis Soutsos, for sure, in one of his poems and in the speech mentioned above given at Argos, uses the image with ease (Soutsos

---

[45] Cf. Van Steen 2007 on private stagings of the play in Constantinople in or shortly after 1821.
[46] A. Soutsos 1996:144.

1834). Alexandros Soutsos, too, mentions the young king, about whom even he remained hopeful at this stage, in a vignette when a farm boy, sent to Nafplio, gradually approaches the noticeably modernizing and changing city:

> On the carriage road to Nafplio, one of the miracle works of Ioannis Kapodistrias, the simple farmhand stood gaping in wonder, saying to himself: "how much, just how much must they have spent building this road!" A little later he passed Tiryns, and then Apovathmoi, where Danaos alighted in old times when he brought the first seeds of community to Greece, and where soon, around 1833, another young Danaos would alight, as king of Greece
>
> A. Soutsos 1996:66

Ostensibly hopeful, there is too much retrospective skepticism (the scene is set in 1831, the time of writing is at least 1834) not to make obvious the signs of Oriental wastefulness and despotism that could attach to Danaos, the king from Egypt, as much as to his modern, European successor.

Conclusion

The situation of Greece around 1830 is framed by a set of mutually overlapping imperial and national geographies. Imperial geographies, as understood in this volume, denote an understanding of space and of place simultaneously one's own and not one's own, a space that is somehow marked by inequality in political and cultural power. The circumstances of the 1830s extend that space one's own and not one's own to the conditions of new national geographies even *within* the boundaries of the state's territory, in which the conflicting demands, the indeterminacy and the volatile locations of identity attach to a Greek geography that is to a large extent first realized in writing. The early 1830s is a moment in time when the capital is not yet determined; Greece has not yet worked out a national rhetoric of its own past civilizing mission in the West and its future civilizing mission in the East (the *Great Idea*), nor has it worked out the status of what land actually belongs to whom. Ludwig Ross, the observer of Queen Amalia's plight as she steps on the Greek shore, would go on, in the 1840s, to write optimistic reviews and opinion pieces for a German audience about the potential for Greek colonization further East,[47] but then he was an archaeologist who believed in benevolent cultural diffusionism and in the precedent of ancient Greece's creative response to other cultures (such as Egypt). Observing

---

[47] Minner 2006:282–290.

what was right in front of his eyes in 1834, however, he may have stood closer to the realities of a queen, an owl, and a geography out of kilter.

Works Cited

Beaton, R. 2009. "Introduction." In Beaton and Ricks 2009:1–18.

Beaton, R. and Ricks, D., eds. 2009. *The Making of Modern Greece: Nationalism, Romanticism & the Uses of the Past (1797-1896)*. Farnham.

Bastea, E. 2000. *The Creation of Modern Athens: Planning the Myth*. Cambridge.

Bridges, E., Hall, E., and Rhodes, P.J., eds. 2007. *Cultural Responses to the Persian Wars: Antiquity to the Third Millennium*. Oxford.

Briffaud, S. 1998. "L'expédition scientifique de Morée et le paysage méditerranéen." In M.N. Bourguet et al. 1998:289–297.

Bourguet M.N. et al., eds. 1998. *L'Invention scientifique de la Méditerranée*. Paris.

Calotychos, V. 2004. *Modern Greece: A Cultural Poetics*. New York.

Clogg, R. 2002 [1992]. *A Concise History of Greece*. 2nd ed. Cambridge.

Cochrane, G. 1837. *Wanderings in Greece*. London.

Eichthal, G. 1836. *«Les Deux Mondes», par M.G.D.E., ... servant d'introduction à l'ouvrage de M. Urquhart, La Turquie et ses resources*. Paris.

Emerit, M. 1975. "Les Saint-Simoniens en Grèce et en Turquie." *Revue des Études Sud-Est Européennes* 13/2: 241–251.

Godlewska, A. 1999. *Geography Unbound: French Geographical Science from Cassini to Humboldt*. Chicago.

Gotsi, G. 2006. "Empire and Exoticism in the Short Fiction of Alexandros Rizos Rangavis." *Journal of Modern Greek Studies* 24/1:23–55.

Gourgouris, S. 1996. *Dream Nation: Enlightenment, Colonization and the Institution of Modern Greece*. Stanford.

Greene, M. 2000. *A Shared World: Christians and Muslims in the Early Modern Mediterranean*. Princeton.

Güthenke, C. 2008. *Placing Modern Greece: The Dynamic of Romantic Hellenism, 1770-1840*. Oxford.

Koliopoulos, J.S. and Veremis, Th. 2002. *Greece: The Modern Sequel. From 1831 to the Present*. New York.

Lianeri, A. 2007. "The Persian Wars as the 'Origin' of Historiography: Ancient and Modern Orientalism in George Grote's History of Greece." In Bridges, Hall and Rhodes 2007:331–354. Oxford.

Leopold, D. 1998. "Saint-Simon, Claude-Henri de Rouvroy, Comte de." *Routledge Encyclopedia of Philosophy*. London.
http://www.rep.routledge.com/article/DC066

Macdonald, G.M. 1995. "Indonesia's Medan Merdeka. National identity and the built environment." *Antipode* 27/3:270–293.

McGrew, W. 1985. *Land and Revolution in Modern Greece, 1800-1881: The Transition in the Tenure and Exploitation of Land from Ottoman Rule to Independence.* Kent, OH.

Machroth, S. 1930. *Das Deutschtum in Griechenland.* Doctoral dissertation. Tübingen.

Miliori, M. 1998. *The Greek Nation in British Eyes 1821-1864: Aspects of a British Discourse on Nationality, Politics, History and Europe.* DPhil thesis. Oxford.

Minner, I.E. 2006. *Ewig ein Fremder im fremden Lande: Ludwig Ross (1806-1859) und Griechenland.* Mannheim.

Papadopoulou-Symeonidou, P. 1996. *Η Επιλογή της Αθήνας ως πρωτεύουσας της Ελλάδος 1833-1834* [The Selection of Athens as Capital, 1833–1834]. Thessaloniki.

Peckham, R.S. 2001. *National Histories, Natural States: Nationalism and the Politics of Place in Greece.* London.

Petropoulos, J.A. 1968. *Politics and Statecraft in the Kingdom of Greece.* Princeton.

Rangavis, A.R. 1892-1930. *Απομνημονεύματα* [Memoirs]. 4 vols. Athens.

Ross, L. 1863. *Erinnerungen und Mitteilungen aus Griechenland.* Berlin.

von Savigny, B. 2002. *Leben in Griechenland 1834 bis 1835: Bettina Schinas, geb. von Savigny, Briefe und Berichte an ihre Eltern in Berlin.* Münster.

Seidl, W. 1981. *Bayern in Griechenland: Die Geburt des Griechischen Nationalsaats und die Regierung König Ottos.* Munich.

Sinarellis, M. 1998. "Bory de Saint-Vincent et la géographie méditerranéenne." In Bourguet 1998:299–310. Paris.

Skopetea, E. 1988. *Το Πρότυπο Βασίλειο και η Μεγάλη Ιδέα: Όψεις του εθνικού προβλήματος στιν Ελλάδα (1830-1880)* [The "Model Kingdom" and the Great Idea. Greek Perspectives on the National Problem (1830-1880). Athens.

Soutsos, A. 1996 [1835]. *Ο Εξόριστος του 1831* [The Exile of 1831] (Ed. N. Vayenas). Athens.

Soutsos, P. 1996 [1834]. *Ο Λέανδρος* [Leandros]. (Ed. A. Samouil). Athens.

———. 1834. *Λόγος εκφωνηθείς εις τον τόπον της ανεγέρσεως του κατ' Αργολίδα μνημείου* [Speech made on the theme/on the place of the establishment of a memorial in the Argolid]. Gennadius Library, Athens, phyll. 69 T.6 no 19.

Steub, L. 1841. *Bilder aus Griechenland.* Leipzig.

Thomas, N. 1994. *Colonialism's Culture. Anthropology, Travel and Government.* Cambridge.

Tonnet, H. 2002. *Études sur la nouvelle et le roman grecs modernes.* Athens.

Tziovas, D. 2003. *The Other Self: Selfhood and Society in Modern Greek Fiction.* Lanham/Oxford.

———. 2009. "The novel and the crown. *O Leandros* and the politics of Romanticism." In Beaton and Ricks 2009:211–224.

Van Steen, G. 2007. "Enacting History and Patriotic Myth. Aeschylus' Persians on the Eve of the Greek Revolution." In Bridges, Hall, and Rhodes 2007: 299–330. Oxford.

Vayenas, N. 1996. "Ο ουτοπικός σοσιαλισμός των αδελφών Σούτσων" ["The utopian socialism of the brothers Soutsos"]. In Soutsos 1996:9–45. Athens.

Witmore, C. and Shanks, M. forthcoming. *From Isthmus to Gulf: A Chorography of the Eastern Morea.*

9

Translation as Geographical Relocation
Nineteenth-Century Greek Adaptations of Molière in the Ottoman Empire

Anna Stavrakopoulou

In short, I learn from the theatre, how to recognize that which is most suited to creating an impression on the mind, to achieving amazement or laughter or *how to ignite a certain charming chuckle in the hearts of men which comes about when one hears the mistakes and idiocies of people with whom one constantly converses naturally*, represented in comedies with much skill from their perspective, of course, without shocking too much through offence.[1]

Fischer-Lichte 2002:137,
quoting Goldoni 1935–1956, I:769

Long before there were modern theater buildings in the geographical area currently inhabited by Greek citizens, even before the formation of a Greek state and an educated middle class that could support theater as an institution, a Greek-speaking intelligentsia was actively interested in theater. On the one hand, all those living in European cities with strong theatrical traditions, such as Paris and Vienna, were familiar with the distinct qualities of this art form, and on the other, those living in cities of the Ottoman Empire with large Greek communities were actively following the developments in countries with unquestioned cultural hegemony, like France and Italy.

This chapter investigates two kinds of empires: cultural empires that are almost without borders, and political ones with a shifting circumference. I will

---

[1]   The italics are mine.

examine the modes of expansion of Molière's poetic empire, two hundred years after his death, in multiethnic cities and societies of the eastern Mediterranean very distant from his domain. My discussion will focus on two plays by Molière, *The Miser* and *Tartuffe*, which in the nineteenth century were adapted successfully for Greek-speaking readers with two major modifications: the time of action was advanced by two centuries, and thus moved to the nineteenth century; and the place "migrated" eastwards by several thousand kilometers, from Paris to Smyrna and Constantinople.[2] So far, the tendency in Greek historiography has been to classify these two adaptations by their language (Greek), and not by their setting (Smyrna and Constantinople), emphasizing thus their Greek aspects and blurring the Ottoman imperial context to which they also belong.

These translations were part of a broader effort made by diaspora Greek intellectuals from 1780 onwards to forge a new Hellenic identity. This effort included a shift in the content of the books published during the last decades of the eighteenth century, as well as a major translating enterprise, which included, among other genres, theater.[3] The institution of theater, in any case, had been considered an educational tool as it could deliver radical messages to literate and illiterate audiences alike. Greek intellectuals started focusing on the forging of a new Hellenic identity, with two major models in mind: post-Renaissance Europe and ancient Greece. They felt that a revival of the glorious past could be achieved only by narrowing the cultural and intellectual gap with contemporary Europe. Given the leading role of France in cultural matters, and due to the impact of figures like Adamantios Korais (1748–1833), the patriarch of the Neohellenic renaissance, who resided in France, it is not surprising that French society and literature formed the main cultural model Greece opted for.

All of us readers, theatergoers and cinema fans of the twentieth and twenty-first centuries, are very familiar with what the two Greek translators undertook in the nineteenth century: apart from productions which attempt historical accuracy (in narrow terms), we have seen several adaptations of Jane Austen's novels and Shakespeare's plays set in different eras and countries, to mention only a couple of adaptation favorites. Two such "translations" involving geographical relocation with an everlasting effect on cultural history are Grigori Kozintsev's *King Lear* (1971) and Akira Kurosawa's *Ran* (1985).[4] Although in these more recent adaptations, in addition to the relocation in Russia and Japan respectively, we witness a "translation" from one medium, theater, to another,

---

[2]   Oikonomos 1816: see Skalioras 1970, Skylissis 1851 and 1871. Although the languages of the primary texts under examination are French and modern Greek, all excerpts are quoted in English.

[3]   Spathis 1986, Tabaki 2007.

[4]   Wood 2005.

cinema, and despite the fact that the play involved, *King Lear*, puts forth a whole set of other issues, the goal of the major film directors is at its core similar to that of the modest, yet daring, Greek translators: to help their readers/viewers understand what is at stake in the specific "foreign" plays.

Before analyzing the ways in which translation functioned as geographical and cultural relocation in adaptations of Molière for mainland and diasporic Greek communities, I will provide a brief overview of theater-related editorial efforts, which prepared the ground for theater as an institution in nineteenth-century Greece. Around the last quarter of the eighteenth century there was a boom in nonreligious publications in Greek, printed by Greek-owned presses in Europe (mainly in Venice and Vienna). Among those publications we find the first dramatic texts, mainly translations of contemporary European authors (like Metastasio and Goldoni); theater was valued as an institution, not only because it was "invented" by the Greeks, but also because major pieces of literature could be accessed by a broader (even illiterate) audience.[5]

Although tragedies were favored during the decades preceding the War of Independence for their educational and inspirational qualities, some often anonymous, learned people did translate Goldoni and Molière.[6] Goldoni revolutionized the genre of comedy in the eighteenth century by introducing several radical changes to the tradition of the Commedia dell'Arte, in the bosom of which he attained his craftsmanship.[7] Thus, he focused on the working classes (promoting servants to center stage), while depicting the aristocrats as slothful and pathetic creatures. Nonetheless, his most endearing and radiant creations were his female characters, who were endowed with all the traditional feminine attributes, supplemented by some enlightened liberties. Thus, Goldoni is the first playwright to glorify a working woman in *La Locandiera*, positioning her not only above idle gentry, but also above working-class men. Apart from their emancipation in the workplace, women in Goldoni comedies choose their husbands prudently, after testing them and often outwitting them.

Around the end of the eighteenth century, Goldoni comedies started being translated and often published, just before the death of the major Italian playwright.[8] In *La vedova scaltra* [*The Cunning Widow*] (1748), rendered in an early Greek translation as "The thoughtful and beautiful widow (η στοχαστική και ωραία χήρα)," the character of Rosaura chooses among four suitors (natives of four leading European nations—Spain, England, France, and Italy) the most

---

[5] Spathis 1986:101–144 and 199–214.
[6] Tabaki 2002:149–157, Hadjipantazis 2002:230–247.
[7] Fischer-Lichte 2002:136–145. The masterful synthesis of Goldoni's achievements in dramatic composition crafted by Fischer-Lichte is most enlightening, despite its brevity.
[8] Spathis 1986:199–214.

appropriate candidate to fill the position of her second husband, who is no other than the Italian, while she marries her sister off to the French (as second best). Nonetheless, although Goldoni's male and particularly female characters enjoy freedom of action, an ideal to which the Greeks aspired, the conservative prerogatives of the society soon forced the translators to find refuge in the less socially threatening comedies of Molière.[9] Ergo, an earlier phase of the European intellectual development was considered more appropriate, and the measured behaviors of the seventeenth century, as reflected in the carefully crafted plots and characters of Molière, provided the ideal answer to questions of moral and social conduct. Starting in the mid-1810s and throughout the century there was a proliferation of translations of Molière's comedies, farcical (as the *Doctor in Spite of Himself*) and philosophical (*The Miser, Tartuffe, The Misanthrope,* etc.). Furthermore, during the second half of the nineteenth century, Molière became the master craftsman for all aspiring Greek comic playwrights.[10] The more professional Greek theater life becomes, the more translators favor adaptations, as opposed to literal translations. In any case, in the sphere of comedy, it has been astutely observed: "theatre translation, as distinct from adaptation, is a very recent phenomenon."[11]

The Miser

The first adaptation, chronologically, is of Molière's *L'avare* [*The Miser*] by Konstantinos Oikonomos. *The Miser* was first performed in 1668 at the theater of the Palais Royal, during a difficult time for Molière, who was struggling with health and family problems, as well as with strong reactions from certain circles regarding *Tartuffe* and *Dom Juan*.[12] *The Miser*, despite its heavy farcical outlook, remains one of Molière's "grand" comedies, in which he ridicules individuals who attempt to impose on others their own obsessions, thus harming not only themselves, but also their immediate circle and society at large. Harpagon, the protagonist, is a sexagenarian widower obsessively preoccupied with his money, "an early modern capitalist in action."[13] Out of extreme thriftiness he is planning to marry his daughter to a rich widower, while he is yearning to wed for a second time choosing the beloved of his son as his ideal bride. During the play, we follow the downfall of the penny-pinching father, after his precious coffer is stolen by a coalition of disgruntled people, including his servant and his

---

9   Hadjipantazis 2002:230–247, Hadjipantazis 2004:20–21.
10 Hadjipantazis 2002 and 2004.
11 Farrell 1996.
12 Gaines 2002:37-39, Jouanny 1960, II:235–237.
13 Gaines 2002:37.

children. The resolution is achieved when the miser concedes to marry his children to the companions of their choice, in exchange for his stolen coffer. The action takes place in seventeenth-century Paris and all the references to material wealth and money-lending involve the currency and habits of the French in the era of Louis XIV (who reigned from 1643 to 1715). Given the tendency to attribute such negative qualities as miserliness to other nations, the miser in Molière's play is compared in three instances respectively to a Jew, an Arab, and a Turk, first by his dumbfounded son who discovers as an incognito customer the high interest rates his father charges, and second by his servant who tries to warn a matchmaker about his master's unrestrained passion for money.

> CLÉANTE. The deuce! What a Jew! what an Arab we have here! That is more
> than twenty-five per cent.[14]

The Miser, Act II, Scene 1

> LA FLÈCHE. All useless here. I defy you to soften, as far as money is
> concerned, the man we are speaking of. He is a Turk on that
> point, of a Turkishness to drive anyone to despair, and we
> might starve in his presence and never a peg would he stir.
> In short, he loves money better than reputation, honour, and
> virtue, and the mere sight of anyone making demands upon
> his purse sends him into convulsions; it is like striking him in a
> vital place, it is piercing him to the heart, it is like tearing out
> his very bowels! And if ...
> But here he comes again; I leave you.[15]

The Miser, Act II, Scene 5

The translator of *The Miser*, Konstantinos Oikonomos, was born in 1780 in Tsaritsani, a small town in Thessaly.[16] His father was a priest who held the administrative position of "Oikonomos" (a dignitary dealing with finances) within the church hierarchy, hence the family surname of Oikonomos. His date of birth falls within the Greek Enlightenment (roughly 1770–1821), and his early education was based on patristic and classical texts. He was reportedly a child prodigy, and his life accomplishments confirmed his brilliant first steps. At an early age he was taught French by a doctor in Ambelakia, and from 1799–1803 he attended the classes of Konstantinos Koumas (1777–1836), one of the most

---

[14] "He [Cléante] makes the shocking discovery that Harpagon is deeply involved in black market finance, floating unsecured loans at usurious rates in order to obtain claims to the estates of young spendthrifts" (Gaines 2002:38).
[15] Both excerpts are from http://www.online-literature.com/moliere/the-miser/2/.
[16] For all information following, see Skalioras 1970:7–16.

prominent and gifted teachers of his time, with a large breadth of knowledge. He married in 1801, and soon after he followed the family tradition and joined the ranks of the church. Upon the death of his father in 1805, he inherited the title and duties of "Oikonomos" and began his career as a preacher. Very soon his fame spread in Thessaly and beyond. His exposure to preaching must have given him a taste of the joys and exultations of acting, as it is known that he was an exceptional orator.[17] In 1806 he was arrested by the men of Ali Pasha and jailed in Ioannina, with the accusation that he was involved in a rebellion coordinated by Papathymios Vlachavas. After he paid the ransom required, he was liberated and returned home. Following his incarceration, after a brief stint in Macedonia, he ended up in Smyrna invited by his old teacher Koumas to teach Greek at the recently established Gymnasium of Smyrna (1809–1819). It is during his tenure at the Smyrna high school that he produced the translation of Molière's *The Miser*. In 1819 the Gymnasium of Smyrna was abolished, following strong reactions by conservative quarters of the Greek community, and Oikonomos was fired.[18] After his expulsion from Smyrna, his career moved steadily upward and honors started accumulating. He was transferred to Constantinople, but during the War of Independence he took refuge in Odessa and stayed in Russia until 1832. He returned to Greece with a very high pension for life from the Russian state, and during the last twenty years of his life, from 1837–1857, he lived in Athens, completely devoted to his writings, which made him one of the most prolific and rigid advocates of Orthodoxy.[19]

Oikonomos was thirty-six years old when he undertook the adaptation of *The Miser*. At the time he was living in Smyrna and was as close to liberal ideas as he would ever get.[20] In the beginning of his introduction, which he addresses "To the Greeks," he explains why he chose to translate *The Miser*, informing his readers that the play had been translated or imitated by all the "wise nations of Europe." Furthermore, he says, "these poems belong mostly to us, by hereditary right [bequeathed by] our ancestors," given that Molière borrowed heavily from the Romans (and more specifically from Plautus' *Aulularia*), who "copied or imitated Greek dramas."[21]

Preempting possible reactions to his modifications of the original (a pattern that is common among several translators of the early 1800s), Oikonomos poses

---

[17] Skalioras 1970:9.

[18] Spathis 2007:33–37.

[19] Skalioras 1970:16.

[20] The play was published anonymously in 1816 in Vienna, with the title Ο Φιλάργυρος [*The Miser*]. For the needs of this article, I have used the 1970 reissue, which includes Oikonomos' 1816 prologue, as well as a valuable introduction by Kostis Skalioras (Oikonomos 1970). All translations are mine.

[21] Skalioras 1970:23.

the question: "If Molière crafted his comedy wonderfully, why didn't you translate it word for word, but instead you initiated changes, and some additions, and omissions?" (ibid., 24). In order to substantiate his argument he composes a brief theory on comedy, combining Aristotelian and nationalist prerogatives and stating its properties and goals:

> Comedy is an imitation of a base and ridiculous act, which intends to cure vice painlessly and to teach virtue. In order to achieve this, comedy must imitate well the mores, rituals and the behavior of the nation for which it is produced. Without this national gain, the playwright cannot attract and move the readers or the spectators of his poem. Molière painted the Miser according to the practices of his compatriots. The Greek must paint him according to the habits of his fellow citizens. It is a necessity for theater to be national, and above all for comedy.
>
> For that reason I often used sentences and opinions and proverbs and some scenes, which differ substantially from the original, so that I adapt the poem to the customs of my compatriots [...] the cloths of Europe we cut them and sew them according to the habit of our compatriots.
>
> Oikonomos 1970:24–25

He provides solid justification for some changed scenes and defends two added episodes, which do not promote the action. With regard to the language, Oikonomos had to face the limitations of the Greek language, which was still being shaped at the time:

> [...] our spoken language is still very unruly and sullied by stains. Until it gets organized and enriched, we have to live with its imperfections. I used some dialects, for instance the common language of the lower classes of Chios in the language of Strovilis [servant of the miser's son], and the vernacular of the Thessalians for Kyr Yiannis [the miser's cook], as well as the vernacular of the Smyrniots for the character of Sofoulio [the matchmaker], and to an extent for the character of the barbaric rich Exintavelonis [very astute rendition of Harpagon]. [...] The comic playwright uses dialects to represent n aiveté, lack of education, and the particularity of the person using the dialect.
>
> Oikonomos 1970:27

In addition, he defends his use of dialects with two arguments. "First, [he uses dialects] because our nation is not thriving yet as far as education, so that comedies are composed in a smooth vocabulary. It is necessary to use a more intense language, and, at times, even light obscenities, so that the text flows and the laughter ensues. Second, the contemporary Greek dialects do not differ so greatly from each other, so as to make a comedy abstruse and obscure." (ibid., 28). His was the first use of dialects in a translation/adaptation, and he set an example that was followed by several translators throughout the nineteenth century.[22] The following comment on Smyrna in connection with the use of dialects is also very important: "in Smyrna, above all, where the action is taking place, because of the frequent interactions with citizens from all over Greece, all the Hellenic dialects are known, in a similar way as once upon a time the dialects of our old language were familiar to the Athenians."[23] Smyrna, one of the biggest port cities of the Ottoman Empire, is compared to classical Athens at the height of its own empire. Oikonomos confesses that he baptized the main character Exintavelonis (connoting a penny-pincher, someone who counts even his needles—*velóni*, meaning "the needle") after painstaking thinking, while he chose all the other names randomly, but very imaginatively, and in a manner that betrays familiarity with the comic tradition. In this lengthy introduction, the reader is impressed by Oikonomos' rare degree of erudition, given that it is evident that he read not only the *Aulularia* [*The Pot of Gold*] by Plautus in Latin, which served as a model to Molière,[24] but was also aware of various French commentaries on *The Miser*, which were indicating several shortcomings of Molière. In fact, for some of his emendations of the original, he claims to have taken into account the criticism of Rousseau and Diderot, among others.[25]

Oikonomos closes his introduction exactly the way he had started it, by addressing the last paragraph to the "fellow compatriots, rich and small and big" asking them to "observe the life and downfall of the misers." His main occupation as a priest and preacher becomes evident in his assessment of the misfortunes the miser causes himself and everyone around him, since "the miser can never become a happy husband, nor a good father, neither a tolerant ruler, nor a peaceful companion, nor simply an honest citizen" (ibid., 30–31). The content of the two scenes he added is considered of paramount importance for the extra vice he pours into an already vicious character. In Act II, after Scene 3, he adds a scene in which some trustees of the hospital knock on the miser's door and ask him for a contribution. In his furiously defensive response to them he curses not only money-collection for the hospital, but also for all common causes, including the schools:

---

[22] Puchner 2001:21; Hadjipantazis 2004:32–33.

[23] Oikonomos 1970:28.

[24] Plautus set the action of his Roman play in Athens (!) and Molière transported it to Louis XIV's Paris.

[25] Oikonomos 1970:25–26.

[...] as if the other heavy expenses of our city were not sufficient, we want to collect money for schools too! And what on earth do we need schools for? So that our children become educated lazy know-alls [...] with my modest ABCs I manage to govern my house fine, while my neighbor, who knows a lot, has gone bankrupt three times.

Oikonomos 1970:71

His last words in that scene constitute a fierce attack against education and its side effects on societies: "the schools above all ruin places [...] look at the Smyrniots, instead of acknowledging their shortcomings, they have opened a big school, so that their children lose their mind and go to France in order to return with hats" (ibid., 71–72). It should not go unnoticed that by endowing the miser with additional negative qualities, pertaining to the health and prosperity of the community, Oikonomos stresses the necessity of education, which revolutionizes individuals and societies. In the second intercalated scene (ibid., 102–103), he juxtaposes the miser to a poor woman (also created by Oikonomos), who cannot pay the rent she owes him because with the few pennies she has she must buy food for her children. In an attempt to show the ultimate debasement of the miser's soul, Oikonomos makes him rigidly deaf to her supplications, insisting on confiscating her only possession (a bathtub). It is clear that these two scenes plant masterfully the old play in the new reality and at the same time render the already risible Molière character even more grotesque; in the first instance, the nastiness of his miserliness is shown on a Greek communal level, with hospitals and schools placed at the top of the agenda, and in the second his lack of humanity is being stressed against a personal backdrop. With two potent strokes Oikonomos makes his fellow Smyrniots gasp while grasping the detrimental effects of stinginess. Furthermore, Dimitris Spathis associates especially the miser's suspicion towards education to current social clashes in the bosom of the Greek community in Smyrna around 1815–1816.[26]

The translation was a huge success and was reprinted several times in the nineteenth century; oddly, in the second edition of *The Miser* (which appeared in 1835 and was the first to be printed in Smyrna), not only was the translator's name once again concealed, but the introduction was also suppressed. By that time Oikonomos, who had returned to Greece from Russia and had become one of the most ardent church spokesmen (in addition to being one of the finer theologians of his time), may have chosen to forget the radical ideas he had adopted in his thirties.

[26] Spathis 2007:33.

This two-hundred-year-old adaptation is still a very lively text. Its language is very close to the Greek spoken in Smyrna two centuries ago, and the characters have a vivacity that has made this translation one of the most popular on the Greek stage, after the development of theater and the formation of the first Greek theatrical groups that toured the coastal cities of the Mediterranean and the Black Sea from the 1830s onwards.[27] As for the handling of the few references to the Turks in the French original, Oikonomos opted to replace them by Jews and Albanians, when it comes to miserly behavior.[28]

Tartuffe

Tartuffe was first staged in 1664, and censored soon after, as it offended a group of *dévots,* or devout Catholics, in the court of Louis XIV. It took several rewrites and changes before the definitive enlarged version of 1669.[29] In five acts, and almost two thousand rhymed verses, Molière denounces religious hypocrisy, by presenting a character of great religious zeal, who finds shelter in the house of a devout naïve fellow, and who manages with a few masterful strokes to become his confidant to the point of controlling the latter's estate. While Orgon, the gullible pious person, wants to marry Tartuffe to his daughter (against her will), Tartuffe courts his host's wife Elmire shamelessly. After several heart-wrenching scenes during which Orgon exposes himself to grave financial dangers, Tartuffe's ruse is unveiled and the mask of virtue and morality is replaced by one of ingratitude and ruthlessness towards his benefactor. The power bestowed upon the hypocrite by the dupe is so destructive that only royal intervention can save the innocent victim from utter ruination; this is one of the rare instances when Molière makes use of the good old *deus ex machina* of Greco-Roman theater.

---

[27] In Hadjipantazis 2002, Appendix II, one can count some twenty performances of the play in the span of roughly forty years, which make it an all-time and all-place favorite, *prior* to 1876, which marks the "birth" of regular theatrical life in Athens.

[28] The only other reference to the Turks in the French original occurs in the words of the matchmaker (Act II, Scene 5), who brags about her skills by referring to two of the mightiest empires ever in the Mediterranean: "There are no two persons in the world I could not couple together; and I believe that if I took it into my head, I could make the Grand Turk marry the Republic of Venice." The Greek translator renders this passage as follows: "I am particularly gifted in marriages: I could even marry the wolf to a ewe-lamb," thus gently expelling from his text any hint that could cause him trouble.

[29] Fischer-Lichte 2002:105–106, Koppisch 2002:448–456, Auerbach 1974:359–394. Needless to say that the literature on *Tartuffe*, one of Molière's finest plays, is more than voluminous: my selection above includes an assessment by a theater historian (Fischer-Lichte), a larger presentation by a Molière specialist (Koppisch in Gaines 2002) and last a lengthy chapter in a seminal text for the field of comparative literature (Auerbach's *Mimesis*), which was written in the 1930s in Istanbul, the place where Skylissis' adaptation sets the action of his *Tartuffe*.

Before we examine how Ioannis Isidoridis Skylitsis (or Skylissis) "transplanted" the play to the Constantinople of the 1850s, let us consider some significant aspects of his life.[30] By a curious coincidence Skylitsis was born in Smyrna in 1819, the year of Oikonomos' expulsion from the city. His father was a rather wealthy merchant from Chios, whose fortune was confiscated after 1821. According to what he claims in an autobiographical note he wrote late in his life, his family wanted him to become a businessman, while he himself longed more for letters than money. Early on he started his career as a journalist, while immersing himself in European literature; although his main aspiration was to become a poet, and he did gain considerable fame in Smyrna and Athens, he devoted almost all of his time to journalism and literary translations, for financial reasons. In the early 1840s, he managed to realize his dream of studying in Europe, and he spent a few years in France (Marseille and then Paris), before heading back to Smyrna in 1844. Starting in the mid-1840s, he translated Eugène Sue, Victor Hugo, George Sand, Alexandre Dumas, as well as Racine, Molière, and others. Given the fact that the Greek language was still being shaped in the middle of the nineteenth century, his achievement in translating *Les Mystères de Paris* by Sue (written in 1842–1843, a very popular *roman-fleuve* with a strong social and political component) for instance, was more than praiseworthy. It was during his most prolific years (1845–1854) that he produced the adaptation in rhyme of *Tartuffe* (Smyrna, 1851). In the mid-1850s, he moved back to Europe (Trieste, Vienna, Paris); it is during this phase that he published the second revised edition of *Tartuffe*, in a volume entitled Μολιέρου άριστα έργα [*Molière's Best Plays*], which also includes the *Misanthrope* and the *Miser* (Trieste, 1871). In the 1870s, Skylitsis returned to the Mediterranean: Smyrna, Alexandria, and Athens. Skylitsis' version of *The Miser* is also set in Smyrna. Nonetheless, a comparison with Oikonomos' *Miser* proves the uncontested superiority of the latter's adaptation; his religious piety notwithstanding, Oikonomos was able to produce a much lighter and brighter text. Skylitsis' language was stiffer with purist undertones, which had worked wonderfully in the rhymed translation of *Tartuffe*, but which sounded strange in the prose of *The Miser*. He died in Monte Carlo in 1890, during a trip there for his ailing health, and rumor has it that he took his own life.[31] Skylitsis' major achievements on the intellectual scene revolve around his precious translations of French classics and of popular literature of his time. His life coincides with the era of the Soutsos brothers, whose

---

[30] Politis 2009. (I am grateful to Alexis Politis for sharing his all-encompassing article on Skylitsis with me before its publication, while I was preparing the oral version of this chapter in the first months of 2009.)

[31] Ibid., 77.

prose is discussed in this volume by Constanze Güthenke; as she has shown, the Soutsoi, as well as Skylitsis, lived in a phase of "transition and of indeterminacy."

In the prologue of his 1851 edition of *Tartuffe*, the thirty-two-year-old Skylitsis argues that the act of translation (as opposed to original creation) was of primary importance for the familiarization of the readers with high-quality drama. He mentions the example of other European countries (like Prussia), whose intelligentsia undertook massive translations of classical and European drama in order to cure similar shortages. He states clearly that there are plenty of major masters of drama whose works had not been rendered in Greek ("where are the good translations of Shakespeare, Schiller, Alfieri, Molière, Sophocles, Euripides and Aristophanes?").[32] He confesses: "one needs to toil hard, of course, and it takes time; but I don't know of any difficulty which cannot be overcome by the perseverance of a sharp and hard-working translator."[33] As Politis has shown, hardworking is one unquestionable characteristic of Skylitsis. As for his method in adapting *Tartuffe*, he says that he "reshaped [the play] according to the customs of the place, where the language of translation is spoken" (ibid.). It is interesting to see how he describes his decision to work on the play, as a true child of the Romantic era to which he belonged; speaking in the third person, he confesses that "he saw in front of him a river, a wide one indeed, but it seemed peaceful and shallow near the riverbed. He went in the river, and he advanced with bold and confident strokes, when he noticed that the river was becoming deeper, and that its flow was becoming more rapid" (ibid., 114). Nonetheless, he carried on and when he had translated the largest part of the play, he came across a copy of an earlier translation of the play by Konstantinos Kokkinakis, published in Vienna in 1815. He confesses that the evolution of the Greek language in the thirty-five years that separate the two translations was to his advantage, and that he chose a different kind of verse (with an unstressed last syllable) from his predecessor. He then goes on to attribute whatever value his translation has to the liberties he took with the text: "in order to make the soul of the writer understood by his audience, the translator changed the names, the places, altered the manners of people [because] it is impossible to translate comedy otherwise" (ibid., 116). His predecessor might have kept the setting and the habits of the original, but the "salt and the irony, which shines there is lost" (ibid., 117). To his rhetorical question "whom would the playwright embrace?

---

[32] Skylissis 1871:110. I am using the 1871 reprint of the prologue, which is almost identical to that of 1851; the differences between the two editions are particularly telling especially in the text of the adaptations. Regarding the two spellings of his name: in the Greek bibliography he is known as Skylitsis, but he signed his publications (including the Molière translations) as Skylissis after a certain point in his life.

[33] Skylissis 1871:112.

the one who translates him word for word fearfully, or the one who translates his spirit lovingly," he explains that he followed the example of the translator of *The Miser* [Oikonomos], praising the renaming of Harpagon to Exintavelonis. Last, he admits that he censored some of Molière's expressions "making them more decent, because he owed this to himself and to the public in front of which the play would be performed" (ibid., 119).

Skylitsis set the play in Constantinople, in the Phanari (present day Fener) area of town, and renamed the entire cast, giving them Greek names with a Constantinopolitan twist: for instance, Madame Pernelle of the original, the mother of Orgon, becomes "Kokona Soultanio," his daughter Mariane becomes "Elengo," Dorine (one of the sharpest and most entertaining characters of Molière) becomes "Drossí," while Orgon becomes "Lemvikis." Needless to say, Tartuffe becomes simply "Tartoufos," because, as Skylitsis explains, the name had become synonymous with "hypocrite" in Greek (due to Kokkinakis' earlier translation). In the text he often uses the hellenized versions of Turkish words like *cübbe* (robe worn by imams), *mahkeme* (Turkish court), etc.

Apart from Phanari, other areas of the city are referred to during the action, like Stavrodromi (Peran-Beyoğlu) (ibid., 128, 136) or Kondoskali (Kumkapı) (ibid., 226) and boats and sea transportation replace carriages and strolls in the city in the original text. In addition, there are plenty of significant details: for instance, Tartuffe prays differently—in a manner befitting the Orthodox ritual (ibid., 139). He is supposedly from some rural area where people have no class or manners, while the girl to whom they plan to marry him is a "Πολίτισσα νύφη" [*Politissa nyfi*], a bride from Constantinople, which means a woman as refined as she can get (ibid., 161). Cléante/Nikandros, the brother in law of Orgon/Lemvikis, is chastised for his liberal ideas by a reference to a specific major thinker of the nineteenth century, Theophilos Kairis (1784–1853), who had created a religion of his own, *theoseveia*, meaning respect for God, which was inspired by the French deists and had been excommunicated by the Church.[34] As Politis has shown, Skylitsis himself had been charmed by Kairis' ideas during his youth, but later in life he became more and more conservative.[35]

Skylitsis' translation was highly esteemed and it quickly gained popularity among readers. In the 1870s, during his stay in Trieste, Skylitsis revised and reprinted the work of his youth; a close comparison of these two versions reveals that the translator revisited his text and improved it by meticulous alterations. His revisions include changes in the names of characters, which give them a Panhellenic twist (as opposed to the Constantinopolitan flavor of the 1851 first

---

[34] "Nikandros, you should drop all those atheisms and your connections to Kairis and Freemasonry" (Skylissis 1871:140).

[35] For Skylitsis' correspondence with Kairis, see Politis 2009:70–74.

edition); for instance, Elengo becomes Eleni, Aleko becomes Alexandros, and Lemvikis becomes Lesvikis. It is not surprising that the agent of power (the King as *deus ex machina* in the Molière original) at the end of the play is also changed to "a secretary of the Patriarchate," as opposed to the "translator of the Sublime Porte" who had intervened in 1851.[36] From reviews of performances of this adaptation throughout the nineteenth century for Greek audiences in the broader Mediterranean, it is clear that actors kept the Constantinopolitan flavor of the first edition, where the daughter is Elengo and the son Aleko, and so on, at least when they performed in Constantinople.[37]

Conclusion

The intellectual dilemmas of the first generation of mostly heterochthonous Greek writers like the Soutsos brothers with regard to what constituted a national literature, as discussed by Güthenke in this volume, preoccupied equally Oikonomos and Skylitsis with an emphasis on what constituted a national language. Although they both translated Molière's plays, they made different decisions regarding their language choices. Oikonomos was more daring (despite the conservatism he embraced soon after) in introducing spoken language and dialects, while Skylitsis was more restrained, along the lines set by the very subject of *Tartuffe*. However, they both moved the action to nineteenth-century Ottoman cities, proving how well Molière characters and plots were equipped for traveling in time and space. Furthermore, Oikonomos' adaptation was much admired in the nineteenth century by translators who strove to match his masterful achievement; by aspiring comic playwrights inspired by the theme of miserliness;[38] and by actors who clearly favored the comic possibilities of Exintavelonis, the penny-pincher, above all other comic parts.[39]

The adaptations of *The Miser* and *Tartuffe* by Oikonomos and Skylitsis, spanning roughly the fifty crucial years that witnessed the War of Independence and the creation of the Greek state, constitute pieces of evidence for the importance of the financial capitals of the Hellenic world (situated beyond the borders of the young Greek state) as well as for the much desired Westernization of

---

[36] It should not go unnoticed that the solution in the play is executed in the 1851 version by a *translator* of the Sublime Porte, not only because the most eminent Greeks, the Phanariots, were the Sultan's translators, but also because the translator was of primordial importance in the shaping of modern Greek ethos and by extension of Neohellenic literature.

[37] See indicatively, reviews in Νεολόγος [*Neologos*], the major Greek Constantinopolitan newspaper, on December 10, 1878 and on November 13, 1881.

[38] Stamatopoulou-Vasilakou 2005.

[39] Hadjipantazis 2004:74.

Greek society.[40] The next generation of translators (in the late 1870s), instead of focusing on socially and spatially rigid characters, chose Molière comedies dealing with social climbing and nouveau-riche behaviors (like the *Bourgeois Gentleman* or *Monsieur de Pourceaugnac*) and relocated the action to Athens, which had by then turned into the undisputed center of Greek literary and theatrical life.[41] At the same time, Molière's empire kept expanding in Turkey and the Levant, being translated and adapted in Turkish and Arabic, sowing the seeds of Westernization.[42] Interestingly enough "the first ever performance of a play in Arabic [was] an adaptation of Molière's *L'Avare*" and it was performed in Beirut in 1848.[43]

The translators of these two adaptations of Molière reflect through their choices their own, clearly post-Enlightenment, post-Goldoni time, rather than the seventeenth century, during which they were conceived. It has been suggested that the choice of Molière comedies to adapt for reading and staging reflected the reticence and conservatism of nineteenth-century Greek society, but one could also maintain that the translators bridged the time-gap, and instead of "plunging" their readers back to the homogeneously French seventeenth-century universe they "propelled" Molière to the multiethnic Ottoman nineteenth-century medley.

Works Cited

And, M. 1963. *A History of Theatre and Popular Entertainment in Turkey*. Ankara.

Auerbach, E. 1974. *Mimesis: The Representation of Reality in Western Literature* (trans. Willard R. Trask). Princeton. Fourth edition.

Farrell, J. 1996. "Servant of many masters." *Stages of Translation* (ed. D. Johnston) 45–55. Bath.

Fischer-Lichte, E. 2002. *History of European Drama and Theatre* (trans. J. Riley). London and New York.

Gaines, J., ed. 2002. *The Molière Encyclopedia*. London.

Goldoni, C. 1935–1956. *Tutte le opere di Carlo Goldoni,* vol. 1. Milan.

Hadjipantazis, T. 2002. *Από του Νείλου μέχρι του Δουνάβεως: Το χρονικό της ανάπτυξης του ελληνικού επαγγελματικού θεάτρου, στο ευρύτερο πλαίσιο*

---

[40] "Smyrna, Constantinople and Syros, the commercial capitals of the Hellenic world had no reason to coordinate with the Athenian climate; the national elations were indifferent to them, maybe even dangerous" (Politis 2009:68).

[41] Stavrakopoulou 2010.

[42] And 1963:65–71, Puchner 1993:105–113, Makdisi 2006, Spathis 2007:40–45.

[43] Makdisi 2006:6.

της Ανατολικής Μεσογείου, από την ίδρυση του ανεξάρτητου κράτους ως τη Μικρασιατική Καταστροφή [From the Nile to the Danube: A Chronicle of the Development of Professional Greek Theater, within the Broader Framework of the Eastern Mediterranean, from the Founding of the Independent State to the Asia Minor Catastrophe] 2 vols. Heraklion.

Hadjipantazis, T. 2004. Η Ελληνική Κωμωδία και τα πρότυπά της στο 19ο αιώνα [Greek Comedy and its Models in the Nineteenth Century]. Heraklion.

Jouanny, R., ed. 1960. Théâtre complet de Molière 2 vols. Paris.

Koppisch, M. 2002. "Tartuffe." In Gaines 2002:448–456.

Makdisi, I. 2006. Theatre and Radical Politics in Beirut, Cairo, and Alexandria: 1860–1914. Center for Contemporary Arab Studies Occasional Papers. Georgetown.

Molière. The Miser. http://www.online-literature.com/moliere/the-miser/0/ accessed on October 24, 2011.

———. Tartuffe. http://www.online-literature.com/moliere/tartuffe-or-the-hypocrite/ accessed on October 24, 2011.

Oikonomos, K. 1970 [1816]. Ο Φιλάργυρος του Μολιέρου [The Miser of Molière] (ed. K. Skalioras). Athens.

Politis, A. 2009. "Η αγάπη για την ποίηση και οι αναγκαστικές μεταφράσεις πεζογραφίας." Πολυφωνία - Φιλολογικά μελετήματα αφιερωμένα στον Σ. Ν. Φιλιππίδη ["The Love of Poetry and the Unavoidable Translations of Prose." Polyphony—Philological Studies Dedicated to S. N. Philippidis] (eds. A. Kastrinaki, A. Politis, D. Polychronakis) 49–103. Heraklion.

Puchner, W. 1993. Η ιδέα του εθνικού θεάτρου στα Βαλκάνια του 19ου αιώνα. Ιστορική τραγωδία και κοινωνιοκριτική κωμωδία στις εθνικές λογοτεχνίες της Νοτιοανατολικής Ευρώπης [The Idea of National Theater in the Balkans of the Nineteenth Century: Historic Tragedies and Social Comedies in the National Literatures of Southeastern Europe]. Athens.

———. 2001. Η γλωσσική σάτιρα στην ελληνική κωμωδία του 19ου αιώνα: Γλωσσοκεντρικές στρατηγικές του γέλιου από τα «Κορακιστικά» ως τον Καραγκιόζη [Linguistic Satire in Nineteenth-Century Greek Comedy: Language-Centered Strategies of Laughter from "Korakistika" to Karaghiozis]. Athens.

Skylissis, I. 1851. Ταρτούφος. Κωμωδία. Μεταφρασθείσα εμμέτρως και μετεχθείσα εις τα καθ'ημάς ήθη υπό Ι. Ισιδωρίδου Σκυλίσση [Tartuffe. Comedy. Translated in Verse and Adapted to our Customs by I. Issidoridis Skylissis]. Smyrna.

———. 1871. Μολιέρου άριστα έργα. Εξελληνισθέντα υπό Ι. Ισιδωρίδου Σκυλίσση [Molière's Best Plays Put into Greek by I. Issidoridis Skylissis]. Trieste.

Spathis, D. 1986. "Οι μεταφράσεις θεατρικών έργων στον 18ο αιώνα." Ο Διαφωτισμός και το νεοελληνικό θέατρο ["Theater translations in the eighteenth century." The Enlightenment and Neohellenic Theater] 69–75. Thessaloniki.

——. 2007. " Έλληνες φιλάργυροι, εχθροί των Φώτων." *Κοινωνικοί αγώνες και διαφωτισμός. Μελέτες αφιερωμένες στον Φίλιππο Ηλιού* ["Greek Misers, Enemies of the Enlightenment." *Social struggles and Enlightenment. Studies dedicated to Philippos Iliou*] (ed. C. Loukos) 27–60. Heraklion.

Stamatopoulou-Vasilakou, Ch. 2005. "Τρεις ακόμη Φιλάργυροι στη δραματουργία της ελληνόφωνης Ανατολής το 19ο αιώνα" [Three More Misers in the Dramatic Production of the Greek-Speaking East in the Nineteenth Century], *Παράβασις* 6:353–365.

Stavrakopoulou, A. 2010. "Αρχοντοχωριάτης και Αγαθόπουλος ο Ξηροχωρίτης: Όπου ο Παντελής Σούτσας συναντά τον Μολιέρο (1876)" [Monsieur de Pourceaugnac and The Bourgeois Gentleman: Where Molière Meets Pantelis Soutsas (1876)]. *Παράδοση και εκσυγχρονισμός στο νεοελληνικό θέατρο: από τις απαρχές ως τη μεταπολεμική εποχή* [*Tradition and Innovation in Modern Greek Theater: From the Beginnings to the Post-World War Era*] (eds. A. Glytzouris, K. Georgiadi) 43–50. Heraklion.

Spiropoulou, V., Bazini E. 2006. "Conflict within the Greek Orthodox Community of Smyrna (early 19th c.)." *Encyclopaedia of the Hellenic World, Asia Minor*; URL: <http://www.ehw.gr/l.aspx?id=8058>.

Tabaki, A. 2002. Η νεοελληνική δραματουργία και οι δυτικές της επιδράσεις (18ος –19ος αι.). *Μια συγκριτική προσέγγιση* [*Modern Greek Dramaturgy and its Influence on the West (18th–19th Centuries). A Comparative Approach*]. Athens. Second edition.

——. 2005. "'Νεωτερικότητα' και ανάδυση των λογοτεχνικών και δραματουργικών κανόνων. Η Ποιητική (Γραμματικά) του Κωνσταντίνου Οικονόμου" [Modernity and the Rise of Literary and Dramatic Rules. *The Poetics (On Grammar)* by Konstantinos Oikonomos], *Παράβασις* 6:353–365.

——. 2007. "The Long Century of the Enlightenment and the Revival of Greek Theater," *Journal of Modern Greek Studies* 25:285–299.

Wood, M. 2005. "The Languages of Cinema." *Nation, Language, and the Ethics of Translation* (eds. S. Bermann and M. Wood) 79–88. Princeton.

10

In "Third Space"

Between Crete and Egypt
in Rhea Galanaki's *The Life of Ismail Ferik Pasha*

Yota Batsaki

R HEA GALANAKI'S 1989 *The Life of Ismail Ferik Pasha** was the first Modern Greek novel to be listed in UNESCO's Collection of Representative Works.[1] A description of the selection criteria explains that these works, whose translation into—mainly—English and French was funded by the organization, are "representative of the values of their cultures" while at the same time they strengthen "intercultural relations."[2] The publisher's website suggests that the novel's appeal was augmented by the contemporary urgency surrounding "the clash of opposing civilizations, of Christianity and Ottoman Islam."[3] *The Life of Ismail Ferik Pasha*, as a national and international artifact, has thus been enmeshed from the beginning in local and global identity politics. It has also become the focus of debate about the relationship of Modern Greek literature to postcolonialism and postmodernism.[4] Yet even while issues of cultural identity have been thoroughly analyzed, little attention has been paid to the work's geographical complexity. The narrative's protagonist moves across Crete, Cairo, Istanbul, and Europe, while the two poles that especially define his belonging, Crete and Egypt, are particularly fluid and contested, "third spaces" suspended

---

* After this chapter was submitted for publication, the following article came to my attention which I was unable to consult: Ipek A. Çelik, "New Directions for Studying the Mediterranean: Eventfulness in Rhea Galanaki's Novel *The Life of Ismail Ferik Pasha: Spina nel Cuore*," *Clio* 41.1 (2011):75-101.

[1] The UNESCO Collection began in 1948, but direct translation subsidies have recently been suspended. http://www.unesco.org/culture/lit/rep/index.php. Accessed August 20, 2010.

[2] Maunick 1986:5.

[3] Quotation from the publisher's website, http://www.agra.gr/english/04.html. Accessed August 20, 2010.

[4] Calotychos 2003; Aleksiç 2009; Jusdanis 2001.

between empire and nation. Yet Egypt vanishes from the unidentified map that appears on the dust jacket of the English translation. This partial erasure of the novel's intricate spatiality suggests the need for thorough analysis of its "geographical inquiry into historical experience."[5] This chapter will focus on Galanaki's use of "third space" as a key vehicle for her critique of imperial—and national—geographies.

My use of "third space" here is related but not identical to Edward Soja's seminal contribution to the "Spatial Turn." In *Thirdspace*, Soja distinguishes between material "Firstspace," amenable to a quantitative "formal science of space," and "Secondspace," the sphere of subjective and aesthetic experience mediated by representation.[6] The elusive "Thirdspace" is a third term, an example of Soja's "thirding-as-othering," whose aim is the "sympathetic deconstruction and heuristic reconstitution of the Firstspace-Secondspace duality" (ibid., 81). Soja's heavily theoretical language proposes space as a corrective to what he views as the long-dominant dialectic of "historicality" and "sociality," the chief explanatory categories favoured by modernity. He advocates instead a "trialectics of spatiality-historicality-sociality" (ibid., 10) that would combine the intricacies of material geography, social production of space, and subjective experience. Soja's "Thirdspace" has much in common with the postcolonial and poststructuralist emphasis on difference. Both the spatial and the ontological approaches to hybridity, marginality, and indeterminacy actively seek out the third term to undermine a polar opposition that is perceived as ideologically suspect. Their common aim: "The disordering of difference from its persistent binary structuring and the reconstituting of difference as the basis for a new cultural politics of multiplicity" (ibid., 93). Galanaki's protagonist, caught in a dual and oppositional belonging to Crete and Egypt, similarly calls not for "pity, but the acceptance of difference."[7] The novelist's strategy resembles Soja's thirding-as-othering, repeatedly introducing third spaces and hybrid identities to destabilize the oppositions of Greek/Turk, Christian/Muslim, center/periphery, even nation/empire. Nevertheless, my use of "third space" is discursively simpler than Soja's: I employ the term to denote those spaces in Galanaki's novel that are portrayed as resistant to clear-cut political, ethnic, or cultural definition. "Third spaces" of this kind persistently defy their emplotment into a linear historical narrative, suggesting instead a model of both geography and identity determined by layered, overlapping, and often contradictory influences.

---

[5] Said 1994:7.
[6] Soja 1996:75;78–79.
[7] Galanaki 1996:84.

Postcolonial theory has contributed significantly to the current attention to space, both as the site for tracing past relationships of power, and as a formative influence on subjectivity. It has also often drawn on literary texts for its inquiry into the diverse experiences of colonization. In *Culture and Imperialism*, Edward Said drew attention to the "geographical notation, the theoretical mapping and charting of territory that underlies Western fiction"[8] and suggested that this notation reflects "the protracted, complex, and striated work of empire" (ibid., 60). Underpinning this link between the representation of space and the forging of identity is a strong sense of geography's past complicity with imperialism. Geography is here understood both as material practice and as academic discipline. From the eighteenth to the early twentieth centuries, the projections of the cartographic imagination—surveys, descriptions, maps—accompanied and accommodated colonial conquest, while "its idiom" of "exploration and comparison" was "suffused and structured by Eurocentrism."[9] "Imperial geography" therefore implies that spatial representations are a disciplinary formation in the Foucauldian sense: systems of order that also circumscribe and exclude, thus enacting relationships of power. This is the argument of Timothy Mitchell's *Colonising Egypt*, a study that preceded Said's *Culture and Imperialism* and resembles it in bringing a colonial angle to the politics of representation. Whereas Said is mainly interested in imaginary geographies (gleaned from scholarship, literature, opera), Mitchell tracks the combined effect of modernization and colonization on nineteenth-century Egypt through the reorganization of its material space (urban planning, agricultural restructuring, the construction of barracks and military academies). In this chapter, I draw on their complementary accounts of how nineteenth-century geographies, real and imaginary, reflect imperial dynamics of power. But Said also writes that if "there is anything that radically distinguishes the imagination of anti-imperialism, it is the primacy of the geographical element,"[10] signaling a possibility of resistance that is usually muted in early postcolonial theory. The pioneering work of Mitchell and Said connected geographical representations to imperial knowledge-power, but achieved this on the basis of oppositions that have come to seem somewhat rigid and stultifying. In literary writing that is attuned to the imaginative richness of "third spaces," space emerges from its geographical cooptation as both amenable and resistant to the project of empire—and, in Galanaki's novel, also of nationalism.

---

[8] Said 1994:58.
[9] Bonnett 2003:57.
[10] Said 1994:225.

The Displaced Orphan:
Filiation versus Affiliation

The novel's main setting is Crete during the half-century that follows the Greek War of Independence (1821–1832), an arena for competing historical forces in the eastern Mediterranean. The location suggests, at the outset, a familiar narrative of Greek revolution against Ottoman rule. This is immediately complicated, however, by the novel's subtitle, *spina nel cuore* [*di Venezia*], which alludes to the island's past as a Venetian colony. Now an Ottoman territory, the island scrambles the line between east and west. Empires are by definition diverse conglomerates where hybridity flourishes. But this is also an era of revolution and modernization, of the forging and hardening of new political identities, of Ottoman reform and the "cult of nationality in the European nineteenth century."[11] Crete, divided between its Christian Orthodox and Muslim populations (while also containing Jewish and Catholic groups), is the stage of frequent insurrections to join the nascent Greek state. While the Ottoman Empire is increasingly dependent on European intervention, it also embarks on its own modernization (Tanzimat). Two reform edicts (1839, 1856) promised equal judicial and fiscal treatment of all creeds (*millets*), while the constitution of 1876 attempted to introduce a notion of common citizenship, *Osmanlí*.[12] To this fluid and combustible mix of waning empire and dynamic nation-state formation Galanaki adds Tanzimat Egypt, which exists in uneasy relation both to the Ottoman Empire and to the rising European hegemony. The Egypt where Galanaki's protagonist finds himself forcibly displaced, then integrated, is not the oriental periphery, but the space of rapid and radical transformation: it aspires to nationalist self-definition, indulges in its own dreams of empire against the Ottoman Porte, while also emerging as an attractive candidate for European colonization.

Galanaki weaves her narrative around scant historical information, supplemented by oral traditions and legends. Her protagonist is a Cretan-Greek orphan captured and reborn as an Ottoman-Egyptian general—multilingual, bicultural, a traveler between East and West. Ismail Ferik Pasha, born Emmanuel Papadakis, is separated from his family and taken to Egypt, where he rises to the post of Minister of War. He follows Crown Prince Ibrahim, the son of Muhammad Ali, on various military campaigns, and accompanies him in his extensive travels throughout Europe. Many years later, Ismail is ordered to suppress another Cretan uprising, stoked by mainland Greeks and European philhellenes. Obliged

---

[11] Francesco de Sanctis quoted in Brennan 1990:48.
[12] Davison 1963.

to return to his native soil as an enemy and conqueror, he dies there during the Cretan revolution of 1866–1868. The novel's titular reference to the traditional genre of the βίος or "saint's life" (to recount the life of an Ottoman Pasha) is an ironic, even blasphemous, statement of difference.[13] Ismail's difference is further accentuated by the contrast with his brother Antonis, a fellow captive who prospers as a merchant in the Black Sea and becomes a leading figure and benefactor of the nascent Greek state. What Ismail perceives as his brother's straightforward and "authorized" life narrative serves as a foil to his own mixed identity. If nationalist ideology seeks to forge a natural connection between a population, its sovereign body, and the land they both occupy, then Galanaki's protagonist is an unwieldy specimen out of place everywhere.

For all its poetry, Galanaki's work also seems finely attuned to postcolonial and postmodern sensibilities. She shares with Said a deep interest in the potential of hybrid, contested spaces to produce similarly complex and multiple subjectivities.[14] In an earlier work that presented texts as "worldly" entities enmeshed in the various political and ideological networks of culture, Said offered a dual model of identity informed by the productive potential of exile.[15] Exile in this reading is not merely geographical displacement, but an eviction from "home" whose negative effect is alienation, but whose positive valence is distance from all-too-familiar structures of thought and feeling. Said calls these two models of identity "filiation" and "affiliation." The first refers to the ties and continuities that are perceived as natural (family, ethnicity, nationality), while the second may encompass the adopted identities of travel and immigration, the new institutional frameworks experienced in academic and professional apprenticeships, even religious conversion. Said does not privilege one model over another: his point is that both are ideologically inflected, their value lying in their oppositionality. The theme emerges again in *Culture and Imperialism*, where Said emphasizes the "contrapuntal" identities[16] that arise from cultural and geographical syncretism. This tug between filiative and affiliative foundations of subjectivity is, I would argue, exemplified in the figure of the orphan, who is provisionally severed from natural ties; once the origin is under erasure, the orphan is free—or constrained—to adopt alternative identities. The orphan therefore exemplifies both the tenacity of inherent or inherited properties, and the possibilities of self-construction. This potential is accentuated by Ismail's captivity and forced displacement, and realized in his ambitious ascent of the meritocratic Egyptian military hierarchy. It is also thrown into stark relief by

[13] Calotychos 2003:272.
[14] Said 2000.
[15] Said 1983.
[16] Said 1994:52.

the parallel trajectory of his brother, Antonis, whose own captivity takes him to the diasporic communities of the Black Sea, and from there to Athens as a main supporter of the Cretan war of independence. Structurally, therefore, Ismail is his brother's foil and enemy.

The novel's opening stages the passage into orphanhood at a moment of communal crisis and in a liminal space. As the Turkish-Egyptian troops retaliate against yet another Cretan rebellion, the boy Emmanuel seeks shelter, along with the rest of the women and children, in a cave. Described as a womb that enables his second birth, the cave also reverberates with the legends that Greek rural communities reserved for their boundaries, the supernatural places that defined inclusion and exclusion.[17] Its shelter engenders guilt by removing Emmanuel from his "natural place"[18] next to the dead bodies of his father and the other men at the village square. This primary displacement is terrifying, shameful, but also life-giving. Emmanuel's orphanhood and rebirth in the cave enacts the transition from filiation to affiliation, from the "natural" ties of family and community to the—partly imposed, partly embraced—ties of his Egyptian military training, rise through the ranks, and intimate friendship with Crown Prince Ibrahim. The transition is marked by the discovery of a "rusty green blade" whose "shape evoked none of the Christian or Arab types of knife known to him." Emmanuel/Ismail describes it proleptically as a sign that his life will "revolve within the orbit of knives" (ibid., 15), but its indeterminate shape also prefigures his own future ambiguity. In Modern Greek, the knife alludes to violence and harm, but also to the clear-cut, the unambiguous; κόψιμο με το μαχαίρι ("cutting with the knife") signifies closure, σπαθί ("sword") denotes someone who is straight, upfront, and can be trusted. In a Cretan account cited by Stewart, one protects oneself from the ξωτικά (*"exoticá"*), the demonic inhabitants of liminal spaces, by drawing a circle around oneself with a knife.[19] The rusty blade, however, is useless as a tool for making distinctions.[20] Galanaki makes an important linguistic choice in likening the blade to the sword of an ανεξίθρησκος angel. The word does not mean "creedless,"[21] as the English translation would have it. Rather, it is a compound of ανέχομαι ("tolerate") and θρησκεία ("religion"), and it encapsulates Galanaki's preoccupation with the toleration of difference in all its most difficult religious and ethnic manifestations. The adjective is also suggestive of the Ottoman practice of religious

---

[17] Stewart 1991.

[18] Galanaki 1996:16.

[19] Stewart 1991:168.

[20] In a later commentary on the novel, Galanaki identifies the knife as Minoan, adding yet another layer to the island's imperial history (Galanaki 1997:31).

[21] Galanaki 1996:15.

toleration, ανεξιθρησκεία, extended to various semi-autonomous religious groups (*millets*) that were subject to imperial taxation. The effect of this unusual word is to link Ismail's subsequent trajectory to specifically Ottoman practices for accommodating difference within the sprawling frame of empire.

The unusual longevity of the Ottoman Empire has been attributed to a flexible and ongoing management of difference, a dual policy of relative "toleration" punctuated by occasional forceful assimilation.[22] Unlike European colonizers, the Ottomans did not as a rule proselytize their subject populations, in particular those other "peoples of the book"—the Greeks, Jews, and Armenians. Gregory Jusdanis notes that as a rule "the Ottoman Empire did not isolate the private identities of the subject peoples for control or indoctrination."[23] But there were significant advantages for the "orphan" who did convert. The European policy of limiting the careers of colonial subjects in the imperial bureaucracy has been posited by Benedict Anderson as a contributing factor to modern nationalism, generating "imagined communities" of resistance made up of dispossessed Creole functionaries.[24] The Ottomans, by contrast, encouraged assimilation of handpicked individuals into their military and administrative hierarchies. Karen Barkey identifies various practices "both marking difference and accommodating its existence,"[25] such as conversion and forceful recruitment of Christian boys into the janissary corps (*devshirme*). Although the *devshirme* had significantly declined by the seventeenth century, Galanaki mines its tenacity in national lore, evoking it through Ismail's capture and forceful assimilation into the Ottoman military. But whereas the *devshirme* in national rhetoric is steeped in the language of cultural trauma, Galanaki's fictional account features several displaced "orphans" who invariably prosper. (Ismail's deadly enemy, Omer Pasha, converted as a young man and was quickly promoted in the Ottoman army, while the Egyptian ruler, Muhammad Ali, was an orphan from Macedonia adopted by a Turkish commander.) Historical evidence suggests that the attitudes of subject populations to conversion or the *devshirme* varied, because although these were acts of violence they could also be "a way for elites and their followers to enhance their status and ensure social advancement" (ibid.). Viewed against a background of relative toleration, and contrasted to nationalist myths of autochthony and ethnic purity, the Ottoman management of difference suggests the advantages and payoffs of affiliation.

At the same time, the processes of filiation and affiliation are rarely clear-cut, but rather overlap and interpenetrate. This is evident both in the historical

---

[22] Barkey 2008.
[23] Jusdanis 2001:110.
[24] Anderson 1991:114.
[25] Barkey 2008:127.

experience of Ottoman conversion and conscription, and in the fictional reimag-
ining of Galanaki's novel. Barkey gives the example of two Serbian brothers
separated by the *devshirme*, who followed different but intertwined trajectories
within the Ottoman hierarchy, "one becoming Grand Vizier (Mehmed Sokullu)
and the other becoming the head of the Serbian Orthodox Church (Makarius),
with his brother's help. One brother, a converted Muslim, headed the Ottoman
State; the other brother, a devout Christian, led the Serbian Church." Like the
fictionalized Ismail and his brother, Antonis, who wrote to each other in Greek,
Sokollu and Makarius corresponded in Serbian (ibid., 124). But there the similarity ends, for Ismail and Antonis experience a deeper, historical separation.
Their respective locations in the territories of empire and emerging nation-
state seem to require a straightforward ascription of political and cultural
identity that eludes the novel's protagonist. The relationship between the two
brothers is brought to an end by a hardening of the categories of difference that
the Ottoman *millet* system had sought to integrate within the broader scheme
of empire. Faced with conflicting allegiances to his Greek origins and Ottoman-
Egyptian upbringing, and unable or unwilling to translate them into a single
ethnic, cultural, and political identity, Ismail is orphaned anew.

Between Crete and Egypt:
Modernization and Its Discontents

Emmanuel's transformation into Ismail occurs in the "third space" of Egypt,
itself undergoing radical transformation in the nineteenth century, marked
by the recent collision of cultures and already in the grip of European influence. Galanaki refers explicitly to the Napoleonic occupation that preceded
Muhammad Ali's rise to power and the subsequent modernization of the country
("new order" or *nizam jadid*), emphasizing changes in infrastructure and the reorganization of the military. Said's *Orientalism* offered the Napoleonic expedition
as a seminal example of the imperialist power-knowledge nexus, while Mitchell
described Egyptian modernization as the importation of European disciplinary
technologies that were ostensibly advantageous to the sovereign, but ultimately
catered to external interests. The new order dictated the organization of agriculture, urban planning, and the military according to the rational model of the
grid, where mastery of space and control of its inhabitants came together. After
1815, the defeated officers and engineers of the Napoleonic "new order" made
their way to Egypt and placed their expertise at the service of Muhammad Ali.
According to Mitchell, "the object at the heart of this plan [was] a new infantry
corps, to be trained and organised according to the new techniques developed
by the Prussians and the French ... Egypt was the first province of the Ottoman

Empire to introduce successfully the new kind of army." In 1822, around the time that Ismail would have begun his army training, new training camps had been built, including one military school in Cairo for 1500 students, organized like a barrack. In April 1822, "regulations were issued bringing all the barracks, military schools, and training camps under a common code of discipline and instruction. The confinement to barracks, the discipline, and the instruction were all innovations."[26]

Ismail's transplantation to Egypt thus makes him, ironically, the subject of European models of discipline and surveillance that he thoroughly internalizes. These, in turn, become a platform for establishing his difference from the Ottoman Turks. Upon his return to the island to fight the Cretan Greeks, Ismail quarrels with his Turkish superior, the brutal Omer Pasha, over atrocities committed by irregular Ottoman troops. His high-minded objection to a conception of the army as "a mindless horde, not to say a collective carnivorous brute"[27] reveals his allegiance to an imported European principle of uniform disciplined action.[28] It also sets him apart from his Turkish counterpart, Omer Pasha, whom he thoroughly orientalizes as a double-crossing "serpent of the desert"[29] and a poisoner. Internal differences open up within the Ottoman army, complicating the handling of the rebellion: Ismail's only direct action in favor of the islanders is an order to the "regular" Ottoman army to fire at the marauding "irregulars." Galanaki's attention to the Egyptian context of Ismail's military training and its adoption of European models of discipline and surveillance creates a complex model of the "oriental" subject as internally differentiated: both the product of European influence and, ironically, the carrier of its fundamental values and practices.

Ismail is deeply conscious of his interpellation, and when he finds himself caught in the struggle between geography and power, he tries to turn it to his advantage. When he returns to the island as enemy and conqueror, he is forced to confront his sympathy for the insurgents. The trope of *nostos* or homecoming is, in the literary tradition from the Homeric *nekyia* to modern Greek folk song, colored by gloom and death. Ismail's stealthy return to the old family home is figured as incongruous regression; he feels himself "shrunk to the size of a child" (ibid., 145), sucking at the air like an infant at the breast. Because the pull of the origin threatens to annul his Egyptian accomplishments and mutilate his rich indeterminacy, Ismail tries instead to fit his conflicting emotions into a Western narrative of modernity and progress: "Astounded, I dragged up from

[26] Mitchell 1988:36.
[27] Galanaki 1996:121.
[28] Mitchell 1988:38.
[29] Galanaki 1996:119.

the depths of my being a liberal European citizen ... who refused to subscribe to the recurrent pattern of the Orient's destiny ... I was amazed at the extent to which the European way of thinking had won over my sun-bred soul, as if such things had more to do with nations than with individual souls.... I thus found myself on the side of the revolutionaries" (ibid., 112–113). Ismail adopts here a narrative of nationalism as a progressive force pitted against an ossified oriental empire. Jusdanis summarizes this position when he records nationalist resistance both to imperialist violence and to the more insidious forms of Enlightenment universalism, and describes it as a motor of modernization: "contrary to the claims of postcolonial theory, nationalism has resisted political and cultural universal systems from the beginning and has sought in national culture the resources for modernization. The nation-state itself has always been seen both in Europe and in its colonies as a vehicle to modernity."[30] Modernity for Jusdanis has a positive valence, but remains premised on notions of political self-definition and economic progress that are themselves distinctly European. In Galanaki's narrative, suspicious as it appears to be of any ideological solution to the vagaries of identity, this recourse to European ideas is experienced instead as a different kind of gloomy interpellation.

Ismail's attempt to circumvent the lethal trap of *nostos* by recasting it as membership in modernity is short-lived: "I derided the pliancy of my own thought: in my desire to ... return to my former life—while knowing full well that no myth had ever shown something of the kind coming to pass without bloodshed—I had had recourse to the most progressive political ideas."[31] It is not only that the novel's persistent representation of the eastern Mediterranean as the epicenter of rapid transformations undermines Ismail's orientalist stereotypes. His appeal to the "European spirit" is also troubled by his own experiences westward. In the course of their European travels, Ibrahim and Ismail admire the scientific supremacy of the West but also reflect on the poverty lurking in the dark corners of the metropolis. Although undermining the center-periphery binary through the experience of travel has become commonplace in postcolonial studies,[32] our understanding has been enriched by ever more varied perspectives that reveal the center to be uneven, disappointing, even "provincial" in its turn.[33] Here, too, Galanaki appears theoretically savvy, positing travel not as a two-way trajectory across a single axis, but as a criss-crossing pattern that involves multiple nodes (Istanbul, Paris, Cairo, Athens). These "centers," invested with different degrees and kinds of authority, are all

---

[30] Jusdanis 2001:9.
[31] Galanaki 1996:113.
[32] For a seminal contribution, see Pratt 1992.
[33] Khuri-Makdisi in this volume.

nevertheless ironically cut down to size. In a letter to Antonis, Ismail advertises both his cosmopolitanism and his city's urban planning by telling his brother to picture one of Cairo's most magnificent squares as being three times the size of the Place de la Concorde.

Nowhere at Home:
Self and Representation

Nowhere is the novel's ironic attitude to the center more evident than in the treatment of Athens as the capital-under-construction of the new Greek state. The choice of Athens (over Nafplio) reflects the need to "establish continuity with a suitable historical past," to bolster the national narrative of autochthony and uniqueness.[34] Yet, as Constanze Güthenke shows in this volume, Athenian space is inherently unstable because its ownership is uncertain and contested. Güthenke's analysis underlines the provisionality of the capital's geography, as well as its artificiality and derivativeness. Antonis writes to Ismail about the rebuilding of the city as it had been dreamed up by the Europeans, spun around the two symbolic poles of the Acropolis and the new palace of the Bavarian sovereign.[35] With the wealth obtained by buying cheap Russian grain and selling it at a profit to the war-ravaged Greeks, Antonis buys lands that are themselves transformed into treasure when they are included in the urban plan and become "the heart" of the new city. He subsequently describes himself to his brother as putting out roots in the "Westernized society of the capital" (ibid.). Antonis builds a neoclassical house decorated by German artists, furnished with European plate and crystal, and encircled by a veranda supported by Doric columns, to house the ghosts of their parents and the wounded and displaced of the Greek War of Independence. He lives like a European, traversing the new boulevards on foot or in his carriage, and joining the other "apprentices" (ibid., 67) of the Athenian urban middle class.

Different as their geographical locations are, the brothers are both exposed to European modes of representation that mediate their experience of "home." To Antonis's Athenian frescoes, painted by German artists, Ismail responds with a narrative of his own encounter, during his European travels, with "the blossoming of oriental fashion" that followed the rediscovery of ancient Egypt and the decoding of the hieroglyphic script. This "breakthrough ... had occurred when the two boys were spending their last summer on the plateau," setting lime-twigs for birds. From these lime-twigs Ismail's description moves beautifully to

---

[34] Hobsbawm 1992:1.
[35] Galanaki 1996:57–58.

the "great arboreal branches" of the European paintings, "resting ... upon imaginary supports, unfolding their coils as far as they could reach," encompassing
both the Pharaonic and the Ottoman Orient. Thinly supported but far-reaching,
these aesthetic representations are a different kind of snare, and they baffle
Ismail with their archetypal splendor. "The works of art Ismail Ferik Pasha had
admired in Europe depicted battles, odalisques, bazaars of such beauty that he
concluded they were deliberately presented so; and he admired them for this
very reason, for he had never come upon anything as beautiful and as real in
Egypt itself" (ibid., 66). Back in Egypt, the splendid interiors of Egyptian officials
are lavishly decorated with European furniture, French porcelain, Venetian
mirrors, and Western paintings of "home." Ismail's house in Cairo is no exception: "In the frames, Egyptian landscapes, painted in the manner of the most
classicizing French school, endowed the stuffy room with imaginary outlets."[36]
While Galanaki's narrative strives to convey the intricacies of hybrid identities, their encasement in these mirrored and painted interiors is also suggestive of inauthentic colonial bricolage. The importation of European luxury
goods is conflated with the invasion of European modes of representation. Both
brothers record—with different degrees of ambivalence—Europe's material and
ideological penetration of their environments. Antonis seems to view this as
an opportunity for the newly forged Greek nation to take its rightful place as
the origin and reincarnation of "the legendary image which had exerted such a
lasting influence on the European spirit."[37] Ismail, on the other hand, finds that
the material geography of Egypt falls short of its depiction in the paintings that
surround him, just as Ibrahim's "golden victories" had been "exchanged for a
handful of copper coins on the international market" and the cities that he had
helped him conquer vanished again from their grasp like "foam-crested waves"
(ibid., 37–38). "Nothing pure," he concluded, "even in its purity."[38] If European
mediation is an inevitable effect of modernization, its respective effects on
Greek and Egyptian national aspirations are distinctly opposite.

Fundamental to the analyses of Said and Mitchell is the argument that the
problem of representation needs to be situated within an imperialist context.
Mitchell uses the term "enframing" to describe what he regards as a particularly European order of representation that he explicitly associates with imperialism, the age of high capitalism, and the era of the world exhibition. Mitchell

---

[36] My translation. Cicellis renders the passage: "The medallions pictured Egyptian landscapes,
painted in the manner of the purest classicizing French school, opening up illusory vents of
escape in the cloistered room" (Cicellis 1996:49). Her translation loses the notion of "enframing"
and inauthenticity that are important to my discussion.

[37] Galanaki 1996:57.

[38] Galanaki 1989:58, my translation.

uses the example of the nineteenth-century staging of Egypt in the world exhibitions to argue that "enframing" works by rendering the world "out there" as a picture, organized with the individual viewer in mind. This spatial organization implies that a vantage point is always available, and that it coincides with the central, sovereign position of the western subject as viewer. The will to mastery inherent in this position is satisfied through the provision of predictable forms of otherness, summarized in Ismail's description of orientalist painting as uniting the "forbidden" with the "desirable." Said's *Orientalism* enumerated some of the attributes that relegate the oriental "Other" to a subservient position, as feminine or effeminate, sensual, irrational, perverse, etc. At the same time, aesthetic pleasure licenses other, more material forms of exploitation. For Mitchell, the claim that the "real" lies just outside the frame of representation doubles as a technique for "rendering history, progress, culture and empire in 'objective' form,"[39] encouraging the assumption that everything can be "made picture-like and legible ... available to political and economic calculation" (ibid., 33). The argument put forward by Said and Mitchell is that western strategies of representation are both imbued by and complicit in the construction of imperial geographies as spaces amenable to aesthetic consumption and economic exploitation.

When the viewer is transported from the representation to its referent, the result may be disappointment at the chaotic actuality of what had hitherto been only an imaginary landscape, or distaste at its unpicturesque modernity. But it can also lead to another strategy for managing the disruption of the viewer's expectations: the claim that the material geography fails to match up to its ideal representation. In a letter to Théophile Gautier that is exemplary of this confrontation between material and imaginary geographies, Gerard de Nérval laments that while his friend was "deploying all the splendours of the Opera" to construct the Cairo of his imagination, Nérval himself could only find "in the real Cairo ... the baroque rudiments of some pantomime show."[40] Asked by Gautier to describe the Cairo dances, he proclaims himself stumped by the cafés "with no trefoils, no delicate columns, no porcelain panelling, no suspended ostrich eggs. It is only in Paris that one comes across cafés this Oriental" (ibid.). Egypt is driven from his imagination by his travels, replaced by "this stockroom of the India trade, this thriving showcase of Egypt's new business class, this warehouse of its new manufacturers!" (ibid., 196). Nérval's eloquent disappointment is of course redolent of the Romantic imagination's privileging of metaphor over its literal referent. But his negative assessment of

[39] Mitchell 1988:7.
[40] Nérval 1999:192.

Cairo's economic modernity—as though European models of progress had no place in the "oriental" "periphery"—invites a more troubling political reading. Regretting the many lands that vanished under his footsteps, "torn down like stage sets," he looks forward to his return home: "It's at the Opera that I will rediscover the true Cairo, the immaculate Egypt, the Orient that escapes me" (ibid.). For Mitchell, "enframing" is premised on the assumption that reality is separate from its representation; the effect of the frame is "to order things, but also to circumscribe and exclude ... To 'determine the plan' is to build-in an effect of order and an effect of truth."[41] Paradoxically, Nérval's longing to recover the real Cairo at the Paris Opera suggests that truth is located not in the material geography of his travels, but in the power of the metropolitan center to generate imaginary geographies. Orientalist fashion is both an export industry (as in the exotic landscapes by the German and French schools that decorate the interiors of Antonis and Ismail) and a lure to bring the wayward traveller back home.

By contrast, for Galanaki's protagonist it is the experience of return that feels inauthentic. Having left the "third space" of Egypt, Ismail's first reunion with the Cretan landscape is suffused by a strong sense of artificiality; he likens the Cretan harbor, scene of his captivity and separation from his brother, to an opera set. Ismail would have been familiar with opera both through his European travels, and through the contemporary construction of the Cairo opera, as part of the Viceroy's celebrations of the opening of the Suez Canal in 1869. Verdi's *Aida* was commissioned by Khedive Ismail, the son of Ibrahim, for the occasion, although *Rigoletto* was the first work to be performed. For Said, the orientalist influences on Verdi's opera (the librettist, Auguste Mariette, was the principal designer of antiquities at the Egyptian pavilion in the Paris International Exhibition of 1867) make it a "hybrid, radically impure work."[42] But whereas for Said the impurity of *Aida* derives, in part, from its colonialist and orientalist contexts, thrown into relief by its first performance in Cairo, Galanaki stages the nationalist trope of return as an equally inauthentic and artificial experience. Ismail's allusion to the opera reflects both his status as a doubly colonial subject (of the sultan, and of the European powers that influence Ottoman and Egyptian politics), and his impatience with nationalist narratives. His Egyptian life is, he insists, a reality, not a representation; what comes closest to mimesis for him is the felt cultural burden to enact a *nostos*, the cultural fantasy of belonging structured as a return to the origin. Since this is a return that he is forced to realize in the oxymoronic guise of a foreign conqueror, his experience is one of depletion, nostalgia as bodily illness. "I cannot keep them alive," complained a French

---

[41] Mitchell 1988:33.
[42] Said 1994:115.

doctor of Muhammad Ali's peasant army conscripts, "when they begin to think of home."[43] If longing for the "true Egypt" propelled Nérval back to the imperial center, for Ismail his departure from Egypt and return to Crete operates in the manner of a death wish. Reducing the hybrid to one of his constituent elements amounts to his erasure.

But Europe does not feature in Galanaki's narrative as a monolithic and omnipotent power operating behind the scenes. It, too, is an internally differentiated entity subject to curious displacements. Ismail, for instance, is not the only one who has difficulties negotiating the Cretan terrain; he is joined by the European philhellenes that suffer from the mountain cold and are bewildered by the internal conflicts of the rebels they have come to help. Galanaki allows herself a moment of wry humor in a wonderful image of displacement that blends the unruly features of the Cretan landscape with the volatile Romanticism of progressive ideals: "A Garibaldian Italian, unaccustomed to leaping over crags, was captured and executed on the spot."[44] Displacement here is both physical and ideological: unable to effect political change in their own countries, nationalists join the philhellenic cause. The reference to Garibaldi is particularly ironic, because Antonis had invoked the Risorgimento leader as a covert test of Ismail's national feeling. Geography, Galanaki hints, resists just as much the conquering aspirations of nationalism as of colonialism. The stubborn recalcitrance of the landscape is conveyed in the colloquial κατσάβραχα ("crags"), which always indicates incongruous positioning, as in the negotiation of rough mountain territory by an urbanite in the wrong shoes.

Conclusion:
The Grid Revisited

Galanaki's crags seem designed to filter out foreign elements. Yet, at the same time, the novel's geography is always already furrowed by some "foreign" power. Unlike Mitchell, who sees the grid as a nineteenth-century imposition on the Egyptian landscape, Galanaki repeatedly refers to the perpendicular lines of the Venetian drainage canals that have crisscrossed Ismail's native Lasithi plateau for centuries. Their imprint structures his recollections of home: "The canals of the Venetian irrigation system, dividing the land into large brown squares, invested the orderliness of peaceful autumnal husbandry with an unworldly

---

[43]   Mitchell 1988:42.
[44]   My translation. Cicellis renders this passage: "One of Garibaldi's Italian partisans, unaccustomed to leaping about on the rocky mountain-slopes, was captured and executed on the spot" (Galanaki 1996:107).

harmony reminiscent of the angel of death."[45] The Venetian grid on the Lasithi plateau is a good example of how geography in Galanaki's novel incites inquiry into historical experience. A primary source of grain for the Venetians, Lasithi was also a refuge for insurgents, and settlement of the plain was harshly banned in the thirteenth and fourteenth centuries. The ban continued until 1463, when the Venetian Senate required Lasithi grain for its military campaigns against the Turks. To improve grain yield, the Senate colonized the plateau with Venetian settlers and sent engineers to construct a drainage grid, probably in 1631–1633.[46] A Roman artificial drainage system may have antedated the Venetian engineering project (ibid., 24). Ismail's landscape of memory thus bears the impression of past occupations and disciplinary formations. Galanaki's subtle but repeated references to the Venetian grid deliberately prevent it from fading into a natural feature of the landscape. Once colonial undertakings and their traces are shown to be overlaid like palimpsests, they undermine those competing imaginary geographies of nationalism that are predicated on fantasies of autochthony and ethnic purity.

Continuity and repetition on the diachronic level are matched by contiguity and overlap on the synchronic level: this is one important way in which spatiality modifies the putative linearity of historical narrative. Galanaki encapsulates both these insights in her frequent allusions to the flag as a condensed expression of politics and geography. Upon entering the Cretan harbor, Ismail notices the Venetian standard inscribed in marble yet ravaged by time, next to the silk flag of the Porte. Both are imbued with impermanence: "The marble standard of the lion of St. Mark endured through the centuries, though mutilated by time and almost unrecognizable, while the silk flag of the Sublime Porte still fluttered in the breeze of the present day."[47] The proximity of marble standard and silk flag, representative of successive colonial powers, is matched by their fragile provisionality ("mutilated," "still"). Another flag, that of the Cretan revolutionary committee, doubles as a map of regional politics, "displaying in its four corners representations of the flags of England, France, Russia, and Greece, and a cross surmounting a crescent in the middle" (ibid., 139). Not quite a national flag, the product of a moment of violent historical flux, the revolutionary banner expresses the political modernity of the moment: emerging nation-states closing in on older imperial forms of community, denoted by the religious symbols in the center. The three Great Powers lurking in the corners are major colonial forces in the new "age of empire," and give their names to the three major political parties of the Modern Greek state. The flag is a stark

[45] Galanaki 1996:17.
[46] Watrous 1882:25–29.
[47] Galanaki 1996:126.

example of the overlapping and conflicting claims that inscribe Galanaki's "third spaces," and a reminder of the messiness of nation-state formation.

Galanaki's exploration of the "fatal intersection of time with space"[48] crystallizes in the novel's concluding image of the site of Ismail's cenotaph. An essay that provided a major source of inspiration for Soja's "Thirdspace" can also illuminate Galanaki's description here. In "Other Spaces," Michel Foucault gives an early description of his version of "third space," which he terms "heterotopia." Heterotopias, for Foucault, have the "curious property of being in relation with all the other sites, but in such a way as to suspect, neutralize, or invert" them (ibid., 24). This makes them both representative and subversive of the culture that surrounds and produces them. Foucault's heterotopias are both isolated and penetrable: entrance into them can be mandatory or restricted, and hides "curious exclusions" (ibid., 26). They have a "precise and determined function within a society," but this function can change along with the "synchrony of the culture in which it occurs." Heterotopias are therefore uniquely "capable of juxtaposing in a single real place several spaces, several sites that are in themselves incompatible" (ibid., 25). Moreover, they are "most often linked to slices in time ... they open onto what might be termed, for the sake of symmetry, heterochronies" (ibid., 26). Foucault's examples of heterotopias include the cemetery, the library, and the museum, but he wonders "if certain colonies have not functioned somewhat in this manner" (ibid., 27). Their characteristics match Galanaki's description of the cenotaph site as the novel's most condensed and striking figure for the spatialization of history:

> Ismail Ferik Pasha's cenotaph was ... erected in the precincts of the Vizir mosque, which was about to be completed at the time. It had been destroyed by a great earthquake eleven years earlier, and was now being rebuilt on the old foundations, on the same site where many years ago there stood a Christian church, alternately Orthodox or Catholic, according to the sovereign's creed.... The Byzantines used to bury governors, archbishops and generals ... while the Venetians used the space for the burial of dukes, Commanders-in-Chief and Latin archbishops, and the Ottomans, at a later date, for their Pashas and other notables.
>
> Galanaki 1996:164-165

Even posthumously, Ismail Ferik Pasha is the subject of conflicting interpretations, with his bust displayed in the War Museum in Cairo and legends of his crypto-Christianity circulating in Crete. His cenotaph, next to a rising mosque,

---

[48] Foucault 1986:22.

took its place on a stratum that was previously occupied by eminent Byzantines and Venetians. The imperial nomenclature changes but is eminently translatable from one layer to the next, supporting Anderson's connection of nationalism to the "large cultural systems that preceded it ... the *religious community* and the *dynastic realm*."[49] Like a museum or a library, spaces designed to compress and render historical time available to representation, the "third space" of the cenotaph becomes in Galanaki's description an imaginary geography of the island's colonial past. Its material location has always had an important social function, half-political, half-sacred, yet its uses have changed "according to the synchrony of the culture in which it occurs" and its description thus doubles as "a sort of general archive, the will to enclose in one place all times, all epochs, all forms."[50] Now occupied by a Greek public school, where unified and linear national narratives are consecrated and disseminated, the site appears to follow a trajectory of historical progress culminating in the nation-state. Novels, after all, are verbal artifacts unfolding in time, and their very mode therefore seems closer to the discursive historicality that Soja decries, than the intricate spatiality this chapter has been trying to untangle. Yet Galanaki's description of the site restores the layers figuratively erased by the physical building of the school, and possibly also discursively muted within it. Throughout, she restores to the landscape the contiguity and contingency of historical forms, traces their relentless overlap. Her fiction is certainly of its historical and cultural moment, for according to Said: "we have never been as aware as we now are of how oddly hybrid historical and cultural experiences are, of how they partake of many often contradictory experiences and domains, cross national boundaries, defy the *police* action of simple dogma and loud patriotism."[51] Perhaps her novel's most original and imaginative contribution lies in giving these contradictory experiences and domains a powerful geographical form.

---

[49] Anderson 1991:12.
[50] Foucault 1986:26.
[51] Said 1994:15.

Works Cited

Aleksiç, T. 2009. "The Sacrificed Subject in Rhea Galanaki's *Ismail Ferik Pasha*," *Modern Greek Studies* 27:31–54.

Anderson, B. 1991. *Imagined Communities: Reflections on the Origin and Spread of Nationalism.* London.

Barkey, K. 2008. *Empire of Difference: The Ottomans in Comparative Perspective.* Cambridge.

Bhabha, H., ed. 1990. *Nation and Narration.* London.

Bonnett, A. 2003. "Geography as the World Discipline: Connecting Popular and Academic Geographical Imaginations," *Area* 35:55–63.

Brennan, T. 1990. "The National Longing for Form." In Bhabha 1990:44–70.

Calotychos, V. 2003. *Modern Greece: A Cultural Poetics.* New York.

Çelik, Z. 1992. *Displaying the Orient.* California.

Davison, R. 1963. *Reform in the Ottoman Empire, 1856–1876.* Oxford.

Foucault, M. 1986. "Of Other Spaces," *Diacritics* 16:22–27.

Galanaki, R. 1996. *The Life of Ismail Ferik Pasha. Spina nel cuore* (trans. K. Cicellis). London and Chester Springs.

———. 1997. *Βασιλεύς ή Στρατιώτης: Σημειώσεις, σκέψεις, σχόλια για τη λογοτεχνία* [*King or Soldier: Notes, Thoughts, Comments on Literature*]. Athens.

———. 1989. *Ο Βίος του Ισμαήλ Φερίκ Πασά.* Athens.

Hobsbawm, E and Ranger, T., eds. 1992. *The Invention of Tradition.* Cambridge.

Johnson, B. 2003. *Mother Tongues: Sexuality, Trials, Motherhood, Translation.* Cambridge, Mass.

Jusdanis, G. 2001. *The Necessary Nation.* Princeton.

Maunick, E. 1986. "A Library of World Classics," *UNESCO Courier* (Jan):5–8.

McKee, S. 2000. *Uncommon Dominion: Venetian Crete and the Myth of Ethnic Purity.* Pennsylvania.

Mitchell, T. 1988. *Colonising Egypt.* Cambridge.

Nérval, G. de. 1999. *Selected Writings* (trans. R. Sieburth). Harmondsworth.

Pratt, M.L. 1992. *Imperial Eyes: Travel Writing and Transculturation.* London.

Said, E. 1994. *Culture and Imperialism.* New York.

———. 2000. *Out of Place: A Memoir.* New York.

———. 1983. *The World, the Text and the Critic.* Cambridge, Mass.

Soja, E. 1996. *Thirdspace: Journeys to Los Angeles and Other Real-and-Imagined Places.* Oxford.

Stewart, C. 1991. *Demons and the Devil: Moral Imagination in Modern Greek Culture.* Princeton.

Watrous, L. V. 1882. *Lasithi: A History of Settlement On a Highland Plain in Crete.* Princeton.

11

The Discursive Mapping
of Sectarianism in Iraq

The "Sunni Triangle" in the
Pages of *The New York Times*

Sahar Bazzaz

O N MARCH 19, 2003, the United States and a small group of supporting
nations known as the "Coalition of the Willing" launched "Operation Iraqi
Freedom" with the expressed intent of removing the authoritarian regime of
then President Saddam Hussein and establishing a democratic government in
Iraq. A few weeks later US President George W. Bush gave a jubilant address to
American troops aboard the battleship USS Lincoln, announcing the successful
termination of combat operations and the beginning of reconstruction in Iraq,
declaring proudly: "America sent you on a mission to remove a grave threat and
to liberate an oppressed people, and that mission has been accomplished."[1] Yet
despite the optimism that followed President Bush's declaration of the cessation of combat operations in April 2003, and contrary to the oft-cited belief
that Iraqis would surely welcome US troops, a violent insurgency began to
spread throughout Iraq. By the end of summer 2003, the security situation in
that country had greatly deteriorated as insurgents began to target occupation
forces, civilians, foreign contractors, and members of the newly formed Iraqi
police. On August 19, insurgents bombed the United Nations headquarters in
Baghdad resulting in the death of, among others, the UN Chief in Iraq, Sergio
Vieira de Mello. By late August, the insurgency was attacking vital infrastructure, including water lines and oil pipelines, and many of the foreign contractors who had come to Iraq to participate in reconstruction were already leaving.
Less than a year later, the *New York Times* declared, "War's Full Fury is Suddenly

---

[1]   Cited in Hashim 2006:xv.

Everywhere," as violence spread throughout Iraq, resulting in unprecedented numbers of American and Iraqi dead.[2] Administration officials, political analysts, and US troops stationed in the country were forced to concede that something had gone terribly wrong. Then Deputy Secretary of State, Paul Wolfowitz—a major supporter of regime change in Iraq and an architect of the invasion—declared his surprise that such fierce resistance to the US presence in Iraq was emerging.[3] Anthony Cordesman—a leading policy analyst and well-respected member of the Center for Strategic and International Studies in Washington, DC—went so far as to declare the US occupation a "dismal failure."[4]

The emergence of an insurgency in Iraq spawned a dizzying search for answers regarding its sources. What could explain a seemingly puzzling paradox—namely, that Iraqis who were brutalized for so long by the regime of Saddam Hussein and his ruling Ba'ath party were resisting "liberation"? Some analysts sought immediate answers with instrumental value for understanding the insurgency in order to crush it. Others hoped to expose what they believed to be the folly of neoconservative policies in the Middle East. And for still others, violent resistance by the Iraqi "Other" elicited existential questions about the essence of the American "Self." Was the Bush administration's policy of regime-change and exportation of democracy a new trajectory in American politics? Or was it simply a continuation of the US imperial character in a different guise?

As pundits opined about the situation, Americans began a process of *discovering* Iraq as unfamiliar and virtually unknown places, such as Falluja, Samarra, and Najaf, entered center-stage, while sectarian and ethnic divisions within Iraqi society—Sunni, Shi'ite, and Kurd—gained heightened importance in political and strategic analysis. For US troops on the battlefield, this process of discovery occurred through a combination of direct combat experience, on one hand, and military education, on another; in December 2003, for example, the United States Department of Defense Intelligence issued a pocket-sized guide entitled, *The Iraq Transitional Handbook,* which was intended to provide US military personnel with "basic reference information on Iraq, including its geography, history, government, military forces, and communications and transportations networks." Reflecting "the coordinated U.S. Defense Intelligence Community position," the *Iraq Transitional Handbook* was meant "to familiarize military personnel with local customs and area knowledge to assist them during their assignment in Iraq."[5] Meanwhile, the print media, blogosphere, and other communications outlets broadcast the war to the American public back home. A

---

[2]   *Gettleman*, April 11, 2004.
[3]   Hashim 2006:28–29.
[4]   Cordesman cited in Hashim 2006:34.
[5]   United States Department of Defense Intelligence 2003:ii.

Lexis-Nexis Academic search using the word 'Iraq' as the search criterion reveals that within the first year following President Bush's declaration of victory, more than three thousand articles and editorials discussing Iraq appeared in the *New York Times* alone.[6]

The remarkable proliferation and generalization of knowledge about Iraq is surely a testimony to the power of the media in the global age. More significant, however, is the fact that a body of knowledge—an "archive"—about Iraqi state and society is taking shape as a result of this encounter. By the term "archive" I refer to a bourgeoning set of discourses about Iraq, its people, history, culture, geography, government, and religious traditions. Informed by the work of post-colonial studies and post-structuralism, scholars of early modern and modern European empires have demonstrated the multiple ways in which systems of knowledge have been implicated in imperial conquests and legitimation.[7] They argue that the conquest, control, and administration of new lands and peoples by imperial powers were predicated on the simultaneous conquest of "an epistemological space."[8] Moreover, "facts" about conquered territories and indigenous societies produced through disciplines such as cartography, geography, and anthropology aided in translating *terra incognita* into a comprehensible and readable whole amenable to control and efficient administration.[9]

In this chapter, I consider the implications of prolonged US military occupation and administration of Iraq in shaping American public discourse about Iraqi state and society during the early years of the conflict. With its emphasis on sectarianism—the notion that Iraqi politics is determined exclusively by sectarian identity—the emerging discourse offered a lens through which to define Iraq as an "epistemological space," and therefore to make it legible to the American public. I argue that sectarian categories of analysis gained a degree of intellectual coherence through a process whereby different regions of Iraq have become associated with specific sectarian groups. The concept of the "Sunni Triangle," a term referring to a geographical region in Iraq that appeared in the print media in conjunction with the emergence of an Iraqi insurgency in 2003, was key to this normalization. Through a close reading/literary analysis of one US newspaper, the *New York Times*, I trace the evolution of the term "Sunni Triangle" between 2003 (when it first appears) and 2005, when elections for

---

[6] The search parameters were April 1, 2003 to April 1, 2004. Compare this number with other contentious political and social issues in the *New York Times* such as "abortion rights" (164 articles), "no child left behind" (226 articles), or "gun control" (202 articles). I would like to thank Aws Shemmari for his work in collecting this data. I also wish to thank Leila Farsakh and Yota Batsaki for their invaluable comments on various versions of this chapter.

[7] For example, Cañizares-Esguerra 2001; Said 1978; Stoler and Cooper 1997; Stoler 2009.

[8] Cohn 1996:4–5.

[9] Asad 1973; Cohn 1996:4–5; Edney 1997; Stocking c1987; Wolff 2007.

an Iraqi interim government were held. As a discursive construct, the "Sunni Triangle" was a means to localize the threat of violence against and resistance to US occupation forces by confining them (that is, violence and resistance) to a geographic region northwest of Baghdad.

My contribution is necessarily a modest and largely incomplete one since it is impossible within the scope of this chapter to discuss the vast discursive production resulting from US involvement in Iraq, which includes publications of political think-tanks, intellectuals and experts, returning veterans whose accounts of service in Iraq abound, bloggers, government issued press releases and reports, newspaper editorials, and works of fiction and film, to name only a few.[10] In addition, it is virtually impossible to ascertain the intentions and personal opinions and views of published authors without understanding the process by which *New York Times* articles and editorials surveyed in this chapter were selected for publication. How the *New York Times* readership understood and interpreted the information they culled from these articles is also difficult to know. And, moreover, the fact that I analyze discourse as it emerges and evolves in real time, so to speak, makes any conclusion about its historical significance provisional at best. Nevertheless, I maintain that a glimpse into an "archive-in-the making" provides a unique opportunity to analyze the nexus of knowledge, power, and discourse formation as it develops within the context of the US use of military force to radically reshape Iraqi society, economy, and politics along neo-liberal and liberal democratic lines. This is especially true since the *New York Times*, like other mainstream US media sources, shores up its legitimacy as a reputable news outlet by regularly drawing on the expertise of technocrats and intellectual elites.

Sectarianism as an Analytical Framework

Sectarian analysis of Iraq displays several general characteristics and assumptions. The first is the notion that religious and ethnic identities are mutually exclusive. The second is that there is a consensus among members of different ethnic and religious groups over how political power should be divided among them. In other words, social, regional, or gender hierarchies within these groups do not influence politics or undermine sectarian identity or solidarity. The third is that in pre-liberation Iraq political power was exclusively reserved for Sunnis while Shi'ites and Kurds were victims. And finally, the fourth assumption—one that is paradoxical in that it seems to undermine the Coalition's desire

---

[10] Recently, the Library of Congress has launched the "Iraq War 2003 Web Archive." See http://memory.loc.gov/diglib/lcwa/html/iraq/iraq-overview.html. I would like to thank Susan G. Miller for bringing this website to my attention.

to transform Iraq into a democracy—is that an Iraqi national identity as a basis for political cohesion does not exist. Instead, only the authoritarianism of the Saddam Hussein regime prevented Iraq's disintegration through the suppression of sectarian centripetal forces. These elements are most clearly summed up in an editorial that appeared in the *New York Times* on December 24, 2003, outlining the main features of Iraqi society since Iraq's creation by Britain in 1921:

> For most of its modern existence Iraq has been a forced amalgam of three different *peoples* [my emphasis] ruled by a privileged Sunni Arab minority and held together by force. The failure to arrange a fair balance of power among Shi'ite Arabs, Sunni Arabs and non-Arab Kurds helped doom Iraq to dictatorship. Saddam Hussein pushed the formula of Sunni dictatorship to the ultimate extreme, terrorizing the Shi'ite majority and unleashing wholesale murder against the minority Kurds.
>
> *New York Times* Editorial Desk, December 24, 2003

Other *New York Times* articles similarly sketch Iraq in terms of minority-majority relations. However, instead of emphasizing the modernity of Sunni political dominance as in the quote above, these articles radically de-historicize sectarianism by presenting it as an immutable feature of the Iraqi social and political landscape. For example, in the new democratic Iraq, reports the *New York Times* in 2003, Sunnis would lose "the advantages they enjoyed for centuries."[11] One year later, *New York Times* reporter Dexter Filkins explained that the Sunnis represented "a minority that has dominated the country for five centuries."[12] And, in the lead-up to the Iraqi elections in 2005, the *New York Times* also reported, "Iraq's Sunni Arab minority has dominated the ruling class through all Iraq's transformations, from the Ottoman era through the British mandate and the reign of Mr. Hussein."[13]

Elements of the sectarian analytical framework also appear in other forms. For example, Amatzia Baram, a professor of Middle Eastern history at the University of Haifa, proposed that the inability to quell the violence and govern Iraq was related to poor knowledge on the part of Coalition authorities about the "tribes" of the country. In an editorial entitled, "Victory in Iraq, One Tribe at a Time," Baram advocates the establishment of "a bureau for tribal affairs to serve as a repository for knowledge of the tribes and their traditions" by the Coalition authority. Although Baram does not mention sectarian affiliation directly, he specifically identifies the tribes of "central Iraq"—an area associated

---

[11] MacFarquhar, August 10, 2003.
[12] Filkins, July 11, 2004.
[13] Tavernise, October 8, 2005.

with Sunnis—but makes no mention of the southern tribal confederations in Iraq many of whose members identify themselves as Shi'ites.[14] In other words, while "tribes" constitute a basic feature of Iraqi society according to Baram's analysis, American military personnel should focus their attention on the tribes of a certain geographical location roughly corresponding to the purported "Sunni Triangle." Sandra Mackey, author of a book on Iraq, also emphasized the sectarian-tribal framework in an article she wrote for the *New York Times* in April 2004. Mackey argues that as conquerors of Iraq, the Ottomans—presumably like the Americans today—were forced to contend with Iraqi tribal dissidence and un-governability in their efforts to establish control over the region. Her efforts to draw parallels between sixteenth-century Constantinople/Istanbul and twenty-first-century Washington, DC reveal contemporary American concerns about the outbreak of violence in the city of Fallujah that spawned a broader insurgency throughout Iraq at the time her article was published. "When the Ottomans arrived in the 16th century," writes Mackey, "Istanbul co-opted the tribes of Falluja and the Sunni Triangle rather than conquer them."[15] Mackey's employment of the term "Sunni Triangle" suggests its existence as a geographical region of concern for would-be conquerors four centuries before the United States occupation of Iraq.

In "Rebuilding Iraq Is ...Nothing a Few Middle Class Guys Couldn't Solve," we find a rare example of the intersection of sectarian and economic analyses during the period under investigation. A young Iraqi entrepreneur explains that, whereas Saddam Hussein's regime stifled the entrepreneurial spirit among Iraqis, the new order must nurture it. Only the support of an indigenous capitalist class could save Iraq. The interviewee explains, "Politics divides people because you compete for dominance. You please the Shi'ites, the Sunnis won't like it. You please the Kurds, the Arabs won't like it. But business unites people. If you're a Sunni and I'm a Christian, we can always make a deal. When we make money together, everybody gets a dividend. It's like a dinner with enough food for everyone."[16] The tone of the article is both striking in its hopefulness about the future of Iraq and in its validation of American entrepreneurial ideals. Moreover, in contrast to the articles discussed previously, in which sectarianism functions covertly within the analysis, this article overtly assumes sectarianism as a defining feature of Iraqi society.

It is important to emphasize that other ways of analyzing Iraqi society exist in tandem with the sectarian framework as I have outlined it above. One particularly interesting example can be found in the *Iraq Transitional Handbook*

[14]   Baram, October 28, 2003.
[15]   Mackey, April 29, 2004.
[16]   Tierney, December 21, 2003.

to which I referred earlier in the chapter. The *Handbook*, which the United States Department of Defense Intelligence published in December 2003, long after violence had erupted in Iraq, explains that although Iraqi society is diverse in terms of ethnic and sectarian identity, it would be incorrect to emphasize this division in understanding the country. "Sunni Arabs in Iraq comprised the country's ruling elite under the Hussein regime. It is difficult, however, to speak of a strict or cohesive Sunni political identity. Sunnis subscribe to a broad spectrum of ideologies and affiliations, many of which have little to do with religion."[17] This rather subtle reading of the role of sectarian identity in Iraqi politics is curiously countered by a significantly less nuanced explanation also found in the *Handbook* about the behavior of Iraqi Arabs. In what seems like a regression to nineteenth-century Orientalism, the *Handbook* explains that the "Arab's view of the world is based on one of five concepts: atomism, fatalism, wish-versus-reality, extremism, and paranoia" (ibid., 67). Military personnel who deal with Iraqis while on their tour of duty should adjust their behavior accordingly, because "Arabs do not address challenges the way Americans would" and "do not generally subscribe to the Western concept of cause and effect" (ibid., 67–68). In other words, irrespective of the sectarian distinctions among Iraqis, they collectively form the unknown "Other," which is clearly distinct from the American "Self." The fundamental category of analysis is therefore a national one rather than one based on internal sectarian divisions among Iraqis.

In "Postcards from Iraq," commentator and Pulitzer Prize-winning author Thomas Friedman also highlights the relationship between the American "Self" and the Iraqi "Other" instead of focusing on sectarian and ethnic divisions within Iraqi society. Nevertheless, sectarianism is implicit in his argument, despite his avoidance of the terms "Sunni" and "Shi'ite." According to Friedman the difficulties of "plant[ing] the seeds of decent, consensual government" in Iraq reflect broader regional problems. The "Arab world" lacks the "minimum of tolerance and respect for majority and minority rights" necessary for democracy. "We are trying to plant the seeds of decent, consensual government in some very harsh soil," explains Friedman. He contrasts the integration and ethnic diversity of US armed forces to those of the Iraqis, thereby making a broader comparison between these societies. The US armed forces in Iraq represent "a Noah's Ark of Americans: African-Americans and whites, Hispanic Americans and Asians, and men and women I am sure of every faith." Friedman defers to arguments about "American Exceptionalism" in order to explain and then justify the US agenda in Iraq. "The fact that we can take for granted the trust among so many different ethnic groups, united by the idea of America—and

---

17   United States Department of Defense Intelligence 2003:204.

that the biggest rivalry between our Army and Navy is a football game—is the miracle of America." Friedman concludes in a self-congratulatory tenor that Iraq lacks the distinguishing characteristics of US society—they "are not in the drinking water." With a sense of relief he adds, "So let's thank God for what's in our drinking water," and hope "that maybe some of it washes over Iraq."[18]

The two previous examples—with their emphasis on an undifferentiated Iraqi "Other" as a foil to the North American "Self"—closely reflect Edward Said's by now widely-known description of relations between colonizer and colonized in which the Eastern/Muslim/indigenous/barbaric "Other" acts as foil to the Western/Christian/colonial/civilized "Self."[19] When viewed together with Friedman's views, the sectarian analysis, which emphasizes differentiation and diversity among the Iraqi population rather than homogeneity, seemingly offers a way out of the Saidian binary (colonized/colonizer), by allowing for the possibility of alliances between Americans and Iraqis. What transpired in 2003, therefore, is indicative neither of a colonial relationship between Iraq and the United States nor of a war of competing national interests between them.

By highlighting the rhetoric of sectarianism in the discussion above I am not suggesting that sectarian tensions are a creation of the US media or that such distinctions did not exist among Iraqis before 2003. Nor am I refuting the fact that Saddam Hussein's regime committed unspeakable atrocities against specific communities and ethnic groups in Iraq. In other words, I do not suggest that sectarian distinction is simply a discursive phenomenon. "Sunni" and "Shi'ite" *are and have been* markers of identity in contemporary Iraqi society and in the past.[20] Furthermore, these identities have been mobilized and become politicized toward different ends by various states and political actors from the Ottomans and their neighboring rivals, the Safavids (and later, the Qajars) during the early modern and modern eras,[21] to British mandatory authorities after World War I,[22] to the Ba'ath regime of Saddam Hussein during the Iran-Iraq War.[23] The sectarian argument has also been adopted by non-state actors such as Ahmad Chalabi (the now somewhat notorious Iraqi exile, vocal critic of Saddam Hussein's regime, leading figure in the London-based Iraqi National Congress, and a major advisor to members of the Bush administration regarding preparations for the 2003 invasion of Iraq), who has repeatedly emphasized sectarian

---

[18]   Friedman, November 21, 2004.
[19]   Said 1978.
[20]   Nakash 1994.
[21]   Çestinsaya 2006; Nakash 1994; Stump 2008.
[22]   Batatu 1980 on British policy towards Shi'ite tribes.
[23]   On fears of a Shi'ite uprising against the Sunnis, see Hashim 2006; Nakash 1994.

politics in his vision of the new Iraq following the fall of the regime.[24] What I do wish to emphasize, however, is that in the early years of the occupation of Iraq by Coalition forces, *New York Times* articles exhibited an overwhelming tendency to frame Iraqi state and society in terms of sectarian and (in the case of the Kurds) ethnic separateness and distinction. In the process, "Sunni" and "Shi'ite" seemed to become normalized as ontologically coherent and inert analytical categories withstanding the passage of time and the conquest or intervention of foreign powers from the Ottomans to the British to the Americans, on one hand, and the ideology, institutions and policies of the Iraqi nation-state, on the other. The fact that successive colonialist and nationalist interventions could themselves be instrumental in the re-constitution or shaping of sectarian identities according to specific historical or geographical circumstances is completely absent from this view. This analytical framework has played a crucial strategic and political role in helping to explain Iraqi responses to foreign intervention while also inadvertently justifying the actions of the United States and its Coalition partners as both moral and necessary.

Violence, the Sunni Triangle, and the Mapping of Iraq

Denis Cosgrove and others have argued that "mapping"—that is, "acts of visualizing, conceptualizing, recording, representing, and creating spaces graphically"—"are creative, sometimes anxious, moments in coming to knowledge of the world."[25] Such a process of discursive mapping occurred with the emergence and regularization of the geographic term "Sunni Triangle," which between mid-2003 and 2005 appeared a total of two hundred and thirty times in the pages of the *New York Times*. On one hand, cartographic authority aided

---

[24] Roston 2008: 36–38, 222, 279–284; Ahmad Chalabi, "The Future That Iraq Deserves," *Wall Street Journal* (Europe), December 22, 2004 cited in Roston 2008:323. The territory that is now known as Iraq served as a buffer zone between the Ottoman-Sunni and Safavid-Shi'ite (and later, Qajar) empires. At times, political rivalry and competition between these neighboring empires was instrumental in normalizing and politicizing sectarian divisions within Iraq (Stump 2008) as in the final decades of the nineteenth century, when Ottoman officials in Baghdad noted with some concern a trend toward the adoption of Shi'ism among (mostly southern) tribal populations of Iraq and began identifying Shi'ism as an obstacle to modernization and a threat to the Ottoman Sultan Abdulhamid's call for Muslim unity. Furthermore, border conflicts with Iran, as well as the competing imperial ambitions of Great Britain and Russia with regard to the region, created tensions during the nineteenth and twentieth centuries. Finally, during the mid- to late-nineteenth century, theological and legal debates among Shi'ite *mujtahids* occurred, which encouraged political engagement among the Shi'ite clergy. The shift had lasting effects for Iraqi Shi'ites, their clergy, and their relationship with Sunnis (Çestinsaya 2006: 27 and 101; Nakash 1994).

[25] Cosgrove 1999:1–2.

in the visualization of a sectarian political reality defined by mutual exclusivity among sectarian groups and the domination of the minority over the majority group. On the other hand, it made the highly abstracted sectarian landscape of Iraqi society, as described above, more concrete by associating "Sunnis" with a specific geographical region of Iraq. However, it was within the context of the eruption and spread of violence against US forces—a little more than a month after President George W. Bush's declaration that hostilities in Iraq had officially come to an end (May 1, 2003)—that the term "Sunni Triangle" began to appear with regularity in the mainstream US media. The *New York Times* first used the term in an article on June 12, 2003, and shortly thereafter, it appeared in other US newspapers, such as *Newsweek* (July 12, 2003) and the *Wall Street Journal* (July 21, 2003). This was almost six months after it had first occurred in the international English-language print media in September 2002.[26] That the term became normative within US public discourse in parallel with the eruption of violence in Iraq is evinced by the fact that between 2003 and 2005, the "Sunni Triangle" appeared a total of two hundred and thirty times in the pages of the *New York Times*, whereas from January 2006 until 2010, its usage had decreased substantially, occurring only thirty-five times in total.

How did the *New York Times* discuss the "Sunni Triangle" between 2003 and 2005? More often than not, *New York Times* articles provided information about its location, topography, and distinguishing ethnological or sociological characteristics. The term "Sunni Triangle" clearly suggests a region inhabited by Sunnis, although it is not clear whether non-Sunnis reside there. This confusion is particularly evident in reference to the city of Samarra, whose geographical location within the "Sunni Triangle" precludes any mention of the city's historic importance as a Shiite pilgrimage site. Although Samarra's population was historically and remains today largely Sunni, it is important to the spiritual geography of Shi'ism as the alleged burial site of revered Shi'ite imams.[27] But while attempting to map its location onto Iraq's material geography, articles often refer to the region as "the so-called Sunni Triangle," also suggesting jour-

---

[26] The *Weekend Australian* and the *National Post* (Canada) carried an interview with former UN Weapons inspector and a critic of the war, Scott Ritter, in which he used the term "Sunni Triangle" in a discussion of military strategy. "We may be able to generate support for an invasion among some of the Shi'ites and some of the Kurds," explained Ritter, "but to get to Baghdad you must penetrate the Sunni Triangle. Sunnis will not rise up against Hussein" (Wallis, September 14, 2002). The *New York Times* made no mention of a geographical location known as the "Sunni Triangle" during the first Gulf War in 1991 (known as "Operation Desert Storm"), when American and international forces sought to oust the Iraqi army from neighboring Kuwait, thereby suggesting its invention sometime after the cessation of hostilities and the imposition of U.N. sanctions and creation of the "No-Fly" zone in northern Iraq.

[27] Nakash 1994; Stump 2008.

nalistic trepidation or uncertainty about the term. For example, in an August 10, 2003 article, Neil MacFarquhar discusses Sunnis "inhabiting what is referred to as the Sunni Triangle around Saddam Hussein's ancestral homeland."[28] In a description of the cities of Khalidiyya and Habbaniyya, Patrick Tyler explains "both Iraqi towns lie along the Euphrates River in the so-called Sunni Triangle, an area of intense resistance to American occupation forces."[29]

A defining characteristic of the "Sunni Triangle" is the prevalence of violence, insurgency, and rebellion within its limits. The region is variously described as "restive,"[30] "volatile,"[31] "forbidding terrain,"[32] a place where "fighting flare[s] up,"[33] and "guerilla war [is] simmering."[34] It is sometimes inhospitable to westerners. *New York Times* reporter John F. Burns explains that Iraqi "amiability ... greets a Westerner almost everywhere *outside* [my emphasis] the Sunni Triangle."[35] The Sunni Triangle also has the potential to export violence to otherwise peaceful areas of Iraq. When conflicts erupted in the northern city of Mosul—an "ethnically diverse city of two million people"—the *Times* reported that Coalition troops believed insurgents were coming from the Sunni Triangle in order to "spoil" the region. "It was not supposed to be this way in Mosul," explained *New York Times* reporter Dexter Filkins. Unlike "places like Ramadi and Falluja and Tikrit"—all of which have been identified by the *New York Times* as falling within the nebulous Sunni Triangle—which "burned," adds Filkins, "Mosul stayed calm, the one city with a Sunni Arab majority where most people seemed to regard the Americans as their friends."[36] Other commentators, such as Tammy Arbuckle, a military analyst who specializes in limited war and insurgency, focused on the actual terrain of the Sunni Triangle—defined, that is, as a geographical locale—as a natural breeding ground for insurrection and militancy. Her analysis implies that this terrain could also sustain insurgencies from various other sectarian groups. She explains:

---

[28] MacFarquhar, August 10, 2003.

[29] Tyler, September 30, 2003.

[30] Wong, June 7, 2004; Sengupta, August 23, 2004; Wong, October 18, 2004.

[31] Wong, June 9, 2004. Between 2003 and 2005, nine *New York Times* articles use the term "volatile" to describe the city of Falluja, which is located in the region identified as the Sunni Triangle.

[32] Wong, June 9, 2004. According to the Brookings Institute website, with which Kenneth M. Pollack was (and continues to be) affiliated at the time that he wrote this article for the *New York Times*, Pollack "is an expert on national security, military affairs and the Persian Gulf. He was Director for Persian Gulf affairs at the National Security Council. He also spent seven years in the CIA as a Persian Gulf military analyst. He is the author of *A Path out of the Desert: A Grand Strategy for America in the Middle East*." *http://www.brookings.edu/experts/pollackk.aspx* accessed March 9, 2010.

[33] Wong and Sengupta, June 20, 2004.

[34] Berenson, October 2, 2003.

[35] Burns, November 16, 2003.

[36] Filkins, November 27, 2003.

The Iraqi guerrillas' area of operation is restricted to the agricultural limits of the Euphrates and Tigris River Valleys to the north and west of Baghdad. This so-called Sunni Triangle—with its maize, tomato and sunflower fields, palm and citrus groves, large farms and small towns— provides the insurgents with food, hiding places and recruits. But beyond it lies arid land, fit only for sheep and goats.

Arbuckle, October 2, 2003

If, as the analysis above suggests, the defining attribute of the Sunni Triangle is its proclivity to spawn violence, its location as a geographical space is more indeterminate and uncertain. *New York Times* articles reveal that the boundaries of the Sunni Triangle continuously shifted according to the movement of the insurgency (see Figure 8). In June 2004, for example, the city of Falluja represented the "heart of the Sunni Triangle."[37] Several months later, in September, after the outbreak of violence in the city of Samarra, the *New York Times* proclaimed Samarra to be the "heart of the Sunni Triangle."[38] And finally in the following month, the city of Ramadi, "the restive capital of Anbar province," had become "the heart of the so-called 'Sunni Triangle'."[39] By the closing months of 2004, the northern city of Mosul also seems to have been absorbed into the Sunni Triangle, significantly expanding its parameters and reflecting the alternative geography outlined in the *Iraq Transitional Handbook*.[40] Writing for the *New York Times* in November, 2004, James A. Marks, a retired army general and the senior intelligence officer for Coalition forces during the invasion of Iraq, alluded to the widening scope of the Triangle's geography when he predicted that "American units that are training in the United States today will absorb the lessons learned in Falluja into their training and deployment in the coming months. These troops will in turn conduct operations throughout the Sunni Triangle: Ramadi, Tikrit, Mosul."[41] In fact, the slipperiness of the Sunni Triangle—its center constantly shifting according to the outbreak of violence— evokes a moving target that is elusive, changing location at a moment's notice, and altering position like the enemy combatants who challenge and undermine US strategy in Iraq. In other words, the roving center (the "heart") of the Sunni Triangle acts as a graphic illustration of the inability to understand the insur-

---

37 Gettleman, June 13, 2004.
38 Filkins, September 5, 2004.
39 Wong, October 18, 2004.
40 The quote is: "Iraq's Sunni Arabs inhabit the valleys of the Euphrates above Baghdad, and of the Tigris between Baghdad and Mosul. This region forms a triangle between Baghdad, Mosul, and the Syrian and Jordanian borders." United States Department of Defense Intelligence 2003:204.
41 Marks, November 10, 2004.

gency, to define and isolate it, and ultimately, to eliminate it. Whether through the crosshairs of a firearm telescope or through the discursive mapping of the Sunni Triangle, Americans must first locate and identify the enemy in order to defeat it, bring stability to Iraq, and ensure a sense of victory.

April 2004 was a decisive turning point in the occupation as violence spread beyond the vague and shifting boundaries of the Sunni Triangle to the south of Iraq. In that month, four US contractors had been killed in the Iraqi city of Falluja (a city located within the Sunni Triangle) and their mutilated bodies suspended from a bridge in the city. While the gruesome event shocked American and Iraqi audiences alike, the broad-scale explosion of violence beyond the Sunni Triangle greatly complicated analysis of the Iraq situation. "How did the slaughter and mutilation of four American civilians in Falluja set off a chain reaction that reverberated beyond the Sunni Triangle and jolted the entire country?" What had previously been "a fading guerilla war," explained the *New York Times*, "ha[d] exploded into a popular uprising."[42] If the Sunni Triangle had helped to localize the insurgents in the early months of the occupation, even if their exact identity was unclear, the outbreak of violence in the "Shi'ite Heartland" rendered tenuous even this military and discursive strategy of control.

It is too soon to conclude about the cultural, intellectual, and policy impacts of the mapping of Iraq in terms of violence and sectarianism. What seems certain, however, is that sectarianism has come to occupy the center-stage in media analysis of the Middle East and Islam since the beginning of Coalition operations in Iraq in 2003. This was true to such an extent that Thomas Friedman cast Sunni identity in global terms in an article he wrote for the *New York Times* about a far-off event: namely, the London subway bombings of 2005. In "A Poverty of Dignity and a Wealth of Rage," Friedman expatiates on the relationship between Islam and violence. He asks: "Why are young *Sunni* [my emphasis] Muslim males, from London to Riyadh and Bali to Baghdad, so willing to blow up themselves and others in the name of their religion?" The answer, according to Friedman, lies in "Sunni Islam's struggle with modernity." Sunni Muslim males are "humiliated by Western society because while Sunni Islamic civilization is supposed to be superior," it has suppressed innovation.[43] An analytical category—"Sunni"— that was meant as a lens in the analysis of a localized problem associated with Iraqi political and religious life in 2003 had become generalized as a means of explaining the violence that occurred in London in July 2005.

These preliminary observations regarding the process of sectarian discourse formation since 2003 raise important questions for scholars interested in the

---

[42] Gettleman, April 11, 2004.
[43] Friedman, July 15, 2005.

knowledge/power nexus in the context of empire. By turning our attention to the "mapping" of Iraq and its implications for shaping the Iraqi archive, on one hand, and on the ways in which sectarian discourse has impacted contemporary Iraqi society on multiple levels (including concepts of space, geography, and their reformulation),[44] on another, scholars may begin to reconsider a number of issues that have informed the study of empires generally and of the eastern Mediterranean, specifically. What are the implications of an analysis that is based primarily on notions of "culture," defined in terms of ethnicity, religious difference, and/or sectarianism? Is this a broader indication of a trend in historical studies away from class, social, and economic history? Or is it a persistent anachronism that sees the Middle East/Islamic (and non-western societies generally) as outside of history and unexplainable by paradigms and methods considered appropriate for "western/developed/modern" societies? And finally, given the importance placed on "diversity" in contemporary US liberal discourse, what does the focus on sectarian divisions within Iraq reflect about US society at the turn of the twenty-first century, particularly in the aftermath of 9/11?

Works Cited

Asad, Talal, ed. 1973. *Anthropology and the Colonial Encounter.* London.

Arbuckle, Tammy. 2003. "Think Small in Iraq." *New York Times,* October 2; Section A, Column 2, Editorial Desk, 31.

Baram, Amatzia. 2003. "Victory in Iraq, One Tribe at a Time." *New York Times,* October 28; Section A, Column 1, Editorial Desk, 25.

Batatu, Hanna. 1978. *The Old Social Classes and the Revolutionary Movements of Iraq.* Princeton, N.J.

Berenson, Alex. 2003. "The Struggle for Iraq: Anatomy of an Ambush; Iraqi Civilians Caught in Crossfire of Guerilla War." *New York Times,* October 2; Section A, Column 3, Foreign Desk, 14.

Burns, John F. 2003. "Witness: The New Iraq is Grim, Hopeful and Still Scary." *New York Times,* November 16; Section 4, Column 1, Week in Review Desk, 1.

Cañizares-Esguerra, J. 2001. *How to Write the History of the New World: Histories, Epistemologies, and Identities in the Eighteenth-Century Atlantic World.* Stanford, Ca.

Çetinsaya, Gökhan. 2006. *Ottoman Administration of Iraq, 1890–1908.* New York.

---

[44] For example, how residents of Baghdad now move through and within neighborhoods where sectarian conflict has resulted in a form of ethnic "cleansing"; or how they navigate the largely inaccessible "Green Zone," which houses the Iraqi government, Coalition offices, and serves as the hub for foreign journalists.

Cohn, Bernard. 1996. *Colonialism and its Forms of Knowledge: the British in India.* Princeton, N.J.

Cooper and Stoler, eds. 1997. *Tensions of Empire: Colonial Cultures in a Bourgeois World.* Berkeley and Los Angeles.

Cosgrove, Denis, ed. 1999. *Mappings.* London.

——. 1999. "Introduction: Mapping Meaning." In Cosgrove 1999:1–23.

Editorial Desk. 2003. "Inventing a New Iraq." *New York Times*, December 24; Section A, Column 1, 20.

Edney, Matthew H. 1997. *Mapping an Empire: the Geographical Construction of British India, 1765-1843.* Chicago and London.

Filkins, Dexter. 2004. "One by One, Iraqi Cities Become No-Go Zones." *New York Times*, September 5; Section 4, Column 1, Week in Review Desk, 10.

——. 2003. "Tough Guy Tries to Tame Iraq." *New York Times*, July 11; Section 4, Column 2, Week in Review Desk, 1.

——. 2003. "A Region Inflamed: Northern Iraq; Attacks on G.I.'s in Mosul Rise as Good Will Fades." *New York Times*, November 27; Section A, Column 4, Foreign Desk, 1.

Friedman, Thomas L. 2005. "A Poverty of Dignity and a Wealth of Rage." *New York Times*, July 15.

——. 2004. "Postcards from Iraq." *New York Times*, November 21; Section 4, Column 1, Editorial Desk, 13.

Gettleman, Jeffrey. 2004. "War's Full Fury is Suddenly Everywhere." *New York Times*, April 11; Section 4, Column 1, Week in Review Desk, 1.

——. 2004. "Iraqis Start to Exercise Power Even Before Date of Turnover." *New York Times*, June 13; Section 1, Column 4, Foreign Desk, 1.

Hashim, Ahmed S. 2006. *Insurgency and Counter-Insurgency in Iraq.* Ithaca and New York.

MacFarquhar, Neil. 2003. "Iraq's Anxious Sunnis Seek Security in the New Order." *New York Times*, August 10; Section 4, Column 1, Week in Review Desk, 3.

Mackey, Sandra. 2004. "A City that Lives for Revenge." *New York Times*, April 29; Section A, Column 2, Editorial Desk, 25.

Marks, James A. 2004. "Rebels, Guns and Money." *New York Times*, November 10; Section A, Column 2, Editorial Desk, 25.

Nakash, Yitzhak. 1994. *The Shi'is of Iraq.* Princeton, N.J.

Pollack, Kenneth M. 2005. "Five Ways to Win Back Iraq." *New York Times*, July 1; Section A, 17. ProQuest Historical Newspapers: *The New York Times* (1851–2007).

Roston, Aram. 2008. *The Man Who Pushed America to War: the Extraordinary Life, Adventures and Obsessions of Ahmad Chalabi.* New York.

Said, Edward. 1978. *Orientalism.* First edition. New York

Sengupta, Somini. 2004. "Violence Surges in Baghdad and Sunni Area to the West." *New York Times,* July 23: Section A, Column 3, Foreign Desk, 8.

Stocking, George W. 1987. *Victorian Anthropology.* New York and London.

Stoler, Ann Laura. 2009. *Along the Archival Grain: Epistemic Anxieties and Colonial Common Sense.* Princeton, NJ.

Stoler, Ann Laura and Frederick Cooper. 1997. "Between Metropole and Colony: Rethinking a Research Agenda." In Cooper and Stoler 1997:1–56.

Stump, Ayfer Karakaya. 2008. "Subjects of the Sultan, Disciples of the Shah: Formation and Transformation of the Kizilbash/Alevi Communities in Ottoman Anatolia." PhD Dissertation. Harvard University.

Tavernise, Sabrina. 2005. "Sunnis Wary as Turning-Point Vote Nears." *New York Times,* October 8; Section A, Column 1, Foreign Desk, 8.

Tierney, John. 2003. "Rebuilding Iraq Is ... Nothing a Few Middle-Class Guys Couldn't Solve." *New York Times,* December 21; Section 6, Column 1, Magazine Desk, 48.

Tyler, Patrick E. 2003. "The Struggle for Iraq: Resistance; U.S. Forces Ambushed in Two Towns." *New York Times,* September 30; Section A, Column 1, Foreign Desk, 14.

United States Department of Defense Intelligence. 2003. *Iraq Transitional Handbook: Country Handbook, A Field-Ready Reference Publication.* n.p.

Wallis. 2002. "Iraqi Threat: Take it with a Grain of Salt." *New York Times,* September 14; Features, 21.

Wolff, Larry and Marco Cipolloni, eds. 2007. *The Anthropology of the Enlightenment.* Stanford, Ca.

Wolff, Larry. 2007. "Discovering Cultural Perspective: the Intellectual History of Anthropological Thought in the Age of Enlightenment." In Wolff and Cipolloni, 2007:3–32.

Wong, Edward. 2004. "In Ramadi, U.S. Seizes 17 Accused of Aiding Insurgency." *New York Times,* October 18; Section A, Column 3, Foreign Desk, 11.

———. 2004. "60 Years Later, a Division Takes Stock on Different Sands." *New York Times,* June, 7; Section A, Column 1, Foreign desk, 9.

———. 2004. "Car Bombs in 2 Iraqi Cities and Exploding Mines Kill at Least 18 More in Iraq." *New York Times,* June 9; Section A, Column 1, Foreign Desk, 9.

Wong, Edward and Somini Sengupta. 2004. "Strike Aimed at Terrorists Kills 17 in Falluja." *New York Times,* June 20; Section 1, Column 1, Foreign Desk, 11.

Figure 8: Map of Iraq showing the advancing and shifting "Sunni Triangle." (Louise Buglass)

Contributors

Antonis Anastasopoulos is Assistant Professor of Ottoman History at the Department of History and Archaeology of the University of Crete, and a research associate of the Institute for Mediterranean Studies of the Foundation for Research and Technology-Hellas (IMS/FORTH).

Dimiter Angelov is Professor of Byzantine History at the University of Birmingham.

Yota Batsaki is the Executive Director of Dumbarton Oaks Research Library and Collection, Washington, DC.

Sahar Bazzaz is Associate Professor of History at the College of the Holy Cross, Worcester, Massachusetts.

Mevhibe Pınar Emiralioğlu is Assistant Professor of History at the Department of History, University of Pittsburgh.

Constanze Güthenke is Associate Professor of Classics and Hellenic Studies at Princeton University.

Dimitris Kastritsis is Lecturer in History at the University of St Andrews.

Ilham Khuri-Makdisi is Associate Professor of History at Northeastern University.

Paul Magdalino is Professor of Byzantine History, Koç University, Istanbul and Fellow of the British Academy.

Anna Stavrakopoulou is Assistant Professor in Theatre Studies at Aristotle University, Thessaloniki.

Sibel Zandi-Sayek is Associate Professor of Art History at the College of William and Mary.

Index

Abdülaziz (Ottoman sultan), 148
Abdülhamid II (Ottoman sultan), 10, 169, 173, 174; Yıldız, 174
Abdülmecid (Ottoman sultan), 147, 148
Achaia (Roman province), 51
Aegean islands, 27
Aegean Sea, 7, 43, 56; Aegean Sea Chart by Mehmed Reis of Menemen, 84
Aeneas, 43
Aeschylus, 201
Aesop, 28
Africa, 43, 44, 45, 57, 60, 61; North Africa, 4, 5, 7
ahkâm defterleri, 111
Ainos, 43
Alexander (Byzantine emperor), 34
Alexander the Great, 50
Alexandria, 137
Alexios I Komnenos (Byzantine emperor), 58
Alfieri, Vittorio, 218
al-Hilāl, 161
Âli Pasha, 139–40, 212
al-Idrisi, 23
Ali Macar Reis, atlas of, 83
al-Jawa'ib, 162
Amalia (queen), 183, 185, 186, 203
Amaseia, 28
Ambelakia, 211

Anastasios I (Byzantine emperor), 26
Anatolē, 56, 57, 59, 60; Orient, late Roman diocese, 56; Orient, late Roman prefecture, 56
Anatolia, 113, 116
Anatolikon (Byzantine theme), 57
Anderson, Benedict, 231, 242
Antioch, 4
Apokaukos, Ioannes, 55
Aphrodite, temple of. *See* Knidos
"Arab Awakening", 10
Arabs, 29, 31, 33, 35, 38, 211, 250, 251
archive, 247
archive-in-the making, 248
Ardanaoutzin, 36
Arethas of Caesarea, 46
Argolid, 193, 198, 202
Aristophanes, 218
Aristotle, 51
Armenia/Armenians, 31, 33, 38
Asafi Dal Mehmed Çelebi: *Şeca'atname*, 119
Asia, 43–44, 45, 54, 56, 57, 58, 60, 59–64; late Roman diocese, 56, 61; Roman province, 28;
Asia Minor, 2, 3, 4, 5, 28, 31, 34, 37, 49, 57, 59
askeri, 10, 114, 115, 120
Athens, 16, 183, 186, 187, 188, 191, 199, 200, 201, 234-35; medieval, 6
Atlas-ı Hümayun (Imperial Atlas), 84

Attaleia, 37
Attaleiates, Michael, 58
Austen, Jane, 208
Avars, 32
ayan, 120 and n34, 121, 122

Ba'ath, 246, 252
Baghdad, 248, 256
Baku, 119
Balkan Mountains (Haimos), 49.
Balkan Slavs, 31
Balkans, 2, 4, 7, 16, 32, 33, 35, 57, 59, 116, 121
Balsamon, Theodore, 55
Baltic, 31
bankruptcy, 138, 139, 140
Bapheus, 113
Baram, Amatzia, 249
Basil I (Byzantine emperor), 32, 36, 38
Basil II (Byzantine Emperor), 5
Basil of Caesarea, 56
Beirut, 172, 173
Belgrade, 37, 124
beylik, 6
Bithynia, 113
Black Sea, 7, 30, 31, 33, 34, 35, 36, 59, 111, 116n15, 216, 229, 230
Blaeus, Willem and Joan, 118; *Atlas Maior*, 118
Blemmydes, Nikephoros, 47
Book of Ceremonies. *See under* Constantine VII Porphyrogenitus: *De cerimoniis*
Bory de Saint-Vincent, Jean Baptiste: *Expédition scientifique de Morée*, 195
Bosporus, 58
Bracciolini, Poggio, 63
Bulgaria, 5, 32, 33, 35, 50, 52, 61
Bush, George W., 245, 247, 252, 254
Byzantine Empire: European provinces of, 27

cadastral survey. *See* mapping technologies
Caesarea (in Cappadocia), 27
Cairo, 161, 225, 233–35, 237–38
Cappadocia, 28
categories of analysis, 247
Caucasian/Caucasus, 33, 35, 36, 38
census. *See* mapping technologies
Chalabi, Ahmad, 252
Chaldiran, 123
Charles V (Holy Roman Emperor), 74
Chazars, 33
Cherson, 31, 34, 35, 37; Chersonitai, 34
Chios, 217
Chonai: sanctuary of the Archangel Michael, 28
Christian Topography, 23
Christians, 114, 122, 250, 252
çiftlik 193-94
Ciriaco d'Ancona, 43n1
civilization, 162, 166, 170, 172, 178, 179
Claudius Ptolemy, 46, 47, 48, 50
coffee shops. *See* coffeehouses
coffeehouses, 165, 166, 175
Commedia dell'Arte, 209
Congress of Paris, 139
Congress of Vienna, 144, 146
Constantine I, the Great (Roman emperor), 30, 31, 37, 38
Constantine VII Porphyrogenitus (Byzantine emperor), 14, 49, 57; *De administrando imperio*, 26, 28, 29–39; *De cerimoniis*, 35, 39; *De thematibus*, 26–29; *Life of Basil* I, 36
Constantinople (Istanbul), 2, 4, 5, 6, 9, 14, 15, 24, 25, 26, 28, 29, 31, 34, 35, 38, 43–64, 208, 217, 219, 225; church of Hagia Sophia, 38, 166, 176; church of the Chalkoprateia, 38; church of the Holy Apostles, 28; Great Palace, 54; Hippodrome,

38; imperial palace, 34, 38; prae-
torium, mosque at, 38; treasury,
28
Cordesman, Anthony, 246
Cosgrove, Denis, 253
Cosmas Indicopleustes. See *Christian
Topography*
courts: Austrian, 138; British, 139;
consular, 137–40, 138; division of
labor between, 138; hierarchy of,
137; *kadı*, 137–38
Crete, 17, 35, 225, 228
Crimea, 31, 34
criticism, literary, 11, 13–14
Croatia/Croats, 32, 39
Cyprus, 27, 31, 34, 37
Cyzicus, 31

Dalisandos, 28
Dalmatia/Dalmatian, 31, 32, 34, 36,
37, 38
Damaskenos Stoudites, 61
David (biblical king), 33
devshirme, 231
dialects, 213
Diderot, Denis, 214
Digenis Akritis, 49
Diocletian, 30, 32, 37
Dionysios of Halikarnassos, 43
Dionysios Periegetes, 46, 47, 48, 50
diplomacy: equivalence and reciprocity, 146–47, 149; friction,
136, 141, 147; gun salute, 143–44,
145, 146, 149; and rivalry, 144–45;
tools and conduct of, 135, 143–44,
146–47, 150
display and spectacle, 133, 145,
148–50; illumination, 145, 148–50;
of national flag, 143–49, 240; of
national sentiments, 144–46; of
uniforms, 144, 149–50
Doctor in Spite of Himself, 210
Dom Juan, 210

Don-Volga canal, 92, 95
Doukas, John (*epi tōn deēseōn*, son of
Andronikos Kamateros), 47, 48
Doukas, John (Caesar) 29
Doukas, John (*sebastos*), 25n10;
Description of the Holy Places, 24
Doxapatres, Neilos, 60
dragoman, 138–40, 149
Dumas, Alexandre, 217

Eastern Question, 135
Ebubekir Dimişki, 118
Edirne, 116, 124
Egypt, 4, 8, 15, 17, 53, 116, 117, 225,
228, 232-33, 235–38
Eichthal, Gustave, 197, 198
empire, 247, 258; 'age of', 11;
Byzantine, 1, 2; classical, 2;
comparative study of, 2–4,
German, 35; Minoan, 230n20;
Ottoman, 1, 2, 6–10; Roman, 3, 4;
Trebizond, of, 59; Venetian, 240
England/English. *See* Great Britain
Enlightenment, 9, 15, 221, 234;
Greek, 211
Ephesos, 6, 61
Epiphanios Hagiopolites, 45
Epiros-Thessaloniki, empire of, 58–59
epistemological space, 247
Erzerum (Theodosiopolis), 33
ethno-religious community (*millet*),
140. See also *millet*
Euripides, 218
Europe, 5, 43–44, 45, 54, 56, 58, 59–64,
225, 234, 236, 239; eastern,
34, 36; as a Roman province,
61; western, 29. *See also under*
Byzantine Empire: European
provinces of
Eustathios of Thessaloniki, 47, 48
Evliya Celebi, 23
exile, 229

extraterritorial agreements (capitulations), 135–36, 138

Falluja, 246, 250, 255, 256, 257
feasts and ceremonials: for Bastille day, 146; for Duchess of Edinburgh, 146; of foreign states, 143–46; for Napoleon III, 145; Ottoman imperial, 135, 143, 147, 148–50; for Queen Victoria, 145, 146; for Victor-Emmanuel, 145; for visit of the sultan, 148
fermans, 124
Filkins, Dexter, 249, 255
Fisher, C., 138
Fisher, J.K., 138
flag. *See under* display and spectacle: of national flag
foreign states: actions of, 136; Austria, 142, 144, 145, 147; Austro-Hungarian Empire, 144; Britain, 142, 144–45; claims of, 142–43, 147; competition among, 135; concession to, 141; consulates of, 138–39, 144–49; cultural influence of, 146; France, 142, 144–45; Greece, 142, 144; Italy, 142, 144–45; national day of, 135; Netherlands, 142, 144; protection granted by, 135, 142, 144; Prussia, 142, 145; Russia, 142, 144–45; Spain, 144–45; United States, 142, 144–45, 149
foreign subjects, 141; claiming status of, 142; immunities of, 137, 139, 143; legal status of, 137; population, 135
Foscolo, Ugo: *The Last Letters of Jacopo Ortiz*, 188-89, 199
Foucault, Michel, 12, 241; heterotopia, 241
France, 116, 240
Franks/Frankish, 32

Friedman, Thomas, 251, 257

Galanaki, Rhea, 225–26
Gattilusio, Palamede, 43
Gautier, Théophile, 237
gaza, 114; *gazi*, 16
geographers, Ottoman ,72
geography: academic, 11; contested, 226; imaginary, 11, 12, 14, 17, 227, 235–38, 242; imperial, 1, 11–12, 136, 194, 227; material, 12, 237
George of Trebizond, 63
George the Monk (chronicler), 30
Georgia/Georgian, 31, 33, 36, 38
Gerald of Wales, 23
Germany, 118; German empire, 35
Goethe, J. W.: *Sorrows of Young Werther*, 188–89
Gog and Magog, 50
Goldoni, Carlo, 207, 209, 221; *Cunning Widow, The*, 209; *Locandiera, La*, 209;
grand vizier, 113, 118, 124, 232
Great Britain, 240, 249, 252, 253; English ambassador, 124
Greece (nation-state), 8, 183-86, 240-42
Greek fire, 31, 34, 35
Gregory of Nazianzos, Saint, 28, 29, 54, 56

Habbaniyya, 255
Habsburgs, 97, 100
Hacı Ahmed Map, 83
Hajj, 94–96
Halikarnassos, Mausoleum at, 28
Hellas, 50–52; Byzantine theme of, 51
Hellenic identity, 208
Hellespont, 60
Heraclius, 27, 32
Herakleia Thrakikē (Thracian Herakleia), 61

Herodotus, 62
Hierokles, 49, 51; *Synekdemos*, 23, 26, 27, 34
Himerios, 54
Hobsbawm, Eric, 11
Homer, 27
Hugo, Victor, 217
Hungary, 39, 116, 117, 118
Hussein, Saddam, 245, 246, 249, 250, 251, 252, 255
hybridity, 3, 226, 228, 239, 242

Ibn Hauqal, 23
İbrahim Pasha, 74
imperial decrees, 122, 123, 124, 125
India, 50, 57, 116
Indian Ocean, 94, 95
insurgency, 245, 246, 247, 250, 255, 256, 257
Iran, 116
Iran-Iraq War, 252
Iraq, 5, 7, 8, 17; liberal democracy in, 248
Iraq Transitional Handbook, 246, 250, 256
Iraqi National Congress, 252
Isidore (cardinal), 56
Islam, 31; reformism, 169
Istanbul, 14, 116, 120, 123, 124, 134, 137, 143, 147, 234; Beyoğlu, 166, 171; comparison with Egyptian and Syria cities, Riḍā on, 171; and diversity, Zaydān on, 176; Galata, 163, 164, 171; Kadiköy, 176; and modernity, Zaydān on, 175; modernization, 125n53, 166, 167; Riḍā on, 169; Shidyāq on, 163, 164, 168; urban changes in nineteenth century, 162; Zaydān on, 172, 174 . *See also* Constantinople
Italy, 29, 31, 32, 34
Izmir, 14: Archbishop's House, 144; Caravan Bridge, 148; Church of

St. Mary, 144; Frank Street, 148, 149; Greek and Armenian patriarchate, 148; harbor, 148, 149; as international center, 134, 137; Kemeraltı Street, 148; Konak, 148; quay, 149; rabbinical residence, 148. *See also* Smyrna

janissaries, 114, 115, 120, 121, 123
Jerusalem, 7, 24, 45
Jews, 211
jihad, 114
John the Lydian: *De magistratibus*, 27
John VI Kantakouzenos (Byzantine emperor), 62–63
Jordanes, 28
Jusdanis, Gregory, 231
Justinian I (Byzantine emperor), 26, 28, 30, 47, 55
Justinian II (Byzantine emperor), 34, 37

Kairis, Theophilos, 219
Kamateros, Andronikos, 48
Kamateros, Petronas, 33
Kanavoutzes, Ioannes, 43–44, 43n1, 60, 61, 62
Kapodistrias, Ioannis, 189, 195, 196, 201, 202
Kara Mustafa Pasha, 118, 124
Karabakh, 123
Karaferye (Veroia), 121, 122, 123n44
Karbones, George, 55, 56
kazasker, 111
Kephalas, Constantine: anthology of, 27
Khalidiyya, 255
Kiev, 119
Knidos, temple of Aphrodite, 28
knowledge: cartographic, 11, 227; geographical, 2; imperial, 227
Kokkinakis, Konstantinos, 218

Kolettis, Ioannis, 185, 187
Komnene, Anna, 49, 50, 58
Korais, Adamantios, 208
Kosmas Indikopleustes, 50, 52
Kotyaeion, 28
Koumas, Konstantinos, 211
Kozintsev, Grigori, 208; *King Lear*, 208, 209
Kurds, 246, 248, 250, 253
Kurosawa, Akira, 208; *Ran*, 208

lakes: Lake Van, 36
Lasithi plateau, 239-40
law: differential legal status, 134; extraterritorial, 134, 136; inter-twined jurisdictions, 137; Islamic, 138; of nationality, 135; partial overlap and conflict of, 134, 138; plurality of, 133, 134; territorial, 134, 136, 141
Lefebvre, Henri, 12
legal pluralism. *See under* law: plurality of
Leo VI (Byzantine emperor), 26, 34, 36
Lepanto, 92, 96
Levant, 4, 15
Libya, 60
Lips, Constantine, 33
Lombards, 31, 32
London Protocol, 184
lords of the frontiers, 120, 121
Louis XIV (king of France), 211, 216

Macedonia (Roman province and Byzantine theme), 48-49
MacFarquhar, Neil, 255
Madaba mosaic map, 25
Magyars, 33
Malalas, John, 52
Malta, 116, 119
Mamluks, 117
Mani, 37

Manuel I Komnenos (Byzantine emperor), 48
Manzikert, 5
mapmaking, 118
mapping, 253, 257, 258; technologies, 133, 135
maps, 118, 119, 114n7, 118n28; porto-lans, 16; isolaria, 16 *See also names of individual maps*
Marco Polo, 23
Mardaites, 37
Mariette, Auguste, 238; Pasha, 179
Marmara, Sea of, 38, 39
Marsigli, Count Luigi Ferdinando, 117, 118
Masalmah, 38
masses. See '*amma*
Mausoleum. *See* Halikarnassos, Mausoleum at
McCoan, J. C., 141
Mecca, 7, 8, 9; and Medina, 7, 8, 9, 94, 98, 106; Sharifate of, 6
Medina, 7, 8, 9. *See also under* Mecca: and Medina
Mediterranean Sea, 1, 2, 4, 5, 7, 13, 31, 111, 116n15, 119, 216, 220, 228, 234; *Mare Nostrum*, 16; in Ottoman geographical consciousness, 76; and Ottoman imperial aspira-tions, 78; and Ottoman imperial claims, 77
Megali Idea, 185, 203
Mehmed I (Ottoman sultan), 104–6
Mehmed II (Ottoman sultan), 5, 7
Mehmed IV (Ottoman sultan), 124
Metastasio, 209
Metochites, Theodore 51, 55, 62
Metropole, 159
millet, 9n26, 140, 228, 231-2. *See also* ethno-religious community
mission civilisatrice, 11, 15; civilizing mission, 170, 203
Mitchell, Timothy, 227, 232, 236, 239

modernity, 2, 8, 11, 12, 159, 226, 228, 232, 233, 234, 238
Molière, 208, 209, 210, 212, 214, 215, 216, 220; *Bourgeois Gentleman*, 221; *Misanthrope, The,* 210; *Miser, The*, 208, 210, 212, 214, 215, 219; *Monsieur de Pourceaugnac*, 221; *Tartuffe*, 208, 210, 216;
Mongols: invasions, 3; Turko-Mongol, 16
Moravia, 33
Morea, 49
Mosul, 255, 256
Mount Olympos, in Bithynia (Uludağ), 38
mountains, 4, 36
Muhammad Ali, 228, 231, 232, 239
Murad III (Ottoman sultan), 80
Mushtāq, Ṭālib, 180
Mustafa II (Ottoman sultan), 124
Muwaylihi, Ibrāhīm, 173
Myra, 29
myron, 29

Nafplio, 16, 186, 187, 190, 191, 192, 195, 197, 200, 202, 203, 235
nahda, 159, 160. *See also* "Arab Awakening"
Najaf, 7, 246
Napoleon, 8, 195, 232
Nasuh, Matrakçı, 80, 119; *Beyan-ı Menazil*, 80
nation: concept of, 28, 37–38
nationalism, 8, 9–10, 227, 231, 234, 239, 240, 242
neo-liberal, 248
Nérval, Gerard de, 237–38
newspaper press, 141, 143–45, 147; as a critical organ, 140, 147; *Journal de Constantinople, L'Écho de l'Orient*, 145; *Levant Herald*, 141
Newsweek, 254
Nicaea, empire of, 58–59

Nicholas, Saint, 29
Nicomedia (Izmit), 38
9/11, 258
non-Muslims, 114, 115. *See also under* Ottoman Empire: non-Muslim subjects of
nostos, 233-34, 238
Notitia (of Constantinople), 25

Odessa, 212
Oikonomos, Konstantinos, 211, 212, 213, 214, 215, 217
oikoumenē, 53, 54
Orhan I (Ottoman ruler), 62, 93, 103
Orient. See *Anatolē*
Orientalism, 251
Orthodoxy, 212
Osman Pasha, Özdemiroğlu, 119
Otranto, 7
Otto (king of Greece), 183, 184, 193, 196
Ottoman Empire: 140, 143, 150; diplomatic protocols, 147, 149; imperial ideology, 70; and modern sovereignty, 139; nationality law, 142; non-Muslim subjects of, 162, 163; resilience of, 143
Ottoman subjects: and foreign naturalization, 142; foreign women passing as, 137, 140–41; non-Muslims, 135, 139; as third party owners, 137
Ottomans, 43, 44, 45, 56, 59, 63, 249, 250, 252, 253
Ouranos, Nikephoros, 26

Pachymeres, Georgios, 113
Palaiologoi (Byzantine dynasty), 55–56
Palatine Anthology, 27
Paris, 234: Shidyāq on, 166, 167; Zaydān on, 177

Parisinus Graecus 2009 (manuscript), 29
Pausanias, 23
Pechenegs, 31, 33, 37
Peloponnese, 31, 34, 36, 51, 56, 191, 194, 195, 202
people: concept of, 28
Pergamon, 7
periphery, 6, 14, 226, 228, 234, 238
Persians, 62, 63
Petrarch, 63
Phanari, 219; Phanariots, 9, 190, 220n36
Phokaia, 43 and n1
Photios, 46, 48, 52
Piccolomini, Aeneas Silvius (Pope Pius II), 63
Piri Reis, 72, 118; *Book of the Sealore*, 76; world map of, 73
Pisani, Etienne, 140
Planoudes, Maximos, 46
Plautus, 212, 214; *Pot of Gold, The*, 214
politeia, 39
political economy: Shidyāq on, 167, 168
Pontos (late Roman diocese), 56
Portugal, 94
postcolonialism, 11, 225, 226, 227, 229; postcolonial studies, 234, 247
post-structuralism, 247
Procopius: *Buildings*, 26
progress, 166
pronoia, 3
property (real), 136; and citizenship, 142; as collateral, 136–38; control of, 135; disputes, 135, 138, 139; and foreign subjects, 134, 135–37, 139–41, 150; freehold, 136; lease-hold, 136; and Ottoman subjects, 139–40; registration, 138, 140; rights, 137, 139, 142, 150; third-party ownership, 139–40; transfer, 137–38, 140
protégé, 135; immunities of, 135, 139;
    as legal status, 139, 141–42
Prousa (Bursa), 38
Psellos, Michael, 46, 47
Ptolemy, 23
public good. *See* public interest
public interest, 164, 167
public transportation, 166, 167, 177
Publius (proconsul of Asia), 28
Pythia (Yalova), 38

Qajars, 252
Racine, Jean, 217
Ramadi, 256
Rangavis, Alexandros Rizos, 192
reaya, 10, 115, 120
rebellion, 123, 124; Cretan 230, 233
reform, 164, 228
Renaissance: in Italy, 45, 63
Rhegion (Küçük Çekmece), 38
Rhōmania, 52
Riḍā, Muhammad Rashīd, 169; on Islam and modernity, 170; *Maʿhad al-Daʿwa waʾl-Irshād*, 169; on *muta-farnijin* (see *tafarnuj*)
rivers, 4, 36; Danube, 4, 5, 32, 34, 35, 36, 37; Dnieper, 36, 38; Euphrates, 58, 256; Granikos, 28; Nile, 57; Rhine, 4; Sangarios, 28; Tigris, 58, 256
Roger II (Norman king of Sicily), 60
Romanos I (Byzantine emperor), 34, 36
Romanos II (Byzantine emperor), 27
Romans (Byzantines), 30, 32, 34, 37
Rome, 2, 4, 7, 15, 43, 53, 56, 62; New Rome (Constantinople), 5, 53, 64
Ross, Ludwig, 183, 184, 203
Rousseau, Jean-Jacques, 214
Rozaites, Michael (scribe), 29
Rus, 31, 38
Russia, 121, 240

Safavids, 7, 99–100, 101, 106, 123, 252

Said, Edward, 11, 12, 62, 227, 229, 236, 252; *Culture and Imperialism*, 227, 229, 238; *Orientalism*, 12, 237
Saint-Simon, Comte de, 193, 197, 198
Salona, 38
Salonica, 118, 137
Samarra, 246, 254
Samothrace, 43
Sand, George, 217
Saracens (Arabs), 38
Sarkel, 33
Schiller, Friedrich, 218
Schinas, Konstantinos, 186
sectarianism, 247, 250, 251, 252, 257, 258
Selim I (Ottoman sultan), 71, 106–7, 117, 123, 124n48
Seljuks, 3, 5, 103
September 11. *See* 9/11
Serbia/Serbs, 32, 39, 49, 61
Shahrukh (Timurid ruler), 104–6
Shakespeare, William, 208, 218
Shi'ites, 7, 8, 246, 248, 250, 253, 257
Shidyāq, Aḥmad Fāris, 161; and Istanbul, 161; modernist approach, 168
sipahis, 114, 116
Sirmium, 37
Skylitsis, Ioannis Isidoridis, 217, 218
Slavs, 32, 36; Peloponnesian, 37
Smyrna, 28, 208, 212, 214, 215, 217; Gymnasium, 212. *See also* Izmir
Soja, Edward, 12, 226, 242; *Thirdspace*, 226, 241
Ṣoḳollu Meḥmed Paşa, 81, 92–97, 108–9
Sophocles, 218
Soutsos, Alexandros, 188, 190, 192, 196, 201, 202, 203, 220; *The Exile of 1831*, 188, 189, 190, 200
Soutsos, Panagiotis, 188, 190, 192, 198, 199, 200, 202, 220; *Leandros*, 188, 189, 192, 193, 199

sovereignty, 150; assertion of, 134–35, 141, 143, 147; conflict of, 135; expression of, 144; and property, 140, 143; recognition of, 141, 144; and territoriality, 141, 143, 147, 150; Westphalian notion of, 133
space: contested, 12, 13, 16, 235; 'third', 17, 225–26, 227, 232, 238, 241
Spain, 31, 116
spatial turn, 12, 226
Split, 37
state power: and geography, 133; instruments of, 143; as negotiated, 134–36, 143; and territoriality, 135, 141
Stephanos, 47, 48, 51
Stephanos of Byzantium: *Ethnika*, 23, 26, 27, 31
Strabo, 23, 27, 28, 46, 47, 48
Stoudites, Theodoros, 55
Sue, Eugène: *Les Mystères de Paris*, 217
Suez Canal, 92, 95
Süleyman I (son of the Ottoman ruler Orhan), 62, 73, 116, 124n48
Sunnis, 8, 246, 248, 250, 251, 253, 254, 257; Sunni Triangle, 17, 247, 250, 253, 254, 255, 256, 257; Sunnism, 94–96, 102–3
Syria, 31, 117

Tabula Peutingeriana, 25
tafarnuj, 171
Taktika. See Leo VI; Ouranos, Nikephoros
Tanzimat, 8, 16, 112, 162, 228; government, 135, 139, 141, 150; reforms, 135
Taron (Armenian principality), 38
territoriality: of the modern state, 133–34, 150; as uneven control, 134

themes (*themata*), 27–29, 39, 57;
  Aegean, 27; Anatolian, 27;
  Anatolikon, 27, 28, 29, 57;
  Armeniakon, 27, 28; Hellas, 51;
  Kibyrraioton, 29; Lykandos, 28;
  Macedonia, 48–49; Mesopotamia,
  27; Paphlagonia, 27; Sebasteia,
  27; Seleukeia, 28; Thrakesion, 28
Themistius, 54
Theodore, Saint (the Great Martyr),
  28.
Theodore II Laskaris (Byzantine
  emperor), 51, 52, 59
Theodosiopolis. *See* Erzerum
Theophanes Continuatus, 33
Theophanes the Confessor (chroni-
  cler), 30, 35, 58
Theophilos (Byzantine emperor) 33,
  34
Thermopylae, 201
Thessalonike, 35
Thomas (mayor of Lykandos), 28
Thrace, 49, 56, 63, 116; late Roman
  diocese, 56, 61; Roman province,
  48
Thucydides, 62
Tikrit, 255, 256
timar, 3
tolerance, 231; religious, 3
Topkapı, 7
Trajan's Gate: Trajan's bridge at, 37
travel, 14, 15, 234
Trebizond, empire of, 59
Troy, 43–44, 62
Turkmen, 5
Turks, 211

uc begleri. See lords of the frontiers
Ukraine, 39
ulama, 170, 176
umma, 169, 171, 172
Umur Beg (emir of Aydin), 62
UNESCO, 225

United States: Department of Defense
  Intelligence, 246; 251; liberal
  discourse, 258; military occupation, 247
universality, 4, 15–16
Üsküdar, 116
Uz, 33

Vapopoulo, Manoli, 139
Venetians, 118, 125n53
Venice, 32, 92, 96, 100, 116
Vienna, 116, 118, 124; Congress of,
  146
von Savigny, Bettina, 186, 191

Wall Street Journal, 254
Walters Sea Atlas, 83
War of Independence: Greek, 185, 188,
  209, 212, 220
Wolfowitz, Paul, 246
women: foreign, 140–41; French, 178;
  Istanbul, 171; Ottoman, 171; as
  property owners, 137, 140–41;
  and prostitution, 178
World War I, 114

Young Turks: Revolution, 10, 161, 169,
  173, 174

Zadar: church of Saint Anastasia, 38
Zaydān, Jirjī, 173; *al-Inqilāb
  al-'uthmāni*, 161, 173
zimmis, 115. *See also* non-Muslims;
  Ottoman Empire: non-Muslim
  subjects of
Zygos (mountains), 49–50

ʿOs̱mān I (Ottoman sultan), 93, 103